ATIQPUT

McGILL-QUEEN'S INDIGENOUS AND NORTHERN STUDIES

(In memory of Bruce G. Trigger)
John Borrows, Sarah Carter, and Arthur J. Ray, Editors

The McGill-Queen's Indigenous and Northern Studies series publishes books about Indigenous peoples in all parts of the northern world. It includes original scholarship on their histories, archaeology, laws, cultures, governance, and traditions. Works in the series also explore the history and geography of the North, where travel, the natural environment, and the relationship to land continue to shape life in particular and important ways. Its mandate is to advance understanding of the political, legal, and social relations between Indigenous and non-Indigenous peoples, of the contemporary issues that Indigenous peoples face as a result of environmental and economic change, and of social justice, including the work of reconciliation in Canada. To provide a global perspective, the series welcomes books on regions and communities from across the Arctic and Subarctic circumpolar zones.

1 *When the Whalers Were Up North*
Inuit Memories from the Eastern Arctic
Dorothy Harley Eber

2 *The Challenge of Arctic Shipping*
Science, Environmental Assessment, and Human Values
Edited by David L. VanderZwaag and Cynthia Lamson

3 *Lost Harvests*
Prairie Indian Reserve Farmers and Government Policy
Sarah Carter

4 *Native Liberty, Crown Sovereignty*
The Existing Aboriginal Right of Self-Government in Canada
Bruce Clark

5 *Unravelling the Franklin Mystery*
Inuit Testimony
David C. Woodman

6 *Otter Skins, Boston Ships, and China Goods*
The Maritime Fur Trade of the Northwest Coast, 1785–1841
James R. Gibson

7 *From Wooden Ploughs to Welfare*
The Story of the Western Reserves
Helen Buckley

8 *In Business for Ourselves*
Northern Entrepreneurs
Wanda A. Wuttunee

9 *For an Amerindian Autohistory*
An Essay on the Foundations of a Social Ethic
Georges E. Sioui

10 *Strangers Among Us*
David Woodman

11 *When the North Was Red*
Aboriginal Education in Soviet Siberia
Dennis A. Bartels and Alice L. Bartels

12 *From Talking Chiefs to a Native Corporate Elite*
The Birth of Class and Nationalism among Canadian Inuit
Marybelle Mitchell

13 *Cold Comfort*
My Love Affair with the Arctic
Graham W. Rowley

14 *The True Spirit and Original Intent of Treaty 7*
Treaty 7 Elders and Tribal Council with Walter Hildebrandt, Dorothy First Rider, and Sarah Carter

15 *This Distant and Unsurveyed Country*
A Woman's Winter at Baffin Island, 1857–1858
W. Gillies Ross

16 *Images of Justice*
Dorothy Harley Eber

17 *Capturing Women*
The Manipulation of Cultural Imagery in Canada's Prairie West
Sarah Carter

18 *Social and Environmental Impacts of the James Bay Hydroelectric Project*
Edited by James F. Hornig

19 *Saqiyuq*
Stories from the Lives of Three Inuit Women
Nancy Wachowich in collaboration with Apphia Agalakti Awa, Rhoda Kaukjak Katsak, and Sandra Pikujak Katsak

20 *Justice in Paradise*
Bruce Clark

21 *Aboriginal Rights and Self-Government*
The Canadian and Mexican Experience in North American Perspective
Edited by Curtis Cook and Juan D. Lindau

22 *Harvest of Souls*
The Jesuit Missions and Colonialism in North America, 1632–1650
Carole Blackburn

23 *Bounty and Benevolence*
A History of Saskatchewan Treaties
Arthur J. Ray, Jim Miller, and Frank Tough

24 *The People of Denendeh*
Ethnohistory of the Indians of Canada's Northwest Territories
June Helm

25 *The* Marshall *Decision and Native Rights*
Ken Coates

26 *The Flying Tiger*
Women Shamans and Storytellers of the Amur
Kira Van Deusen

27 *Alone in Silence*
European Women in the Canadian North before 1940
Barbara E. Kelcey

28 *The Arctic Voyages of Martin Frobisher*
An Elizabethan Adventure
Robert McGhee

29 *Northern Experience and the Myths of Canadian Culture*
Renée Hulan

30 *The White Man's Gonna Getcha*
The Colonial Challenge to the Crees in Quebec
Toby Morantz

31 *The Heavens Are Changing*
Nineteenth-Century Protestant Missions and Tsimshian Christianity
Susan Neylan

32 *Arctic Migrants/Arctic Villagers*
The Transformation of Inuit Settlement in the Central Arctic
David Damas

33 *Arctic Justice*
On Trial for Murder – Pond Inlet, 1923
Shelagh D. Grant

34 *The American Empire and the Fourth World*
Anthony J. Hall

35 *Eighteenth-Century Naturalists of Hudson Bay*
Stuart Houston, Tim Ball, and Mary Houston

36 *Uqalurait*
An Oral History of Nunavut
Compiled and edited by John Bennett and Susan Rowley

37 *Living Rhythms*
Lessons in Aboriginal Economic Resilience and Vision
Wanda Wuttunee

38 *The Making of an Explorer*
George Hubert Wilkins and the Canadian Arctic Expedition, 1913–1916
Stuart E. Jenness

39 *Chee Chee*
A Study of Aboriginal Suicide
Alvin Evans

40 *Strange Things Done*
Murder in Yukon History
Ken S. Coates and William R. Morrison

41 *Healing through Art*
Ritualized Space and Cree Identity
Nadia Ferrara

42 *Coyote and Raven Go Canoeing*
Coming Home to the Village
Peter Cole

43 *Something New in the Air*
The Story of First Peoples Television Broadcasting in Canada
Lorna Roth

44 *Listening to Old Woman Speak*
Natives and Alternatives in Canadian Literature
Laura Smyth Groening

45 *Robert and Francis Flaherty*
A Documentary Life, 1883–1922
Robert J. Christopher

46 *Talking in Context*
Language and Identity in Kwakwaka'wakw Society
Anne Marie Goodfellow

47 *Tecumseh's Bones*
Guy St-Denis

48 *Constructing Colonial Discourse*
Captain Cook at Nootka Sound
Noel Elizabeth Currie

49 *The Hollow Tree*
Fighting Addiction with Traditional Healing
Herb Nabigon

50 *The Return of Caribou to Ungava*
A.T. Bergerud, Stuart Luttich, and Lodewijk Camps

51 *Firekeepers of the Twenty-First Century*
First Nations Women Chiefs
Cora J. Voyageur

52 *Isuma*
Inuit Video Art
Michael Robert Evans

53 *Outside Looking In*
Viewing First Nations Peoples in Canadian Dramatic Television Series
Mary Jane Miller

54 *Kiviuq*
An Inuit Hero and His Siberian Cousins
Kira Van Deusen

55 *Native Peoples and Water Rights*
Irrigation, Dams, and the Law in Western Canada
Kenichi Matsui

56 *The Rediscovered Self*
Indigenous Identity and Cultural Justice
Ronald Niezen

57 *As affecting the fate of my absent husband*
Selected Letters of Lady Franklin Concerning the Search for the Lost Franklin Expedition, 1848–1860
Edited by Erika Behrisch Elce

58 *The Language of the Inuit*
Syntax, Semantics, and Society in the Arctic
Louis-Jacques Dorais

59 *Inuit Shamanism and Christianity*
Transitions and Transformations in the Twentieth Century
Frédéric B. Laugrand and Jarich G. Oosten

60 *No Place for Fairness*
Indigenous Land Rights and Policy in the Bear Island Case and Beyond
David T. McNab

61 *Aleut Identities*
Tradition and Modernity in an Indigenous Fishery
Katherine L. Reedy-Maschner

62 *Earth into Property*
Aboriginal History and the Making of Global Capitalism
Anthony J. Hall

63 *Collections and Objections*
Aboriginal Material Culture in Southern Ontario, 1791–1914
Michelle A. Hamilton

64 *These Mysterious People*
Shaping History and Archaeology in a Northwest Coast Community, Second Edition
Susan Roy

65 *Telling It to the Judge*
Taking Native History to Court
Arthur J. Ray

66 *Aboriginal Music in Contemporary Canada*
Echoes and Exchanges
Edited by Anna Hoefnagels and Beverley Diamond

67 *In Twilight and in Dawn*
A Biography of Diamond Jenness
Barnett Richling

68 *Women's Work, Women's Art*
Nineteenth-Century Northern Athapaskan Clothing
Judy Thompson

69 *Warriors of the Plains*
The Arts of Plains Indian Warfare
Max Carocci

70 *Reclaiming Indigenous Planning*
Edited by Ryan Walker, Ted Jojola, and David Natcher

71 *Setting All the Captives Free*
Capture, Adjustment, and Recollection in Allegheny Country
Ian K. Steele

72 *Before Ontario*
The Archaeology of a Province
Edited by Marit K. Munson and Susan M. Jamieson

73 *Becoming Inummarik*
Men's Lives in an Inuit Community
Peter Collings

74 *Ancient Pathways, Ancestral Knowledge*
Ethnobotany and Ecological Wisdom of Indigenous Peoples of Northwestern North America
Nancy J. Turner

75 *Our Ice Is Vanishing/Sikuvut Nunguliqtuq*
A History of Inuit, Newcomers, and Climate Change
Shelley Wright

76 *Maps and Memes*
Redrawing Culture, Place, and Identity in Indigenous Communities
Gwilym Lucas Eades

77 *Encounters*
An Anthropological History of Southeastern Labrador
John C. Kennedy

78 *Keeping Promises*
The Royal Proclamation of 1763, Aboriginal Rights, and Treaties in Canada
Edited by Terry Fenge and Jim Aldridge

79 *Together We Survive*
Ethnographic Intuitions, Friendships, and Conversations
Edited by John S. Long and Jennifer S.H. Brown

80 *Canada's Residential Schools: The History, Part 1, Origins to 1939*
The Final Report of the Truth and Reconciliation Commission of Canada, Volume 1

81 *Canada's Residential Schools: The History, Part 2, 1939 to 2000*
The Final Report of the Truth and Reconciliation Commission of Canada, Volume 1

82 *Canada's Residential Schools: The Inuit and Northern Experience*
The Final Report of the Truth and Reconciliation Commission of Canada, Volume 2

83 *Canada's Residential Schools: The Métis Experience*
The Final Report of the Truth and Reconciliation Commission of Canada, Volume 3

84 *Canada's Residential Schools: Missing Children and Unmarked Burials*
The Final Report of the Truth and Reconciliation Commission of Canada, Volume 4

85 *Canada's Residential Schools: The Legacy*
The Final Report of the Truth and Reconciliation Commission of Canada, Volume 5

86 *Canada's Residential Schools: Reconciliation*
The Final Report of the Truth and Reconciliation Commission of Canada, Volume 6

87 *Aboriginal Rights Claims and the Making and Remaking of History*
Arthur J. Ray

88 *Abenaki Daring*
The Life and Writings of Noel Annance, 1792–1869
Jean Barman

89 *Trickster Chases the Tale of Education*
Sylvia Moore

90 *Secwépemc People, Land, and Laws*
Yerí7 re Stsq̓ey̓s-kucw
Marianne Ignace and Ronald E. Ignace

91 *Travellers through Empire*
Indigenous Voyages from Early Canada
Cecilia Morgan

92 *Studying Arctic Fields*
Cultures, Practices, and Environmental Sciences
Richard C. Powell

93 *Iroquois in the West*
Jean Barman

94 *Leading from Between*
Indigenous Participation and Leadership in the Public Service
Catherine Althaus and Ciaran O'Faircheallaigh

95 *Against the Current and Into the Light*
Performing History and Land in Coast Salish Territories and Vancouver's Stanley Park
Selena Couture

96 *Plants, People, and Places*
The Roles of Ethnobotany and Ethnoecology in Indigenous Peoples' Land Rights in Canada and Beyond
Edited by Nancy J. Turner

97 *Fighting for a Hand to Hold*
Confronting Medical Colonialism against Indigenous Children in Canada
Samir Shaheen-Hussain

98 *Forty Narratives in the Wyandot Language*
John L. Steckley

99 *Uumajursiutik unaatuinnamut / Hunter with Harpoon / Chasseur au harpon*
Markoosie Patsauq
Edited and translated by Valerie Henitiuk and Marc-Antoine Mahieu

100 *Language, Citizenship, and Sámi Education in the Nordic North, 1900–1940*
Otso Kortekangas

101 *Daughters of Aataentsic*
Life Stories from Seven Generations
Kathryn Magee Labelle in collaboration with the Wendat/Wandat Women's Advisory Council

102 *Aki-wayn-zih*
A Person as Worthy as the Earth
Eli Baxter

103 *Atiqput*
Inuit Oral History and Project Naming
Edited by Carol Payne, Beth Greenhorn, Deborah Kigjugalik Webster, and Christina Williamson

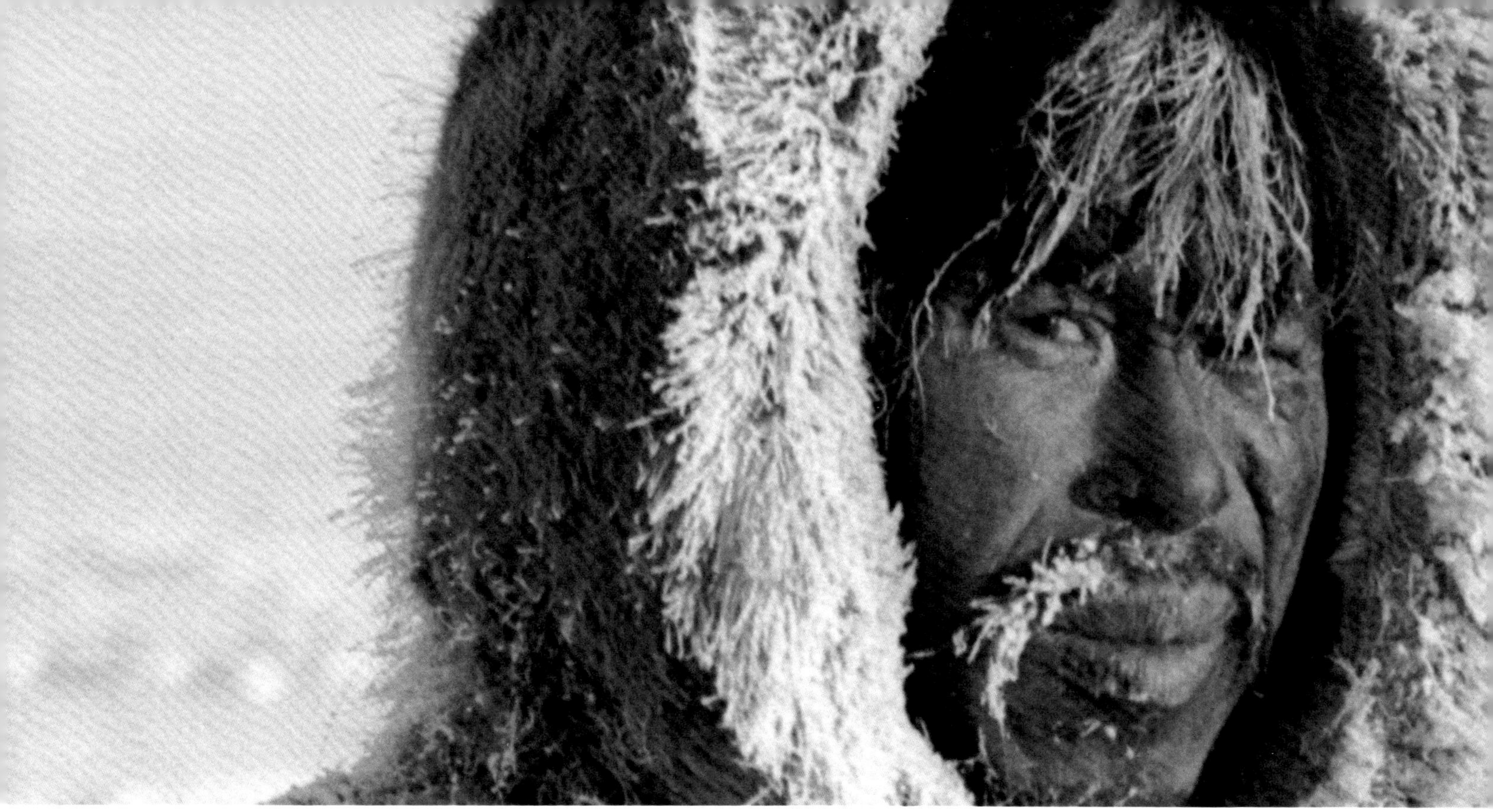

ATIQPUT

Inuit Oral History and Project Naming

Edited by Carol Payne, Beth Greenhorn, Deborah Kigjugalik Webster, and Christina Williamson

McGill-Queen's University Press
Montreal & Kingston | London | Chicago

ISBN 978-0-2280-1105-7 (cloth)
ISBN 978-0-2280-1335-8 (ePDF)

Legal deposit third quarter 2022
Bibliothèque nationale du Québec

Printed in Canada on acid-free paper

This book has been published with the help of a grant from the Canadian Federation for the Humanities and Social Sciences, through the Awards to Scholarly Publications Program, using funds provided by the Social Sciences and Humanities Research Council of Canada.

Funded by the Government of Canada | Financé par le gouvernement du Canada | Canada | Canada Council for the Arts | Conseil des arts du Canada

We acknowledge the support of the Canada Council for the Arts.

Nous remercions le Conseil des arts du Canada de son soutien.

Library and Archives Canada Cataloguing in Publication

Title: Atiqput : Inuit oral history and Project Naming / edited by Carol Payne, Beth Greenhorn, Deborah Kigjugalik Webster, and Christina Williamson.
Names: Payne, Carol J., editor. | Greenhorn, Beth, editor. | Webster, Deborah Kigjugalik, editor. | Williamson, Christina, editor.
Series: McGill-Queen's indigenous and northern series ; 103.
Description: Series statement: McGill-Queen's Indigenous and northern studies ; 103 | Includes bibliographical references and index.
Identifiers: Canadiana (print) 20220175624 | Canadiana (ebook) 20220181330 | ISBN 9780228011057 (hardcover) | ISBN 9780228013358 (PDF)
Subjects: LCSH: Names, Inuit. | LCSH: Names, Personal—Social aspects—Canada, Northern. | LCSH: Inuit—Portraits. | LCSH: Library and Archives Canada—Photograph collections. | LCSH: Inuit—History. | LCSH: Inuit—Social life and customs. | LCSH: Inuit—Biography.
Classification: LCC E99.E7 A85 2022 | DDC 971.9004/9712—dc23

Set in 10.5/14 Calluna with Calluna Sans and Ilisarniq
Book design & typesetting by Garet Markvoort, zijn digital

This book is dedicated to all Inuit who pass on Inuit naming traditions to the next generations.

Matna. Nakurmiik. Qujannamiik. Quana.

CONTENTS

PART TWO | ATIQPUT: INUIT ELDERS SPEAK ABOUT NAMING

PART THREE | EXTENDING PROJECT NAMING

FOREWORD

I am very honoured to be asked to write this foreword for this book about Project Naming.

My ataatatsiaq (grandfather) Peter Pitseolak (1902–1973) was an advocate of Inuit culture. He had many stories to tell, mostly about day-to-day happenings, and while hardly anything was recorded on paper, as there was hardly any paper to write on, he managed to keep a daily journal. As many of you know, Peter Pitseolak was an accomplished photographer and took many photographs. His life story and photographs resulted in the publication of the book *People from Our Side*.[1]

In 1961, my ataatatsiaq Peter Pitseolak moved to the small settlement of Cape Dorset, now called Kinngait, when government, nursing station, Anglican and Catholic churches, and most importantly Hudson's Bay Company, where all fur trapping was sold, were already established. Fellow Inuit from over twenty outpost camps in the surrounding area moved around the same time. Children then attended school, including his daughter Annie. This was a great time of transition for our people, and ataatatsiaq Pitseolak wanted to show this with his photographs.

Much before this time, I remember ataatatsiaq Pitseolak taking pictures at his outpost camp, located on the trail line where other people were travelling from their outpost camps much further [away]. His pictures were of people from his camp and others who were passing through.

At Peter Pitseolak's camp there was no running water, so all of his developing was done manually. When he was developing his pictures, we were not allowed to come in and out from his wooden house as the natural light was not allowed. Otherwise, it would overexpose the printing.

It was so amazing to see the pictures he took earlier developed. There was lots of setting before pictures [were taken], and some people had to wear their beautiful skin clothing, which was very important in the photographs. It is clear to me that when you look at my grandfather's photographs, he intended to ensure that traditional clothing was depicted so that this information would be available for future generations to learn from.

Like my ataatatsiaq, in 1968, I started taking photographs with an instamatic camera. I sent the negative films south for developing. It took such a long time to get the slides back. By the time I received them, I had forgotten what I had taken.

I would like to thank all the contributors who took part in the creation of this book. I also want to assure all readers making use of this Project Naming book how very valuable it is.

Jimmy Manning
Photographer, former studio manager,
Tortuga print shop
Kinngait, Nunavut

NOTE

1 Pitseolak and Eber, *People from Our Side*.

ACKNOWLEDGMENTS

All books appear in print with the help of many hands. But *Atiqput: Inuit Oral History and Project Naming* has been a particularly collaborative publication. Centring around the sharing of images, names, and conversations between Inuit, as well as those between Inuit and Qallunaat, the knowledge exchanges it describes have collaboration at their core. Indeed, for many Inuit participants, Project Naming reflects a key value of Inuit Qaujimajatuqangit, the principle of Pilimmaksarniq (Pijariuqsarniq), and defined by the Government of Nunavut as the "development of skills through observation, mentoring, practice, and effort."[1] We, the collaborative team of four editors, are delighted to publicly thank all those who worked together in the spirit of Pilimmaksarniq to bring this book together.

First and foremost, we want to acknowledge with deep gratitude all of the authors who have contributed to this volume. Elders are literally at the centre of this book and they are also the centre of Project Naming as a whole. Many thanks to Elders Sally Kate Webster, Piita Irniq, Manitok Thompson, Ann Meekitjuk Hanson, and David Serkoak who welcomed the opportunity to share their reflections with younger generations of Inuit and to introduce Qallunaat readers to Inuit culture and history. The editors of this volume are also indebted to the Elders for their guidance in the editorial process and throughout the history of Project Naming. As a project and book in which photographs are key catalysts in the retelling of histories, we are grateful to artists Jimmy Manning, Barry Pottle, and asinnajaq, as well as art historian

Heather Igloliorte, who generously shared their own images and reflections on images and the significance of naming. Project Naming was an idea first developed by Murray Angus and Morley Hanson, faculty at the Inuit post-secondary school Nunavut Sivuniksavut, based in Ottawa. We are grateful for their recounting of the project as it grew from an idea. We are also grateful to former NS students Kathleen Ivaluarjuk Merritt and Paula Ikuutaq Rumbolt for discussing their experiences. And many thanks to Frank Tester, Curtis Kuunuaq Konek, Sandra Dyck, Sheena Ellison, and Alexandra Haggert for discussing the ways that Project Naming has been extended since its formation.

This volume has its origins in a two-day workshop in March 2017, hosted by Library and Archives Canada (LAC) and Carleton University. We gratefully acknowledge the Social Sciences and Humanities Research Council of Canada's Connections Grant program for its support of the gathering and this publication. Darlene Gilson guided us through the application with her usual acumen. Additional support for the workshop was provided by LAC and Carleton University. At LAC, the workshop was made possible by the support of William Benoit, Vicky Brisson, Julie Dobbin, Alexandra Haggert, Sarah Hurford, Gordon Jung, Raphaëlle Joanisse, Karen Linauskas, Harriett Mathews, Jessica Ouvrard, and Amy Tector. Tom Thompson of LAC skilfully documented the event in photographs and video. At Carleton University, we thank contributor Sandra Dyck and the Carleton University Art Gallery for hosting one day of the gathering. The workshop came alive through the involvement of many Inuit and Qallunaat participants. For their participation, thanks to then Nunavut Sivuniksavut students, including Tetra Aaluk, Dione Adams, Yvon Aliyak, Surya Angatajuak, Candace Barnabas, Jeanina Barrieau, Aislyn Bolt, Olaph Christensen, Chantal Emiktaut, Dustin Joanas, Sebastian Kanayuk, Jillian Kaviok, Lily Kilabuk, Gabriel Klengenberg, Brandon Mannik, Amber Nukadlaaq, Senna Oolooyuk, Cathy Pikuyak, and Jamie Takkiruq. And for assistance, we are also grateful to then Carleton University students Christina Williamson, Alexandra Nahwegahbow, Robert Comeau, Emily Putnam, Jessie Raymond, and Leah Snyder as well as Clara Haskell from Concordia University. Leah Snyder and France Rivet took beautiful photographs of the event, some of which appear in these pages. And a special thank you to Elder Manitok Thompson and Ed Atkinson, director of the Nunavut Archives, for supplying and preparing country food for the workshop.

We thank Carleton University for its support of this publication, including through a Development Grant. We also received invaluable editorial assistance from Carleton University students Emily Putnam and Jessie Raymond. Many thanks to Katie Lydiatt for editorial work and assisting Beth with the index.

For ongoing support of Project Naming and its aligned research collaborations, we have many other partners to thank. First and of utmost importance, Project Naming would not exist without the generosity and knowledge-sharing of Inuit communities. Nunavut Sivuniksavut faculty and students not only initiated the project and contributed to this volume, but they have been engaged with these discussions for years. At LAC, which began a collaboration with Nunavut Sivuniksavut over twenty years ago, colleagues from across the organization have supported the project in so many ways. Project Naming is truly a team effort at LAC. Its longevity has been made possible through the dedication of a core group of colleagues and practicum students who have worked directly with Beth over the years. Through their commitment, Project Naming has developed into a nationally based initiative that includes First Nations, Inuit from across Inuit Nunangat, and the Métis Nation. These individuals include: Angèle Alain, Carrie Alexander, Marie Blake, Vicky Dalrymple, Sophie Dazé, Jill Delaney, Julie Dobbin, Kim Dubois, Michael Eamon, Nancy Fay, Caroline Forcier-Holloway, Susan Globensky, Gerry Ippersiel, Kayley Kimball, Carla Kluck, David Knox, Cédric Lafontaine, Harriett Mathews, Eric Mineault, Kaelen Murray, Patrick Osborne, Michael Rajzman, Gillian Sullivan, Tom Thompson, and Irene Van Bavel. Special thanks goes to Alexandra Haggert, who took over from Beth in 2017, and to Ellen Bond, the current coordinator. We also acknowledge Eli Brown, Jim Burant, Peter Robertson, Andrew Rodger, Guy Tessier, and Ed Tompkins, the photo archivists at LAC who saw the need for and supported Project Naming from its inception.

At McGill-Queen's University Press, we have had an indefatigable advocate in Jonathan Crago. Thank you for your astute guidance and support throughout. We are grateful to the peer review readers whose thoughtful feedback has helped us shape the volume and particularly to illuminate the Elders' words. At MQUP thanks to Elli Stylianou, Elena Goranescu, Kaitlin Littlechild, Jennifer Roberts, and Jacqueline Davis, plus a particular note of gratitude to Kathleen Fraser.

Carol offers a huge thanks to her family – John, Meg, and Alice – for everything. For help and conversations about these projects over the years, she also thanks Andrea Kunard, Liz Payne, Carol Williams, Catherine Khordoc, Anne Bowker, Anna Hoefnagels, Mitchell Frank, Jill Carrick, Brian Foss, Ruth Phillips, and Miranda Brady.

Beth is grateful to the people in her life who have supported her work on Project Naming over the years: Sean, Shari, Amanda, Sarah, and Elizabeth.

Deborah says *matna* to her mother Sally Kate Qimmiu'naaq Webster who continually shares her family and community history and answers her never-ending questions so she can pass it down to her children Sonja Akilak and Nicole Amaruq. She acknowledges her former mentors Charles Arnold and the late Barnabas Peryour who shared with her the story behind her name, Kigjugalik.

Christina thanks her family, Cathy, David, and Duncan, for their steadfast support over the years, and she is grateful to her academic mentors Michel Hogue, Ruth Phillips, Carol Payne, and Frank Tough. She wishes to acknowledge the students of Nunavut Sivnuniksavut's class of 2017, especially Candace Barnabas, Lily Kilabuk, Olaph Christiensen, Tagalik Eccles, and Jillian Howmik Kaviok. Watching them become mothers, hunters, seamstresses, and leaders over the past few years has been an honour.

Over the years of working on this volume, we four editors have also developed lasting friendships. This volume has been built on that sense of camaraderie.

NOTE

1 "Inuit Societal Values," Government of Nunavut, accessed 25 January 2022, https://www.gov.nu.ca/information/inuit-societal-values.

ABBREVIATIONS

CLEY	Department of Culture, Language, Elders and Youth in the Government of Nunavut (until 2012); now known as the Department of Culture and Heritage
CU	Carleton University
DINA	Department of Indian and Northern Affairs
GN	Government of Nunavut
HBC	Hudson's Bay Company
ITK	Inuit Tapiriit Kanatami
LAC	Library and Archives Canada
NFB	National Film Board of Canada
NGC	National Gallery of Canada
NS	Nunavut Sivuniksavut
NU	Nunavut
NWT	Northwest Territories
QIA	Qikiqtani Inuit Association
QTC	Qikiqtani Truth Commission
RCMP	Royal Canadian Mounted Police
RNWMP	Royal North-West Mounted Police
TRC	Truth and Reconciliation Commission
UBC	University of British Columbia

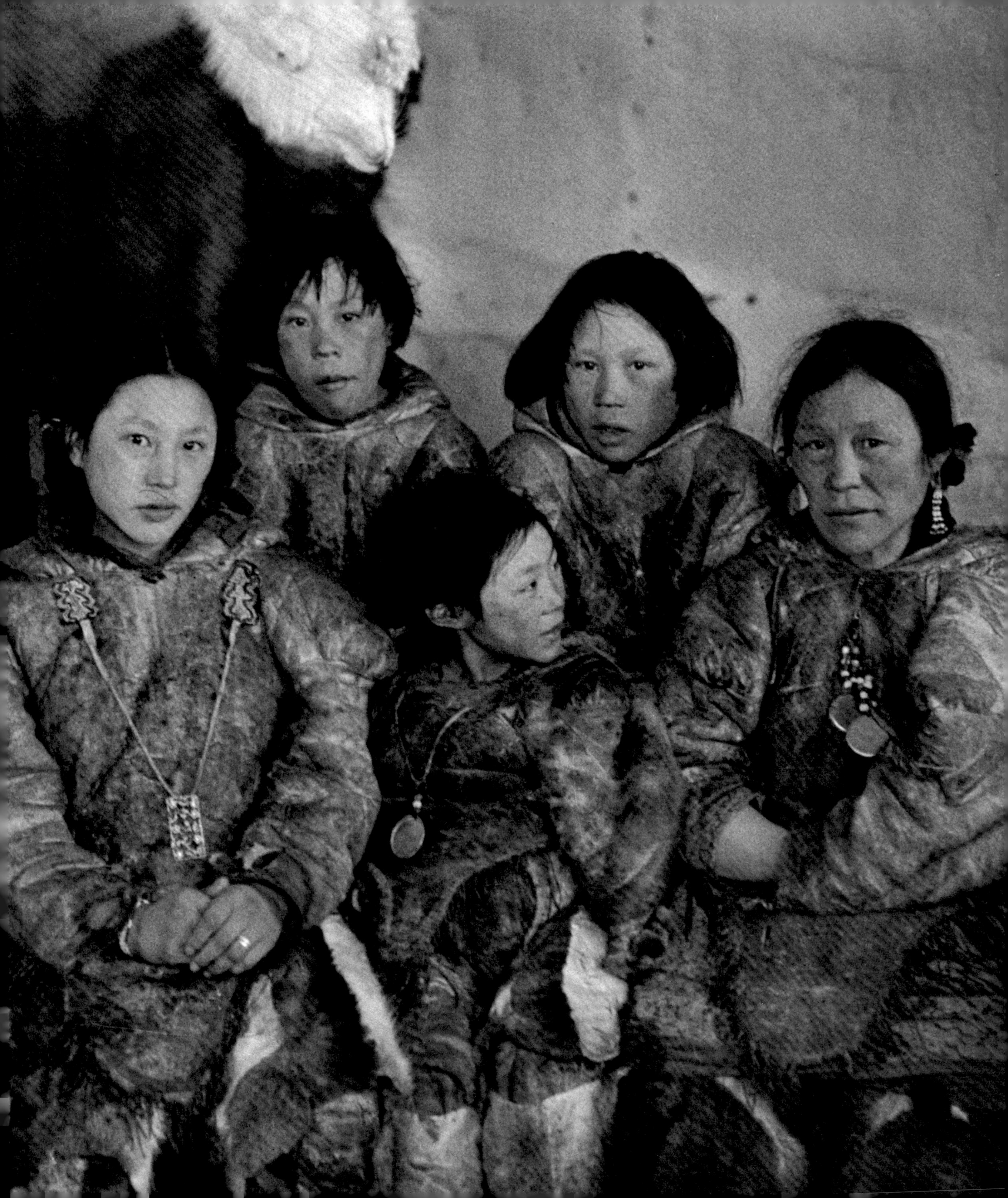

ATIQPUT

INTRODUCTION

Carol Payne, Beth Greenhorn, Deborah Kigjugalik Webster, and Christina Williamson

With contributions from Piita Irniq, Ann Meekitjuk Hanson, Sally Kate Webster, Manitok Thompson, Mathewsie Ashevak, Katrina Hatogina, and Bernadette Elgok

Our names – Atiqput – are very meaningful. They are our identification. They are our Spirits. We are named after what's in the sky for strength, what's in the water ... the land, body parts. Every name is attached to every part of our body and mind.

Yes, every name is alive. Every name has a meaning. Much of our names have been misspelled and many of them have lost their meanings forever. Our Project Naming has been about identifying Inuit, who became nameless over the years, just "unidentified eskimos ..." With Project Naming, we have put Inuit meanings back in the pictures, back to life.

Piita Irniq[1]

Atiqput: Inuit Oral History and Project Naming celebrates Inuit naming practices and through them honours Inuit culture, history, and storytelling. As Elder Piita Irniq, a contributor to this volume, states, "Our names – Atiqput – are very meaningful. They are our identification. They are our Spirits." This is a book about seeing, talking, listening, and remembering, as shared among Inuit across generations. At the same time, it also addresses the often fraught connections between Inuit (in Nunavut, particularly, but also across Inuit Nunangat and in the South) with outsiders or Qallunaat. These pages are filled with conversations between generations of Inuit as well as reflections by southern partners that have taken place across Nunavut and in Ottawa over several years. Those identifications and discussions were prompted by long-forgotten archival photographs, usually shot by southerners and intended for southern audiences, in an effort to reclaim Inuit names and identities.

The engagement with Inuit names discussed in these pages has been facilitated through Project Naming, the photo-based Inuit history research program founded by the Inuit college Nunavut Sivuniksavut (NS) and its faculty members Murray Angus and Morley Hanson, initially with funding from the Government of Nunavut. Project Naming is rooted in the Inuit-centred pedagogy of NS (see Chapter 1 in this volume for the history of NS and the origins of Project Naming). Beginning in the 1980s (in a kind of pre-history of Project Naming as a formalized initiative), NS students interviewed Elders in their home communities across Nunavut about photographs depicting Inuit from the vast collections housed at Library and Archives Canada (LAC). Those conversations helped to identify Inuit by name while forging cross-generational connections and kindling the students' deep engagement with their own culture. As Angus and Hanson state in this volume, "these images really started something."[2] By the early 2000s, the initiative became formalized when LAC began coordinating Project Naming in collaboration with NS and the Government of Nunavut's Department of Culture, Language, Elders and Youth (CLEY), as it was known at the time. Inuit collaborators from across Nunavut identified hundreds of people in historical photographs as Canada's federal archive developed innovative, dialogic means of amassing and disseminating information.

Beth Greenhorn managed Project Naming for LAC from 2003 to 2017 and is one of the co-editors of this volume. She created digital links between images and Inuit culture through LAC's website, at gatherings in Ottawa, and in communities across Nunavut as well as through social, broadcast, and print media. With Project Naming, NS and LAC aimed to establish models for Inuit-settler collaborations. It has also sparked several collaborative research initiatives including Deborah Kigjugalik Webster's research into the history of Inuit special constables, the Nanisiniq and Nanivara History Projects, and Views from the North, in which young Inuit learned how photographs created by Qallunaat could be reframed to tell Inuit stories on Inuit terms (see Chapters 11, 12, and 13).

Indeed, "these images really started something."

How do Inuit participants in Project Naming "put Inuit meanings back in the pictures, back to life"? How does it facilitate Inuit-centred knowledge? Since the early 2000s, it has involved hundreds of participants and taken varying forms, as a few anecdotes from across the project's history reveal. One of the first youth to participate in the project at that time was Mathewsie Ashevak, then an NS student. In December 2003, Mathewsie travelled to his home community of Kinngait in the Qikiqtaaluk region of Nunavut with a DVD containing several hundred digitized photographs from the collections at LAC. The images depicted Inuit from the area around present-day Kinngait. Mathewsie showed them to his step-grandfather, Pauta Saila, Saila's wife, Petalusie, as well as his grandmother, the artist Kenojuak Ashevak (see Chapter 14 in this volume and Figure I.1). The images sparked memories from these Elders. The experience was meaningful for Mathewsie, too. Reflecting on his conversations with the Elders, and the impact they had on him, he wrote:

> Before now, I had not talked much with Elders. This experience was new to me, and I really enjoyed it. Each time they named a person in the picture, it made me want to go back to the time that they remembered. The most interesting thing I heard was how nice it was in the past, when there were few houses and roads ...

1.1 | [Udluriak (left) and Kenojuak Ashevak (right) on board the Eastern Arctic Patrol ship MV *Regina Polaris*], 1948. Original title: Another picture of Oolooreak and a friend.

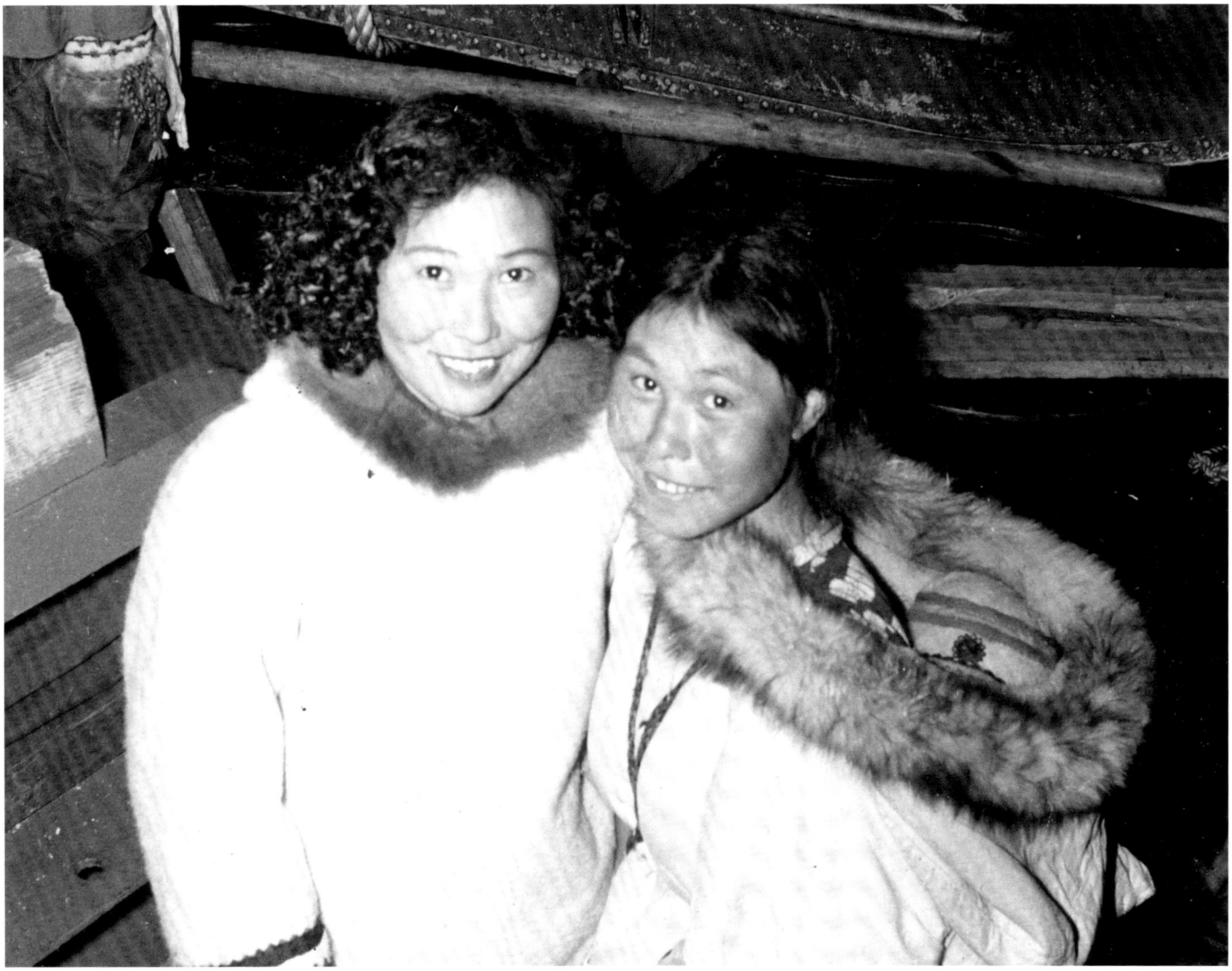

> walking from one camp to another … that's what our Elders were like, working to live.[3]

Mathewsie's encounter in 2003 reveals how the private experience of sharing archival images strengthened bonds between Inuit Elders and youth.

But through its institutional partner, LAC, Project Naming has also prompted encounters in more public ways.[4] For several years, *Nunavut News North*, a weekly newspaper distributed across Nunavut, published "Do You Know Your Elders?" (see Figure 3.10). This popular feature included an archival photograph of Inuit culled from the collections held by LAC. Each week, Inuit recognized relatives and friends. In this volume, for example, Elder Sally Kate Webster recalls opening a copy of *Nunavut News North* to find a picture of her mother and sisters Janet and Lucy (see Figure 5.2). Moments of recognition, like Webster's, not only prompted personal memories but in turn these recollections changed the southern historical record. Since the Project Naming collaboration between NS and LAC began in 2001–02, several thousand individuals, places, and events have been identified in photographs held at LAC, and, by extension, the institution's approach to cataloguing – to creating archival records – has itself been changed.

Most often, encounters prompted by Project Naming – and its affiliated partners – are private conversations that engage in identifications, local histories, and caring relationships between participants. Almost a decade after Mathewsie Ashevak sat down with his Elders in Kinngait, another Project Naming conversation took place 1,800 kilometres away in the Kitikmeot region. In January 2012, then NS student Katrina Hatogina and Elder Bernadette Elgok sat down in Elgok's home in Kugluktuk, both women's home community. As Hatogina later explained, because Elgok is her best friend's grandmother, she is at the Elder's home almost every day.

Resting between Hatogina and Elgok was a digital audio recorder and a simple three-ring binder filled with about forty new photographic prints made from archival images from the collections at LAC with additional images from collections at the National Gallery of Canada. The photographs had been shot by southern photographers during the 1950s and 1960s when the area was called "Coppermine" by southerners and renowned as a centre of the fox fur trade. They depicted various people and places in and around the area: young Inuit women modelling fox fur; a camp on the land; the view out to an island; an old church; and community members posing for the camera or greeting a biplane. As with the other photographs, these pictures were all originally intended for southern audiences.

Yet in 2012, in Elgok's home, these southern-made images prompted an intimate conversation about local Kugluktuk people and history while simultaneously bridging two generations. Elgok, who moved to Kugluktuk in 1948, was engrossed by the pictures. She identified a few people in them, described how Inuit hunted at the time, and remarked about changes in the shoreline. Her conversation moved from the 1950s to life in the hamlet today. Even when the faces were unfamiliar to her, she was moved by revisiting her community through photographs and, even more, having an opportunity to share her recollections with a young woman with whom she held a strong bond.

At one point, the conversation paused as Elgok recognized a very familiar face in the album: her own. Two of the photographs in the album featured her, then in her twenties,

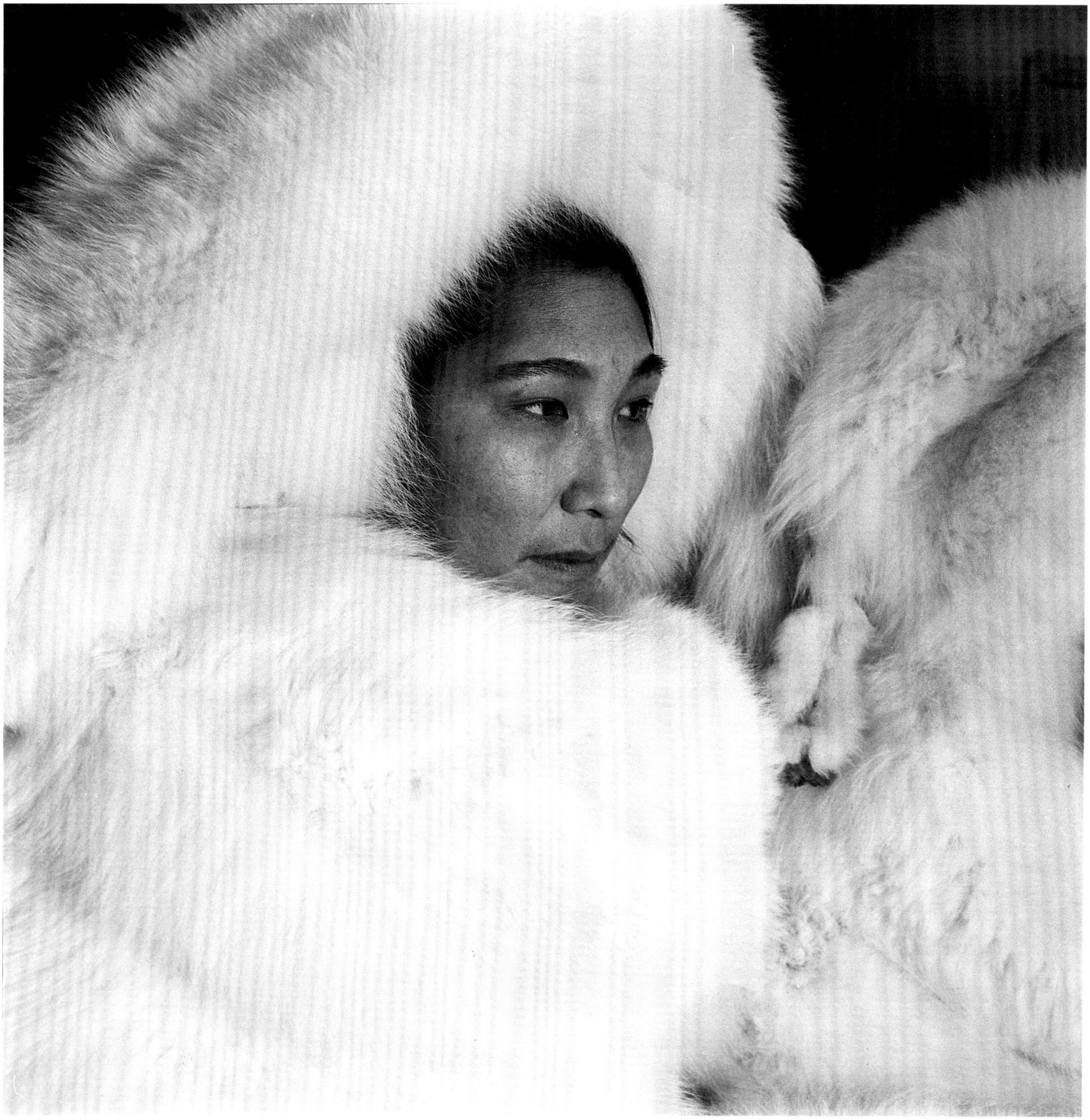

1.2 | [Bernadette Elgok], 1966. Original title: woman in furs.

modelling (Figure I.2). As Hatogina recalled, "When she [Elgok] saw herself, she was like 'Boy, I was such a beautiful young lady,' and I noticed that she felt good about it, after seeing herself. I told her afterwards, I'm like, 'You're always pretty!' She was really smiling as I walked out."[5] The two women spoke for about an hour, with the younger one recording parts of their encounter for the Views from the North website, an affiliate of Project Naming. Their conversation bridged generations of Inuit while challenging conventional historical readings of historical photographs of Inuit.

Nothing, it seems, could be homier than the three anecdotes we have just recounted: an Elder happening upon a picture of her family and two youth chatting with their Elders. We imagine that most readers – Inuit and non-Inuit alike – turning this page have participated in conversations somewhat like the one just described, perhaps with grandparents or elderly aunts or uncles or with a young child curious about your own past. They are conversations typically couched in nostalgia or a sense of familial duty. But this book will suggest that those cozy, familiar conversations between generations or when an Elder recognizes her own family in print, discussions that revolved around naming, photographs, place, Inuit culture, and memory, are also culturally and politically charged events, acts of decolonization.

For Inuit in Nunavut – like many Indigenous groups – the act of memory is, indeed, politically and culturally significant. In these pages, memory work takes the form of reclaiming lost names and, through them, honouring Inuit traditions and intergenerational connections. Memory is a key strategy for reaffirming cultural identity as well as reclaiming and reshaping western and southern historical narratives about their culture and communities. In so doing, memory work augments ongoing struggles toward self-governance, land claims, language retention, and the repatriation of Indigenous material culture, while reasserting cultural bonds and knowledge.[6] And, at the same time, it complements the guiding principles, traditional knowledges, skills, and attitudes that encompass Inuit Qaujimajatuqangit (IQ).[7]

Project Naming, like Indigenous memory work more broadly, also speaks to the complexity of exchanges: temporal, generational, and cultural. Not only do the images reach across generations of Inuit but they also participate in an interchange between Inuit and Qallunaat. Ironically, the images that prompted those intimate discussions about family, community members, and Inuit culture were photographed by outsiders and are now mainly housed at LAC, Canada's federal archive in the National Capital Region, or other collections, thousands of kilometres from the Nunavut communities they depict. Elders and youth became acquainted with these photographs through the work of LAC staff, particularly that of Greenhorn, and other southern researchers. In short, the photo-based conversations narrated above were at once community-oriented discussions of Inuit culture and part of an intercultural network.

This volume discusses the central cultural importance of Inuit names – Atiqput. It does so through the work of Project Naming, the Inuit cultural history research initiative founded by NS and expanded by LAC in which many Inuit Elders, youth, and community members from across Nunavut, as well as southern researchers, have participated or are now participating. An ongoing initiative, this collaboration centres on the use of photography as an agent of Inuit cultural consolidation. It is built on a partnership between NS and LAC with the subsequent involvement of community groups in Nunavut and researchers from Carleton University (CU) and the University of British Columbia (UBC). At the core of Project Naming and the initiatives that it has engendered are Elders' commentaries on and identifications of Inuit in archival photographs depicting communities in what is now Nunavut.

Project Naming also provides valuable lessons to Qallunaat about Inuit culture and heritage, Nunavut, and northern research. Participating Elders and younger Inuit have asserted Inuit names and meanings into photographs and history; in doing so, they have also challenged how research with Inuit is conducted in the South. In creating a mechanism for dialogic identifications of the photo collections held at LAC, Project Naming has strived to develop a model for institutions to work with Indigenous communities and develop more collaborative approaches. In this way, Project Naming responds to calls – from Inuit Tapiriit Kanatami and the Truth and Reconciliation Commission of Canada, among other bodies – toward responsibility and reciprocity.[8] At the same time, it establishes a mode of working that replaces conventional extractionist research approaches used by many southerners in the North. Instead, it models collaborative work that privileges Inuit contributions and cultural forms, including prominently Oral History.

As a network between Inuit and Qallunaat, Project Naming provides intercultural dialogue, but it is also punctuated by silences. By design, most identification sessions conducted for Project Naming were not recorded; instead, they were private, intimate conversations. While participants have shared thousands of image identifications with LAC, and in doing so have "restoried" the colonial historical record, the details of their conversations were usually not made available publicly. Indeed, it is instructive to think of those intimate identification sessions in terms of what Métis scholar and artist David Garneau calls "irreconcilable spaces of Aboriginality." Garneau defines these spaces as

> sites of epistemological debate. In the exchange of stories, gestures, touches, thoughts, feelings, and laughter the very nature of contemporary Aboriginality is subtly tested, reconsidered, provisionally confirmed, or gently reconfigured, composed, and played in rehearsal. This requires separate discursive territories for First Nations, Métis, and Inuit folks to be themselves and to work themselves out.

These spaces are irreconcilable in the sense that their function depends upon a difference from settlers.[9]

We acknowledge and respect those "irreconcilable spaces," which at times take the form of silences in the southern (settler) historical record. They remind us of the limits of both intercultural dialogue and archival knowledge as well as the ephemeral, fluid nature of Oral Tradition. But, at the same time, there has long been a great deal of interest within Inuit communities in recording Elders' recollections as important means of maintaining traditions, language, and historical knowledge among Inuit (and also asserting Inuit ways of knowing into the southern record). As discussed below, these efforts have resulted in several well-known Oral History initiatives across Nunavut. In this volume, we have attempted to contribute to those efforts through recorded reminisces of Elders and other Inuit. Indeed, some research conducted in affiliation with Project Naming – including Deborah Kigjugalik

Webster's work on the history of special constables (see Chapter 11), the Nanisiniq and Nanivara History Projects (see Chapter 12), and Views from the North (see Chapter 13) – includes recorded interviews between youth and Elders as key components of their work. In these ways, *Atiqput: Inuit Oral History and Project Naming* acknowledges "irreconcilable spaces" of Inuit culture while employing select recorded Oral Histories to support Inuit ways of knowing and restory the southern historical record.

Collaborative, intergenerational, intercultural, and interdisciplinary, Project Naming is located at the intersections of Inuit culture, memory studies, Nunavummiut political strategies, Indigenous pedagogy and research methodologies, interventions into archival practice, visual anthropology, and the history of photography.

Many of the names or identifications, images, and conversations prompted by these undertakings are available on the web. On LAC's Project Naming website as well as through social media and on websites developed for the Nanisiniq and Nanivara History Projects and Views from the North, visitors can browse archival photographs, read new identifications of people in the images, watch videos, listen to audio recordings, and read participants' reflections. The Internet has been deployed to reach the projects' key participants and audiences: Inuit in the communities of what is now Nunavut depicted in the archival photographs. Through those linked sites, cultural knowledge is shared across Nunavut as well as throughout Inuit Nunangat and among Inuit living in the South. The web allows this information to be modified in a dynamic model of collaborative research and dissemination that reflects and makes virtual the flow of Inuit Oral Tradition. Indeed, as many Inuit acknowledge, interactive web-based technology is a particularly effective tool for geographically dispersed but Internet-connected communities across the North. According to celebrated Inuit filmmaker Zacharias Kunuk, for example, the web is "the most important media tool of the twenty-first century to protect Inuit language and culture."[10]

Yet the concerns addressed in Project Naming also call for the analytic space of a book that enters Inuit Knowledge onto the academic record and considers the implications of this multifaceted research. As such, this volume is intended to complement material on the websites. In *Atiqput: Inuit Oral History and Project Naming*, the reader will encounter a mix of words and images: reidentifications of archival photographs by Inuit participants; reflections on Inuit naming practices, culture, and history by Elders and other participants; perspectives from NS faculty and LAC staff, the two core institutional participants; and reflections by Inuit and Qallunaat participants on methodology, the history of photography among Inuit, and the uncertain space of the southern researcher in these conversations. In sum, *Atiqput: Inuit Oral History and Project Naming* is a book about connections: intergenerational bonds and exchanges among Inuit as well as between the South and the North, between Inuit Knowledge and southern academic scholarship. Ultimately, it is a book about learning. These pages are filled with what young Inuit have learned, what the Elders have relearned, and what southern researchers and institutions can learn. In these ways, it connects scholarship and pedagogy, North and South, youth and wisdom gained with age.

Project Naming's core goal is returning names to Inuit represented in archival photographs and through that process acknowledging the deep significance of the naming process in Inuit culture, as discussed below around the concept of atiqput. This book, *Atiqput: Inuit Oral History and Project Naming*, has four goals related to that overarching concern. First, the volume provides a record for Inuit communities (in Inuit Nunangat and in the South) of names and naming that will render aspects of Project Naming's and aligned research initiatives' websites into a more permanent form. Second, it attempts to insert Inuit Knowledge into the southern historical record by addressing both an academic audience and a wider southern public. To this end, the volume mainly comprises Inuit contributions with identifications of images and excerpts from interviews, in addition to the archival photographs that initiated this discussion. Third, it offers a detailed discussion of the methodologies used in Project Naming and aligned research programs; in this way, *Atiqput: Inuit Oral History and Project Naming* builds on important work in several areas to provide guideposts for future projects. Finally, it is a book of cultural analysis in which the experiences of Inuit – including Elders and youth – as well as those of southern researchers are examined.

Atiqput, "Our names"

Elder Piita Irniq, one of the contributors to this volume, crafted the title by suggesting the word *atiqput*. He translates atiqput as "our names" and notes that it also relates to the word *aqiqaqpuguttauq* ("We also have names"). As quoted at the opening of this introductory essay, Elder Irniq asserts that "Our names – Atiqput – are very meaningful. And Project Naming reflects that. They are our identification. They are our Spirits. We are named after what's in the sky for strength, what's in the water … the land, body parts. Every name is attached to every part of our body and mind."

Indeed, a name and the act of naming are central to Inuit culture. The indispensable volume *Uqalurait: An Oral History of Nunavut*, for example, prioritizes Elders' discussions of naming as the first of its twenty-three themes on Inuit identity.[11] As Uqalurait editors John Bennett and Susan Rowley state, "Three essential parts made a human in the Inuit view: body, soul, and name. A nameless child was not fully human; giving it a name, whether before or after birth, made it whole."[12]

The use of the Inuktitut word atiqput in the title of this volume is intended to capture the cultural importance of naming for Inuit. Further, it signals the rich and varied meanings of Inuit names and naming practices across generations. As Elder Ann Meekitjuk Hanson, also a contributor to this volume, states, atiqput "says everything about our names, naming tradition, naming today and tomorrow, why we have names, who we are."[13] Asserting the importance of atiqput is also a way of asserting Inuit culture while challenging widespread historical erasures, misidentifications, misspellings and derogatory labels.

With those eloquent comments about the meaningfulness of atiqput from Elders Piita Irniq and Ann Meekitjuk Hanson in mind, we pause and ask, what is in a name? Within Inuit culture, responses to this question reveal the complexity of naming traditions as well as the significance and weight that each name carries. This question also underscores the significant changes imposed upon Inuit names beginning with the first European contact, followed by Christian missionaries, and subsequent colonial identification schemes imposed by the Canadian federal government. As scholar Valerie Alia summarizes, "conquered subjects may be colonized in different ways, but renaming is almost always part of their colonization."[14] Describing the intricacies of naming practices and the significance of namesakes in Inuit culture, Pauktuutit, the Inuit Women of Canada Association, asserts:

> Inuit believe that when a child is born, the "soul" or spirit of a recently deceased relative is taken on by the newborn. The newborn is then named after this relative. This "soul" manifests in the child in a variety of ways, including certain physical characteristics, skills or personality traits. Since the child is, in a sense, part of the person after whom they have been named, they are deserving of the same respect and treatment as this person received while they were alive.[15]

Related to the practice of creating namesake relationships, Inuit culture does not observe gendered distinctions used in most southern societies. Inuk artist and arts administrator Heather Campbell[16] explains:

> If a boy was named after a deceased woman with children, those children would address the boy as "my mother" or "my little mother" to acknowledge that special relationship. Bonds are often formed between people who are not related. It's a lovely way of creating a strong sense of belonging and strengthening interconnectedness within a community. Inuit believe some of the unique characteristics of someone who has passed can live on in their namesake.[17]

In this way, naming in Inuit culture connects generations profoundly.

The arrival of European explorers, as early as the sixteenth century, and later European and American whalers brought the first of many renaming systems imposed on Inuit by outsiders. Unable to pronounce names in Inuktut,[18] the earliest Qallunaat to visit Inuit Nunangat gave Inuit they met foreign names. Subsequently, Qallunaat missionaries – as part of their efforts to convert Inuit to Christianity – bestowed them with biblical names. While many Inuit adopted Christian names, as Ann Meekitjuk Hanson discusses in Chapter 8, they also *Inuktized* them, demonstrating resistance to southern culture. For example, John became Joanasie; Mary, Miali; Abel, Ipeelie; and Elizabeth, Ilisapie.

Beginning in the late nineteenth century, the resource-rich North attracted yet more Qallunaat, many affiliated with the federal Canadian government. This period saw an influx of employees from the Department of the Interior,[19] the Royal Canadian Mounted Police, and other federal government officials. They established administrative centres throughout the North.

Southern interventions accelerated further following the Second World War. Government bureaucrats depended upon the cooperation and assistance of Inuit to carry out their claims to sovereignty. These devastating interventions included forced relocations to permanent settlements and to the High Arctic, as well as the establishment of the Distant Early Warning (DEW) Line, to name just a few. The following quote from a 1975 report prepared for the former Department of Indian and Northern Affairs (DINA) exemplifies the government's justifications for their administration of Inuit in the loaded language and attitudes of the day:

> For centuries the Eskimos of Canada's Arctic, or Inuit as some people preferred

to be called, lived their lives in almost total isolation ... most did not enter into permanent contact with other societies until the twentieth century when the spread of trading posts across the Arctic brought *once and for all the white man with his institutions, his bureaucracy and his passion for order.*[20]

In its quest to impose forms of southern management, the Canadian government devised several methods to enumerate the Inuit population, often by erasing Inuit names. As Natan Obed, Inuit Tapiriit Kanatami president, has recently stated, "The erasure of our names became commonplace, with wide-ranging effects throughout Inuit Nunangat. It was a colonial tactic that caused disruption in Inuit naming practices and family connections, while stripping us of our identities."[21] The first system to enumerate Inuit began in the Eastern Arctic in 1932 with fingerprinting.[22] This practice was followed by mugshots of Inuit holding slates with an early identification number system, as captured in the three photographs of a family from Mittimatalik (Pond Inlet) taken in 1945 (Figures I.3, I.4, I.5).

The "problem" with naming and identification of Inuit persisted among southern officials, who maintained surveillance of Inuit to document hunting, trapping, education, hospitalization, and misdemeanors.[23] After years of debating various identification systems, officials devised "Eskimo Disc Numbers" (ujamiit) as a way to keep track of every Inuk. They divided Inuit Nunangat into twelve districts, separated into west and east, and issued each Inuk a unique numeric identifier.[24] Discs were stamped with an "E" for east or "W" for west, and numbers designated each district, community, and individual (see Inuk artist Barry Pottle's photographic responses to the disc numbers in this volume). Recalling authoritarian rules of this system, Apphia Agalakti Awa (E5-345) recounts:

> The Qallunaat told us to carry them [discs] with us at all times and never get them dirty. They told us that if we went to hospital down South, we had to take our numbers with us. That was the only way the government could recognize us, was by our number ... If a person died in the hospital down South, before they buried that person, the government would put the E5 number on the coffin ... Today, when people go out down South to look for their relatives' graves, they use the E5 number to locate the grave.[25]

Opponents compared this numbering system to dog tags, arguing that it was dehumanizing. The disc number system was eventually discontinued. In its place, the federal government, along with the Northwest Territories Council, introduced "Project Surname" to replace the disc numbering system. Under this new initiative, conducted from 1968 to 1971, every Inuk was required to adopt a surname, even though this practice was foreign to Inuit culture and society (see David Serkoak's account of Project Surname in Chapter 9).[26]

Many Qallunaat who travelled North took photographs of Inuit they encountered. As the national repository of federal government records and private collections of national historical significance, LAC holds thousands of photographs depicting Inuit.[27] In general, photographers did not record their names (or the names of other Indigenous Peoples). Where names exist on photographic records, either as captions in albums, or written below or on the back of a photograph, they are

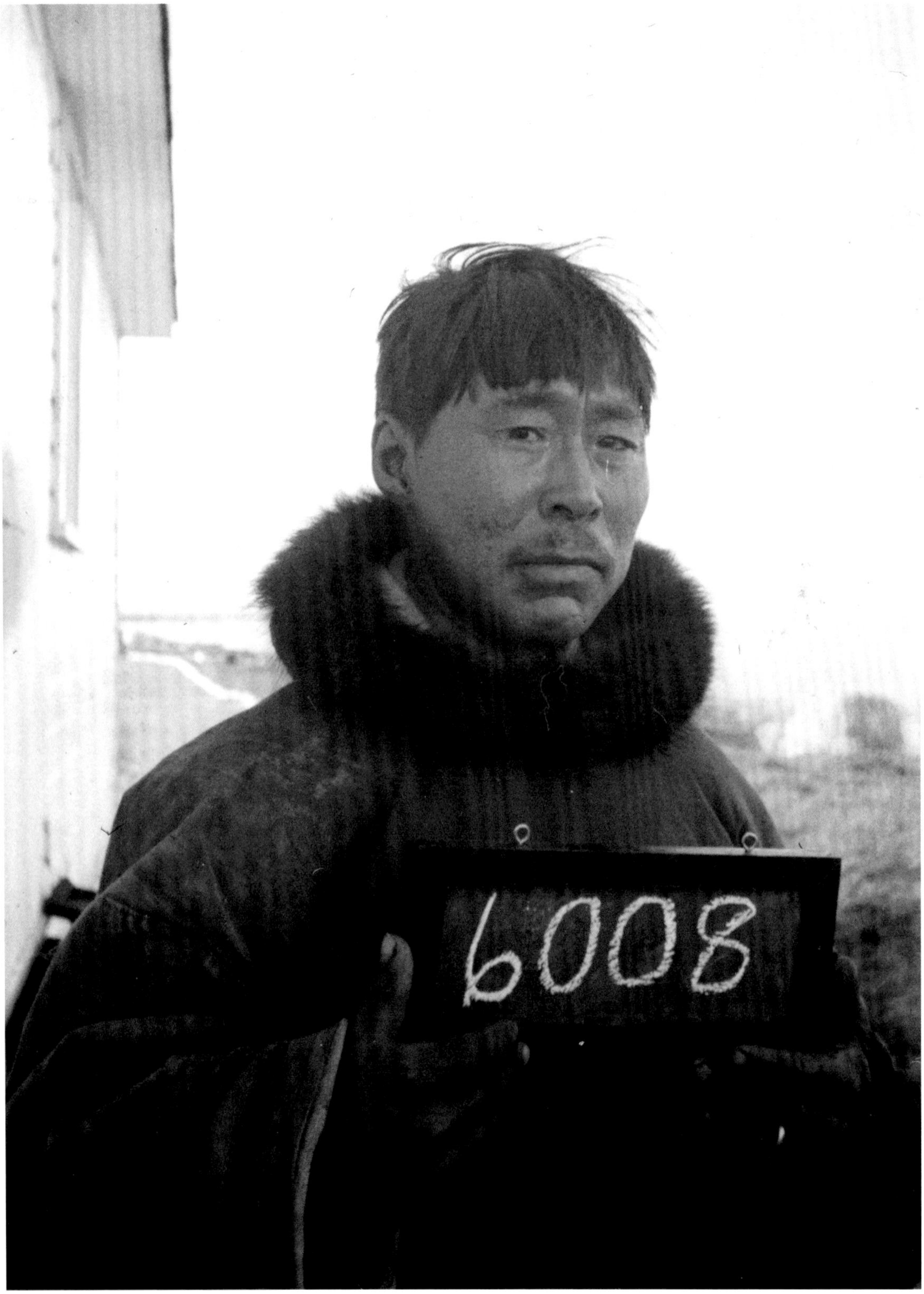

1.3 | [David Arnatsiaq], Mittimatalik. Original title: Pond Inlet, 1945.

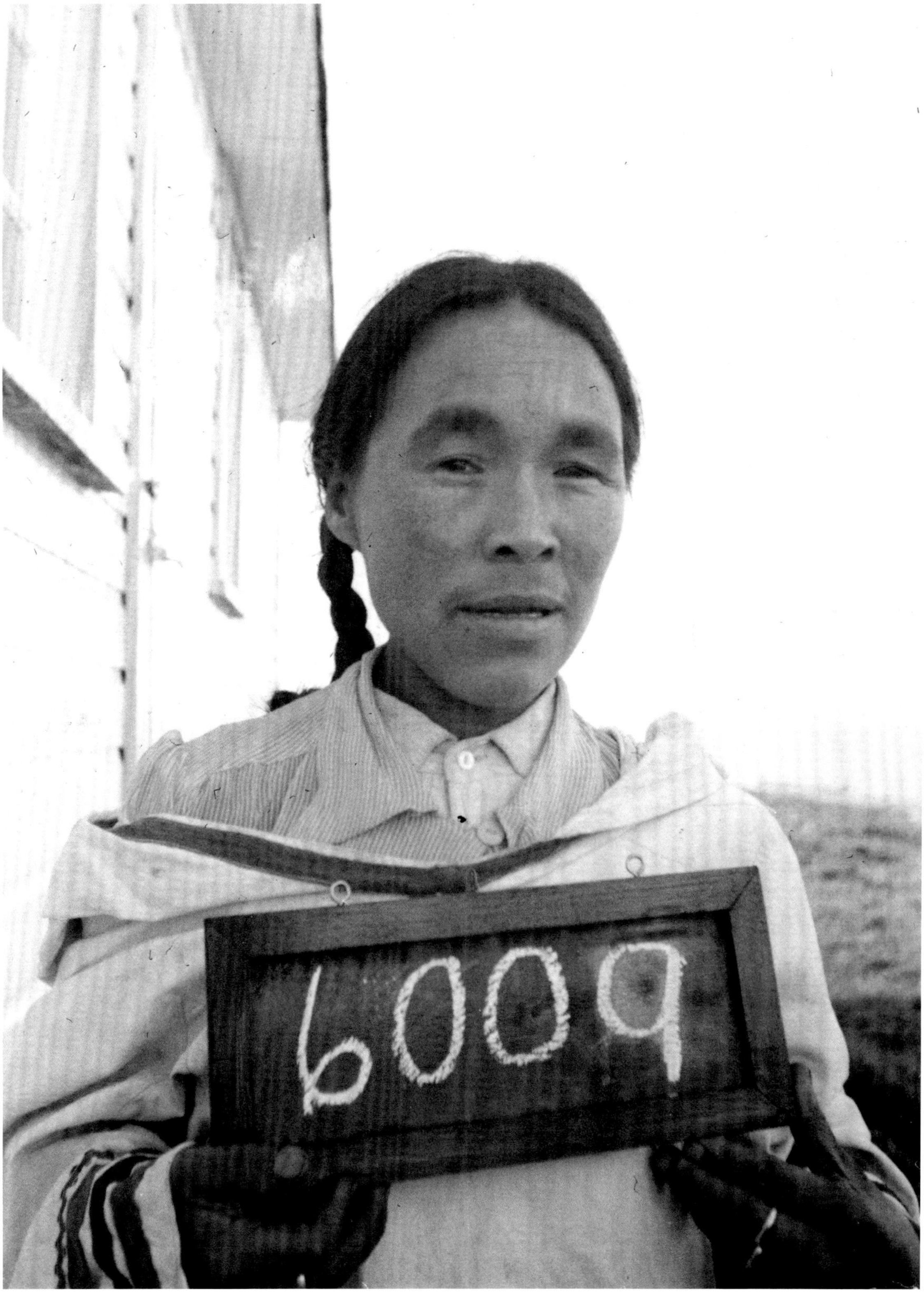

1.4 | [Tuurnagaaluk], Mittimatalik. Original title: Pond Inlet, 1945.

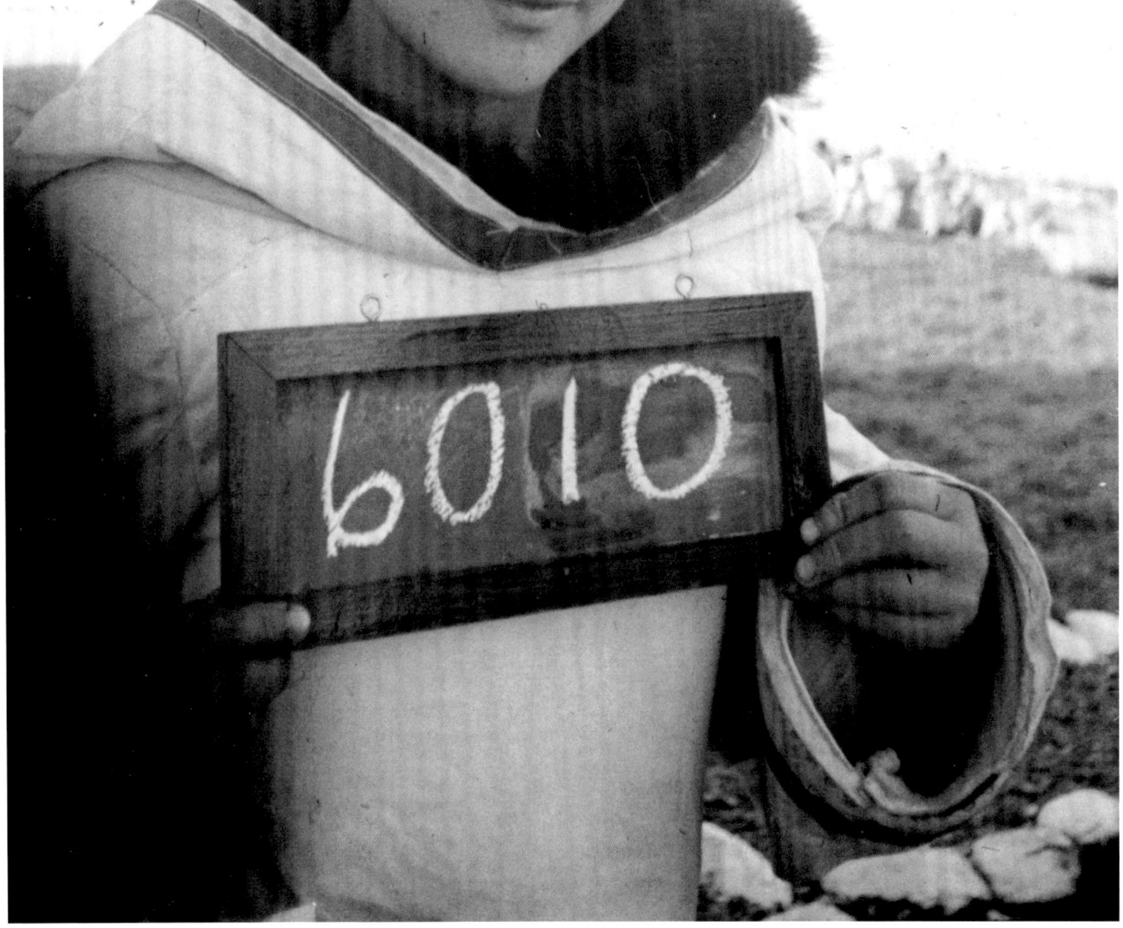

1.5 | [Juunaisi (also identified as Eunice Kunuk Arreak)], Mittimatalik. Original title: Pond Inlet, 1945.

1.6 (*opposite*) | [Five women seated in an iglu; Niviaqsarjuk is second from the left], Qatiktalik. Original title: "Arctic Bells" [*sic*] Cape Fullerton, Hudson Bay: Rosa, Hattie, Nellie, Cooper and Tidley Winks, March 22, 1905.

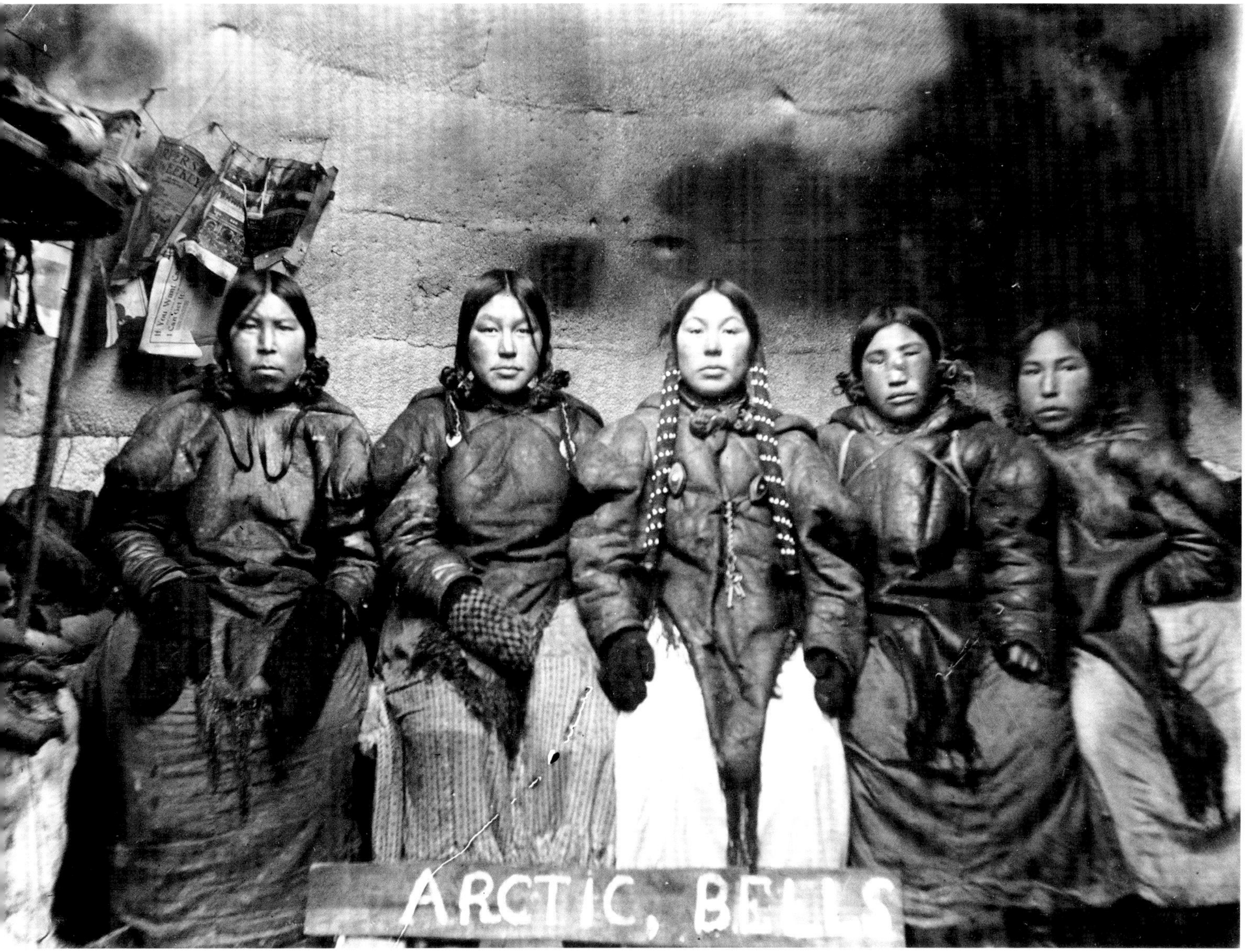

usually Anglicized, and in some cases include demeaning epithets. Typical is a 1905 image of five women taken inside an iglu (Figure I.6). Joseph-Elzéar Bernier, the photographer of this portrait, officially titled "Arctic, Bells [*sic*]," identified the women with names and nicknames unrelated to their language and traditions: "Rosa, Hattie, Nellie, Cooper and Tidley Winks."[28]

As the contributors to this book explore, Inuit names have a special significance that connect individuals to their ancestors, lineage, and culture. The loss of knowledge about one's namesake has had detrimental effects upon younger generations of Inuit. According to Elder Armand Tagoona, "An Inuk believes that when you name your child after the dead one, then the dead one lives again in the name, and the spirit of the dead one has a body again."[29] And as Alia argues, "in Inuit society, names literally create and continue life."[30] Fundamentally, the power of names is intricately woven into the fabric of individual and social identities. Suzanne Steele, a participant in Project Naming, posted on Facebook: "Through our names we have agency and dignity and cease being 'subjects.'"[31] The concept of atiqput, the naming and the reclamation of Inuit identities, is a key goal of Project Naming.

Unikkaat

Atiqput: Inuit Oral History and Project Naming is also a book about knowledge passed on from generation to generation by Oral Tradition. Here, knowledge is particularly focused on the significance of naming practices within Inuit culture. In this way, the book – and Project Naming as a whole – also reflects the IQ values of Piliriqatigiingniq (the development of collaborative relationships or working together for a common purpose) and Pilimmaksarniq (skills and knowledge acquisition).[32] And, centrally, it shares knowledge through unikkaat.

The word *unikkaat* is defined by Elders participating in Nunavut Arctic College's *Interviewing Inuit Elders* series as "modern stories."[33] The linguist Louis-Jacques Dorais states that the term "applies to any story narrating events that happened recently or in a not-too-distant past."[34] Scholar Keavy Martin, in her innovative study on Inuit literature, uses the term *inuusirmingnik unikkaat* to refer to life stories or memories told from the perspective of personal experiences.[35] In this way, modern or recent stories (unikkaat) differ significantly from the concept of unikkaaqtuat. Unikkaaqtuat is defined by the Nunavut Arctic College oral history program as "very old stories"[36] and according to Dorais "is a legend or a myth (Inuit do not distinguish between the two) considered to have happened a very long time ago."[37] The identifications and conversations sparked by Project Naming engage with Elders' memories of recent histories and, as such, reflect the specific concept of unikkaat.

In recent years, a series of important Oral History projects in Nunavut have been established to gather and keep Elders' life stories. Key among these initiatives are Nunavut Arctic College's Oral History projects (cited above), the volume *Uqalurait: An Oral History of Nunavut*, and the Igloolik Oral History Project, as well as research by Janet McGrath, Louis-Jacques Dorais, and Keavy Martin, among many others.[38] The concept of unikkaat is important across Inuit generations. We note, for example, that the great Inuit filmmaker Alethea Arnaquq-Baril's production company is called "Unikkaat Studios, Inc."[39]

Project Naming contributes to Oral History initiatives and other forms of Inuit storywork through photo-based identifications, which in turn prompt unikkaat. The rich meanings of names and the process of names are always at the core of those conversations.

While Elders' knowledge conveyed through the flow of Oral Tradition – and, specifically, unikkaat – is central to Project Naming, these initiatives also revolve around Inuit experiences and perceptions today. As Alexina Kublu, Frédéric Laugrand, and Jarich Oosten have stated of the Nunavut Arctic College Oral Traditions Project, "in qualifying knowledge of the Elders as 'traditional,' we should never forget that it was always directed to the future, intended to give a perspective to younger generations so that they were better equipped to face the changes they were facing."[40] Naming through photographic identifications and the stories that images elicit are not only about the past but implicitly guide younger Inuit in their lives today and in the future. As a research program rooted in the Inuit-centred pedagogy developed at NS, Project Naming aims to participate in its goal to guide Inuit youth to live life today through Inuit teachings. These photo-based encounters instill a sense of the importance of naming practices and through them, the importance of Inuit cultural heritage and Inuktut language skills that students at NS and other Inuit youth are taking up wholeheartedly.

Readers will find many stories in this book. As co-editor Deborah Kigjugalik Webster puts it, "When we Inuit share our knowledge, life stories or memories with Project Naming we are reclaiming our history." For example, in Chapter 7, Elder Manitok Thompson shows a photograph (see Figure 7.2) taken by naval captain and Arctic explorer Joseph-Elzéar Bernier with the caption "Eskimo Couple, Cape Fullerton, 1904–05." In contrast to that uninformative caption, Thompson's interpretations of the image provide rich context and new meanings. She identifies this couple as her great-grandparents, identifying the woman, her great-grandmother, as Tulugaa, and the man, her great-grandfather, as Tassiuq. Thompson goes on to say that her granddaughter was named after Tulugaa. In this way, naming becomes a powerful link, reaching across six generations. Names also attest to cross-cultural relations. Thompson, for example, explains that her maternal grandfather, Iqungajuq (Tulugaa and Tassiuq's son), was given the name "Dick Wager" by whalers. She talks about how her grandparents took part in the search for Franklin's ship, and she recounts other accounts of her family history.

While the assertion of atiqput is a core aim of Project Naming, Inuit participating also engage with unikkaat. Through those processes of naming, stories are shared, prompted by historical photographs.

Historical Images and Inuit Culture

If Project Naming celebrates Inuit names and intergenerational connections, what role do the archival photographs play in those significant reidentifications?[41]

Paradoxically, the photographs that spark those deep engagements with Inuit culture are, almost exclusively, the work of non-Inuit southerners. Most of the photographs used in Project Naming are ethnographic likenesses and come from the holdings of LAC. As Greenhorn discusses elsewhere, LAC images used in the project range in date from the early 1900s to the early 1970s, though most were taken during the 1940s and 1950s.[42] The emphasis on this relatively recent history was intended to benefit from the living memories of Elders. These images were also made during a period of escalating and damaging contact between Inuit and southerners. Many of the photographs were shot under the auspices of various federal agencies, including the National Film Board of Canada (NFB), the then DINA, and National Health and Welfare, among others. As such, they were harnessed to the colonial mandates of Canada: assimilation, nation-building, and land and resource exploitation. Other bodies of photography used in Project Naming were shot by individual professional or amateur photographers. They were intended for southern audiences, not for Inuit eyes. The photographs often connote, in coded visual form, prevalent southern attitudes toward Inuit at the time.

The photographic raw material of Project Naming is part of a long history of Inuit being visualized by southerners. This history includes images made in the sixteenth century when British explorer Martin Frobisher travelled three times across parts of what is now known as the Eastern Canadian Arctic between 1576 and 1578.[43] Frobisher, his crew, and authorities in England under the reign of Elizabeth I recorded and disseminated their understanding of Inuit Nunangat and of Inuit themselves through the kind of empirical evidence that would have been accepted as credible within the values of sixteenth-century Europe. These included maps, texts about the voyages written by such figures as Richard Hakluyt and George Best, and naturalistic renderings of Inuit (some of whom were famously taken – against their will – to England).[44] The practice of visually documenting European exploration in Inuit Nunangat was continued by those seeking a Northwest passage from members of the ill-fated Franklin Expedition in 1845 to the Norwegian Roald Amundsen's successful navigation in 1903–06. Maps and visual documents were tantamount to planting a flag in the ground to (visually) claim ownership over territory.[45]

When the camera arrived in the North, visual contact between Inuit and Qallunaat escalated. As Richard Condon and Pamela Stern have shown, photographs were made in Inuit Nunangat as early as 1853, but it was not until the 1880s that the region was photographed extensively. Project Naming's understanding of the complex role photography (and film) played historically in Inuit-Qallunaat relations is informed by the work of many scholars.[46] Among them, one key source is *Imaging the Arctic*, an indispensable 1998 collected volume co-edited by J.C.H. King and Henrietta Lidchi.[47]

More often than not, the camera was understood historically as a tool of scientists and social scientists – ranging from geologists, biologists, and geographers to ethnographers.[48] Among ethnographers – and other photographers whose work reflected aspects of ethnography – the camera became a nearly ubiquitous tool by the early twentieth century. At Qatiktalik, around 1903–04 alone, for example, Joseph-Elzéar Bernier, Captain George Comer, an American whaler commissioned by anthropologist Franz Boas, A.P. Low of the Geological Survey of Canada's (GSC) Neptune Expedition, and portrait photographer Geraldine Moodie all depicted Inuit they encountered.[49] A decade later, the GSC's Canadian Arctic Expedition of 1913–18 produced dozens of photographs of Inuit from around Kugluktuk credited to Diamond Jenness, Vilhjálmur Stefánsson, and G.H. Wilkins.[50] Ethnographic-style photography also served missionary efforts in the region. Archibald Lang Fleming, Anglican bishop of the Arctic, photographed and filmed his congregants and other Inuit for publications and films aimed at mass conversions.[51] The most indelible ethnographic images of Inuit may have been those made by Robert Flaherty for the 1922 film *Nanook of the North* and in related still photographs. In filmic sequences and artfully posed portraits, Flaherty created visual emblems of Inuit as Other.[52]

Early twentieth-century ethnographic images of Inuit – and those reflective of the ethnographic gaze – were informed by a salvage paradigm, the effort to preserve vestiges of supposedly vanishing cultures and in doing so implicitly present them as inferior to the West or South.[53] Subsequent photojournalistic depictions of Inuit in the mid-twentieth century and after often perpetuated these tendencies.[54] Such images typically present their Inuit subjects as a primitive and vanishing peoples living outside the modern; in short, they replicate aspects of many colonialist and ethnographic representations of Indigenous Peoples globally.[55]

By the 1950s, photography supported rapidly increasing southern interventions into Inuit Nunangat. Thousands of photographs were made under the auspices of DINA, the NFB, and Health and Welfare Canada, among dozens of other governmental agencies. They illustrated Canadian policies and programs in the North as well as satisfying southern Canadian curiosity about Inuit and supporting the assimilation of Inuit into southern settler life. These interventions by outsiders proved to be devastating to Inuit not only at the time but across subsequent generations. And photography, a seemingly benign documentary tool, played a role in rationalizing and normalizing those ultimately traumatizing and acculturating policies. The photographs used in Project Naming reflect the cultural perspectives of that long history of imaging Inuit by outsiders inflected by a salvage paradigm and a series of devastating policies.

But while these images might at first seem to be expressions solely of a southern, colonialist view of the North, they are complex encounters, produced with the participation – whether willing or coerced – of Inuit. The Inuit sitters' presence and power are always evident in the image. As such, Indigenous scholars and artists as Michelle Raheja, Amy Lonetree, Hulleah Tsinhnahjinnie, Paul Seesequasis, Celeste Pedri-Spade, and Jeff Thomas, among others, have argued that the Indigenous subjects of historical photography and film were always already asserting their power or agency.[56] As Thomas has written of his encounter with ethnographic images: "More than a simple anthropological record, the photographs provide a window to the past, enabling us to become better acquainted with the living and breathing people they portray."[57] While photographic encounters do reveal deeply etched inequities, they can also offer the possibility of a returned gaze, the assertion of a self beyond the imaginings of the colonial photographer, and the idea of the photograph as an encounter.[58]

These understandings of the photograph as an encounter, the agency of the sitter[59] and reception as a means to reframe photographic meaning from Inuit perspectives informs Project Naming. Through identifications and Oral History, its participants recognize the importance and power of hundreds of Inuit pictured by colonial cameras. In returning Inuktut names to sitters and returning their stories to Inuit communities, participants in Project Naming demonstrate that the photographic encounter is always multidirectional and multivalent.[60] And they reframe these archival images with respect, memory, and Oral Tradition, translating settler-colonial images into Inuit unikkaat. In this way, Project Naming's many participants challenge that long history of colonial visualization of Inuit while simultaneously decolonizing archival practice.

Project Naming's goal has never been to provide full analyses of individual colonialist fonds in the archive.[61] Such materials and histories are available through LAC, but they are outside the Inuit-centred mandate of Project Naming. Further, to detail the full histories of these settler-made collections of images and associated archival records would be to privilege settler narratives or risk an unwitting act of recolonization. Archives are malleable entities, reshaped by each person using them.

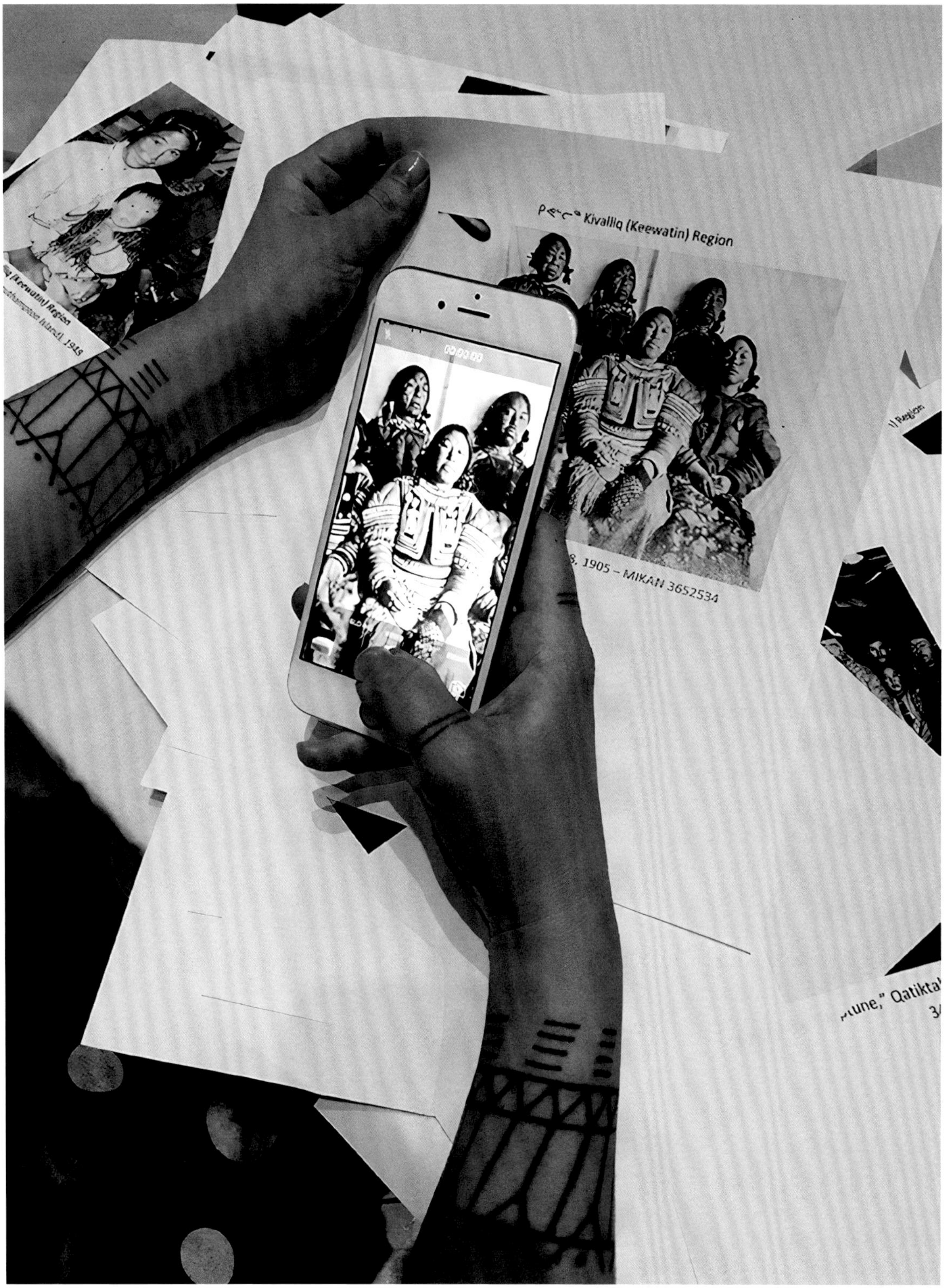

1.7 | Inter/faces with Kathleen Ivaluarjuk Merritt, Ottawa, 2017.

Part of the achievement of these many photo-based encounters is to reconfigure the archival descriptions, from Inuit points of view. Project Naming celebrates atiqput prompted by settler-made photographs, but it resists telling history exclusively through settler narratives.[62]

Reading this Book, Engaging with Layers of Inuit History

Atiqput: Inuit Oral History and Project Naming brings together generations through Oral Tradition and visual representations. At the same time, this book and the interactions it describes reframe settler visual histories from Inuit perspectives. And throughout, the commentaries in these pages offer information about what has been learned from Project Naming as a means of engaging with layers of Inuit history. In many ways, the photograph in Figure I.7 crystallizes that overall approach. It depicts the tattooed hands of contributor Kathleen Ivaluarjuak Merritt (see Chapter 2) taking a photograph with her smartphone of a historical photograph depicting six Inuit women in Qatiktalik in 1905 taken by Joseph-Elzéar Bernier. There are several layers of photographic mediation here: the early twentieth-century image, its subsequent publication, Merritt's re-recording of it, and, less discernibly, the image taken by photographer and digital designer Leah Snyder in March 2017, recording this photo-based encounter. Those multiple translations and mediations seem to collapse as Merritt interacts with these ancestors, sharing the photograph with friends and family.

The women in the 1905 photograph that Merritt is studying were among the last generation involved in the whaling industry. Their made-in-Italy beads and made-in-India calico skirts are testaments to the products accessible to these women and how they embraced new styles and technologies. In Elder Ann Meekitjuk Hanson's term, these women Inuktized these goods for themselves and their community.[63] Merritt, with her made-in-China smartphone, represents the latest generation of Inuit adaptability as she photographs the image to share with family and friends far from Ottawa. Despite Bernier's intentions over a century ago, this colonial image has become a family portrait when it is returned to the hands of descendants.

With layers of historical meaning through photographic image and conversation in mind, we have organized this volume into three sections that tell stories from Project Naming through the voices of its many participants. Each part of the book comprises essays and discussions framed by a brief introduction. Although the book opens with the beginnings of Project Naming, and a history of the initiative, the three sections do not have to be read in order. Instead, like any good conversation, they invite readers to make connections between different voices and pick up the discussion where they wish. Interspersed between the three parts of the book are two image essays featuring the visual art and words of artists Barry Pottle (in conversation with Inuk art historian Heather Igloliorte) and asinnajaq.

Part 1 recounts the story of Project Naming itself from its origins to the present. NS faculty Murray Angus and Morley Hanson discuss how they initiated Project Naming to reflect the acclaimed Inuit-centred curriculum they have developed. That chapter is followed by the words of former students Kathleen Ivaluarjuk Merritt (whose hands appear in Figure I.7) and Paula Ikuutaq Rumbolt who look back on their experiences at NS and their participation in Project Naming and related research. This section closes with an essay by co-editor Beth Greenhorn, who narrates Project Naming's long history at LAC across many media and outreach programs.

Following the first section, we include a photo essay (Chapter 4) featuring contemporary photo-based Inuk artist Barry Pottle's *The Awareness Series*, for which he photographed "Eskimo disc numbers" and paired them with portraits of Inuit they reference, and his series *Foodland Security*, which addresses access to country food among urban Inuit. Pottle's images are illuminated through reflections by the artist himself in conversation with Inuk art historian Heather Igloliorte, both from Nunatsiavut.

Reflecting Elders' position at the heart of Project Naming, the centrepiece of this volume – Part 2 – features the voices of Elders with their reflections on the act of naming and using photographs to reframe Inuit history. Sally Kate Webster narrates several photographs depicting family and friends from around Qamani'tuaq and in doing so, she models how Inuit Qaujimajatuqangit (IQ) principles or Traditional Inuit Knowledge guide learning. Former commissioner of Nunavut (2000–05) Piita Irniq gives his perspectives on the cultural importance of these photo-based conversations. Manitok Thompson, the first female cabinet minister in Nunavut, addresses Inuit youth about the importance of namesakes and clothing to connect to their heritage. Ann Meekitjuk Hanson, a commissioner of Nunavut from 2005 to 2010, engages in a conversation with youth (her three grandsons) about the importance of maintaining connections through namesakes. Educator David Serkoak discusses the importance of song and story to naming in his own life. The emphasis in this section of the book is on Inuit orality. Indeed, the essays by Sally Kate Webster, Piita Irniq, Manitok Thompson, and David Serkoak had their origins in conversations recorded at the same 2017 gathering where Kathleen Ivaluarjuak Merritt captured an archival image on her cell phone. And while Ann Meekitjuk Hanson's essay was written for the volume, it too includes a conversational element as Hanson interviews her grandsons. Each of the Elders' statements is followed by a brief afterword by the editors reflecting further on the implications of Elders' thoughts.

We follow the Elders' words with a second artist's pictorial essay (Chapter 10). Here the Inuit filmmaker asinnajaq, from Nunavik, reproduces stills from her film work while discussing the decision to change her name and how that change was rooted in family and culture.

The final section of the book, "Extending Project Naming," looks to research that has grown from NS and LAC's initial collaboration. Including four different research projects, this section reflects on theory and approach, considering the broader implications of collaborative photo-based research for Inuit advocacy and historical research. Co-editor Deborah Kigjugalik Webster writes about her own experiences researching the history of Inuit Royal Canadian Mounted Police special constables from Nunavut, research that has both benefited from Project Naming identifications and contributed more identifications. Frank Tester and Arviat-based researcher Curtis Kuunuaq Konek discuss the Nanisiniq and Nanivara History Projects, which employ archival records and social media to engage Inuit youth and Elders in reinterpreting their past. Co-editor Carol Payne and Sheena Ellison introduce Views from the North, a 2005–14 collaboration between NS, LAC, and CU that expanded Project Naming's methodology to include photo-based Oral History recordings made by NS students with Elders in their home communities. The final chapter, by Carleton University Art Gallery director Sandra Dyck, draws on Project Naming's recognition that southern photographs of Inuit can be used to enrich knowledge of Inuit history. In her essay, Dyck specifically discusses how the celebrated Kinngait (Cape Dorset)–based artist Kenojuak Ashevak has been seen through the camera's eye.

The volume closes with a detailed glossary of terms and place names, which we hope will keep the conversation going for generations to come. Throughout the book, Inuktut words have been incorporated into the text without italics; in this small way, we hope to signal a normative use of Inuktut rather than presenting it as foreign. We have also privileged Inuktut place names in the volume.[64]

Readers will note that there are variant spellings of many Inuit names included in this volume and throughout Project Naming. Inuit Elders are our guides in identifying Inuktut names and the spelling of those names for individuals as well as for places across Inuit Nunangat. Whenever possible, we have tried to follow Elders' advice respectfully in these identifications. Above all, whenever known, we identify Inuit by their chosen names. But we also recognize that sometimes there are differences of opinion about how to spell names. In cases where the identified person has passed and variant spellings have been suggested, we have used the cataloguing method developed by Project Naming in which the name identified by an Elder or a close family member appears first followed by alternate spellings in brackets. This approach acknowledges that sometimes multiple interpretations of spelling coexist. In relation to this, we note that Inuktut languages were originally oral and that written Inuktut (in syllabics or Roman orthography) was introduced relatively recently by Qallunaat (traders, missionaries, teachers, government officials). As such, any written version of an Inuit name often carries within it both Inuit tradition and the history of colonization.

One of the central goals of Project Naming is to identify Inuit in archival photographs held at LAC. It has an inestimable number of photographs depicting Inuit and the Arctic. A portion of these have been digitized, several thousand of which have been identified. There remain many individuals in photographs still to be named. Yet even when Elders cannot identify people depicted, photographs have much to tell them about Inuit life and communities decades ago. In this volume, we have mainly reproduced photographs in which Inuit represented have been identified through Project Naming; however, the reader will notice a few unidentified photographs that, nonetheless, have guided intergenerational conversations about Inuit culture.

Throughout, *Atiqput: Inuit Oral History and Project Naming* explores the rich and meaningful processes of Inuit naming and, with it, explores Inuit culture as a whole.

NOTES

1 Piita Irniq, personal correspondence with Beth Greenhorn, 13 July 2021.

2 See Chapter 1 in this volume, Morley Hanson and Murray Angus, "Nunavut Sivuniksavut and the Origins of Project Naming: A School Perspective."

3 Also quoted in Chapter 1. Ashevak, "Personal Account of Mathewsie Ashevak," on Project Naming web page.

4 LAC has since published *Nations to Nations: Indigenous Voices at Library and Archives Canada*.

This multilingual eBook features essays by First Nations, Inuit, and Métis Nation staff at LAC that explore published and archival material in the language of their communities. Library and Archives Canada, ed., *Nations to Nations.*

5 Katrina Hatogina, in conversation with Sheena Ellison, Ottawa, 2012.

6 Here, "memory work" is used to evoke both the importance of Inuit narrations of the past and memory studies scholarship. Both provide alternatives to conventional notions of history and insist on the importance of seeing the past in the present.

7 Curriculum and School Services Division, *Inuit Qaujimajatuqangit*.

8 Inuit Tapiriit Kanatami, *National Inuit Strategy on Research*; Nickels et al., *Negotiating Research Relationships with Inuit Communities*; The Truth and Reconciliation Commission of Canada, *Honouring the Truth, Reconciling for the Future.*

9 Garneau, "Imaginary Spaces of Conciliation and Reconciliation," 34.

10 Kunuk, "Keynote Address."

11 Bennett and Rowley, *Uqalurait*, 3–10.

12 Ibid., 3.

13 Ann Meekitjuk Hanson, personal correspondence with Beth Greenhorn, 14 July 2021.

14 Alia, *Names, Numbers, and Northern Policy*, 10.

15 Pauktuutit, *The Inuit Way*, 16; Owlijoot and Flaherty, eds., *Inuit Kinship and Naming Customs*; Bennett and Rowley, *Uqalurait*, 3.

16 Heather Campbell was one of three Indigenous researchers/archivists who worked on We Are Here: Sharing Stories (WAHSS), a mass digitization initiative involving Indigenous content held at Library and Archives Canada (2018–20). For more information about WAHSS and a related initiative, Listen, Hear Our Voices, see Chapter 3.

17 Campbell, "A.P. Low and the Many Words of Love in Inuit Culture."

18 For a short discussion regarding Inuktut and the various dialects and writing systems, see Campbell, "Introduction to Inuktut," 6.

19 This governmental body has changed names and mandates frequently. It was later known as the Department of Indian and Northern Affairs Canada and is currently called Crown-Indigenous Relations and Northern Affairs Canada.

20 Roberts, "Eskimo Disc Numbers," 3. Emphasis added.

21 Obed, "How to Overcome Erasure of Inuit Identity in Archival Photos."

22 Initially, there were no major protests to fingerprinting of Inuit, but the practice was cancelled after the first year after being deemed unethical.

23 The disc identification system began around 1941 for the decennial census. By the time the Canadian Government introduced a Children's Allowances scheme in 1945 (later called Family Allowances), Canada's first universal welfare program, the disc system was in use across the Arctic.

24 The federal government imposed the disc system in northern Yukon Territory, the Northwest Territories (that includes present-day Nunavut), and northern Quebec (Nunavik). The west included three districts, while the east consisted of nine districts east of Gjoa Haven (Uqsuqtuuq).

25 Awa, "The Old Culture," in Wachowich et al., *Saqiyuq*, 129.

26 Greenhorn, "*Project Naming*," in Benoit and Everleigh, *Participatory Archives.*

27 The archival collections at LAC also include vast numbers of photographs of First Nations peoples and citizens of the Métis Nation.

28 While visiting LAC, "Hattie's" great-granddaughters discovered six other photographs of their great-grandmother and provided her Inuit name, Niviaqsarjuk. These photographs include a183439, c001384, c001499, e006581108, e006581109, and e006581111.

29 Tagoona, Aivillingmiut, 1975: plate 10, quoted in Bennett and Rowley, *Uqalurait*, 3.

30 Alia, *Names, Numbers, and Northern Policy*, 8.

31 Posted by Suzanne Steele on Project Naming on Facebook, 11 March 2019.

32 Curriculum and School Services Division, Government of Nunavut, *Inuit Qaujimajatuqangit*, 33.

33 Nakasuk et al., *Interviewing Inuit Elders: Introduction*, 213; Ekho and Ottokie, *Interviewing*

Elders: Childrearing Practices, 136. Also quoted in Martin, *Stories in a New Skin*, 43.
34 Dorais, *The Language of the Inuit*, 162–3.
35 Martin, *Stories in a New Skin*, 42–3, 98–120.
36 Ootoova et al., *Interviewing Inuit Elders: Perspectives on Traditional Health*, 318.
37 Dorais, *The Language of the Inuit*, 162–3.
38 McGrath, "Isumaksaqsiurutigijakka"; Collignon, Therrien, and Duchemin-Pelletier, *Orality*; Dorais, *The Language of the Inuit*; Laugrand and Oosten, *Inuit Shamanism and Christianity*; Oosten and Laugrand, *Introduction: Interviewing Elders*, vol. 1; Bennett and Rowley, *Uqalurait*; Kublu, Laugrand, and Oosten, "Listening to Our Past"; "Igloolik Oral History Centre," Canadian Network of Northern Research Operators, accessed 25 January 2022, http://cnnro.ca/igloolik-oral-history-centre/.
39 Among Arnaquq-Baril's films are *Angry Inuk* (2016) and *Tunniit: Retracing the Lines of Inuit Tattoos* (2011). Unikkaat Studios Inc. website, accessed 25 January 2022, https://www.unikkaat.com/.
40 Kublu, Laugrand, and Oosten, "Interviewing the Elders."
41 In this way, the photographs used in Project Naming support Gabrielle Budach, Donna Patrick, and Teevi Mackay's assertion (in their work with urban Inuit) of "the potential of objects to connect people across contexts, time, space, life worlds, and generations." Budach, Patrick, and Mackay, "Talk around Objects," 447.
42 Greenhorn, "Project Naming / Un Visage, Un Nom," 22.
43 Kublu, Laugrand, and Oosten, "Listening to Our Past"; Distard, "Frobisher, Sir Martin," in Nuttall, *Encyclopedia of the Arctic*.
44 *Septentrionalium*, LAC, e004414662; Best, *A True Reporte*; Hakluyt, *Voyages in Search of the North-West Passage*.
45 For a discussion of Inuit responses to mapping, see Aporta, "The Power of Maps," in Krupnik, *Early Inuit Studies*, 354; Fossett, "Mapping Inuktut."
46 Condon, "The History and Development of Arctic Photography"; Geller, *Northern Exposures*; Adams, "Arctic and Inuit Photography, Part One"; Adams, "Arctic and Inuit Photography, Part Two"; Langford, "Richard Harrington's Guide"; Langford, "Richard Harrington's Indigenous Madonnas"; Racette, "Returning Fire, Pointing the Canon"; Tippett, *Between Two Cultures*; Ross, "The Use and Misuse of Historical Photographs"; Close, "Geraldine Moodie's Arctic Photographs."
47 *Imaging the Arctic* comprises a detailed and multifaceted study of photography in the Arctic and among Inuit. As such, it has provided us with invaluable resources about photographic history; however, photographic history is not central to Project Naming's overall goals of using photographs to foster intergenerational knowledge of Inuit history and culture while also entering Inuit Knowledge into the southern record. King and Lidchi, *Imaging the Arctic*. Of particular relevance here are the essays: Stern, "The History of Canadian Arctic Photography"; Wamsley and Barr, "Early Photographers of the Canadian Arctic and Greenland"; Graburn, "The Present as History."
48 Photographs were sometimes made for aesthetic reasons (as seen in images by such figures as William Bradford, for example) but these are exceptions. Whitman, "Technology and Vision."
49 Harper, "Collecting at a Distance"; White, "In Search of Geraldine Moodie"; Close, "Geraldine Moodie's Arctic Photographs"; Canadian Women Artists History Initiative, "Moodie, Geraldine."
50 Stern, "The History of Canadian Arctic Photography"; Stefánsson, *Report of the Canadian Arctic Expedition*; Hancock, "Diamond Jenness's Arctic Ethnography."
51 Geller, *Northern Exposures*, 51–84; Geller, "Pictures of the Arctic Night."
52 Flaherty, *Nanook of the North*; Flaherty, *My Eskimo Friends*; Flaherty, *Robert Flaherty, Photographer/Filmmaker*; Christopher, "Through Canada's Northland," 9; Adams, "Arctic and Inuit Photography: Part Two"; Flaherty and Flaherty, *Robert and Frances Flaherty*; Raheja, "Reading Nanook's Smile."
53 See Hancock for a nuanced discussion of how Jenness contravened the salvage paradigm: Hancock, "Jenness's Arctic Ethnography"; James Clifford, "On Ethnographic Allegory"; King

and Lidchi, *Imaging the Arctic*; Geller, *Northern Exposures*.

54 Tippett, *Between Two Cultures*; Langford, "Indigenous Madonnas," 28–48; Langford, "Richard Harrington's Guide"; Sangster, *The Iconic North*.

55 Fabian, *Time and the Other*; Pinney, *Photography and Anthropology*; Edwards, "Objects of Affect," 221–34; Edwards, "Photographs and the Sound of History," 27–46.

56 Among others, see Tsinhnahjinnie, "When Is a Photograph Worth a Thousand Words?"; Lonetree, "A Heritage of Resilience"; Seesequasis, *Blanket Toss under Midnight Sun*; Pedri-Spade, "'But They Were Never Only the Master's Tools'"; Raheja, "Reading Nanook's Smile"; Thomas, "At the Kitchen Table with Edward Curtis." See also Williams, *Framing the West*, 138–69.

57 Thomas, "Emergence from the Shadows," 217.

58 This model of experiencing the photograph as an encounter or conversation is also indebted to a wide range of recent literature in photo studies, most prominently in the work of Ariella Azoulay. Azoulay conceptualizes a photograph as "the product of an encounter of several protagonists, mainly photographer and photographed, camera and spectator." This conceptual model argues for the agency of the people who sit for photographs as well as those of us who are their spectators. Project Naming, an initiative that stresses the sitters over the photographers and facilitates the power of reframing photographic history, is indebted to this thinking. Here in reference to the photograph as an encounter, we also draw on Mary Louise Pratt's classic discussion of the "contact zone." For Pratt, the contact zone describes a "space of colonial encounters ... usually involving conditions of coercion, radical inequality, and intractable conflict." When Pratt wrote those still resonant words in the 1992 book *Imperial Eyes*, she was thinking of cultural encounters recounted in travel narratives at geographic sites, including trading posts and border crossings, and she examined these historic locales. In examining European travel writing about southern, west, and central Africa, the Caribbean, and Latin America from the eighteenth to the twenty-first centuries, Pratt was attentive both to Imperial visions of the world, which often takes the form of an Imperial self-image, and "the reverse dynamic, the powers colonies have over their "mother" countries." "A 'contact' perspective emphasizes how subjects are constituted in and by their relations to each other. It treats the relations among colonizers and colonized, or travelers and 'travelees' ... in terms of copresence, interaction, interlocking understandings and practices, often within radically asymmetrical relations of power." Azoulay, "What Is a Photograph?," 11; Azoulay, *The Civil Contract of Photography*; Pratt, *Imperial Eyes*, 6–7.

59 For an important discussion of Indigenous agency in filmic and photographic images, see Evans and Glass, *Return to the Land of the Head Hunters*.

60 For an influential discussion of the photograph as a multivalent encounter, see Azoulay, *The Civil Contract of Photography*.

61 Project Naming has only ever addressed photographic holdings, which in turn come from various government and private fonds or collections within LAC.

62 For an opposing view, see Lett, "Hidden Stories of Colonialism."

63 Ann Meekitjuk Hanson, Chapter 8 in this book; see also Williamson, "Sewing in Arviat."

64 For more on Inuktut language, please see Heather Campbell, "Introduction to Inuktut."

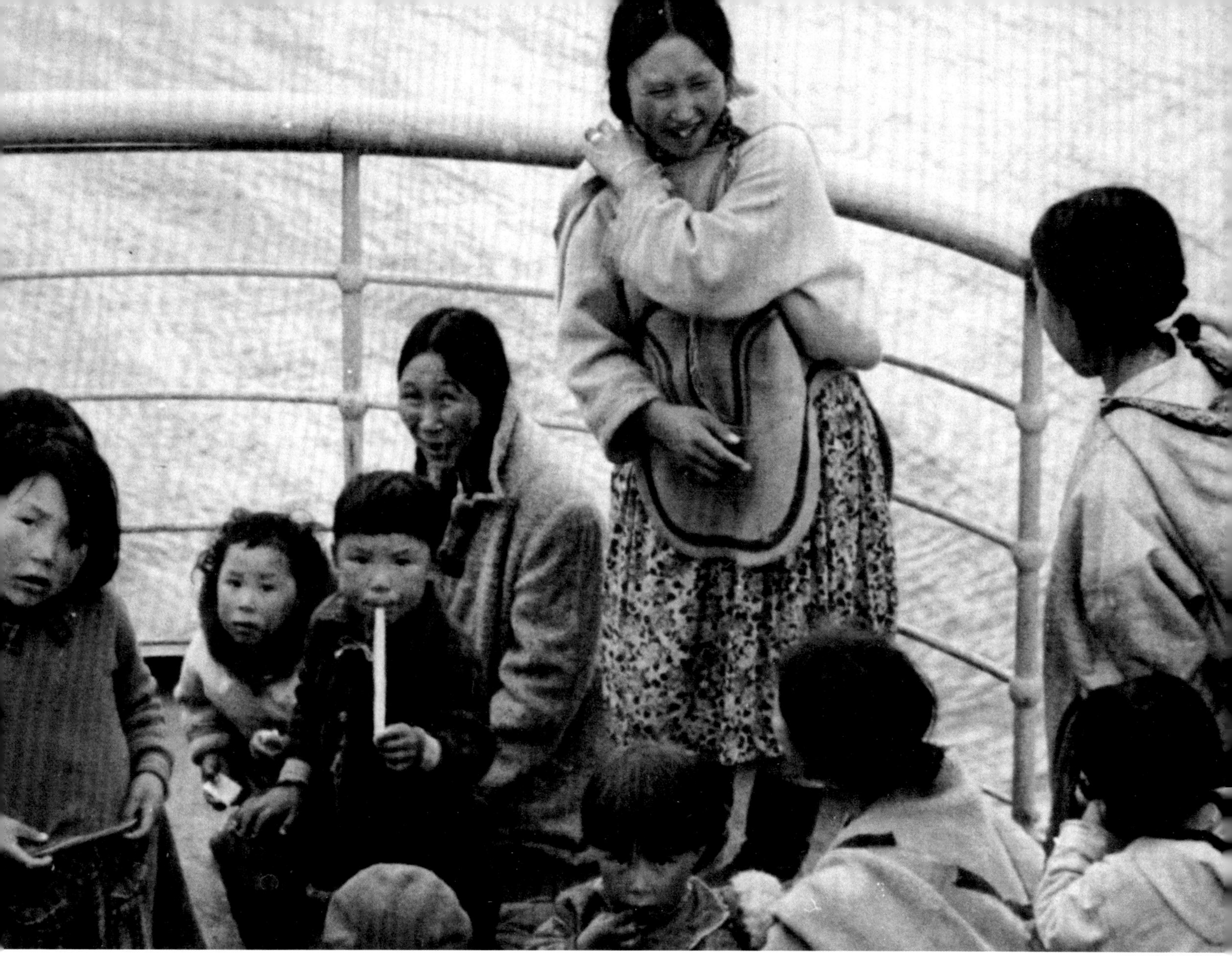

PART ONE

Project Naming: From the Past to the Future

INTRODUCTION

Carol Payne and Alexandra Haggert

We open this volume with three essays narrating the history of Project Naming from its origins to recent activities. They reveal the project's grounding in a combination of Inuit-centred pedagogy, Inuit-Qallunaat institutional collaboration, and decolonizing interventions into the archive.

Project Naming is a collaboration between two institutions: Nunavut Sivuniksavut (NS) and Library and Archives Canada (LAC). In many respects, they are unlikely partners. NS is a small post-secondary Inuit college program located in Ottawa with a curriculum built on Inuit-centred pedagogical principles and a "popular education" model. In contrast, LAC is Canada's federal archive, the country's most influential historical repository and, as such, a key arbiter of historical knowledge framed by the Canadian settler state.

By combining their resources, NS and LAC enhanced knowledge, developing new approaches to and perspectives on knowledge acquisition. For example, access to the photographic collections at LAC and the assistance of archivists and other LAC staff enhanced Inuit students' education at NS, facilitating their learning about Inuit culture and history from their Elders in Nunavut. The archival photographs provided memory prompts and links between the generations for transgenerational discussions. LAC, in turn, was prompted by NS's initiative to engage public partners, and specifically Indigenous groups, more extensively. If the core of Project Naming is the seemingly straightforward act of putting names to faces in archival photographs, within a larger frame, those reattributions – and Project Naming as a whole – might be seen as a series of decolonizing acts and interventions into the colonial archive. Indeed, in identifications carried out by hundreds of Inuit over the years, participants have "restoried" the historical record in Inuit terms, name by name.[1]

The first essay in this section tells the story of Project Naming at Nunavut Sivuniksavut. Written by NS co-founding faculty member (now retired) Murray Angus and retired NS faculty member and coordinator Morley Hanson, it also provides some background on the award-winning pedagogy the school has developed. In this essay, Angus and Hanson recount how Project Naming originated in an assignment in which, every year, each student would bring home a single photograph from the collections at LAC to show an Elder. According to the two faculty members, this was "a prime example of NS's pedagogical approach," one built on Inuit cultural values, attention to student interest, and adaptability. With early support from the Government of Nunavut's Department Culture, Language, Elders and Youth (CLEY) as it was then called, the project expanded through digitization and began formally partnering with LAC. And throughout, as Angus and Hanson explain, the project – and NS's curriculum as a whole – affirmed to students "the richness to Inuit life and culture," helping them to gain "a better understanding of themselves and making familial connections."

Faculty perspectives are followed in the second essay with commentaries by two NS graduates, throat singer Kathleen Ivaluarjuk Merritt and writer Paula Ikuutaq Rumbolt. Merritt and Rumbolt both participated in photo-based conversations with Elders while students at NS, learning about Inuit culture and history. The exercise to interview an Elder was consistent with the life experiences of Paula Ikuutaq Rumbolt, who grew up with her grandparents speaking to her in Inuktitut. As she recalled, "We learned through pictures and it's helped us understand our family tree." In contrast, for Kathleen Ivaluarjuk Merritt, who did not speak Inuktitut fluently at the time, there was (in her words) "a very strong sense of shame and guilt that came with not being able to ask them questions in their own mother tongue." Merritt's education at NS and those conversations opened a door to reconnecting with her Elders and to language.

The final essay in this opening section is by co-editor Beth Greenhorn, a senior project manager at LAC, who oversaw Project Naming from 2003 to 2017. Here, Greenhorn provides a detailed institutional history of LAC's involvement with Project Naming. As she recounts, Project Naming not only had an impact on the maintenance of Inuit historical knowledge but it influenced practices at LAC by prompting the archive to gather research information from Inuit directly as well as changing cataloguing practices. Greenhorn's essay follows Angus's and Hanson's comments chronologically, showing how Project Naming grew from its origins at NS to an initiative that reaches Inuit through the web, social media, and other forms. Today, under the aegis of LAC, Project Naming has been extended nationally to include images and identifications from Indigenous Peoples across Canada.

NOTE

1 Regan, *Unsettling the Settler Within.*

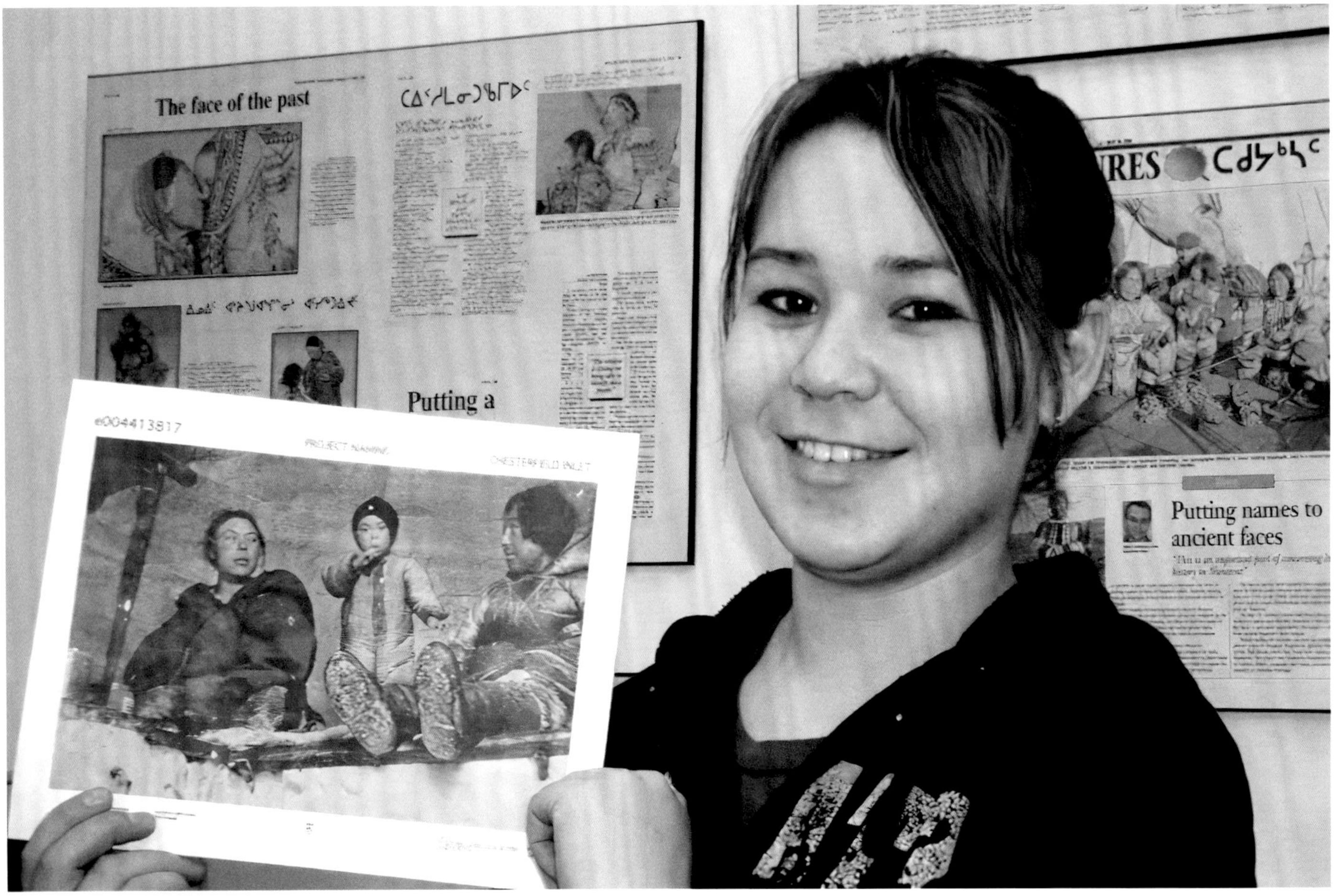

1.1 | Nunavut Sivuniksavut student Rebecca Kunnaat Penney holding a copy of a photograph of Louisa Angugatsiak, Theresie, and Marc Tungilik from Library and Archives Canada, 2003.

CHAPTER 1

Nunavut Sivuniksavut and the Origins of Project Naming: A School Perspective

Morley Hanson and Murray Angus

> It was so exciting showing these Elders the pictures – it was almost like taking them back to the days when they were young. When I clicked on each picture, I watched their eyes. As they recognized an individual, they would have a big smile on their faces. They acted as if these pictures were taken just yesterday.
>
> Mathewsie Ashevak, NS student, LAC's Project Naming website, February 2004

Nunavut Sivuniksavut (NS)[1] is a post-secondary college program for Inuit youth based in Ottawa. While not an official part of the Government of Nunavut's educational system,[2] NS has become one of the flagship programs whose mandate is to teach Inuit youth about their histories, politics, and culture, while preparing them for further post-secondary studies and/or immediate entry into the Nunavut workforce.[3]

NS began in 1985 with two instructors[4] and an enrolment of ten students. Since then, it has expanded significantly, and now has four full-time instructors, one full-time administrator, and several part-time lecturers and support workers, and enrolment has increased to an average of fifty students each year. While the majority are from Nunavut, the program has attracted students from other regions in Inuit Nunangat.[5] It has its own learning facility located at 450 Rideau Street in Ottawa, and its courses are accredited by Algonquin College.

When the program began, educational material relevant to Inuit was extremely limited for alternative post-secondary school programs. Few published resources were available that centred on Inuit history.[6] Following a "popular education" model, the first nine years at NS did not offer courses in the conventional sense. Over the course of the school year, the students studied their own history, as well as the history of the Qallunaat who travelled to and lived in the Arctic over the last two centuries. Focusing on the colonial actions of the Canadian government in the Canadian Arctic, the curriculum covered many issues that Inuit are dealing with today, including the legal provisions of their land claim agreement and other concerns relating to their communities, their regions, and internationally. As we have written elsewhere, "At its core, the program is founded upon the desire to help the students learn about the world they are stepping into as young adults (a.k.a. Nunavut), how it came to be, and their own collective story, which in turns involves

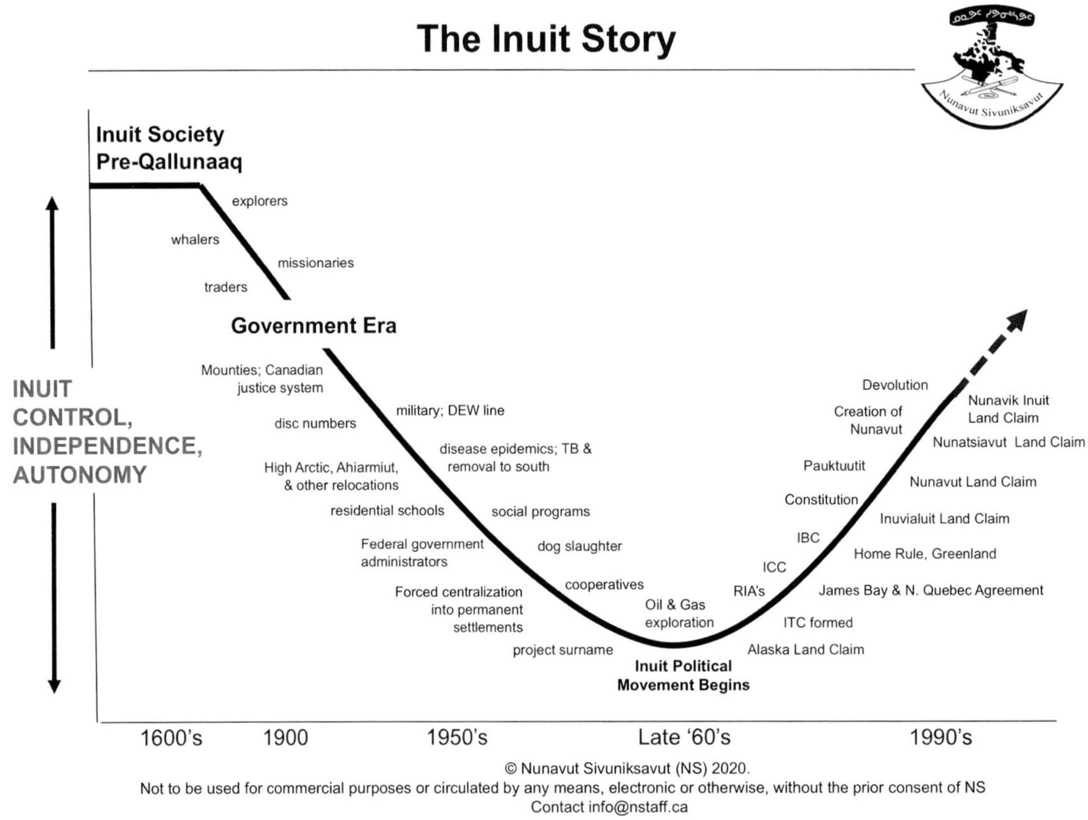

1.2 | Inuit Power Curve.

learning history, land claims and politics from the point of view of the Inuit experience."[7]

Fundamentally, the focus of NS's curriculum is about helping students understand their history. During their first weeks at NS, they often ask: "We see how we're living now. We know that our parents and grandparents were living completely differently. We see some of that still today, but life has changed a lot ... What happened?" For many of these young people, that story was unknown to them. Oftentimes it was unknown to their parents who may have attended residential schools and been forced to speak English, resulting in a disconnect from their history and culture. To visually capture the major events in the North, from pre-contact to the creation of the new territory, NS created the "Inuit History Power Curve." Following nine months of intense study, the students consistently leave the program with a deeper appreciation for who they are, their history, and their culture.

The students who apply to NS take a leap of faith by coming South, far from home and their families. They don't know what to expect except that their peers, their families, and perhaps their teachers have said, "you should apply to NS," "it's a good program," "you'll appreciate it." With this encouragement, they get on a plane that brings them to Ottawa for a year of intense study. While in the South, they also learn presentation skills that enable them to act as cultural ambassadors for Inuit and Nunavut. Many of the graduates have gone into politics, become leaders of Inuit-based organizations, had successful careers in the arts and culture, and served on the board of directors at NS.

Given the lack of educational material about northern history from an Inuit perspective, the early years of the program were spent researching manuscript and textual records at

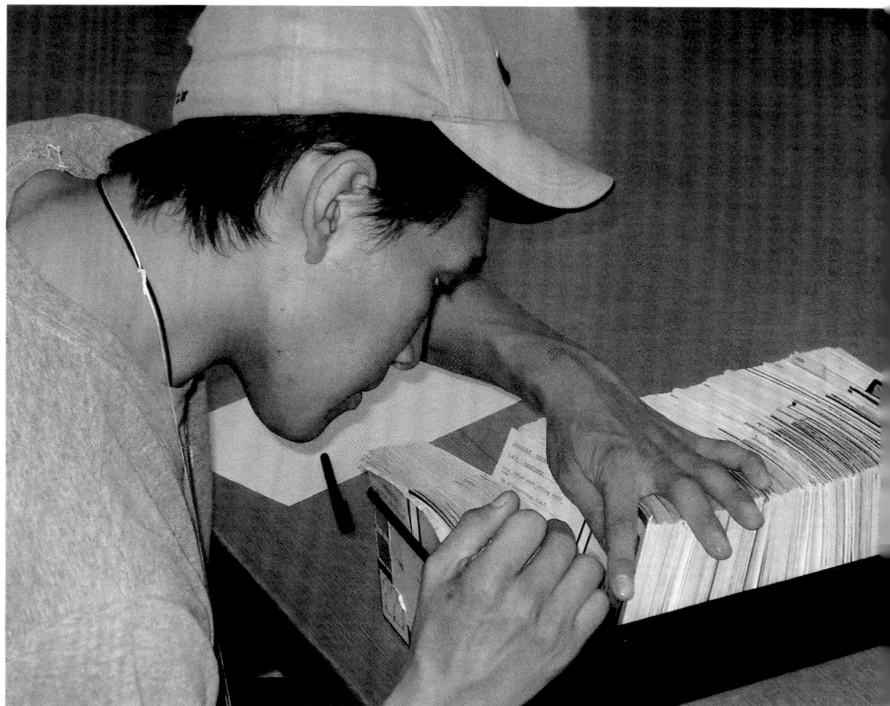

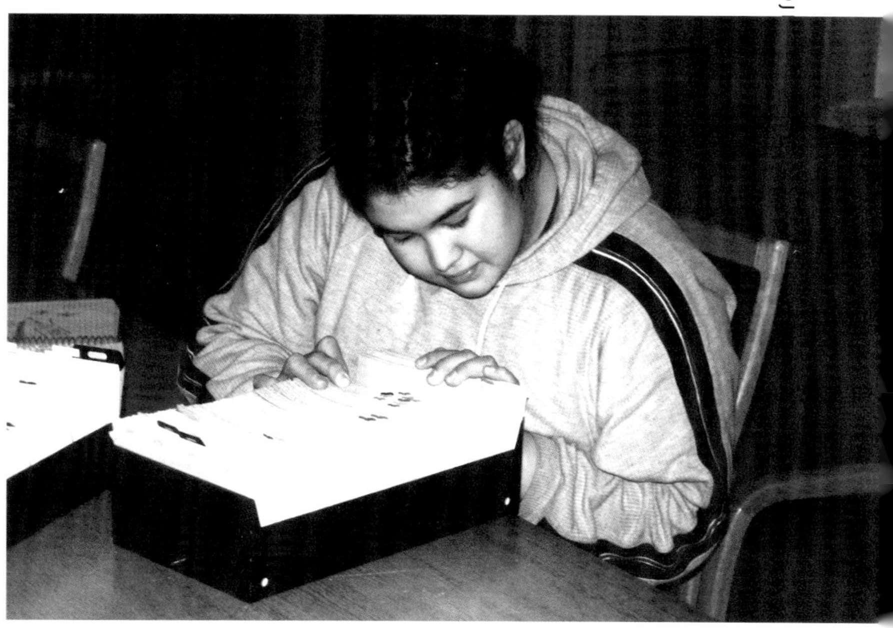

1.3 and 1.4 | Tommy Akulukjuk (*top*) and Neevee Wilkins (*bottom*) researching photographic records in the card catalogues, National Archives of Canada (now Library and Archives Canada), Ottawa, 2002.

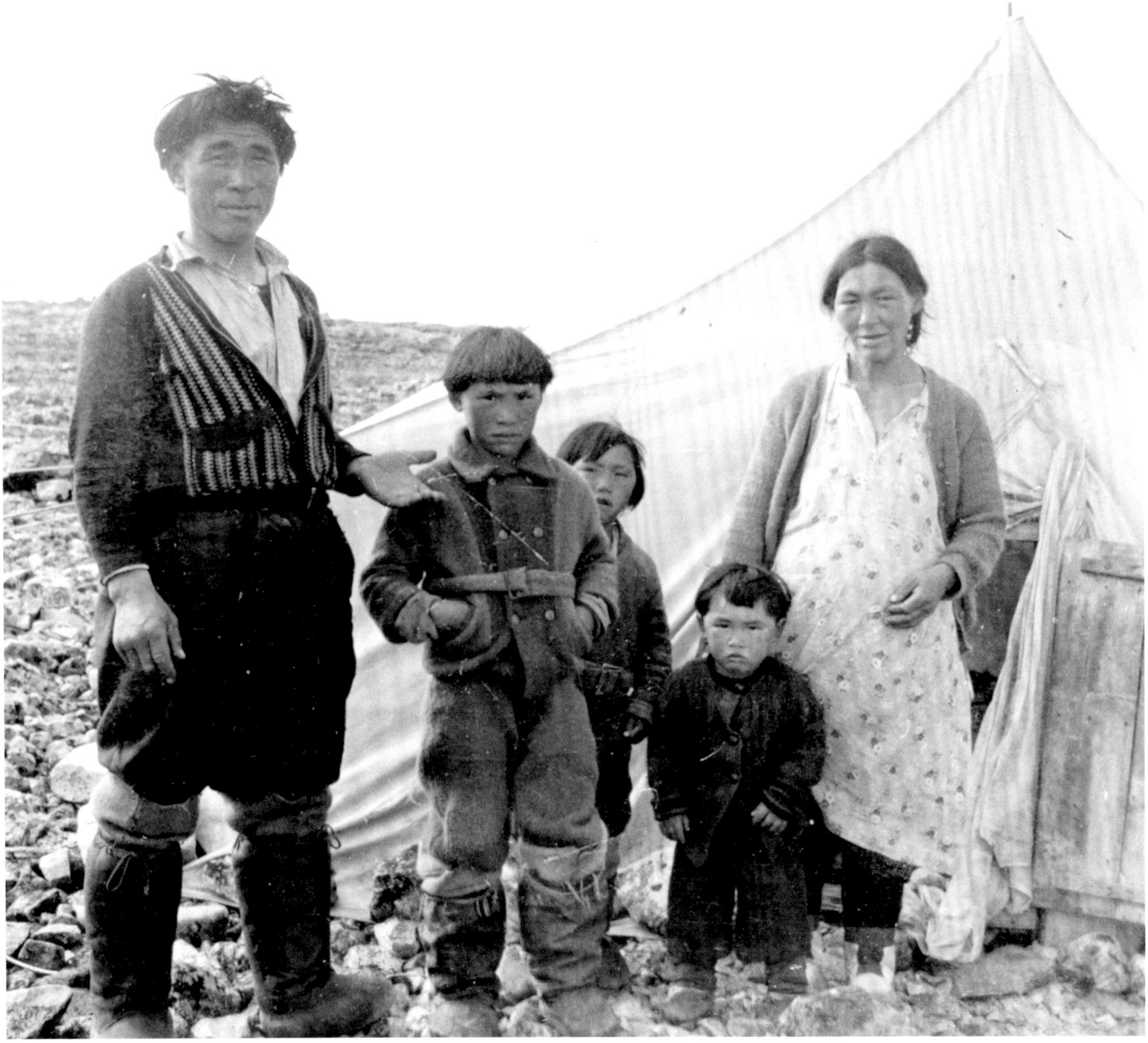

1.5 | [Left to right: Thomas Siatalaaq, Maurice Alikutiaq, Simone Alikaswa, Max Okatsiak, Arnalaaq], Igluligaarjuk. Original title: An Eskimo family residing on the point at Chesterfield Inlet, 1948.

Library and Archives Canada (LAC)[8] with the hope of finding material to talk about in class. This led to the discovery of LAC's photographic collections, which contain tens of thousands of photos taken in the Arctic, produced mostly by Southerners in past decades. To take advantage of this invaluable historical resource, NS began to bring the students to LAC each year, as part of their study into Inuit history (Figures 1.3 and 1.4).

Occasionally, the photographs found in the card catalogue drawers were organized by community area or by region, but generally, the locations where the images had been taken were never recorded. While the photographs provided visual evidence of the past, the majority of captions were generic, such as "Eskimo family." Very often, the information on the cards did not contain much more than that.

The students were fascinated by these glimpses of the past. These were pictures of people who were obviously from their society and culture. Occasionally, they would be excited to find someone in a photograph who they thought might be a relative, but there was no record to confirm their identities. At this point in their studies, the students had been in Ottawa for about four months talking about and trying to reframe the past and its different phases. The photo collections revealed another important gap in information.

As part of their annual trips to LAC,[9] NS invited students to choose a single image of interest and the program would pay for an enlargement they could take home at Christmas. This was in the era before digitization. Several weeks later, they received an eight-by-ten glossy reproduction of their chosen image to show Elders and other relatives back home. At that time, the goal was not about identifying names; rather, it was simply meant to be a conversation starter about the past.

Each year, when the students returned to Ottawa, following their break, they would all report a similar story: that the photo they had taken home had led to conversations between themselves and Elders, conversations they never had before. In the process, they learned new things about their own family's history or the history of their community. Upon returning to school, they would say, "The Elder told me that this is the first time that a young person has come and asked me questions about the past. This is the first time I've had an opportunity to talk about the way life used to be." The images were succeeding not only as conversation-starters but as a bridge between generations.

Throughout the 1990s, NS continued this annual practice of reproducing single photos that students shared with their Elders and families. The local knowledge students gained from their conversations back home was a perfect complement to the broader historical overviews that they were learning in their academic studies at NS. It was also a prime example of NS's pedagogical approach. Rather than having a pre-set curriculum that had to be rigidly adhered to, courses at NS have always evolved in response to the expressed interests of the students and the expanding array of resources available to support their studies. Students found archival photos to be a beneficial part of their learning experience. Thus, the program was adapted to incorporate it: such is the NS pedagogy.

For the first few years of the students' archival research, there was no expectation that the activity would expand beyond a single photo each year. But as the years passed, the benefits of working with the archival photos proved incontrovertible. Year after year, students would record their conversations with the Elders and declare that what they were learning was important to them. When they returned home in the spring, they did so with a renewed confidence in themselves and their identity.

The idea for Project Naming arose in an unusual setting. In the 1990s, NS began organizing an annual international trip to allow students to meet and exchange ideas with other Indigenous Peoples. In April 1998, the students travelled to Sweden to meet with the Sami in its northern regions. During a twenty-hour train ride from Stockholm to Kiruna, students and staff reminisced about their experiences with the archival photographs. This was in the early days of digitization. It was during this conversation that an idea arose: "instead of paying twelve dollars for one photographic reproduction, why not put many digitized photographs onto a computer that students could take home? How amazing would that be!" It was out of this discussion that the idea of a bigger project was born.

By 2001, Project Naming had evolved from a yearly research visit by students to LAC to a broader digitization initiative. LAC had thousands of images taken in the Arctic in its photographic collections, the majority of which had never been catalogued and were largely inaccessible in storage. This presented a huge untapped resource. Digitization would allow people in the North to see photographs of themselves and their history for the first time. How many Canadians even know these photographic records exist, especially those from the North? And, how many Nunavumiut would ever be able to travel to Ottawa for their own research? Project Naming had the potential to change that.

NS was in a strategic position to coordinate such an initiative. Based in Ottawa, it had ready access to the archives and the photo archivists; it also had a relationship with Nunavut, which at the time was a newly created territory. One of the departments in the new Government of Nunavut was Culture, Language, Elders and Youth (CLEY).[10] An expanded archival photo project seemed to be a solid match for the department's mandate.

NS staff contacted LAC officials to test out the idea of digitizing significant batches of photos and they were quick to recognize the potential of such an undertaking. LAC staff described in greater detail the nature of their collection and how most had been taken by Southerners who were travelling or working in the North during the 1940s, '50s, and '60s. The majority of the photos had never been seen by people in the North, and as was the case with the earlier photos students had obtained, Inuit were seldom identified.

In 2001, NS put together a funding proposal to CLEY for a pilot project. The premise was straightforward: LAC would digitize a selection of photos and present them to NS on CDs. NS would then forward the CDs to the communities where the photos had originally been taken and would negotiate with Elders and/or youth groups to work together to identify the people in the photos. NS would also oversee and coordinate the program, administer the funds, and record the information to be sent back to LAC. The project proposal identified six goals: preserve Nunavut's cultural heritage; provide Elders and youth with opportunities to work together; increase opportunities for youth to learn about their past; provide youth with work experience in their own communities; enhance the quality of data at Library and Archives Canada; and contribute to the digitization of the photographic collections at LAC.

To connect the project to recent Inuit history, it was decided to call the undertaking Project Naming, to echo Project Surname. Project Surname was the historic process carried out in the late 1960s when Inuit across the North were invited to choose a surname for themselves for identification purposes. This initiative replaced the earlier government instrument known as E-Numbers – a simple leather tag that identified individual Inuit only by a number. Project Naming would continue this task of naming people, this time moving back into the past.

Officials at CLEY recognized the value of the initiative and provided funding for the pilot to demonstrate the efficacy of the project. It allowed NS to hire a youth field worker and purchase a laptop. A few prominent Inuit at the time, including Piita Irniq (see Chapter 5), saw the potential with digitization and were quick to offer their support.

From the outset, there was an appreciation of the time sensitivity and a sense of urgency associated with Project Naming. When the current generation of Elders passes on, the chances that the younger generation would be able to recognize the people in the photographs would severely diminish. The project also had many benefits. It provided access to the photographic collections at LAC depicting Inuit communities; it was a catalyst that encouraged conversations between Elders and youth. It provided youth with opportunities to learn about their past. And it enabled LAC to correct and improve its archival descriptions.

The Project Naming pilot project began with the digitization of approximately seventy-four images taken in Iglulik by Toronto-based photographer Richard Harrington that dated from the late 1940s. Using the funding from CLEY, NS purchased a laptop and shipped it and the CD with the photographs north. A young Inuk in Iglulik, Sheba Awa, was hired to show the photos to Elders in her community. From October 2001 to February 2002, Elders were able to identify fifty-eight (or 78 per cent) of the people depicted in the seventy-four photographs. These results confirmed that the concept behind the project was sound, and the returns, in terms of information collected, would make it worth continuing (Figure 1.6).

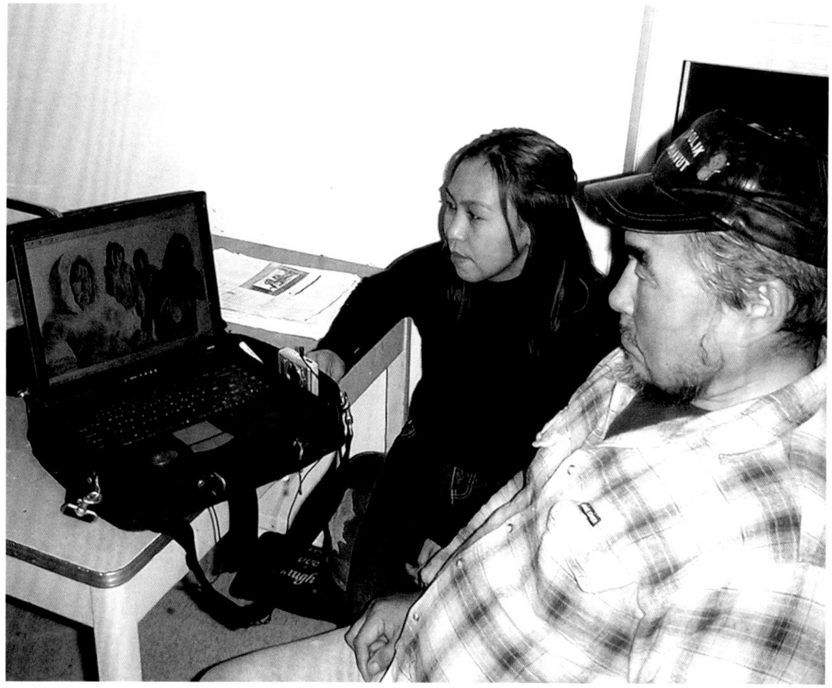

1.6 | Fieldworker Sheba Awa showing photographs to Elder Eugene Ipkangnak during the pilot project, Iglulik, 2001–02.

For the next seven years, NS continued to coordinate the project, with financial support from CLEY. The process repeated itself each year: LAC delivered a CD to NS each fall with a selection of photographs and NS looked through the photographs, which were usually taken in a variety of communities. There were several main communities with the greatest volume of photographs in those early years: Kugluktuk (Qurluqtuq) in the west, Arviat on the Hudson Bay coast, Qamani'tuaq (Baker Lake), Pangniqtuuq (Pangnirtung), Mittimatalik (Pond Inlet), Iglulik, and Taloyoak (Spence Bay). Wherever the largest number of students was

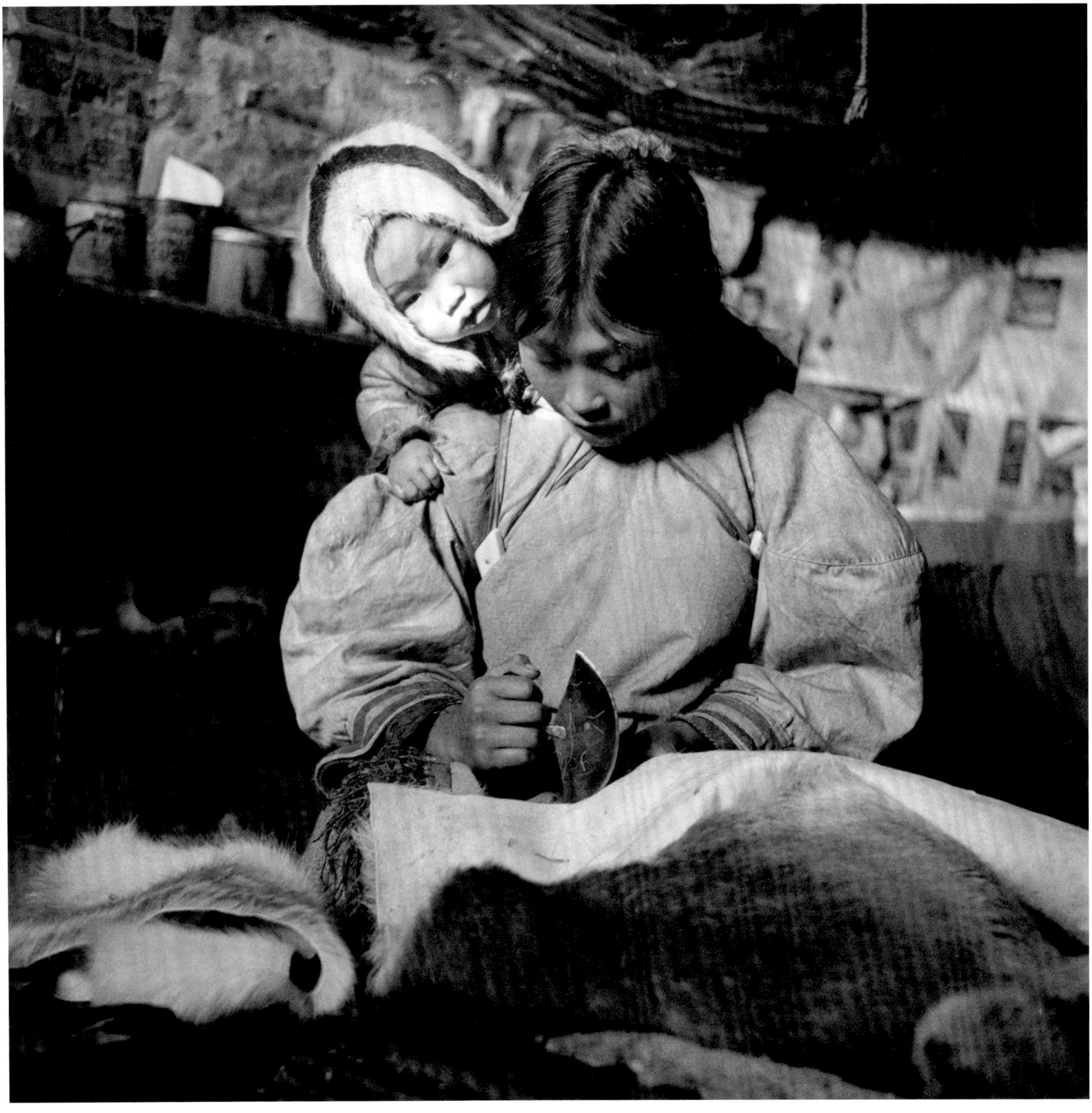

1.7 | [Kuuttikuttuk and either her daughter, Elizabeth, or her son. Kuuttikuttuk was married to Qulaut], Iglulik, c. 1948.

from in any particular year, NS would contact an Elder or a youth group in that community.

Aside from some administrative costs, NS made sure that the funding from CLEY was spent in Nunavut, and that Elders and youth groups were compensated for their collaboration. The photo identification sessions were carried out in different ways. Some consisted of a youth visiting and sitting with an Elder in their home, while others involved community gatherings. If there were no active Elders or youth groups in the community at a given time, the high school would be contacted and grade 12 students would undertake the interviews with Elders as part of their community service hours.

There were notable and even surprising aspects to the data that came back from the interviews with Elders. The first example provided a stark insight into the difference between Inuit and Qallunaat cultures: for NS and LAC staff (all Southerners), the goal of the project was to simply acquire the names of every possible individual in a photograph. Elders, however, could not do this: they could not identify people by their names without also naming the people to whom they were related. In Inuit culture, personal identity cannot be separated from relationships with others. This was consistent throughout each of the naming gatherings. The Elders asked: Whose wife? Whose brother? Whose sister? They described the people in the photographs as somebody's wife, somebody's adopted mother, and so on. They talked about family connections (Figures 1.7 and 1.8).

Learning not just a name but a whole relationship with that person and extended family was very significant for the NS students. Being a minority within Canada and coming from a culture that is not well understood and is seen as being unsophisticated by mainstream society, many of the students at NS lack pride or an understanding of their special place within Canada or the world. During their studies at NS, many gain an appreciation of, and a sense of pride in, their culture and history. Among the many things they learn is not buying into the simplistic image about the Arctic and about Inuit way of life perpetuated by southern Canada. For those in the South, understanding the richness of Inuit life and culture has been long missing. The conversations with Elders during Project Naming gatherings benefitted the students in acquiring a better understanding of themselves and making familial connections. They started to see themselves differently, in a different light.

In contrast to Qallunaat, NS students know their relatives and can name ancestors, often going back five generations. They know who they are genealogically and how they are related to everybody in the community. This knowledge instills a sense of something more than that simplistic image that has been portrayed of Inuit culture. Those connections show a richness to their society, how it was organized, and how they related to each other. This knowledge has been lost by many other societies.

The other thing that stood out was the accuracy of people's memories. The photographs shown in Iglulik in 2001 had been taken fifty years before. There were also pictures taken from a distance, with obscured faces. Yet, the Elders could identify and name individuals based on their clothing, as it was all individually made in that earlier time. The story behind one photograph taken by Harrington is particularly poignant: it shows Sapangaarjuk seated on the qamutiq. During his return trip from Sanirajak (Hall Beach) to Igluglik, his feet had to be amputated because they froze (Figures 1.9 and 1.10).

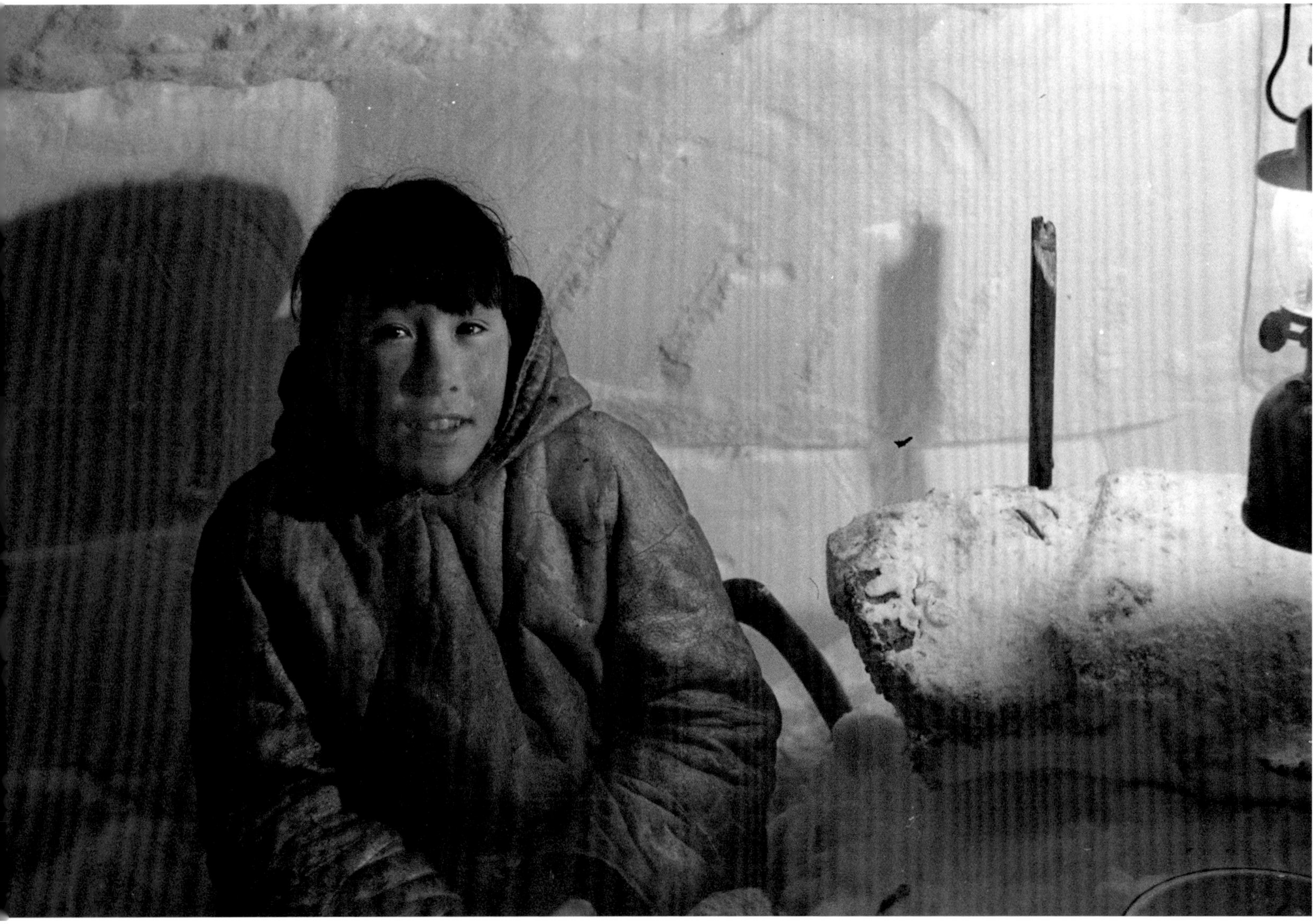

1.8 | [Alorut. He is Pikujak's husband, Leah Ivvalu's brother, Anulik's son, and Kailapi Alorut's father], Iglulik, c. 1948.

1.9 (*opposite*) | [Phillip Napacherkadiak and his qimuksiqtuq], Taloyoak, 1949–50.

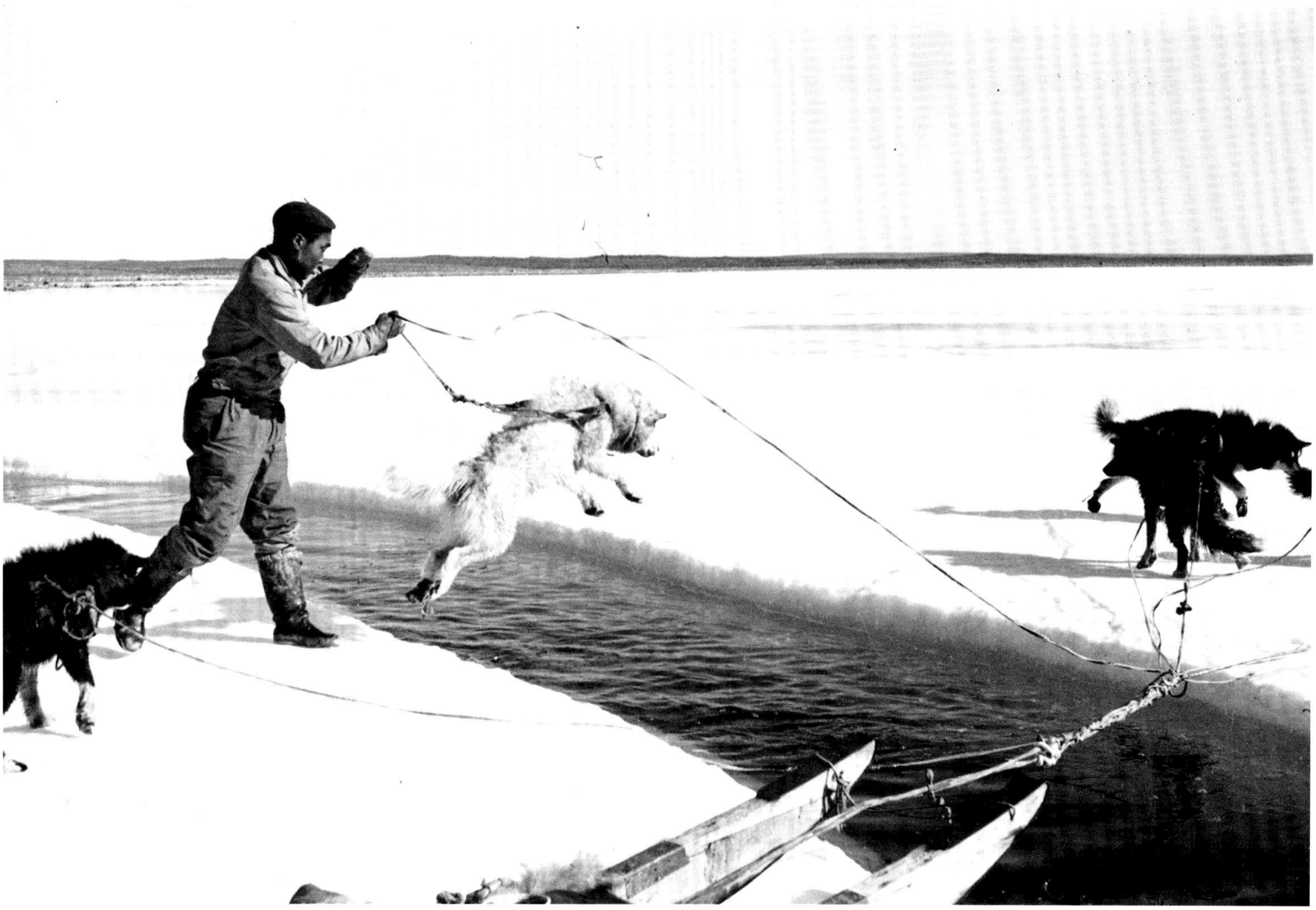

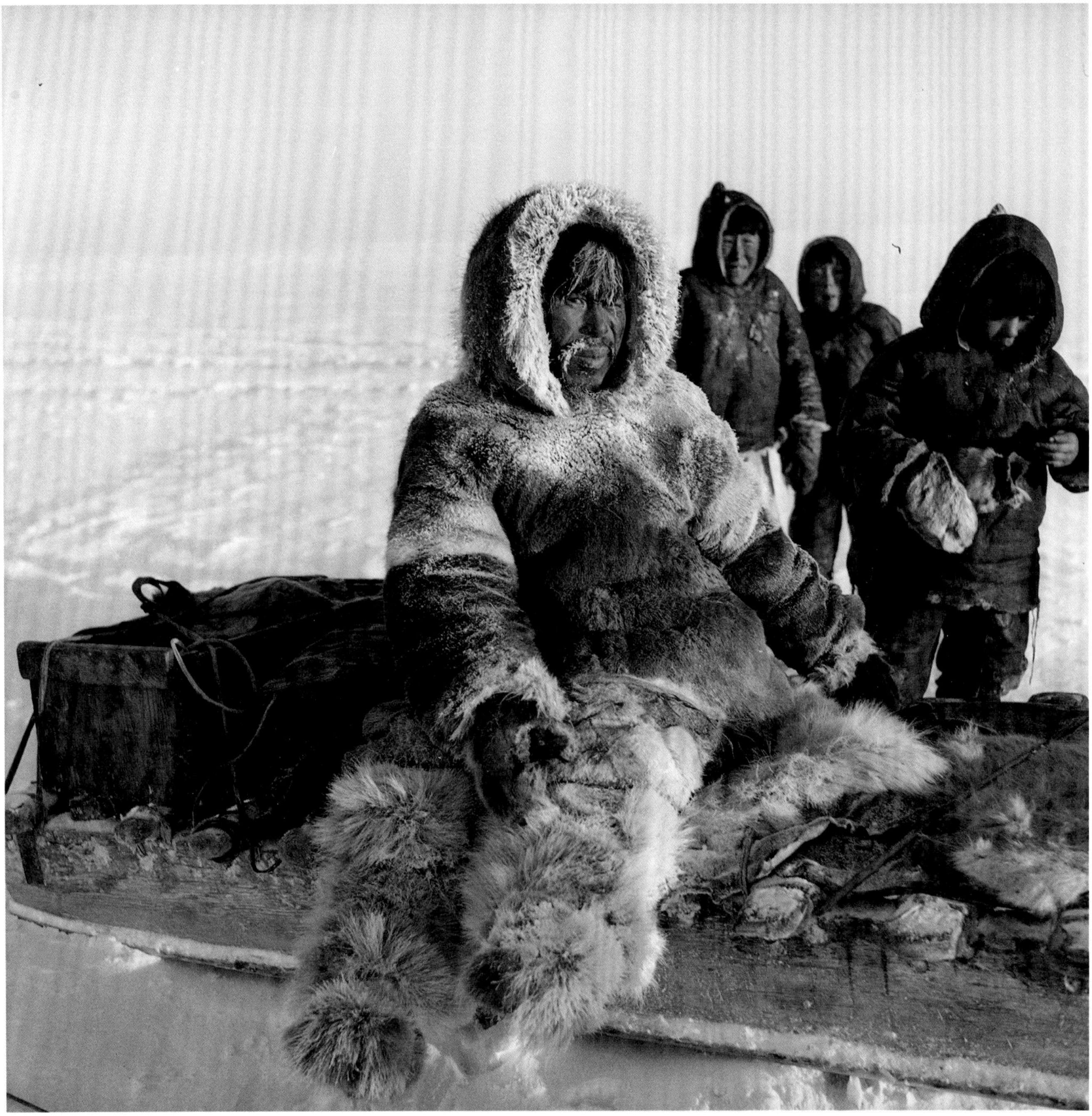

1.10 | [Sapangaarjuk seated on the qamutiq, Apak? (left), unidentified boy (centre), and Lazarus Uttak? (right). Sapangaarjuk, Hannah Uyarak's father, was returning to Iglulik from Sanirajak and froze his feet, which had to be amputated], c. 1948.

Project Naming has been an important initiative, not just for the data it has obtained for Inuit who are yearning to know their past, but as an example of something that can be done for the benefit of all other Indigenous Peoples in Canada. NS is proud to have been involved in the early stages of its development.

We want to acknowledge Beth Greenhorn at LAC for the stability of her presence in the whole project from the get-go and honour her for holding the project together all these years. We are also thankful that LAC has seen the benefit to continue its support for the project because it is one of a kind.

NOTES

1 In 2006, NS was presented a national award for "Innovation and Effectiveness in the area of Aboriginal Learning" by the Canadian Council of Learning, and in 2008, was named as one of Canada's top ten social change organizations by the Tides Canada Foundation. Angus and Hanson, "The New Three R's," 45.

2 As a not-for-profit charitable institution, NS is affiliated with Algonquin College for purposes of accreditation and is funded by Nunavut Tunngavik Inc., Kivalliq Inuit Association, Kakivak Association, Kitikmeot Inuit Association, and the Government of Nunavut's Department of Education.

3 The Nunavut Sivuniksavut program began during the land claims negotiations that led to the Nunavut Land Claims Agreement in 1993 and the creation of the new territory of Nunavut in 1999. Inuit leadership recognized the need for young Inuit to be trained for the land claims negotiations, and later to implement them, and thus, NS was created. Angus and Hanson, "The New Three R's," 32.

4 Murray Angus was one of the original instructors at NS, beginning in 1985. Morley Hanson joined NS in 1998 and has been the leader of the organization for most of the years since.

5 The Inuit homeland, known as Inuit Nunangat, is comprised of four Inuit regions – Inuvialuit, Nunavut, Nunavik, and Nutansiavut. It includes the land, water, and ice contained in the Arctic region.

6 Since NS begin in 1985, there has been an increase in the production of new resources, many of them Inuit-based and Inuit-authored, allowing students a critical look at the past.

7 Angus and Hanson, "The New Three R's," 34.

8 When NS began researching at Library and Archives Canada, it was known as the National Archives of Canada.

9 The annual research visits to LAC were carried out throughout the 1980s and 1990s.

10 CLEY subsequently became the Department of Culture and Heritage.

2.1 | Paula Ikuutaq Rumbolt (*centre*) speaking at the fifteenth anniversary of Project Naming event with Kathleen Ivaluarjuk Merritt (*left*) and Deborah Kigjugalik Webster (*right*).

2.2 | [Left to right: Misiraq, Elizabeth Unurniq (Tapatai), and Kajurjuk], Qamani'tuaq, 1926.

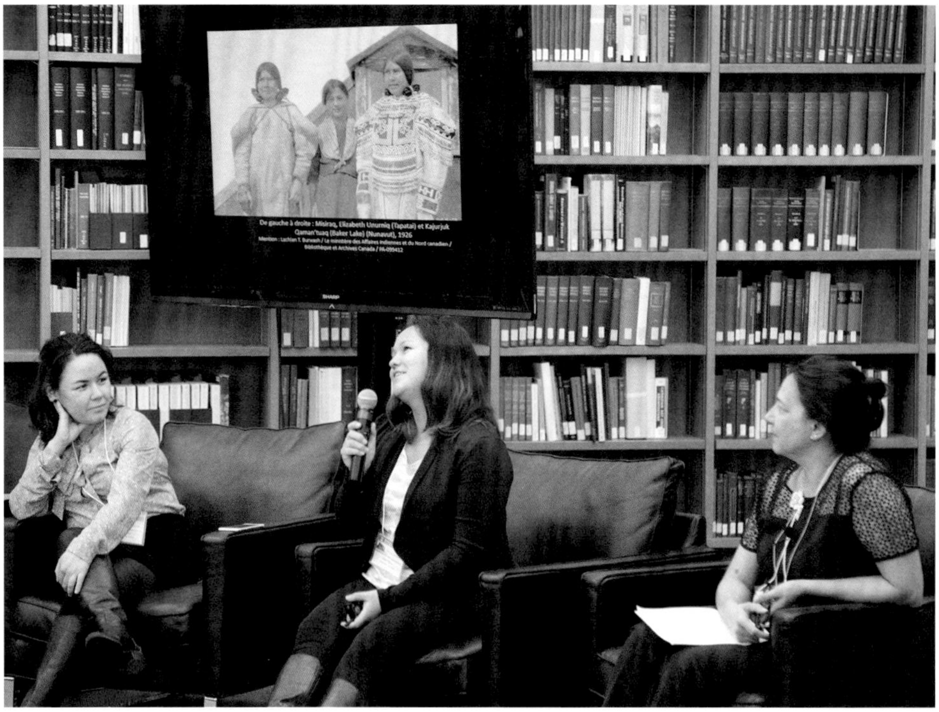

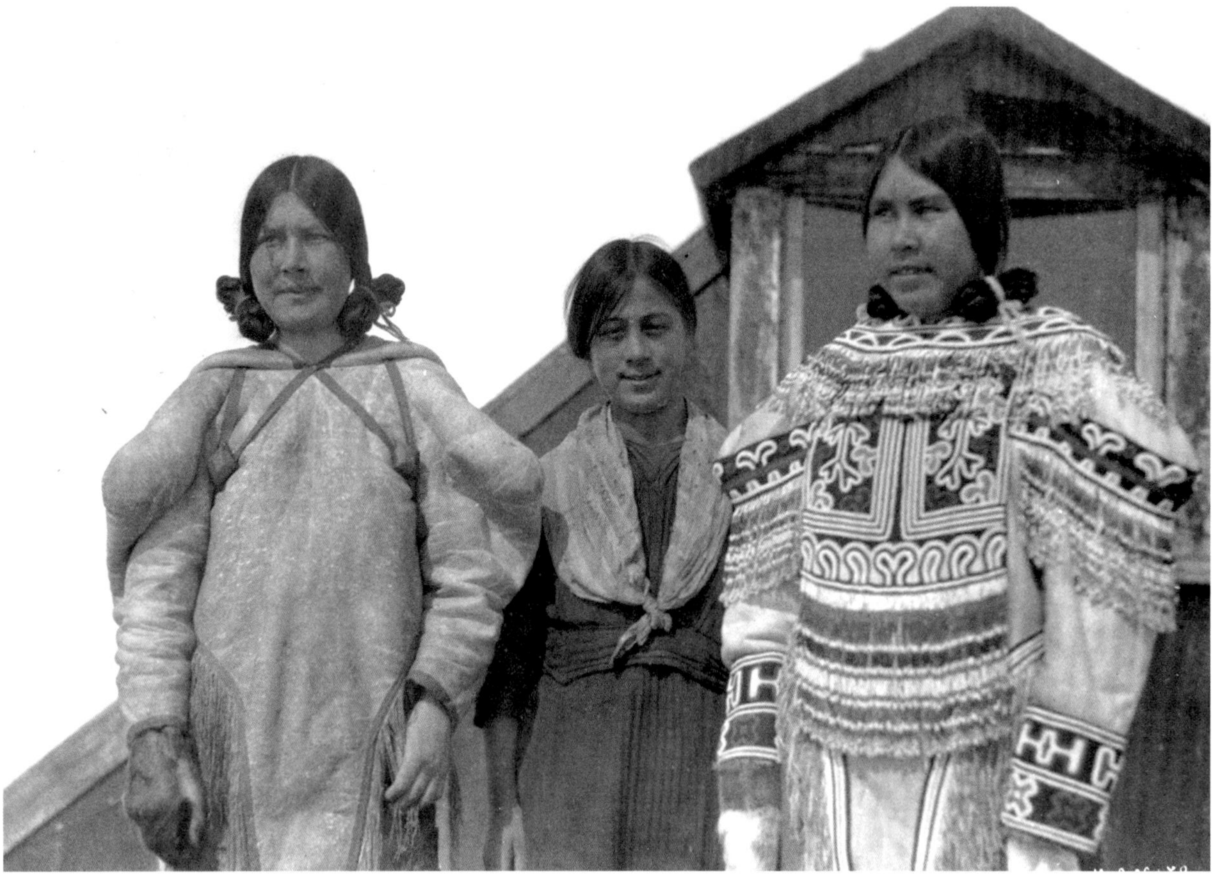

CHAPTER 2

Two Graduates Look Back at Nunavut Sivuniksavut and Project Naming

Paula Ikuutaq Rumbolt and Kathleen Ivaluarjuk Merritt

Paula Ikuutaq Rumbolt

I'm named after my mom's childhood friend who passed away when she was a child. Out of respect for her friendship, my mom thought that I should be named after her. Ikuutaq was my grandfather. My mom was dreaming about my grandfather when she was pregnant with me, so, keeping Inuit tradition of naming alive. I'm named after my grandfather Ikuutaq.

At Nunavut Sivuniksavut (NS), Kathleen Merritt and I were in the same class. I always say that attending NS was probably the best decision I ever made for myself (Figure 2.1).

When we began at NS, we brought back a lot of the pictures when we went home at Christmas. We went to interview Elders and people in the community who might know who the people in the photographs were. I remember when we were interviewing my grandmother. Her name was Janet. There were three of us from Baker (Qamani'tuaq) sitting around a coffee table when my little cousin, who was probably seven years old at the time, decided to

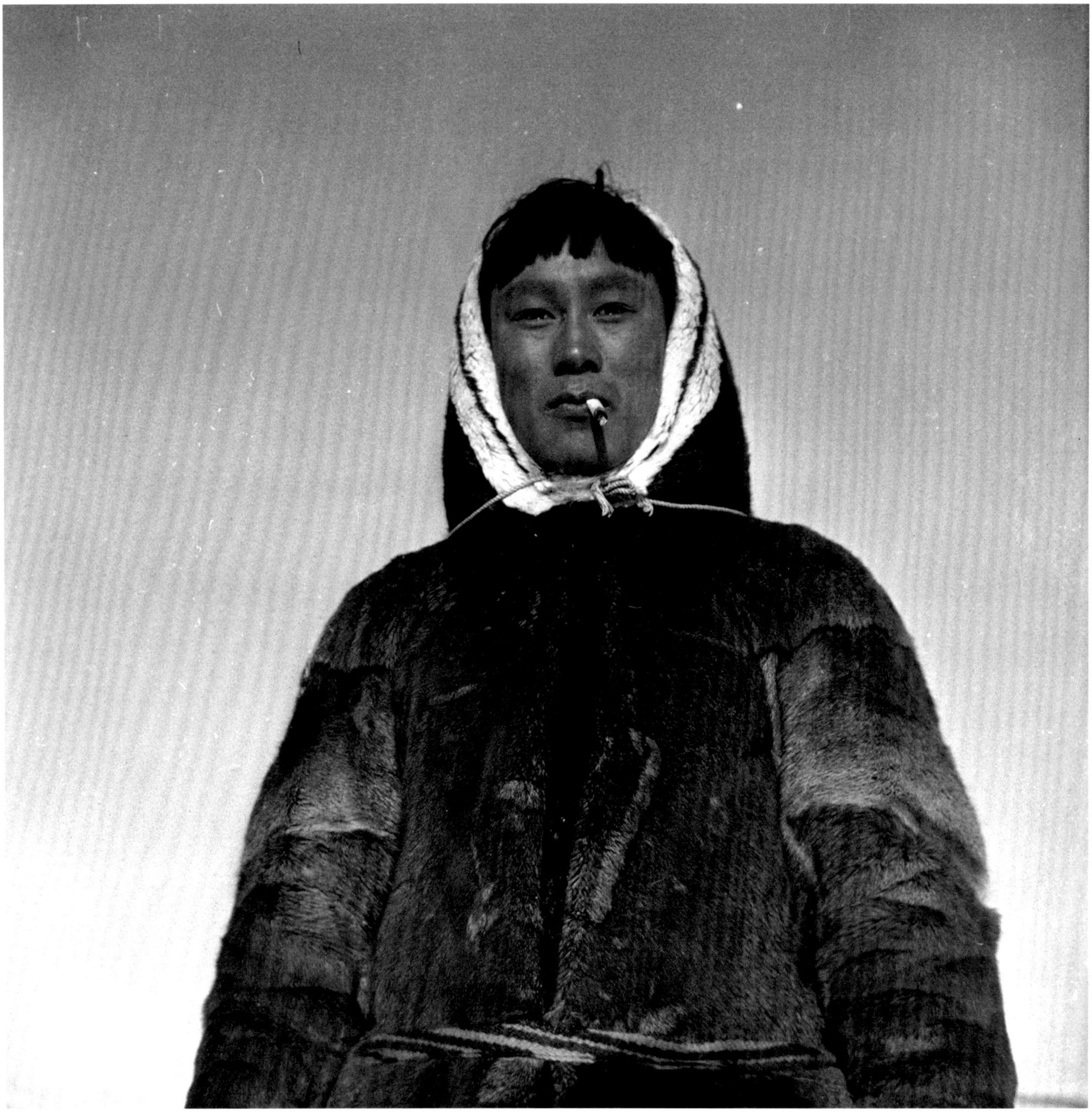

2.3 | [Barnabus Arnasungaaq, a world-renowned soapstone carver], Qamani'tuaq, 1949.

2.4 | Arnasungnark unloading block of soapstone, Qamani'tuaq, 1963.

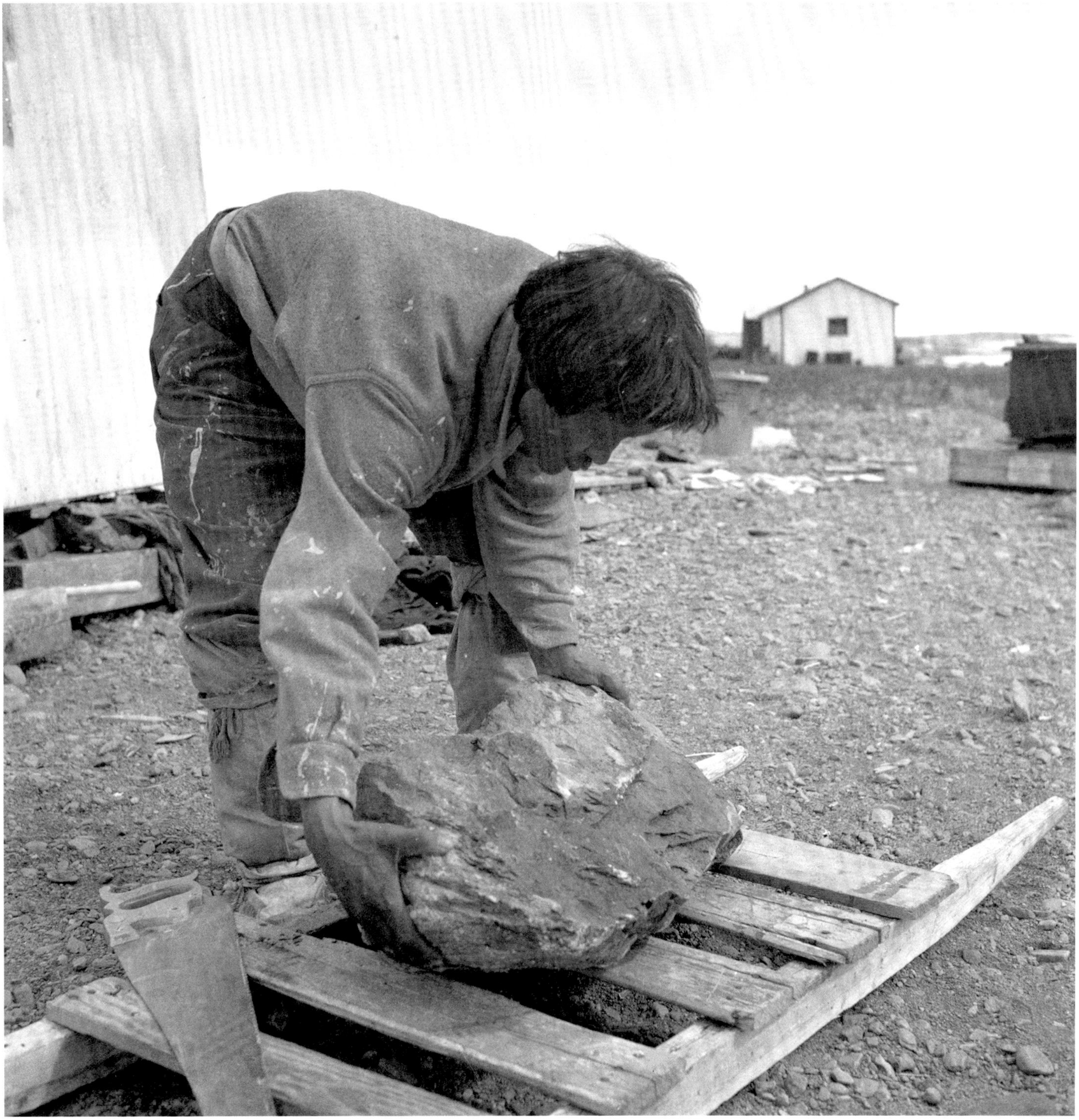

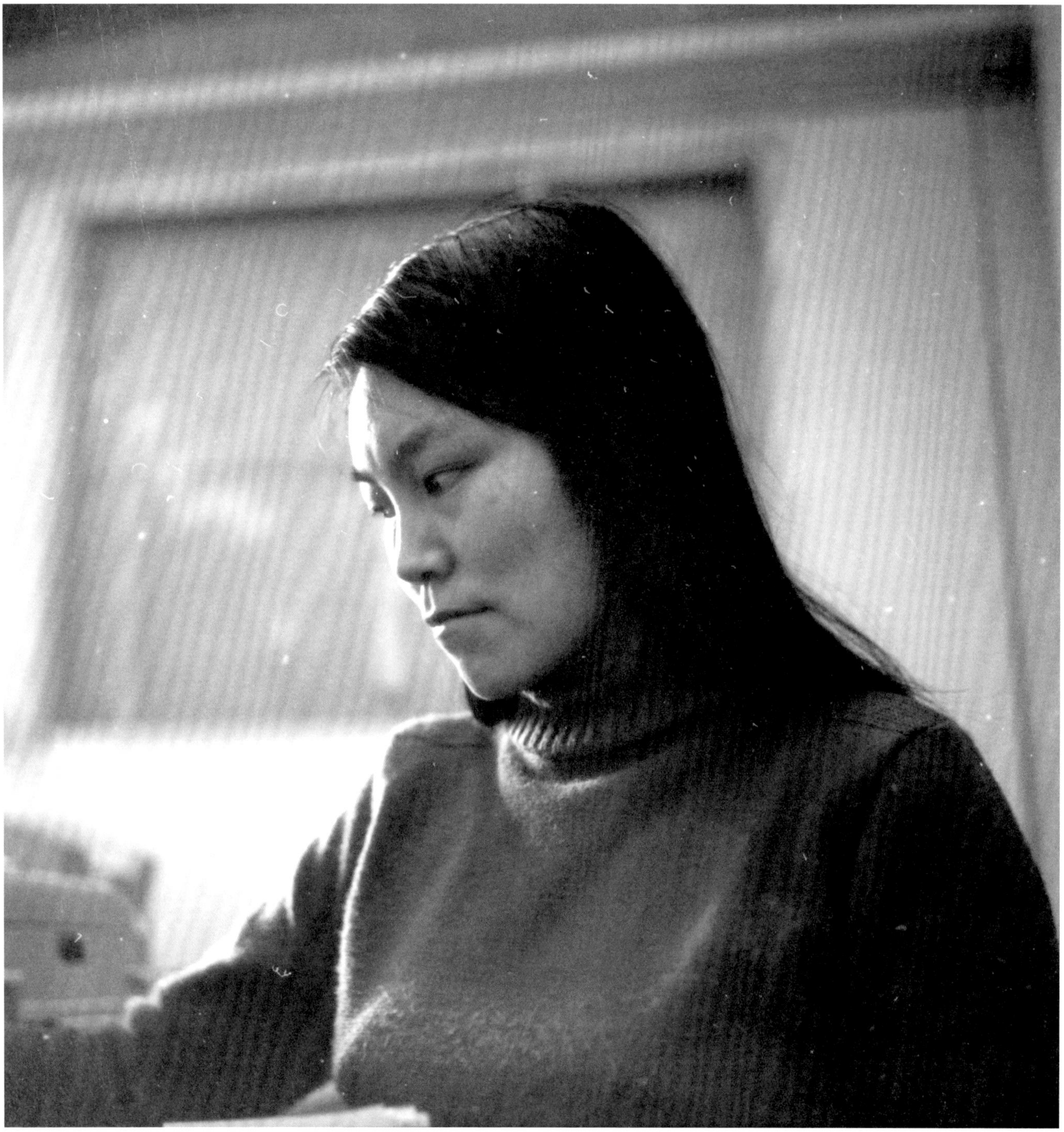

2.5 | [Betty Natsialuk Amarouk Hughson], Qamani'tuaq, 1969.

join us and listen to my grandma's stories of the people in the pictures. I knew he understood Inuktitut so I knew he was understanding the stories that my grandma was telling us. And I just looked at him in the middle of one of her stories. He was sitting on the floor and using the couch as a pillow, and he fell asleep. I think that shows the importance of pictures and stories that are around in my family (Figures 2.2–2.5).

We had a closet in our house that was filled with old photographs, they were stored in these old tins that had two hundred pictures in each of them. And lots of old photo albums, so you'd have to peel off the plastic. Whenever my cousins came over, we would take them though we never knew who these people were that were in the pictures. We would take out these pictures and we'd ask our moms who these people were. There were probably at least ten people in the house every time, and they would just kind of stop what they were doing and we would all look at these pictures together. Our parents would tell us stories about these people that are in the pictures. I was taught, "this is your avaaq, this is your avaaq or who you're named after." We learned through pictures and it's helped us understand our family tree. Like how far back we can go just through these pictures.

Kathleen Ivaluarjuk Merritt

I'm named after my grandmother's late sister Ivaluarjuk. She was alive for a lot of my life and recently passed away. When we're named, we either take on traits of the person we're named after or [take on their] relationships with people. My namesake, Ivaluarjuk, was my grandmother's younger sister; all of her children would call me "mom" growing up. Your sense of relationships with other people, like your family, grows when you're named after somebody in our culture.

I went to Nunavut Sivuniksavut (NS) in 2008 with Paula Ikuutaq Rumbolt for the first year of the program and again in 2009 for the second year of the program, so, from 2008 to 2010.

I remember coming into Library and Archives Canada to look at old photographs. We couldn't really find a lot of Rankin Inlet (Kangiqliniq), so I decided to try and find some photographs from Coral Harbor (Salliq) where my mother is originally from. I took some photos home, for the two weeks over Christmas break. I waited and waited and waited to sit down with Elders to do the assignment.

Paula grew up with her grandmother. So, to speak with her family was an easy experience. In my experience, I found it a lot more difficult. First off, I wasn't able to just go and visit my grandparents; [since] they were in Coral Harbor and I was at Rankin Inlet. So, I went to visit my best friend's grandparents. I brought home some photos to show them. But I waited until the day before I left to go back to Ottawa to interview them. I didn't realize, coming home with the photos, that it would not be so difficult. I think the anticipation of asking the Elders was more difficult than conducting the interviews itself (Figures 2.6 and 2.7).

At that time, I didn't speak Inuktitut fluently. I think there was a very strong sense of shame and guilt that came with not being able to ask them questions in their own mother tongue. I think a lot of young people who aren't Inuktitut speakers or aren't fluent Inuktitut speakers, carry that shame sometimes. I didn't realize how difficult it was going to be for me to approach Elders, to talk about their past and stories without being able to do it in their language. That was one of the points that stuck with me.

2.6 | [Inuit awaiting medical examination aboard the *C.D. Howe* on eastern Arctic patrol. The following individuals are identified: the young girl standing facing the camera with a plaid skirt is Theresa Aklunark; Theresa Aklunark's mother, Tunalaaq Bruce, is standing facing towards the camera and is wearing a floral print skirt; Mary Tagalik is facing the camera and sitting on the boat deck in front of the railing (she was the daughter of Mukkik, and was Kayayuak's first wife); Mary Tagalik's children are sitting on her lap, Emiline Kowmuk is on the left, and her brother, Evasaaq, is on the right and is holding a whistle(?)], Salliq, 1951.

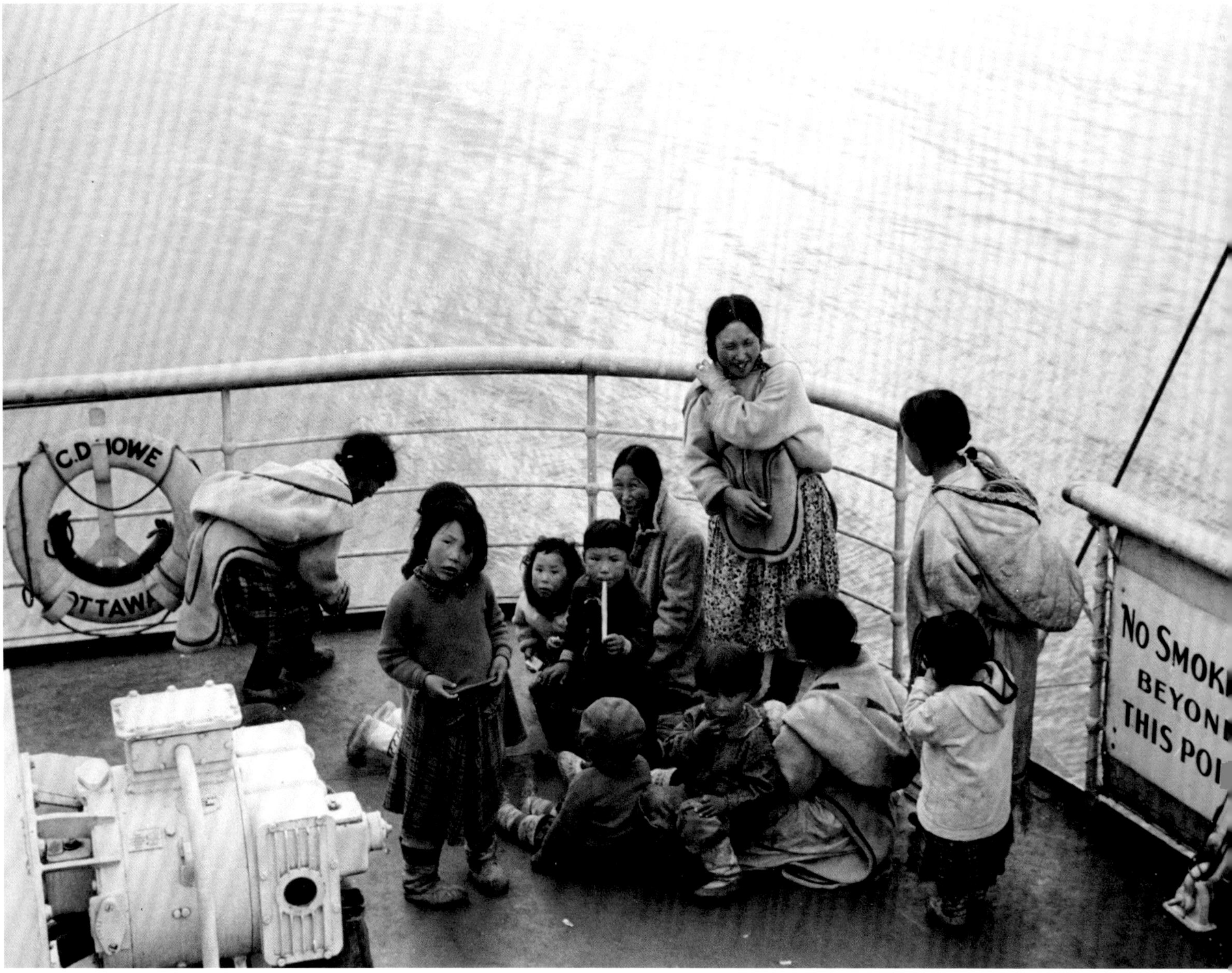

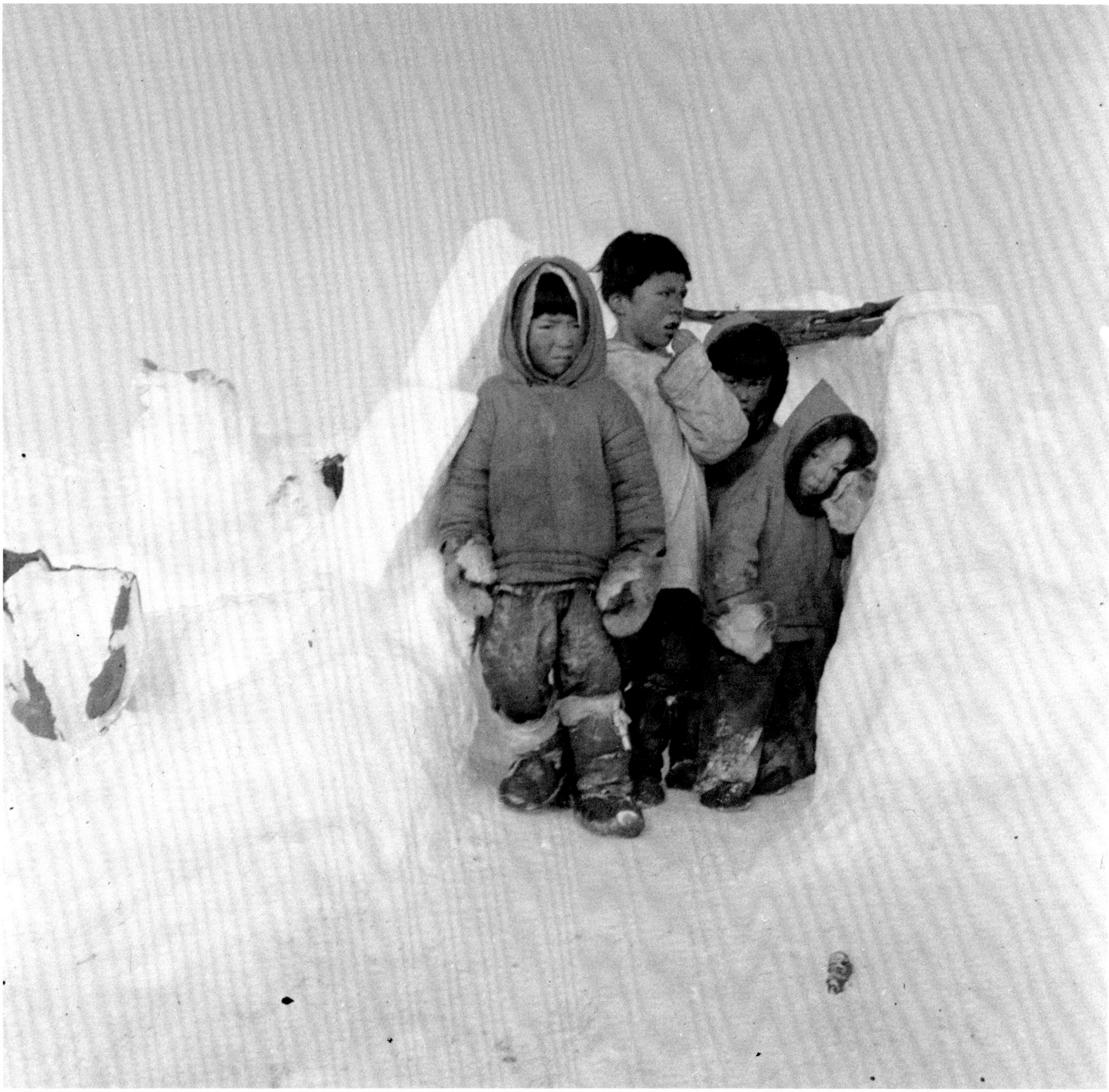

2.7 | [Children in front of their qarmaq, from left to right: Paul Maniittuq (Manitok), Yvo Airut, Michael Kusugaq (Kusugak), Jose Kusugaq (Kusugak). Michael and Jose Kusugaq are from Kangiqliniq, and their uncle is Paul Maniitiuq (Manitok)], Naujaat, 1953.

What I did find when I did the interviews was that our Elders and Story Keepers are so keen to share their stories and so willing. It just takes that initiative, I think, from young people to go and visit our Elders, have tea, and just ask them some questions. So many of them are just waiting for that moment to be able to share all these stories they have. That's one thing I learned from this experience: not to be afraid. Since being a student at NS, I have taken Inuktitut courses and I'm much better at speaking it now than I was ten years ago. I'm happy to say that I can have conversations with my grandmother about growing up.

Having been a student of NS, I learned about the colonial history from Murray Angus, Morley Hanson, and the Inuit Power Curve (see Figure 1.2), with the different waves of changes that happened in the North. I remember coming back from NS and any time I had a chance to visit with my grandmother, I'd really want to ask her, "So, this is what I learned at NS. This is what happened in the 1960s and the 1970s when the land claim negotiations were happening in Canada. I know that this was happening, but what was happening in your community and in your family at that time?" I wanted to ask those questions for a long time, and I didn't because I didn't speak Inuktitut then. But now, I'm proud to say that I can speak it. Not fluently, but much better than before.

This was my experience with Project Naming: at first, I sat down with the Elders and they talked about the different people and the places in the photographs. But that really was … a way to begin. The storytelling just went on and on for a couple of hours about the time period when those photos were taken. The stories weren't necessarily just about the photos, but about the Elders' experience at that time. And they were telling me stories about how the RCMP (Royal Canadian Mounted Police) came into the community, and some were funny stories and some were sadder stories.

I was thinking about how that's so true: how the memory is so strong, but also, the accuracy of those stories. Inuktitut was an oral language for a very long time until it was turned into a written language and so the accuracy of the history just through storytelling is incredible to realize.

I'm now a full-time performer. I also work with the National Arts Centre. But as a full-time performer, I am on the road performing, but also connecting with people, talking about our history and what it's like in the North. Just today, I was making the connection between how the stories and Oral History have to be so accurate for the sake of survival … and the survival of our culture.

When I teach throat singing and do workshops with youth in our communities, I'm starting to learn more and more about how stories of throat singing are just as important as teaching the techniques. When I'm telling stories from back home or from generations before, I'm starting to find within my artistic practice the accuracy of those stories. The only way of keeping those stories alive today is by connecting with Elders. And images are such a wonderful way of doing that.

CHAPTER 3

The Story behind Project Naming at Library and Archives Canada

Beth Greenhorn

I had the honour to lead Project Naming at Library and Archives Canada (hereafter LAC) from 2003 to 2017.[1] Over the years, I have met many Nunavummiut who have offered their time, knowledge, and expertise to help with the identification of the hundreds of anonymous Inuit depicted in the photographic records held at LAC. They have generously shared their community and family histories and the importance behind Inuit names. In this chapter, I recount the story of Project Naming in terms of its development and impact at LAC.

Picking up where Morley Hanson and Murray Angus left off in Chapter 1, I will provide an overview of the impacts Project Naming has had on Inuit communities and archival practice at LAC, at both the operational and institutional levels. Over that time, the project has had many unforeseen twists and turns with several unexpected outcomes. Although Project Naming does not have official stages, it can be grouped into four periods, each addressing a different aspect of the initiative as a whole. I have termed them: Phase I: The Early

Years (2002–04); Phase II: The Naming Continues (2005–14); Phase III: Growth and Expansion (2015–17); and Phase IV: Project Naming and Its Impact at LAC (2017–present).

Phase I: The Early Years (2002–2004)

When Morley Hanson and Murray Angus of Nunavut Sivuniksavut (NS) brought Inuit students to LAC to search for photographs of their communities (see Chapter 1), they encountered a colonial photographic collection. As the nation's archival repository, LAC has an estimated 30 million photographs in its holdings. In addition to photographic records taken by federal public servants, it includes thousands of images from private collections that relate to Canadian history. A large number of these photographers document the three Indigenous Peoples in Canada: First Nations, Inuit, and the Métis Nation. The collections found at LAC – including its photographic holdings – reflect Canada's colonial history with, until recently, prevalent settler attitudes that Indigenous Peoples would disappear or assimilate into the dominant European-based society.

With few exceptions, the names of Inuit depicted in the photographic records were missing or described in ethnographic terms and outdated terminology, such as "Native type" or "Eskimo," while the full names of non-Inuit individuals were usually included in the accompanying captions. A page from a 1936 photo album compiled under the auspices of the then Department of Indian and Northern Affairs (DINA) provides a stark example of this tendency.[2] In the album, the names of Mr G.H. Lawrence (top left) and Constable McQuirter and Mr Robert Betham (bottom right) were included in the captions, while none of the nine Inuit depicted were identified. Discouraged by the anonymity of Inuit depicted in photographs like those in the DINA album, Angus and Hanson proposed Project Naming (Figure 3.1).

LAC's involvement with Project Naming started modestly with the digitization of 485 images taken by the photographer Richard Harrington in four Nunavut communities, Iglulik (Igloolik), Kugluktuk (Coppermine), Padlei (former community near Arviat), and Taloyoak (Spence Bay), in the late 1940s and early 1950s. Digitizing the Harrington photographs was a logical choice. Harrington is well known for his Arctic images, especially portraiture, dating between 1948 and 1953, and other images made during a period of about twelve years that he spent in the region. His photographs of Inuit provide recognizable depictions in either close-up portraits or views of people performing daily activities. However, like the majority of images of Indigenous Peoples in the collections at LAC, the names of most of the individuals captured by Harrington were never recorded. With photographs that had been shot approximately fifty years before Project Naming began, the chances of Elders and community members being able to recognize their family, and in some cases themselves, remained quite high.

In June 2003, just a few weeks after I started working at LAC, I received the list of identifications for the Harrington photographs from NS in the form of a spreadsheet. Elders recognized about three-quarters of the individuals depicted in the images.[3] This number surpassed all expectations. In addition to identifying people portrayed in the photographs, Elders provided names of their relatives and other contextual information. Among them was a photograph of Elizabeth Tatiggat Piugaattuq taken in Iglulik in 1952–53. Thanks to the Elders who recognized her, LAC could now properly acknowledge that

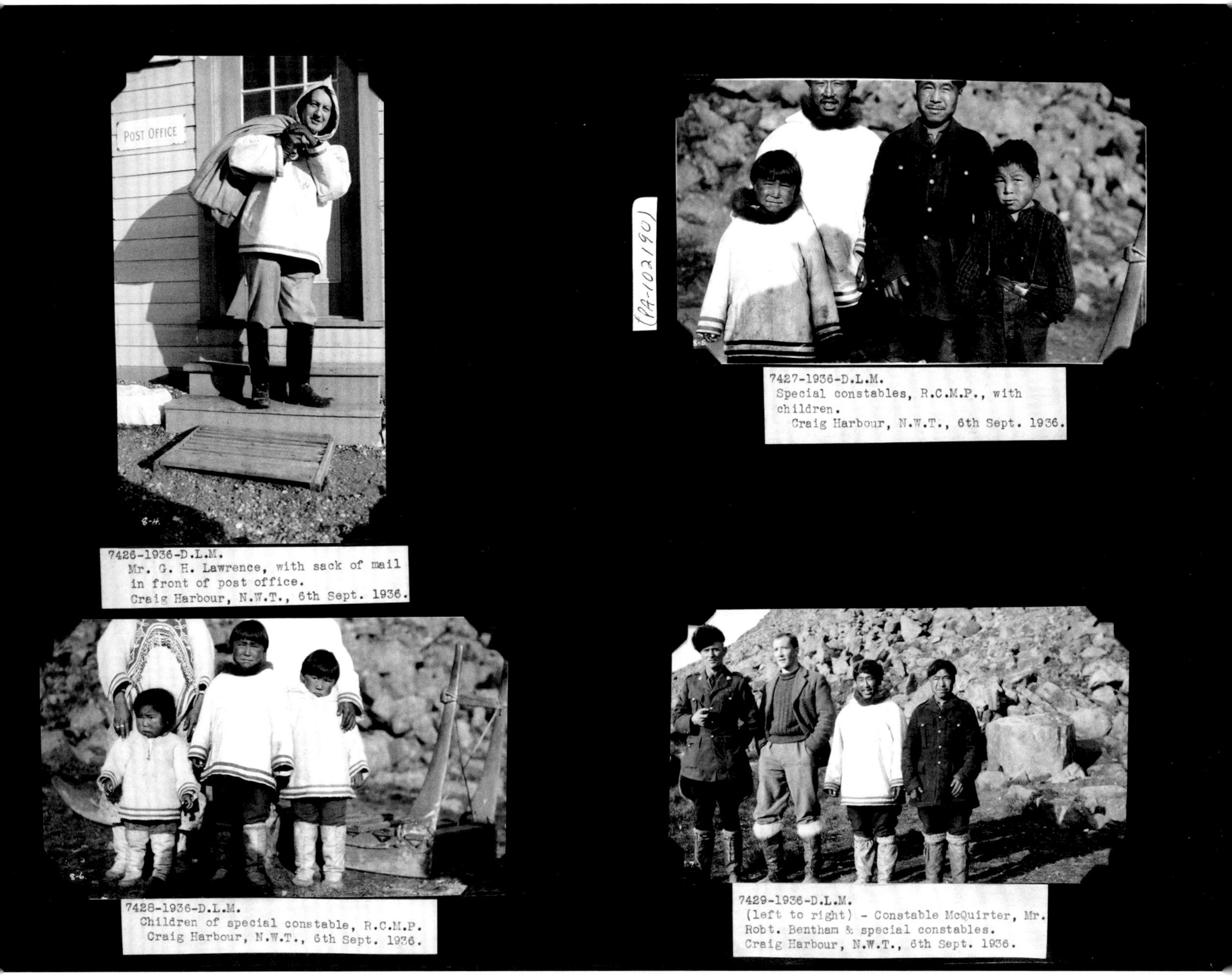

3.1 | [Album 20, page 66 with photographs of G.H. Lawrence standing with a sack of mail outside of a post office, two Inuit RCMP special constables with two boys, a special constable standing in front of a qamutiq with his wife and children, and Constable McQuirter and Robert Bentham with the same two special constables at Craig Harbour], 1936.

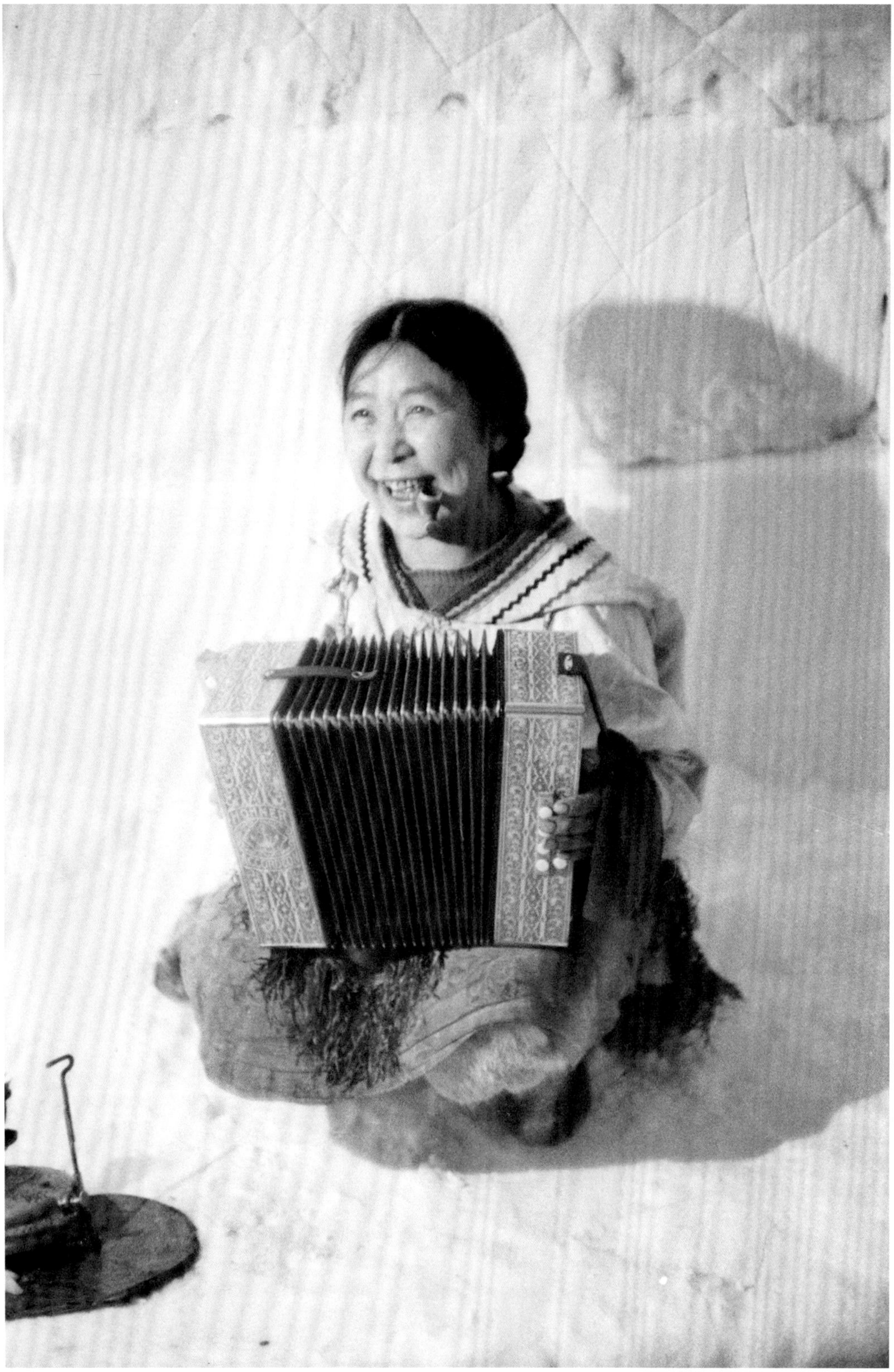

3.2 | [Elizabeth Tatiggat Piugaattuq. She is Noah Piugaattuq's wife and Solomon Mikki's adoptive mother], Iglulik, 1952–53.

Ms Piugaattuq was married to Noah Piugaattuq and was the adoptive mother of Solomon Mikki (Figure 3.2).

Following archival practice and theory, the newly recovered names of individuals and accompanying information were placed in square brackets and added to the Title field in the archival record.[4] An explanatory note was added in the "Additional Information" field stating that the caption in square brackets was the result of Project Naming.

But when it came to the locations where the photographs were taken, the conversation about how to attribute place names was not as straightforward. Inuit have inhabited, hunted, and fished in these places for centuries, and have always called them by their Inuktut names. Unlike place names imposed by outsiders, which often celebrate European explorers and officials from southern Canada, Inuit names are linked inextricably to a specific place or region and describe physical or cultural features in the landscape. Explaining the significance of place names, the Inuit Heritage Trust's website states:

> The land has always been alive with names for all places of any significance to Inuit who have called this environment home for centuries. Until the middle of the 20th century, Inuit depended completely upon animals of the land for food, shelter, clothing, and tools. To understand the land well was to survive. Naturally, Inuit communicated about places using names in their own language. Traditionally this knowledge was captured in a rich oral history.[5]

For example, during Richard Harrington's time in the Arctic (between 1947 and 1959), the region was called the Northwest Territories by settler society and all twenty-five communities (of what is now Nunavut) were labelled in English on maps, atlases, and other official government documents.[6] In the time that Project Naming has existed, following the founding of Nunavut, two of the communities visited by Harrington,Taloyoak and Kugluktuk are now officially called by their Inuktitut names.[7]

After initial discussions with my colleagues in LAC's Photo Division about how to record place names, we consulted Elder Piita Irniq for his advice. To recognize the significance of traditional Inuit place names and show the short time span of European-imposed labels, Irniq urged LAC to adopt the following format: "Kugluktuk, Nunavut (*for a time known as* Coppermine, Northwest Territories)" (emphasis added). In the end, however, LAC decided on a more conservative archival approach and used the colonial name of the community, followed by the traditional Inuit names in square brackets. Joe Ulurksit and Gemma having a tea break in the vicinity of Coppermine (now Kugluktuk) is an example of this early method to revise place names in LAC records.

With the help of Inuit Knowledge, Elders were also able to identify the names of ilagiit nunagivaktangit (camping sites)[8] and other places frequented by Inuit but not listed on settler maps of the region. One of these photographs depicts Piqqanaaq working on caribou meat while he was fox hunting at a settlement in Akunijuaq/Akuniyuaq (Figure 3.4). Piqqanaaq was identified by his daughter, Helen Konek, one of the Elders who participated in the first phase of Project Naming. (See Chapter 12 for a discussion of images depicting Helen Konek by her grandson, Curtis Kuunuaq Konek.) Without the knowledge of Elder Konek, we would never have learned the name of the camp where her father's photograph had been taken, since

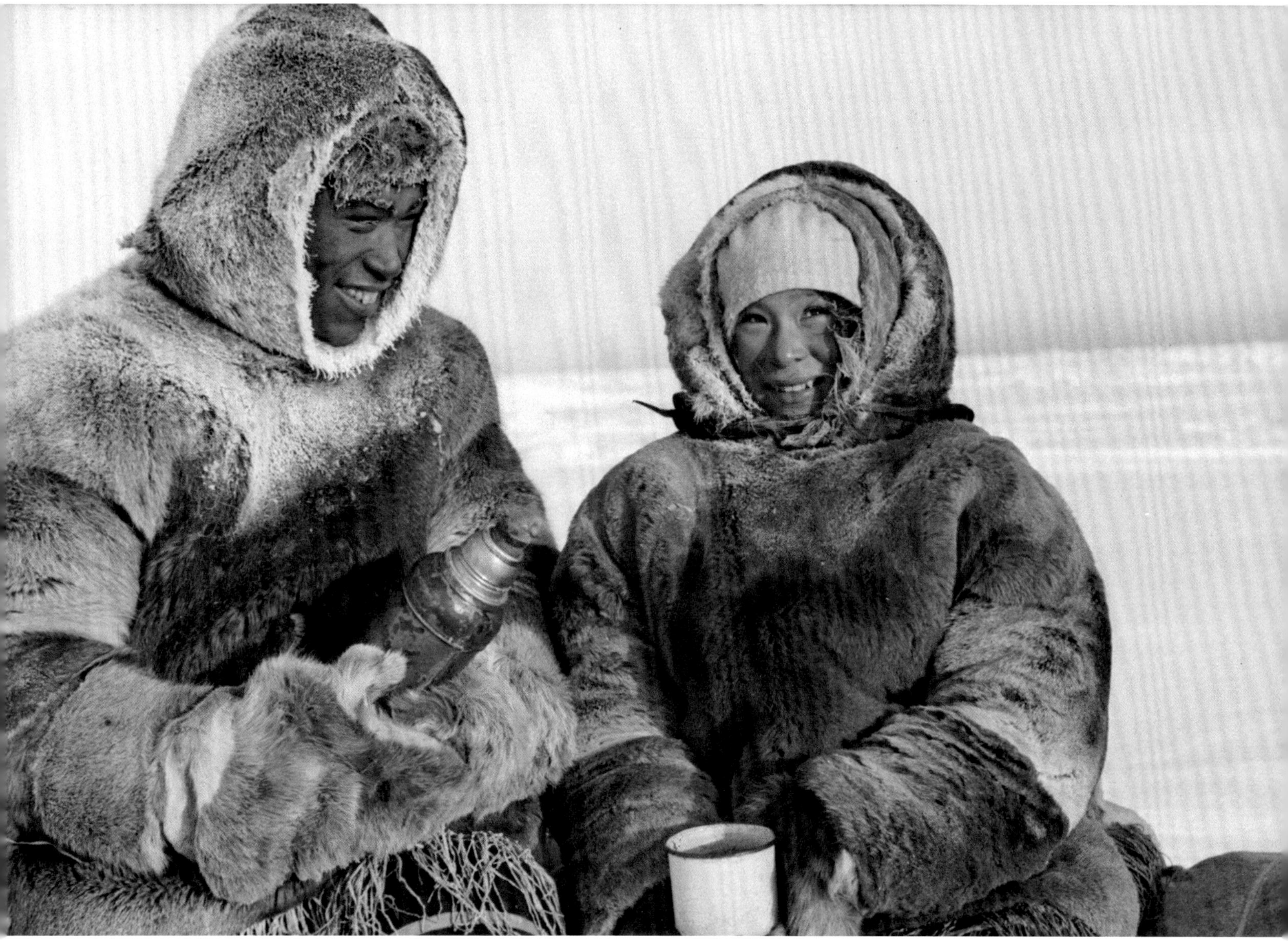

3.3 | [Joe Ulurksit and his wife Gemma], Kugluktuk, 1949.

3.4 (*opposite*) | [Piqqanaaq working on caribou meat. He was Helen Aagatok Konek's father and Curtis Kuunuaq Konek's grandfather. This photograph was taken while Piqqanaaq was fox hunting at a settlement in Akunijuaq/Akuniyuaq], near Padlei, 1949–50.

Akunijuaq/Akuniyuaq does not exist on any "official" maps.

Following the large number of identifications of people in the Harrington photographs, LAC dedicated funding to Project Naming for additional photographic research and digitization beginning in June 2003. That summer, I worked with Elisapee Tatigat Avingaq, a second-year student from NS. Together, we researched and selected approximately 800 photographs from the Qikiqtaaluk (Baffin) region for digitization.[9] In contrast to the first group of photographs digitized, which were all made by Harrington, the second group included photographs from a range of fonds[10] at LAC from private (individual) holdings to government collections, ranging in date from the 1920s to the late 1950s.[11]

As with the first group of photographs taken North, Elders identified the names of individuals in a substantial number of photographs – over two hundred images. To my astonishment, they recognized people whose pictures were taken in the 1920s, more than eight decades earlier! Among the individuals identified was a 1923 image of Qannguq washing an animal skin. Elders also added invaluable information related to kinship. In this case, they noted the

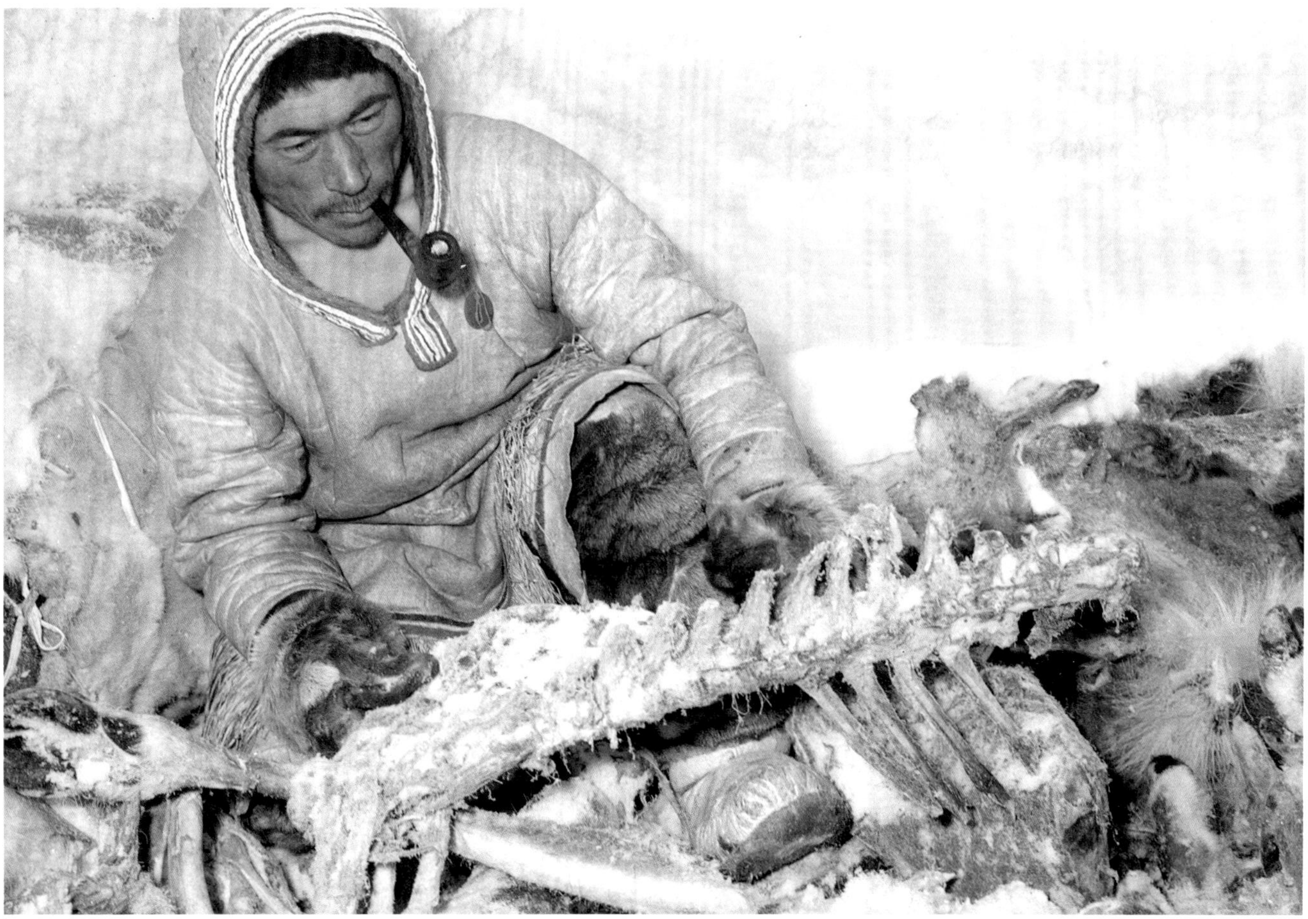

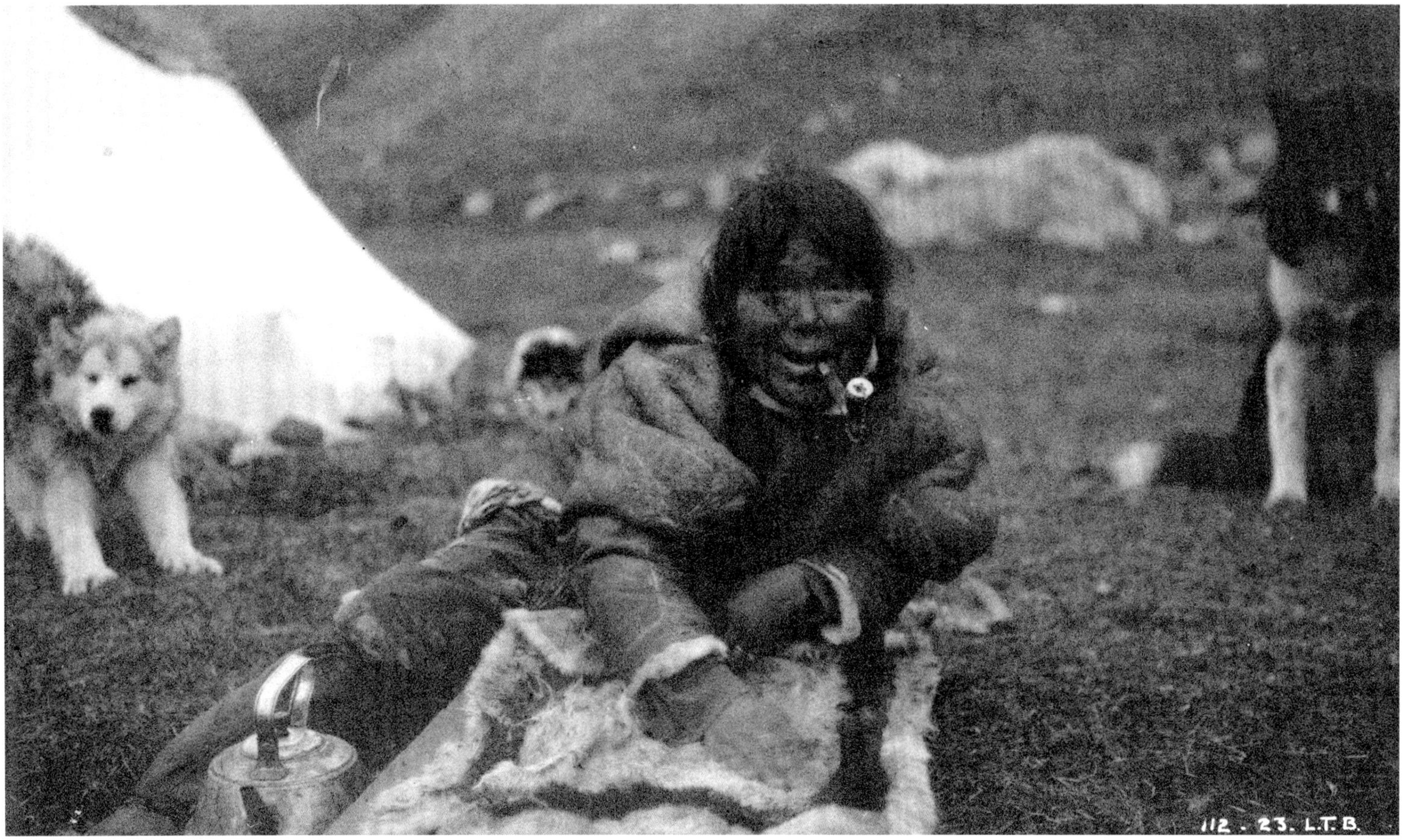

names of Qannguq's first husband, Aula, and her second, Urulu (Figure 3.5).

In October 2004, LAC launched a trilingual web exhibition and database featuring the early work of Project Naming. We included the newly re-identified Harrington photographs as well as the eight hundred additional images that had been digitized in the summer of 2003. [12] As a commitment to the importance of improving archival descriptions and giving people back their identities, LAC added "The Naming Continues," an online form inviting the public to submit names and other information related to the photographs.[13] Over the next year, members of the public identified Inuit portrayed in the archival collections by sharing their knowledge and information via "The Naming Continues" form. Among the many faces identified by the public was the 1929 photograph of Elder Suzanne Singuuri's father, Sappa Aipili, who worked as a guide for the Northwest Territories and Yukon Branch in the Department of the Interior (Figure 3.6). Captivated by his face, Elder Singuuri was certain she knew the man depicted in this photograph. She initially thought it was her brother from Ikpiarjuk (Arctic Bay),

3.5 (*opposite*) | [Qannguq washing an animal skin. Her first husband was Aula, and her second was Urulu], Mittimatalik, 1923. Original title: Old native woman.

3.6 | [Sappa Aipili], Kinngait, 1929. Original title: an Eskimo employee of the Northwest Territories and Yukon Branch, Department of the Interior.

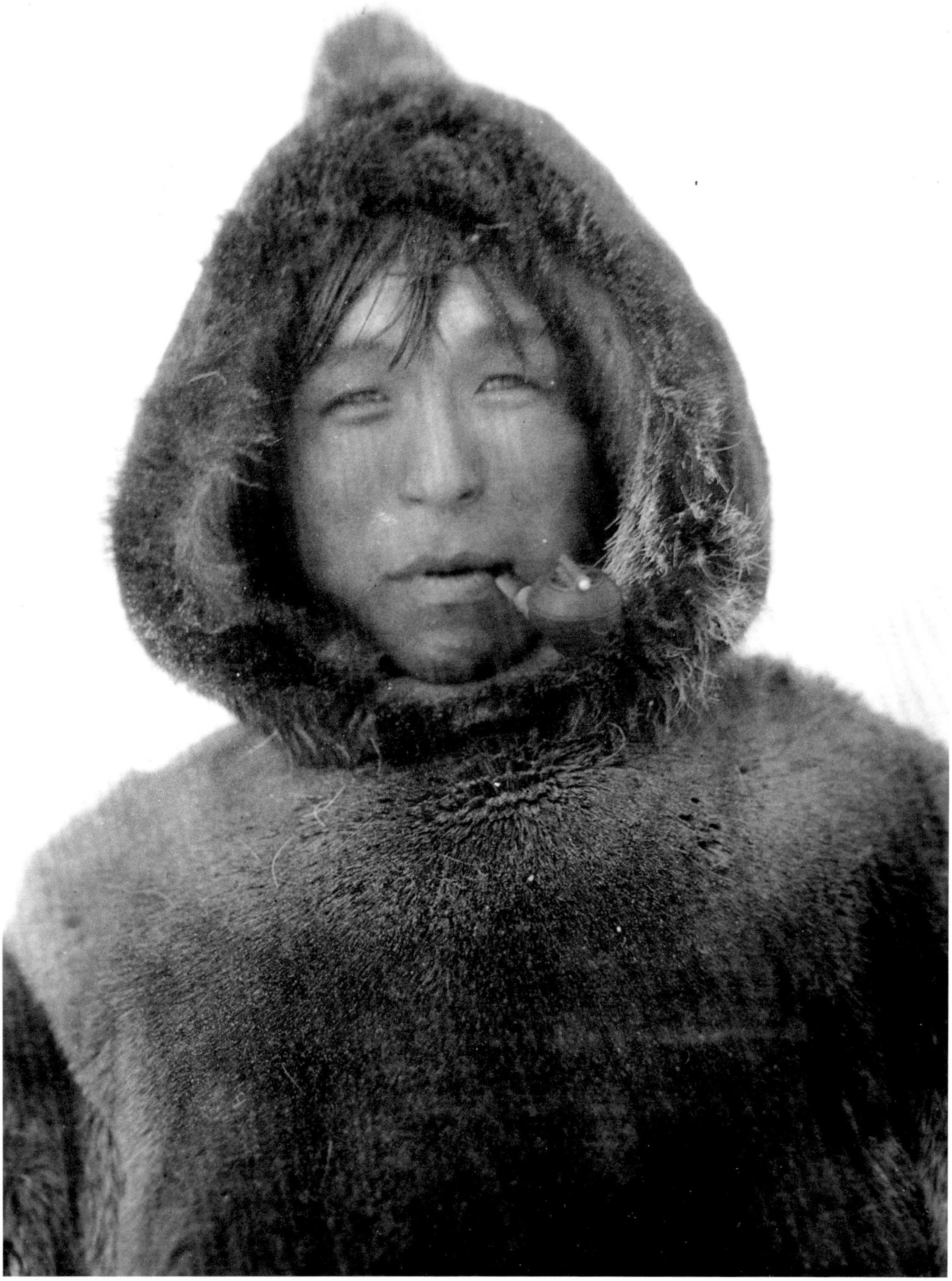

but the date did not make any sense given that the photograph was too old to be him. She then realized why the face looked so familiar: it was her father.[14] Before its digitization, Elder Singuuri had never seen a photograph of her father as a young man.

Phase II: The Naming Continues (2005–2014)

The period from 2005 to 2014 was productive for Project Naming. Public interest and support grew as more images were digitized and LAC launched an expanded web exhibition and database. The project also gained national media interest and collaborations increased with community groups and outreach through national and international speaking events.[15]

Recognizing the relevance of the project as having "unsurpassed qualitative value,"[16] LAC applied for and received a second round of funding from the Department of Canadian Heritage's CCOP program in 2005 to carry out new digitization of photographic records depicting Nunavummiut.

In October 2005, the Government of Nunavut's Department of Culture, Language, Elders and Youth (CLEY) organized a two-week research visit to LAC by two staff, Joanna Quassa and Sylvia Ivalu, along with Iglulik Elders Louis Uttak and Abraham Ulayuruluk (Figure 3.7), and recent NS graduate Jesse Mike. With the assistance of LAC staff, the researchers painstakingly poured through hundreds of analogue images from the Qikiqtaaluk region that ranged

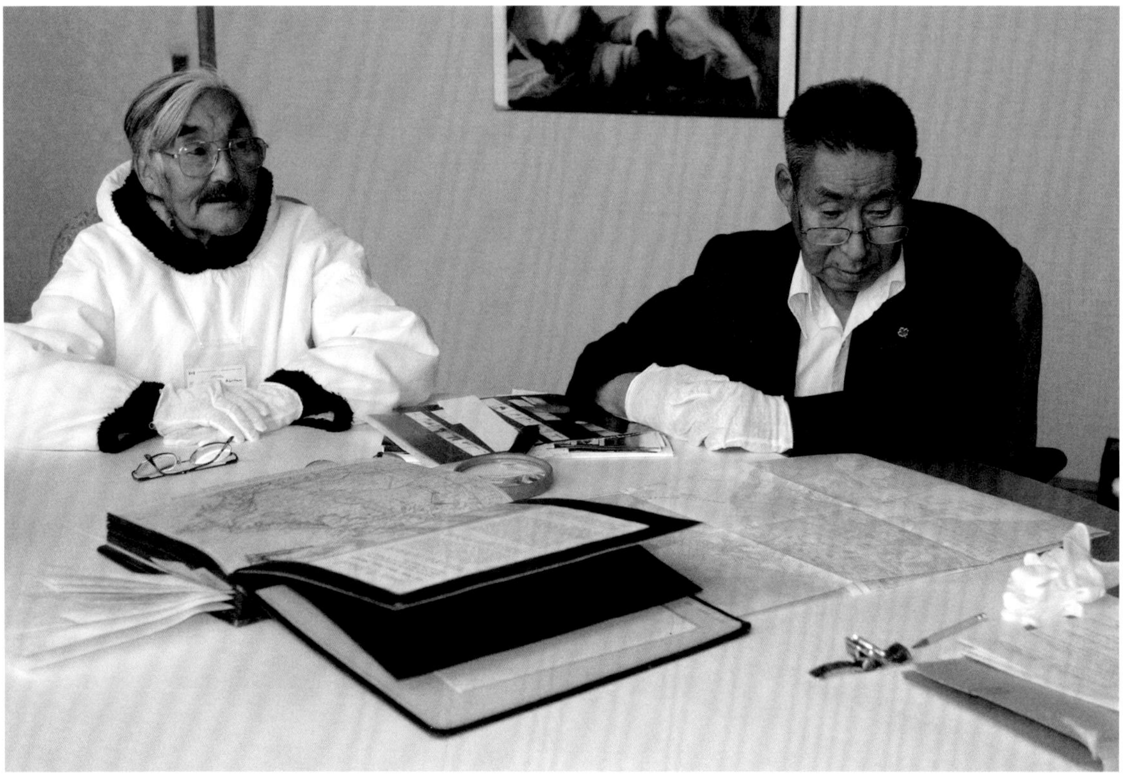

3.7 | Iglulik Elders Abraham Ulayuruluk (*left*) and Louis Uttak (*right*) during their research visit at Library and Archives Canada, Ottawa, 2005.

from photographs mounted in albums to individual prints, 35mm slides, and negatives. Jesse Mike discovered a photograph depicting her grandfather and aunt, while Elders Uttak and Ulayuruluk were able to identify a number of individuals captured in more than thirty images, including a group photograph of Ujaralaaq, Mark Tutat, Amimiarjuk, Arraq Qulitalik, Valentine Auqsaaq, and Tarqtaq taken at an unknown location in the early 1950s.

In 2005, LAC began a collaboration with Views from the North. Led by Carol Payne, a co-editor of this volume and a Carleton University faculty member, this project initially involved the digitization of photographs in the National Film Board of Canada (NFB) collection held at LAC. While Views from the North followed many of the procedures first established by Project Naming – youth taking digitized archival images on laptops to show Elders in remote northern communities – it pushed the boundaries of the project through Oral History interviews on film with Elders. Significantly, Views from the North was the first community-based partnership with Project Naming involving Inuit youth and Elders, but it was not the last. Other notable collaborations that built upon the foundations of Project Naming included the Nanisiniq: Arviat History Project (2010–12) and the Nanivara Project (2013–14), led by community members and UBC faculty member Frank Tester. Using digitized archival photographs as a starting point, the Nanivara and Nanisiniq projects expanded the scope of Project Naming even further by re-telling the histories of the communities of Arviat and Uqsuqtuuq (Gjoa Haven) from an Inuit perspective using social media platforms. These initiatives are described by Carol Payne and Sheena Ellison in Chapter 13 and Frank Tester and Curtis Kuunuaq Konek in Chapter 12 in this volume.[17]

In August 2007, LAC launched an expanded online exhibition of Project Naming that included searchable lists of communities and locations of photographs taken in Nunavut, as well as those depicting places near the borders of the newly formed territory. The inclusion of locales outside the territory of Nunavut was a significant move for Project Naming, signalling its future as a national initiative that would eventually include all three Indigenous Peoples in Canada: First Nations, Inuit, and the Métis Nation.

Soon after launching the updated web exhibition, I created a poster to promote the expansion of Project Naming and distributed it to every contact I had made while working on the project over the previous four years. In my email message, I asked my contacts to share it with friends, family, and colleagues, and to post it in their local community centres, stores, schools, and other public places. The poster featured two rows of photographs of unidentified individuals, with a brief explanation about the project and the URL for the website (Figure 3.8).

To my surprise and delight, the following day I received an email from Betty Novalinga Brewster (née Lyall) who informed me that she and her late sister, Bella Ningyooga Wilcox (née Lyall), were depicted in an image in the second row (Figure 3.9). I was hopeful the poster would generate new Project Naming supporters but never imagined I would receive an identification so quickly, and from someone I had never met living nearly 3,000 kilometres away. That day, I received several other emails from Ms Brewster, who shared photographs of her daughter and grandson. She asked if I could post them on the Project Naming page on LAC's

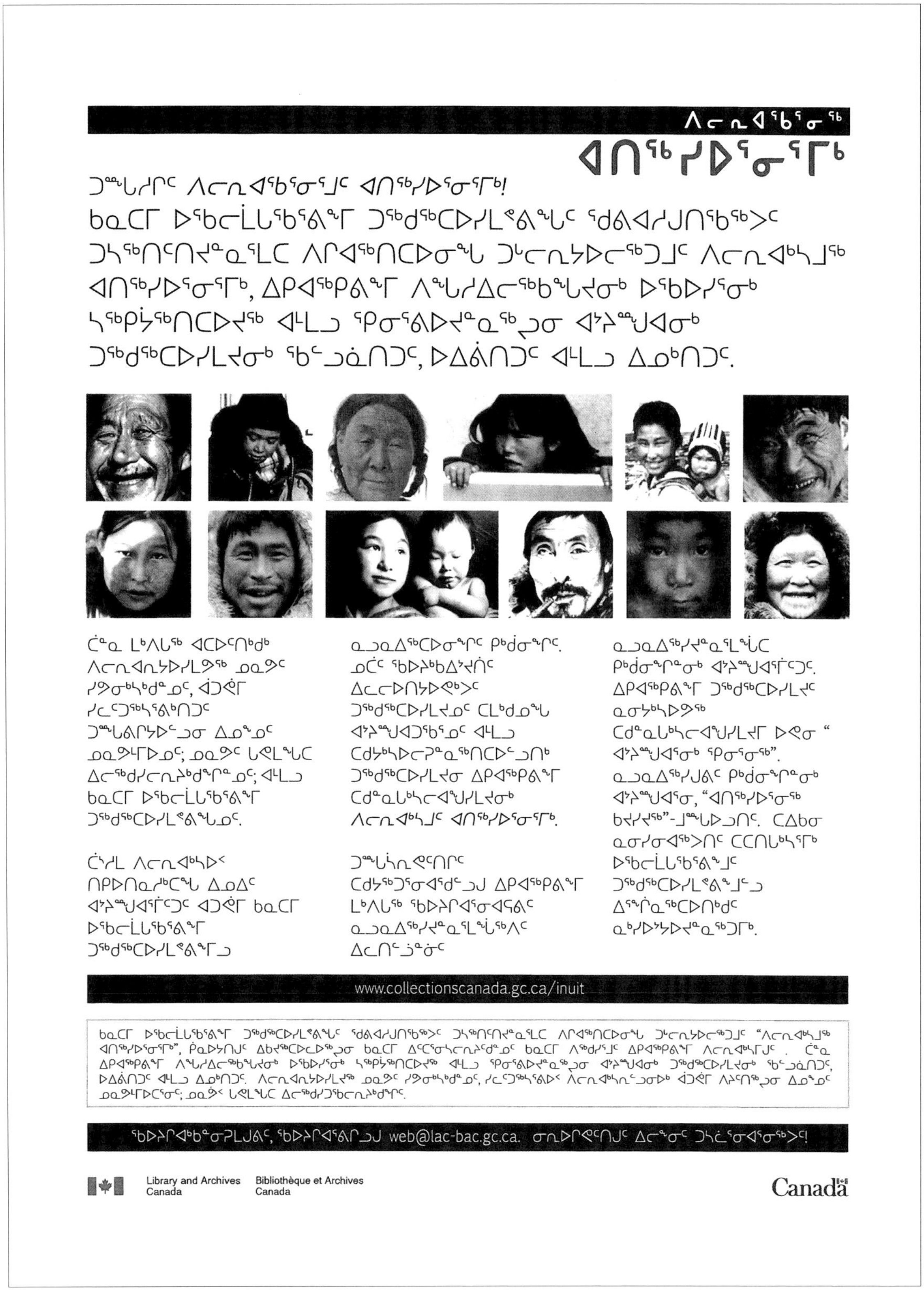

3.8 | Project Naming promotional poster, 2007.

3.9 (*opposite*) | [Bella Lyall-Wilcox carrying her baby sister, Betty Lyall-Brewster], Taloyoak, 1949.

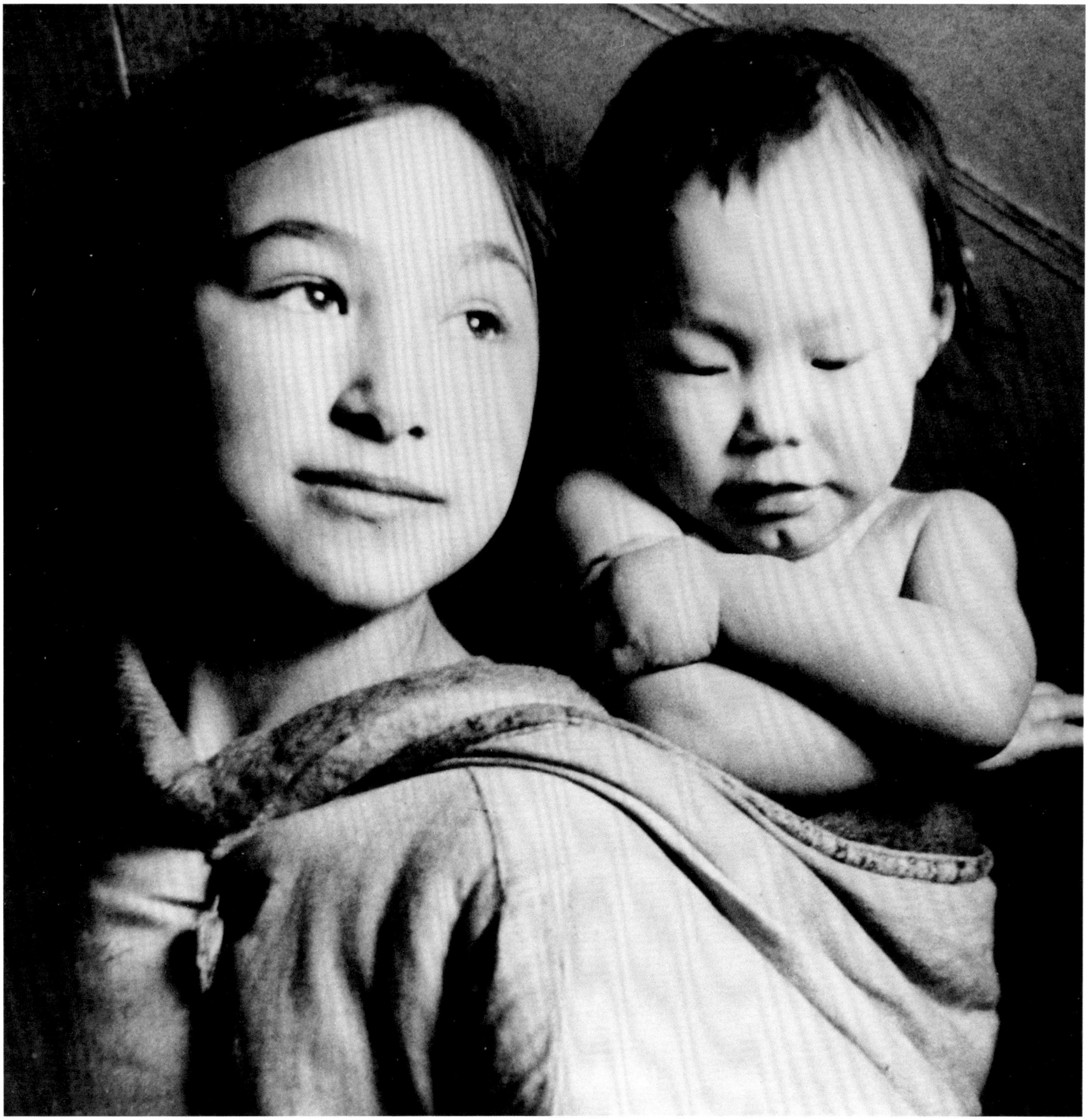

website so the public could see the resemblance between herself as a baby and her grandson. Unfortunately, I could only include images that were part of LAC's collection on the website and was never able to share them publicly.[18]

In September 2007, several weeks after launching an updated version of the Project Naming web exhibition, I was contacted by George Lessard, the former photo editor from Northern News Services Ltd. Based in Yellowknife, Northwest Territories, Northern News Services publishes seven different weekly papers in northern Canada, including *Nunavut/News North*, which is distributed to all twenty-five communities in Nunavut. A supporter of Project Naming, Lessard offered to create a regular feature in *Nunavut/News North* that would showcase an unidentified image from LAC each week. Excited by the opportunity to reach an even wider audience, I sent him an initial selection of about twenty high-resolution images representing various communities in Nunavut. The first photograph was published on 17 September 2007, in the new feature titled "Do You Know Your Elders?" (Figure 3.10). The couple depicted were immediately identified as Saa, who was making tea on a qulliq, and Atamie, who had lost his sight.[19] Their names were given to Lessard, who then sent the information to me by email in Ottawa. I updated the database and mailed copies of the photograph to the family members who identified the couple as an acknowledgment of LAC's gratitude.

Robert Comeau, a young Inuk from Iqaluit, describes his family's enthusiasm for the "Do You Know Your Elders?" feature, and how historical images benefit younger generations of Inuit disconnected from their past:

> Project Naming has been something that's been around since I can physically remember, fifteen years. I was about seven years old back then. I don't remember it starting, but I do remember every time we'd get the paper ... we'd flip over to the Project Naming page and see if it's one of our ancestors, because our grandparents and our great aunts would always be willing to answer those questions.
>
> So just providing that channel for youth to be engaged with the Elders is something of tremendous value. Because as Inuit, we have a social history that not many of us understand that we're still learning about: our shared experiences of colonialism, like with residential schools, relocations, day schools, and the continuing impacts of these events to our people, which may sometimes hinder young people's abilities to have these conversations with Elders.[20]

Given its popularity in *Nunavut/News North*, Northern News Services added a "Do You Know Your Elders?" feature in *Kivalliq News*, a weekly paper distributed to the central Nunavut community of Kangiqliniq (Rankin Inlet) during the winter of 2008. *Nunavut/News North* and *Kivalliq News* published this feature for the next few years. In that time, dozens of people were identified by family members and friends. This collaboration has been beneficial to the newspaper, the communities, and LAC. The papers were guaranteed weekly content that had great popularity among its readerships. Family members and friends were able to reconnect with historical photographs never seen before digitization. And LAC received the names and identities of individuals who would have remained unknown without the knowledge and support of the communities.

In addition to receiving new identifications through "The Naming Continues" online form, communities have provided names through

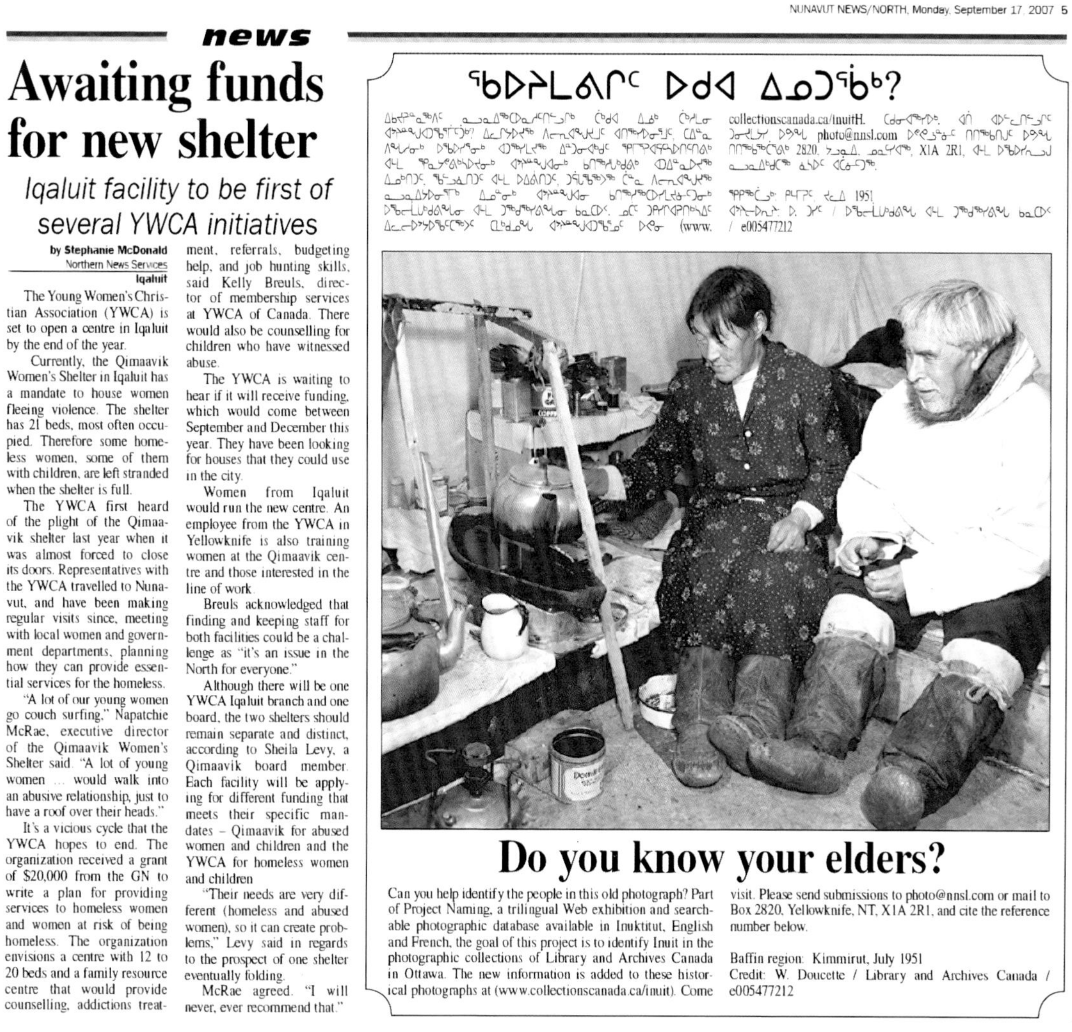

NUNAVUT NEWS/NORTH, Monday, September 17, 2007 5

news

Awaiting funds for new shelter

Iqaluit facility to be first of several YWCA initiatives

by Stephanie McDonald
Northern News Services
Iqaluit

The Young Women's Christian Association (YWCA) is set to open a centre in Iqaluit by the end of the year.

Currently, the Qimaavik Women's Shelter in Iqaluit has a mandate to house women fleeing violence. The shelter has 21 beds, most often occupied. Therefore some homeless women, some of them with children, are left stranded when the shelter is full.

The YWCA first heard of the plight of the Qimaavik shelter last year when it was almost forced to close its doors. Representatives with the YWCA travelled to Nunavut, and have been making regular visits since, meeting with local women and government departments, planning how they can provide essential services for the homeless.

"A lot of our young women go couch surfing," Napatchie McRae, executive director of the Qimaavik Women's Shelter said. "A lot of young women … would walk into an abusive relationship, just to have a roof over their heads."

It's a vicious cycle that the YWCA hopes to end. The organization received a grant of $20,000 from the GN to write a plan for providing services to homeless women and women at risk of being homeless. The organization envisions a centre with 12 to 20 beds and a family resource centre that would provide counselling, addictions treatment, referrals, budgeting help, and job hunting skills, said Kelly Breuls, director of membership services at YWCA of Canada. There would also be counselling for children who have witnessed abuse.

The YWCA is waiting to hear if it will receive funding, which would come between September and December this year. They have been looking for houses that they could use in the city.

Women from Iqaluit would run the new centre. An employee from the YWCA in Yellowknife is also training women at the Qimaavik centre and those interested in the line of work.

Breuls acknowledged that finding and keeping staff for both facilities could be a challenge as "it's an issue in the North for everyone."

Although there will be one YWCA Iqaluit branch and one board, the two shelters should remain separate and distinct, according to Sheila Levy, a Qimaavik board member. Each facility will be applying for different funding that meets their specific mandates – Qimaavik for abused women and children and the YWCA for homeless women and children.

"Their needs are very different (homeless and abused women), so it can create problems," Levy said in regards to the prospect of one shelter eventually folding.

McRae agreed. "I will never, ever recommend that."

Do you know your elders?

Can you help identify the people in this old photograph? Part of Project Naming, a trilingual Web exhibition and searchable photographic database available in Inuktitut, English and French, the goal of this project is to identify Inuit in the photographic collections of Library and Archives Canada in Ottawa. The new information is added to these historical photographs at (www.collectionscanada.ca/inuit). Come visit. Please send submissions to photo@nnsl.com or mail to Box 2820, Yellowknife, NT, X1A 2R1, and cite the reference number below.

Baffin region: Kimmirut, July 1951
Credit: W. Doucette / Library and Archives Canada / e005477212

3.10 | First publication of the "Do You Know Your Elders?," which received this identification: [Saa (left) and Atamie (right) who is blind. They are in a tent at Kimmirut and Saa is making tea or coffee over a qulliq. Atamie (possibly E7-200) and Saa are the adoptive parents of Qasinga (E7-204). Qasinga's daughters are Arniak and Mary]. Original title: Making tea for 80-year-old blind man, Adamee in his tent, Lake Harbour, 1951.

other methods. One of these included a collection of posters created by a family from Pangniqtuuq (Pangnirtung) who organized a community-wide photo identification session. Each person depicted in the photographs was assigned a number on a label, whose names were recorded in Inuktitut syllabics and English in the accompanying legends. In other cases, members of the public emailed PDFs with the names of individuals transcribed onto the image. All of the names were added manually

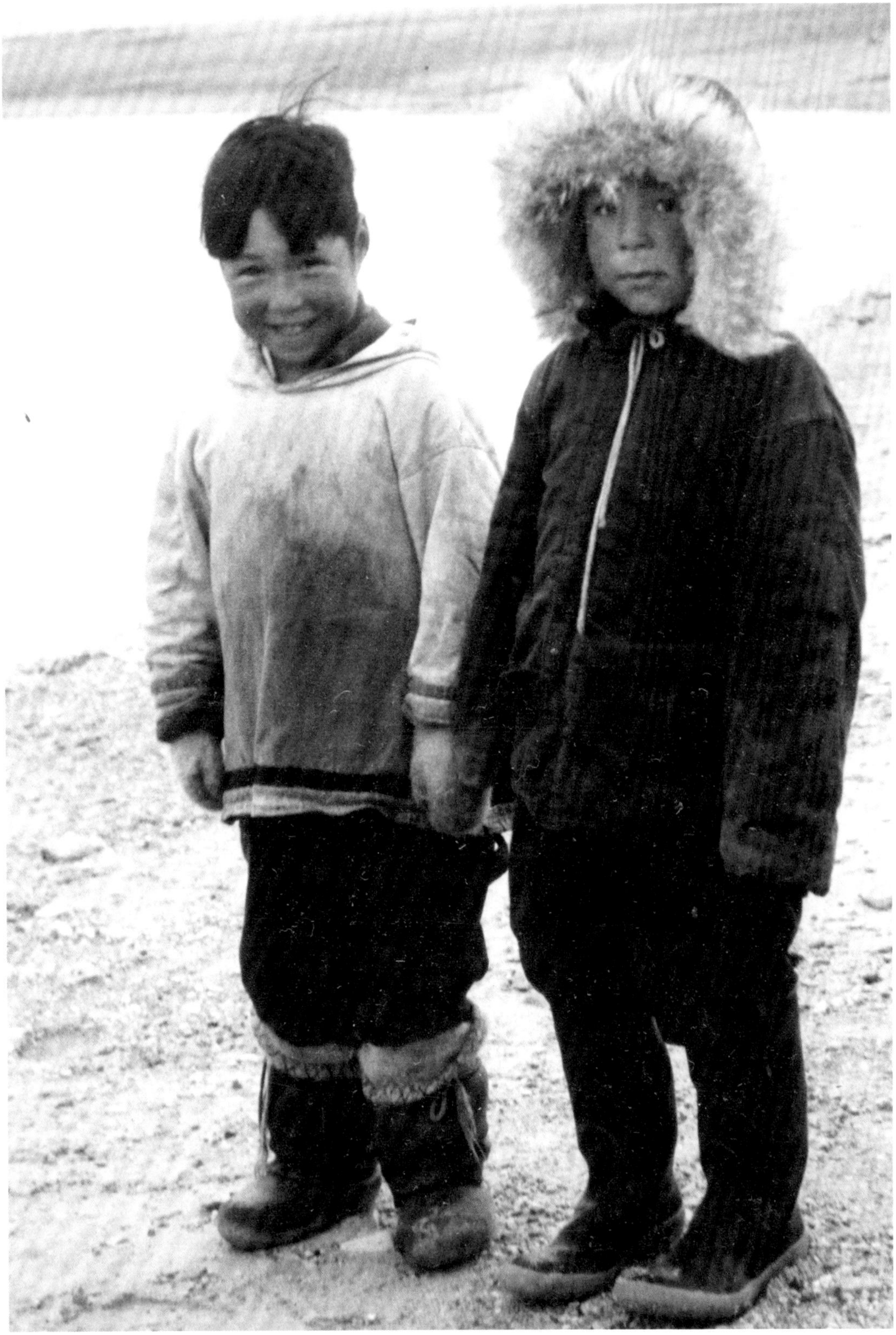

3.11 | [Kutik (Richard Immaroitok) on the left and Louis Tapadjuk on the right in Iglulik just before their departure to Sir Joseph Bernier Federal Day School in Igluligaarjuk], 1958.

to the database records by LAC staff, who have jokingly described Project Naming as LAC's "first crowd sourcing initiative."

Between 2007 and 2014, Project Naming grew steadily, developing into a broader community engagement and photo identification initiative. Although funding from Canadian Heritage had ended in 2007 following the launch of the second phase of the website, LAC continued to support the project by assisting community-led projects and other initiatives at the territorial level with the continued digitization of photographic records from Nunavut.[21] There are many stories to recount from this period; I will focus on just a few that I find particularly compelling.

Community-organized photo identification events have played an invaluable role in reconnecting families with their loved ones, and in some cases, photographs of themselves. In April 2009, LAC organized an event to celebrate the tenth anniversary of the creation of the territory of Nunavut. The day included presentations by various Nunavummiut and LAC staff, performances by NS students, a station with laptops for photo identifications, and a small exhibition of photographic reproductions from the collection. None of the individuals captured in the photographs chosen for the exhibition had been identified before the event.

Kutik (Richard Immaroitok) was among the many people who attended this celebration. One of the photographs I had selected for the exhibition depicted Kutik and his friend, Louis Tapajuk. Unbeknownst to them, their picture was taken just before the boys boarded a plane in Iglulik, which would take them to the federal day school in Igluligaarjuk (Chesterfield Inlet), almost 800 kilometres away from home (Figure 3.11). Before meeting Kutik, I imagined that the boys' apprehensive expressions captured in the photograph were caused by the glare of the sun. After hearing the tragic story behind this photograph, I could now see their faces conveyed a sense of trepidation, but not fully comprehending what was to unfold.

On another occasion, in the winter of 2011, the Kitikmeot Heritage Society in western Nunavut held several community slide shows of photographs from LAC. During one of these gatherings, Mona Tigitkok, an Elder from Kugluktuk, discovered a photograph of her younger self, taken sixty years earlier. Immediately before this photograph was taken, Elder Tigitkok was captured on video where she is seen coming through the doorway into the room with the slide projector. When she saw the projection on the screen, she immediately recognized herself and burst into a huge smile after reconnecting with her portrait as a young woman (Figures 3.12 and 3.13).

In addition to supporting events in communities in Nunavut, LAC has helped with numerous research tours from Nunavummiut, by ordering photographic material beforehand and digitizing records of interest to be taken back to the communities for identification. While there have been many incredible visits, one that was particularly special occurred in June 2012 when a group of Elders and youth from Arviat visited LAC (Figure 3.14). Over the course of a day, with laughter and tears, the group looked through hundreds of photographs and negatives, identifying thirty-one family members in seventeen images. Louisa Gibbons discovered her mother, Catherine Kopak, and her grandmother, Yarat, in a picture taken at Kingayualik, near Padlei, while Elder Eva Muyunaganiak found two photographs of her mother, Utnguuyaq.[22]

There was a bittersweet ending to the photo identification events held in Kugluktuk in 2011 and Ottawa in 2012. Sadly, both Elder

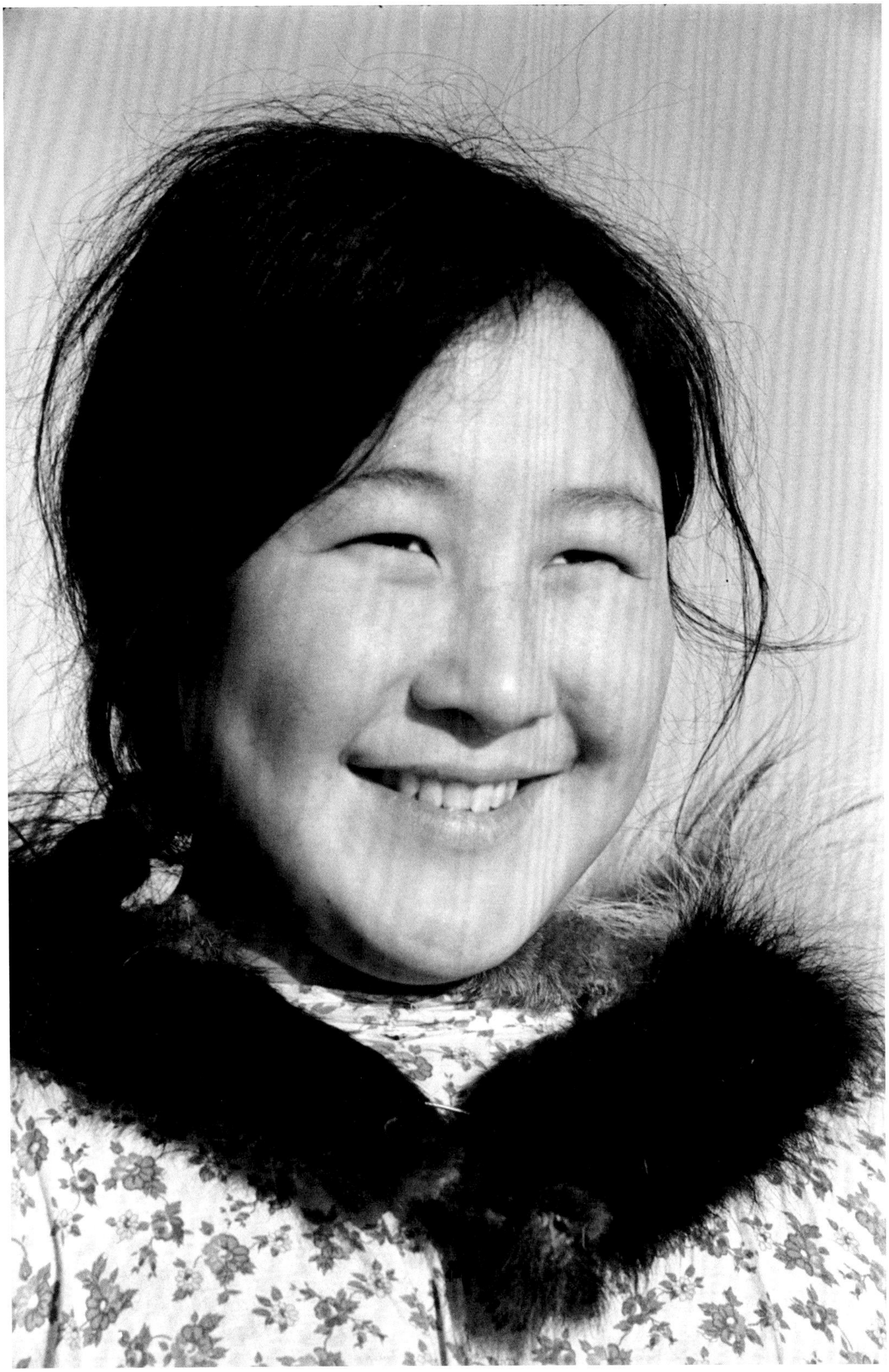

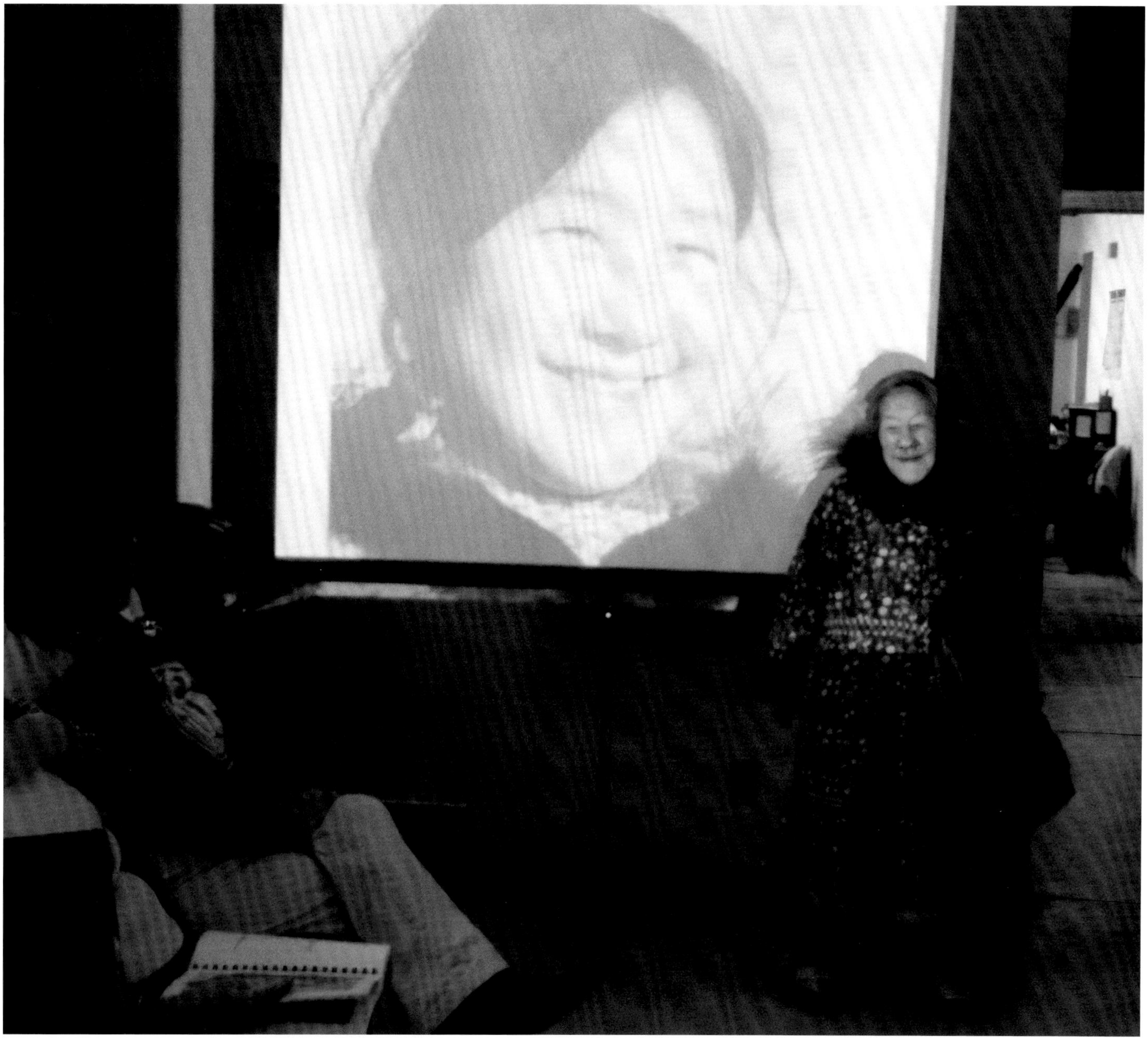

3.12 (*opposite*) | [Mona Tigitkok], Kugluktuk, 1949–1950

3.13 | Mona Tigitkok, at the Kitikmeot Heritage Society, Kugluktuk, 2011.

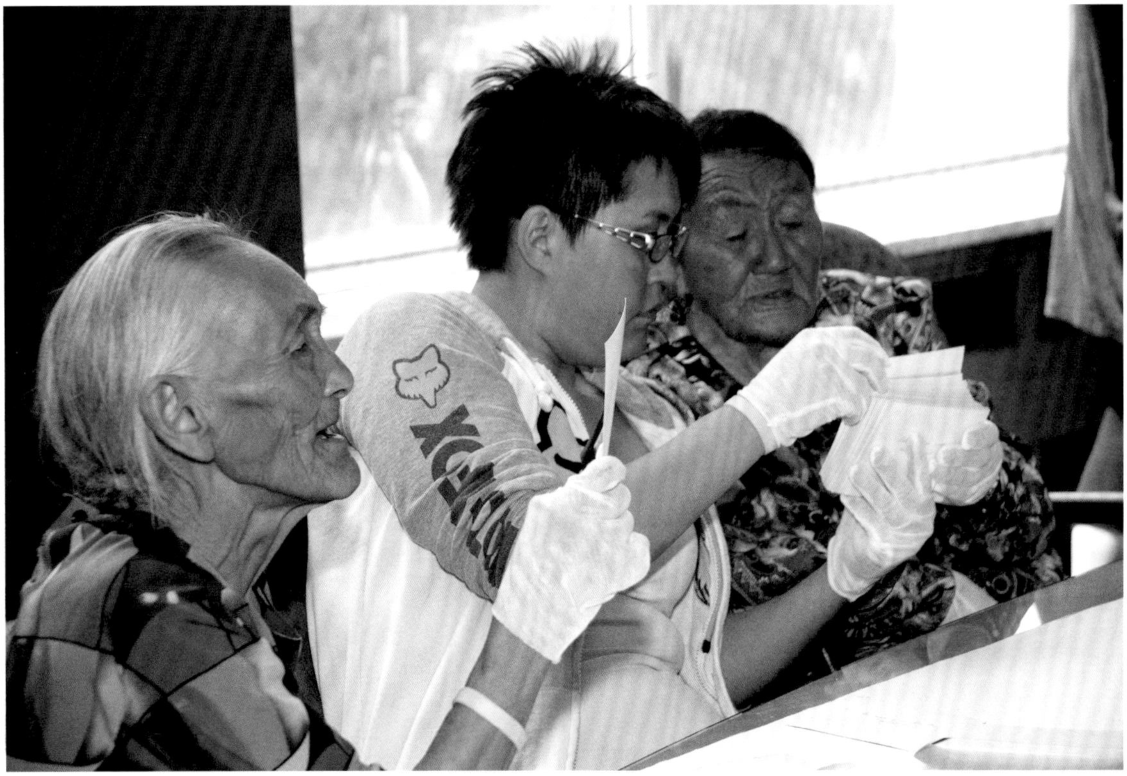

3.14 | Arviat residents Elder Eva Muyunaganiak (*left*), Louisa Gibbons (*centre*), and Elder Mary Anowtalik (*right*) during a research trip to Library and Archives Canada, Ottawa, 2012.

Tigitkok and Elder Muyunaganiak passed away several months after reconnecting with the photographs. Their deaths reminded all of us involved in Project Naming of the urgency and time sensitivity of this work.[23]

Phase III: Growth and Expansion (2015–2017)

In May 2015, LAC officially expanded Project Naming to all three Indigenous groups in Canada – First Nations, the Métis Nation, and Inuit from all four regions (Inuvialuit Settlement Region, Nunavut, Nunavik, and Nunatsiavut). To mark this development, LAC updated the Project Naming website and created several promotional products for community groups, organizations, and the public to share on their websites, social media, or as posters (Figure 3.15).[24]

Within days of launching the newly expanded Project Naming album on Facebook, family members identified the two girls featured in the first post as Rose Anne Hardotte (née Jobb) on the left and Jane McCallum (right) from the Peter Ballantyne Cree Nation in Saskatchewan.[25]

Between June 2015 and February 2017, LAC posted a total of seventy-seven photographs depicting First Nations, Inuit, and Métis Nation individuals in the Project Naming album on Facebook and received thirty-five identifications. The photographs made an impact on communities as evidenced in the heartfelt comments and spirited conversations by friends and relatives on Facebook. Their likes, tags, and shares enabled LAC to reach people from across the country, many of whom had no prior knowledge of Project Naming.

While LAC staff considered the Project Naming album on LAC's institutional Facebook page a success, it was felt the project would attract an even wider audience and receive more identifications if Project Naming had a dedicated account. In February 2017, LAC launched

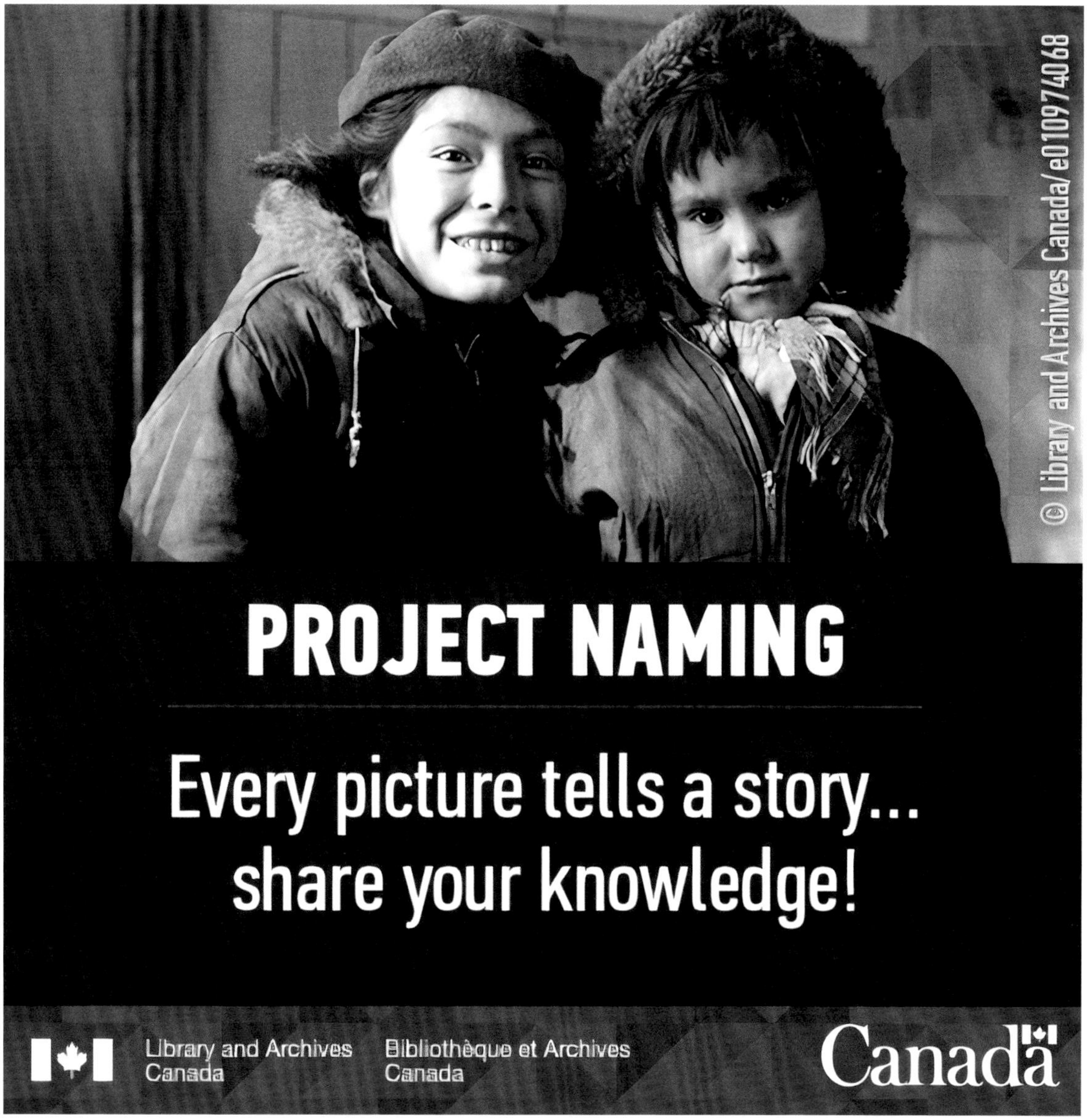

3.15 | Project Naming web banner, 2015.

Project Naming on Facebook and Twitter and committed to posting three photographs each week from a different province and territory. LAC officially announced the launch on 1 March, the first day of the fifteenth-anniversary celebration.

To mark its fifteenth year, in March 2017, LAC collaborated with Carleton University to organize a three-day anniversary event celebrating the contributions of Project Naming. The first two days focused on the achievements of the first thirteen years of the project and its engagement with Nunavummiut. To celebrate the future of Project Naming and to mark its expanded reach to all Indigenous Peoples in Canada, LAC organized a panel on the final day[26] that included Onondaga curator and photographer Jeff Thomas, Métis Nation artist Rosalie Favell, and Inuk filmmaker, visual artist, and writer asinnajaq (see her picture essay in this volume). All three use archival and historical imagery in their artistic practice to retell the stories of their communities. Before Project Naming, Indigenous Peoples depicted in most archival photographs have been anonymous subjects. The work by Thomas, Favell, and asinnajaq signals an exciting shift within the archival community and is an excellent example of how Indigenous individuals are reclaiming their histories.

Phase IV: Project Naming and Its Impact at LAC (2017–present)

Since 2002, LAC has digitized thousands of photographs depicting Indigenous Peoples and has received the names of an estimated several thousand individuals.[27] While some members of the public still use "The Naming Continues" online form, Facebook has become the primary space for intergenerational conversations and the sharing of names and stories. Photographs posted on Project Naming on Facebook offer a popular space for dialogue and identifications. However, it is labour-intensive for LAC as staff must closely monitor posts for names of individuals, which then need to be manually added to the database.

In response to public demand, LAC launched Co-Lab in May 2018, which both supports and extends the work of Project Naming.[28] This long-awaited crowdsourcing tool enables the public to transcribe textual documents and tag photographs online. While Co-Lab showcases archival records containing non-Indigenous content, many of the documents chosen for this interactive virtual space include textual and photographic records related to First Nations, Inuit, and Métis Nation peoples and their histories. The impact that Project Naming has had upon LAC is not unique to this institution. In fact, the evolution of the project and its community engagement, carried out over the last two decades, are part of a broader shift in archival theory and Indigenous scholarship that challenge the authority of archival institutions and their role as gatekeepers. In his 2001 article about archival science, Terry Cook contended that "archives traditionally were founded by the state, to serve the state, as part of the state's hierarchical structure and organizational culture."[29] The assertions put forth by Cook and other critical thinkers within the archival community have been the topics of discussion among LAC staff, particularly those of us working on Project Naming, and more generally on Indigenous content and with Indigenous communities.

More broadly, the developments of Project Naming and Indigenous-related work at LAC have been influenced by the recommendations outlined in the *Final Report of the Truth and*

Reconciliation Commission of Canada, published in 2015.[30] In 2017, LAC received federal government funding for two three-year Indigenous-focused initiatives: We Are Here: Sharing Stories (WAHSS) and Listen, Hear Our Voices (LHOV). Three Indigenous researchers/archivists were hired for WAHSS,[31] a mass digitization project based in the National Capital Region, and seven Indigenous archivists were hired for LHOV,[32] carrying out their work directly in communities across the country. While Project Naming has demonstrated the necessity of creating new descriptions that are respectful towards Indigenous Peoples, the discussion involving the Indigenization and decolonization of archival practices at LAC was further spurred on by the WAHSS team, who were responsible for the creation of thousands of archival descriptions for the newly digitized records.[33] While revisions to archival records were employed by Project Naming through identifications provided by the public, the new procedures spearheaded by the WAHSS team pushed the boundaries of archival descriptions even further. In October 2018, LAC announced new guidelines for the creation of titles of archival records that are more culturally sensitive and inclusive. In cases where original content pertaining to Indigenous Peoples contain offensive, inaccurate, or outdated vocabulary, LAC now creates assigned titles using current vocabulary placed in square brackets, followed by the original caption in the "Title" field. These procedures apply not only to photographic records but are extended to all archival documents pertaining to First Nations, Inuit, and Métis Nation peoples.[34] The guidelines mark a theoretical shift at LAC that privileges Indigenous Knowledge and expertise while recognizing the long history of colonialist subjugation under which the records were created.

Conclusion

First and foremost, Project Naming is a reciprocal project built on collaboration between LAC and Inuit, and now, in its extended form, in collaboration with First Nations and the Métis Nation. Although coordinated by a federal government agency (LAC), it is ultimately community-guided and has managed to survive because of grassroots support. Project Naming has helped support efforts towards decolonizing LAC, with its legacy of erasing the names of Indigenous Peoples and the places they have inhabited for centuries. It is about a restorative history through the reclamation of identities, and, by extension, fosters a sense of dignity by adding names to faces. Through digitization, Inuit, First Nations, and the Métis Nation have voices in the federal archive and play central roles in correcting the historical record. While there remains much work to be done, Project Naming has helped LAC support its efforts towards reconciliation (as outlined by the Truth and Reconciliation Commission of Canada's Calls to Action) by ensuring that Traditional Knowledge is made accessible to Indigenous Peoples, is properly preserved over time, and is appropriately described and disseminated in a manner that respects communities.

Acknowledgments

I would like to acknowledge the archivists at Library and Archives Canada who saw the need for and supported Project Naming before its inception and after its official launch in 2002. They include Eli Brown, Jim Burant, Peter Robertson, Andrew Rodger, Guy Tessier, and Ed Tompkins.

NOTES

1 Project Naming won the Innovation award in the eighth Francophone libraries' Livres Hebdo Grand Prize in Paris, France in 2017 and has been used as an example of community engagement and collaboration in information management/archival studies courses.

2 Inuit men and children in the top right photograph have since been identified as (left to right) Uvvatuattiaq, Mala, Aluluuq Aksakattak, and Aula. These men were employed as special constables with the Royal Canadian Mounted Police.

3 From its beginnings, for privacy reasons, unless an individual specifically asked to have their name added to the database description, LAC does not list the names of people who provided identifications of individuals in the photos.

4 From 2003 to 2015, the following paragraph was added in the "Additional Information" field to explain the project and use of square brackets: "Title of the photograph in square brackets is based on information provided by Project Naming. This project brings Youth and Elders in Nunavut to work together to identify and record the names of people in photographs held at Library and Archives Canada." When the scope of the project expanded nationally in 2015, the statement was modified to: "The title of the photograph in square brackets is based on information provided by Project Naming. The goal of this project is to identify and record the names of people, places, activities and events in photographs held at Library and Archives Canada." Changes in cataloguing protocols are explained at the end of this essay.

5 Inuit Heritage Trust, "Introduction."

6 The territory of Nunavut was created on 1 April 1999.

7 Taloyoak (large caribou blind) officially changed its name from Spence Bay in 1992, and in 1996, the community of Coppermine was officially changed to Kugluktuk (the place of moving water), called Qurluqtuq in Inuinnaqtun.

8 According to the Qikiqtani Truth Commission, ilagiit nunagivaktangit (singular) "means 'a place used regularly or seasonally by Inuit for hunting, harvesting, and/or gathering.' It also includes special places, such as burial sites of loved ones, or sites with abundant game." Qikiqtani Truth Commission, *QTC Final Report: Achieving Saimaqatigiingniq*, 14fn1.

9 The majority of students who started at NS in the autumn of 2003 were from the Qikiqtaaluk or the Qikiqtani (Baffin) region, the easternmost area of Nunavut.

10 Fonds is the term used by archivists to indicate a collection of documents originating from the same source – an individual, agency, or organization.

11 When LAC began researching additional photographic collections in the summer of 2003, the NS instructors recommended only digitizing records taken after the 1940s because the chances of Elders recognizing individuals dating prior to this decade would be small. Given the opportunity to digitize material that had been stored in vaults and only accessible through on-site visits, I included photographs that dated as early as the 1920s. Even if Elders were not able to recognize individuals in the images, I hoped the digitized photographs would provide younger generations of Inuit a visual record of what life was like for their ancestors.

12 The first phase of the Project Naming website was available in English, French, and Inuktitut syllabics, while the database was only offered in English and French. For information about the challenges of creating online content in Inuktitut, see: Greenhorn, "*Project Naming*: Always on our Minds."

13 "The Naming Continues" online form was the first time LAC had created a method that encouraged the public to share information and help improve the archival descriptions.

14 Email from Janet McGrath on behalf of Elder Singuuri to the author, 14 February 2005.

15 Some of the media coverage included a feature on Global Television's genealogy program *Past Lives* (October 2004) and a feature interview on CBC Television's national news show *The National* (January 2005) that aired in April 2005 as part of the CBC's weeklong broadcast from Nunavut. Between 2005 and 2014, Beth Greenhorn presented Project Naming at several national and

international conferences and gatherings, some of which included: Museums on the Web, Vancouver, British Columbia, 2005; Canadian Expo, Nagoya, Japan, 2005; Canadian Historical Association Conference, Saskatoon, Saskatchewan, 2007; Canadian Conservation Institute's International Symposium on Preserving Aboriginal Heritage: Technical and Traditional Approaches, Ottawa, Ontario, 2007; Inuit Studies Conference, Winnipeg, Manitoba, 2008; Arctic College, Iqaluit, Nunavut, 2008; International Polar Year conference, Montreal, Quebec, 2012; Digital Arctic Archives Gathering, Charlottesville, Virginia, 2013; and Association of Canadian Archivists, Winnipeg, Manitoba, 2013.

16 LAC's grant application to the Canadian Content Online Program, March 2005.

17 In addition to collaborations between LAC and partner organizations, Project Naming served as an inspiration and model to other visual repatriation initiatives, including the National Archives in London, England's colonial photographs series that began with "Africa through a lens" in 2012, and the "The Names and Knowledge Initiative," launched by the Hudson's Bay Company Archives (part of the Archives of Manitoba) in 2014.

18 In 2007, I had no mechanism to post photographs such as those shared by Betty Novalinga Brewster from her collection on LAC's website. In May 2015, LAC launched a Project Naming album on Facebook. In November 2016, I posted a photograph of three boys, a young woman, and a baby taken in the late 1940s at Fort Ross, Nunavut, LAC, a066340. I received a text from a colleague that evening who suggested that Bella and Betty were in this photograph. The following day, I emailed Betty's daughter, Janet, who confirmed that her aunt Bella was holding her mother (Betty) in this photograph, along with their brothers Johnny (Kavavow?) Lyall, Pat Napatchee Lyall, and an unidentified boy. By pure chance, I posted this photograph on Betty's birthday. Janet shared a photograph of her mother on the Facebook post taken on her birthday. Before digitization, email, or social media, making the link between the two photographs would likely never have been possible. One is part of the Medical Services Branch, a series in the Department of Health and Welfare containing over 110,000 photographs, while the other is in the "CFJIC" sub-sub-series in the Department of National Defence with over one million photographs.

19 In addition to their names, family members added that Atamie and Saa are the adoptive parents of Qasinga, whose daughters are Arniak and Mary.

20 Comeau, "Healing Journey: *Project Naming* at 15." For more of Robert Comeau's reflections, see Chapter 8 where his grandmother, Ann Meekitjuk Hanson, interviews him and two of her other grandsons.

21 Among these collaborations were the Qikiqtani Truth Commission (Spring 2008), a training workshop organized by Inuit Heritage Trust (September 2008), a second research visit organized by the Government of Nunavut's Department of Culture, Language, Elders and Youth (December 2008), and Know History (CRIIM) (2011–12).

22 Both photographs of Utnguuyaq were taken while she was in labour. Out of respect for Utnguuyaq and her surviving family members, I am not including these images in this paper, nor are they available in the database.

23 During another on-site research visit of the *Nanisiniq: Arviat History Project* team in May 2011, two Elders in their home community of Arviat passed away. In 2011, the Government of Nunavut estimated the population of Arviat was 2,442, and only 75 individuals were over the age of sixty-five. The passing of two Elders represented a terrible loss to the community. Nunavut Bureau of Statistics.

24 The two girls in the photograph are from the Cree community of Buffalo Narrows, Saskatchewan. Gilliat Eaton, LAC, e010974068. At the time of writing this paper, neither girl has been identified.

25 Following this identification, I was able to update the records for another photograph depicting Rose Anne Hardotte and Jane McCallum (Rosemary Gilliat Eaton, LAC, e010974908), and one of Rose Anne Hardotte (Rosemary Gilliat Eaton, LAC, e010975234). Without the identification of both girls in the first Facebook post, the connections

to these other photographs would likely not have been possible.

26 Anishinabe Algonquin Elder Annie Smith St-Georges opened the program with a prayer, which was followed by remarks from Métis National Council president Clément Chartier.

27 The exact number of identifications received from members of the public has been a challenge to track for several reasons. Since Project Naming began, the databases containing archival records, including the photographic collections, have undergone several different migrations. Database developments, shifting institutional priorities, and re-organizations in staffing have further complicated data collection.

28 "Co-Lab: Your collaboration tool."

29 Cook, "Archival science and postmodernism," 18.

30 Article 69 of the Truth and Reconciliation Commission's Calls to Action calls upon LAC to "fully adopt and implement the UNDRIP [United Nations Declaration on the Rights of Indigenous Peoples] and the United Nations Joinet-Orentlicher Principles, as related to Aboriginal peoples' inalienable right to know the truth about what happened and why, with regard to human rights violations committed against them in the residential schools." Article 70 calls upon the federal government "to provide funding to the Canadian Association of Archivists to undertake, in collaboration with Aboriginal peoples, a national review of archival policies and best practices to i. determine the level of compliance with UNDRIP and the United Nations Joinet-Orentlicher Principles." *Truth and Reconciliation Commission of Canada Final Report*.

31 We Are Here: Sharing Stories is a mass digitization initiative. The core team comprised three Indigenous archivists/researchers (two First Nations and an Inuk), and non-Indigenous staff (a project manager, three archival assistants, a lead archivist, and a database administrator). Between 2017 and 2020, the team digitized and described nearly 600,000 archival and published records pertaining to Indigenous Peoples. The creation of an eBook was part of the funding commitment for WAHSS and LHOV. In September 2021, LAC launched *Nations to Nations: Indigenous Voices at Library and Archives Canada*. This electronic publication features twenty-eight essays by First Nations, Inuit, and Métis Nation staff at LAC. The multimedia content was chosen by the authors based on their personal connections to the archival and published material, and includes journals, maps, artwork, photographs, publications, and audiovisual recordings from the collections at LAC. Each essay showcases a variety of media that has been re-contextualized by the authors, providing unique perspectives that challenge the dominant narrative. Where possible, the texts are presented in the Indigenous language related to the content in each section, with English and French versions.

32 The goal of Listen, Hear Our Voices is to support Indigenous organizations in their efforts to digitize their existing culture and language recordings and build the skills, knowledge, and resources required to carry out this work in their communities.

33 To learn more about the considerations undertaken by the Indigenous team members of WAHSS in the creation of culturally sensitive archival descriptions for photographs depicting Indigenous Peoples held at LAC, see Campbell, "Cultural Insensitivity: Reclaiming Our Names." This article was published in *Inuit Art Quarterly* as an extension of ITK president Obed's commentary "Reclaiming Our Names."

34 The new guidelines for the creation of culturally sensitive archival descriptions were adopted following consultations with the Indigenous Advisory Circle (IAC) created at LAC in early 2018. Consisting of fifteen members, the circle includes First Nations, Métis Nation, and Inuit Elders, librarians, archivists, and others working in the cultural heritage sector. Part of the IAC's mandate is providing expertise and guidance to the policies concerning the decolonization of Indigenous archival descriptions.

CHAPTER 4

Pictorial Essay I

Barry Pottle in conversation with Heather Igloliorte

(with contributions from Sally Webster and Deborah Kigjugalik Webster)

Library and Archives Canada, Ottawa
1 March 2017

BARRY POTTLE: I was thinking about my own personal history, and coming from Nunatsiavut in Labrador, and the lack of history and the lack of stories that I don't know because of a number of reasons.

I've been in Ottawa for thirty years. I call myself Ottawa-muit because I've been in Ottawa more than I've been in Labrador these days … Also we have a big urban Inuit population, not only in Ottawa but throughout Canada as well.[1] I wanted to give that a little bit of a nudge to urban Inuit because I think it's important that we are acknowledged and recognized. "Yeah we're here and we're doing some wonderful things as well." Not only from an art standpoint, from a holistic community standpoint I think we're doing really well. So, I just wanted to just acknowledge that.

HEATHER IGLOLIORTE: I'm named after a Kiwi; my mom is white – she's a

Newfoundlander – and my father is an Inuk. And I'm named after my mother's New Zealander pen pal, Heather, who's still alive. Hopefully next year I'll take my mother to meet her pen pal. They've never met … I grew up in Happy Valley–Goose Bay but my father's from Hopedale. My grandmother, Susannah Igloliorte (née Mitsuk), is from Hopedale and my grandfather Matthew Igloliorte is from Nain. Those are the two current most northern communities in Nunatsiavut. There used to be more communities located up the coast but they were relocated, in a different way than other relocations [in Nunavut] but with the same kind of colonial ends. In Nunatsiavut, we have a different history of naming because we were evangelized beginning in 1771, about a hundred and fifty years before other parts of the Canadian Arctic. And so, a lot of my father's generation have Biblical names. My father is James and my uncles are David and Solomon and my aunt is Miriam. We haven't maintained this history of naming [across generations]. The Moravian Church started influencing our names a long time ago.

In the briefest of ways that I can explain our history, when Newfoundland and Labrador joined Confederation, the new provincial government of Newfoundland had written in all the same provisions for Indigenous Peoples as everywhere else in Canada. Then in the final version of the Terms of Union in 1949, they took everything out. And so, First Nations people in our province were not covered under the Indian Act. You might have heard about the Qalipu First Nation, and all the troubles they've had recently [in 2017, around membership and enrolment].[2] It's related. Inuit in Nunatsiavut were not included under any of the federal jurisdiction that all other Inuit in Canada were included in. We weren't under the [federal] Department of Mines and Resources. There was basically no one taking care of us. The province disregarded us and so did the federal government. That has led to, historically, a separation between Inuit in Labrador and Inuit elsewhere. And I think that we were the last to settle our land claims. We settled them in 2005 and became self-governing. I think it's only in the last about thirty years that we've really been able to start connecting and travelling and doing our own thing together. Joining ITK [today, Inuit Tapiriit Kanatami] in the 1970s was a big first move in that direction.

Barry Pottle, *The Awareness Series*

HI: This photo series really struck me because when I first met Barry, which was probably about a decade ago now, we were talking about this project. You were at the time just beginning transitioning from photojournalism into art and artistic practice as a photographer. And this was the body of work that you were working on at the time. See figures 4.1–4.6.

BP: I was inspired to do this project through a story in the news, I think it was *Nunatsiaq News*, about a young student doing a project on the disc numbers. I found out it was actually Norma Dunning who did the project.[3]

HI: I think that a lot of southern Canadians have never really heard this story. We know a lot about the [Indian Act] pass system but we don't know that Inuit had a kind of similar system in the Arctic.

BP: That's right. A lot of people were really surprised that this actually happened. They were not aware of it. This is why I call this "*Awareness 1*" and "*Awareness 2*" because I want to bring

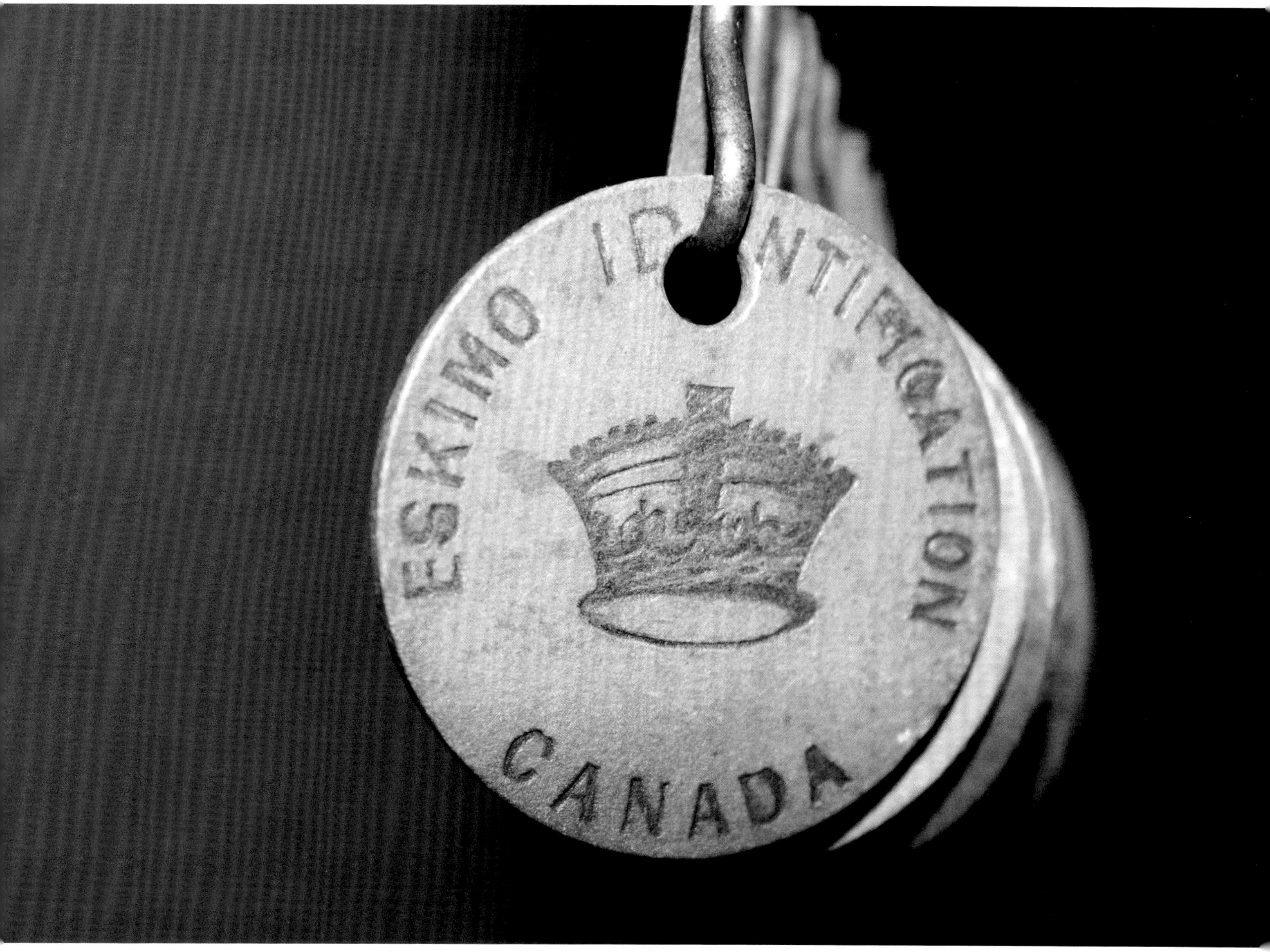

4.1 | *Awareness 1*. Digital photograph. 2011.

4.2 (*overleaf*) | *Awareness 2* (Billy E.6-935). Digital photograph. Southern Qikiqtaaluk Region, Nunavut, 2010.

awareness about this story. A lot of people were really surprised that this had taken place and it's a very recent history, and it's still in living memory. People were really surprised and very supportive of the project.

Here, the E-6 number, just for those of you who don't know: this is the person's number. The first number says which community or area where they're from. Do you know who? This is Billy (Figure 4.2).

HI: There were E and W, right? Like east and west?

BP: Yes, E for east and W for west.

HI: So, 6 might be Baffin Island?

DEBORAH KIGJUGALIK WEBSTER: Yes. This must be a Baffin one. Which community is it?[4]

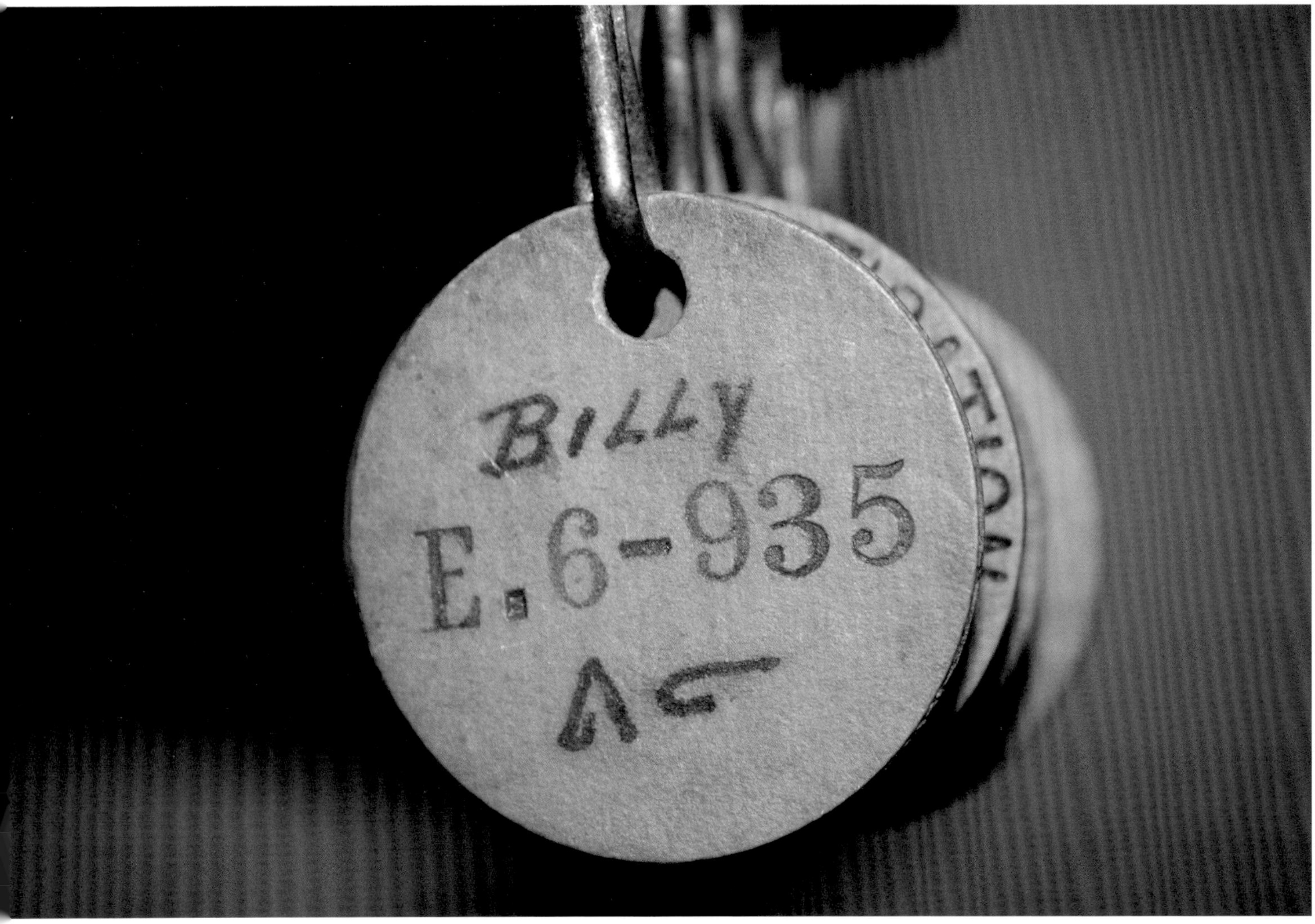

HI: So, the name Billy in the syllabics would have been written in by someone else. That wasn't on the tag, right? Somebody wrote their name.

DKW: In my research on special constables, I found the first Eskimo [Disc Number]: E1–1.[5]

BP: Wow. That's pretty interesting.

DKW: Yes, and Curtis [speaking to Curtis Konek in the audience], you must know who this person is: Special Constable Jimmy Gibbons from Arviat. So, Arviat is community number one, and Gibbons was the first person. I was trying to see if there was a link between special constables and who received the first numbers in a community. There are a few specials that have number one but not all.

SALLY WEBSTER: That's why my dad was E2–4.[6] His father was E2–1 and his wife was E2–2 because he was a special constable, and their daughter [was] E2–3. But my dad was the next one, so he was E2–4. We have a low number because [we] were the first one to have E-numbers.

HI: That's amazing. I've never heard about that before.

BP: *The Awareness Seri*es came about in terms of my study from photography. I'm a self-taught artist: I've never been to any schooling or whatnot for photography. I was all self-taught, although I read manuals and books, but it's still basically self-taught. But this [project] came about through that article and I understand the history of photography within Inuit art is not as prevalent as sculptures and carvings and that. So, I saw an opportunity to explore – through that medium – some of the things I've known over the years and some of the things I came in contact with such as the Eskimo Identification Program while in school. I looked at Norma's project and I said, "I wonder if I could do this using photography?" Having a big community here in town, I started to ask my fellow Inuit if they have their E-numbers or they know their E-numbers or if they didn't care? And if so, can I photograph them? Lo and behold, all the tags here are from Reepa Evik at Carleton, it's her family's, she graciously lent them to me. [It] took about a year in total to photograph the discs as well as a number of Inuit who are part of this project.

I started looking at it from an artistic standpoint to see if I could actually do it [represent the complex history Inuit have with their discs] using photography. And this work, called *The Awareness Series* was the final product of that. My intent was to photograph the tags and then juxtapose Inuit who either know their number or don't know their number, don't really care, or whatever. I just wanted to give that human dimension to it, right? Show that human face to the program. That is what this project is about. There's nineteen images in total. They're all Reepa Evic's family's tags, so she lent them to me. I started photographing them over about a year – probably two years in total. I had intended to follow up with respect to recording the stories from each of the family members and from Reepa Evic herself, but I just haven't got that far into the project yet.

I was very conscious of the fact that am I the right person to do it because I've never really been under this system coming from Labrador. As Heather was saying, we were never under this system because we were under the

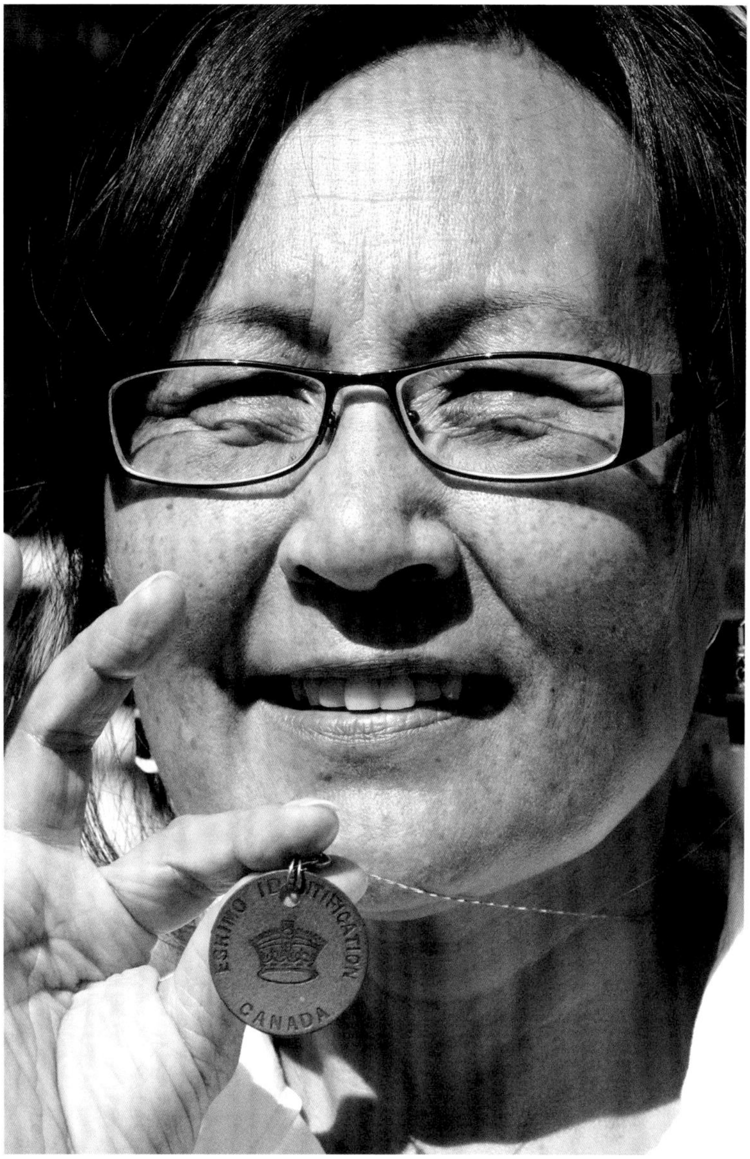

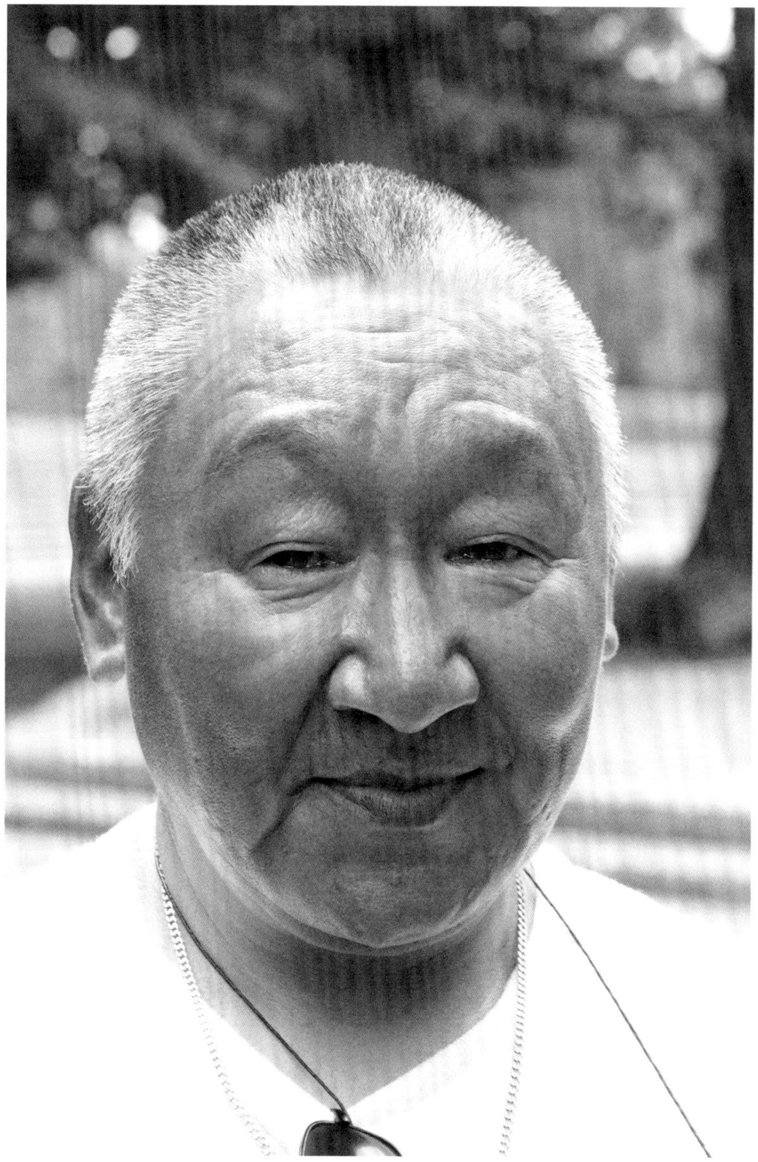

4.3 | *Leena Alivaktuk (E6-741), Very Proud Inuk*. Digital photograph. 2011.

4.4 | *Mattiusi "Mathewsie" Iyaituk*. Digital photograph. 2011.

British rule in Newfoundland and Labrador. Sometimes I'm very hesitant to show these, especially with the Inuit in the room, because it has positive and negative things associated with it. But from an artistic standpoint, I wanted to show if it was possible to do it. I wanted to show that photography itself has never been a recognized Inuit artform by the mainstream art world. I wanted to do that as well: try and build a foundation for photography.

There are a number of individuals who I look to for inspiration, from a photography standpoint. That would be Peter Pitseolak, of course, Jimmy Manning, [and] David Kilabuk. Now there's a bunch of artists coming out of Labrador: Ryan Winters, Jim Andersen, Holly Andersen, and Jenny Williams. These are the inspirations for me to do photography from an artistic standpoint. [As for my educational] background; I went to school at Carleton University [where] I got a BA in Aboriginal studies where half of my credits were art history related. So, there's that connection as well to art.

These are some of the Inuit that I photographed. Leena Alivaktuk Burns. She's very proud. I call that image "Very proud Inuk" because she wears her tag every day and she's very proud of it. And then there's Mattiusi Iyaituk from Ivujivik, Nunavik. I originally asked him if I could use his photograph in this project and he said, yes. Then he came back to me and he said "No, I don't want to do it ... because of the privacy issues" (around his image and his E-number as well). He had real concerns about security: identification theft, that sort of stuff. So, I said, "Can I use it anyway in that perspective?" This is why [his tag is not visible] here. But I also wanted to give that human dimension to this faceless program that was developed in the 1940s and 1950s by the federal government. (Figures 4.3 and 4.4.)

HI: Elders today talk about how everyone knew themselves. They'd say, "I'm E1-1622." I don't know if people understand how ubiquitous it was. If you go into any museum that has a historical collection of Inuit carvings and you turn over a sculpture that was made in the 1940s, the 1950s, the 1960s, the 1970s, you're just as likely – maybe even more likely – to see a disc number carved into the base than someone's signature. It shows just how prevalent this system was and how a whole generation of people were known by numbers and not by [their] names.

4.5 | *Dora Fraser (E9-2485)*. Digital photograph. Nunavik, 2011.

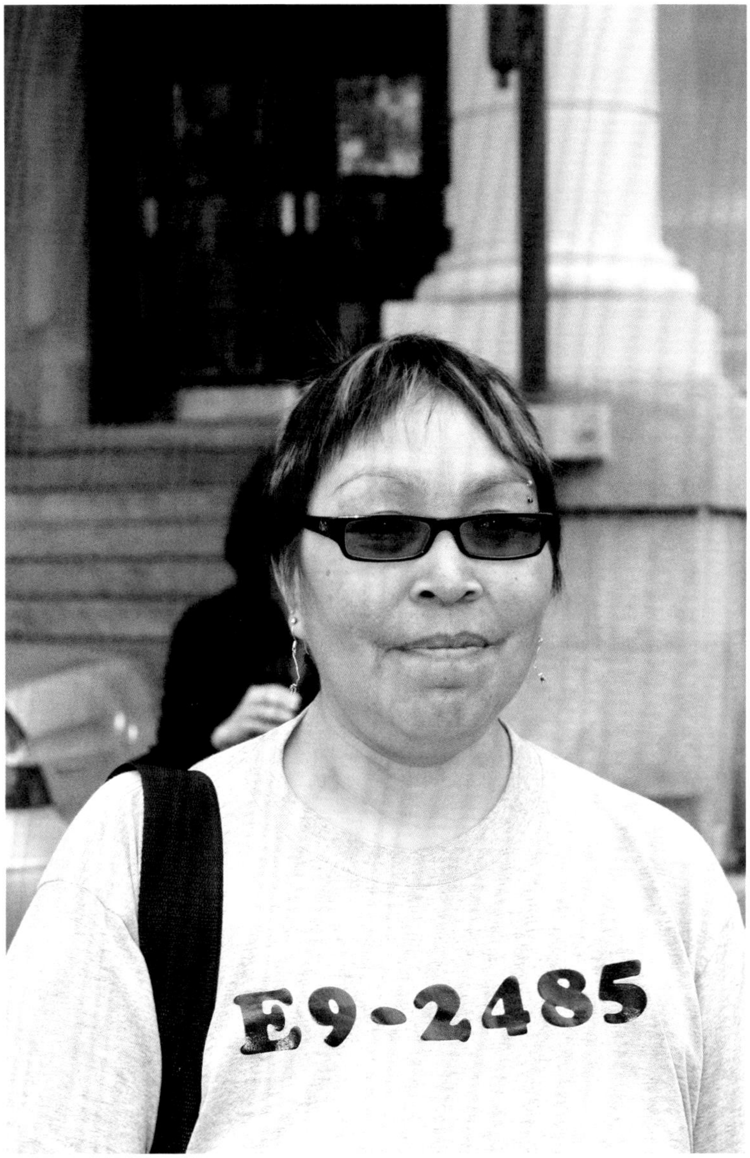

I think what's really interesting about this series, Barry, is how important it was that you were in Ottawa to be able to do it. Not only is this a place where there's a lot of urban Inuit, but also that so many Inuit travel here for medical reasons, and because of all the government organizations that have their offices here. You did this because you were going out and doing photojournalistic work and you could actually meet people with firsthand experience. There's one photo where you met a woman who had her number on a t-shirt, right? You were able to approach her and say, "Would you like pose for this series that I'm working on?"

BP: Yes. Dora Fraser. I met her in Winnipeg at the National Truth and Reconciliation event there. Lo and behold, she was coming up the road with her E-number on her shirt and I got really excited, "Oh, can I photograph you for this project?" (Figure 4.5). What's really positive is how my fellow Inuit [are] willing to do this project with me, to say, "Yes, go ahead and do it." I didn't get much opposition for taking photographs. I'm very fortunate to have had that support. And I thank you [Inuit] very much for it. But like you said, living in Ottawa we do have a large community here and so I was able to draw on and be inspired by and talk to my fellow Inuit. Whether it's at a gallery or just individually, some of them actually come up to me and say their E-numbers. They said, "They mentioned you in the E-numbers and I heard you were doing this project." That was really, really positive, and very, very supportive.

HI: One of the things that you haven't mentioned is that you asked people to think about how they felt about the system as you were taking their photo. And so, you do see some people are smiling and some people are frowning. You can see how they feel about it based on their expression. I often think that this was, therefore, a kind of Oral History project. But it largely lives in the conversation that you had with the person since you didn't write down or record what they said.

BP: Basically, when I first met sitters, I was talking to each individual about the project and what I wanted to do, are you willing to share your E-number but your image as well. Some of them were quite hesitant and I noticed right away. Because I think of the effects of this [identification tag] program has had on them over the years and growing up with this system. I didn't want to push it because I wanted to see if they're willing to help me and the project and be part of it. But I didn't want to really push it because I don't think I was ready to push it at that point. I was more interested in focusing on getting this project together from a visual perspective. My intent was to develop the stories later on. And I'm still hoping to do it, but we'll have to wait and see about that one. But overall, it's been positive, and some people were hesitant, and others were very, very open and willing to share their experiences and their names to this project.

I consciously made a decision not to position myself in this project, as to whether I agree with it or don't agree with it. That wasn't my point. The point was to bring it out. To be able to see if I could do it artistically, and then bring it out into the mainstream society in order to bring some awareness to it by bringing it out to the forefront. I wasn't really interested in saying this was a horrible situation, and I'll leave it up to my fellow Inuit who are, or were, under that system to say that now. I don't feel that I should do that, although I've thought about it. I think from my standpoint and from an artistic standpoint, my goal is just to visually bring that forth into the project under those guidelines.

HI: I think it's a really important part of the work that it's not just the photographs and nametags themselves. It's also people. The tags and the people don't necessarily correspond. But – like you were saying about all the different faces – you can tell that these are Inuit from all across different parts of the Arctic who are talking about this shared experience, but they don't all feel the same way about it.

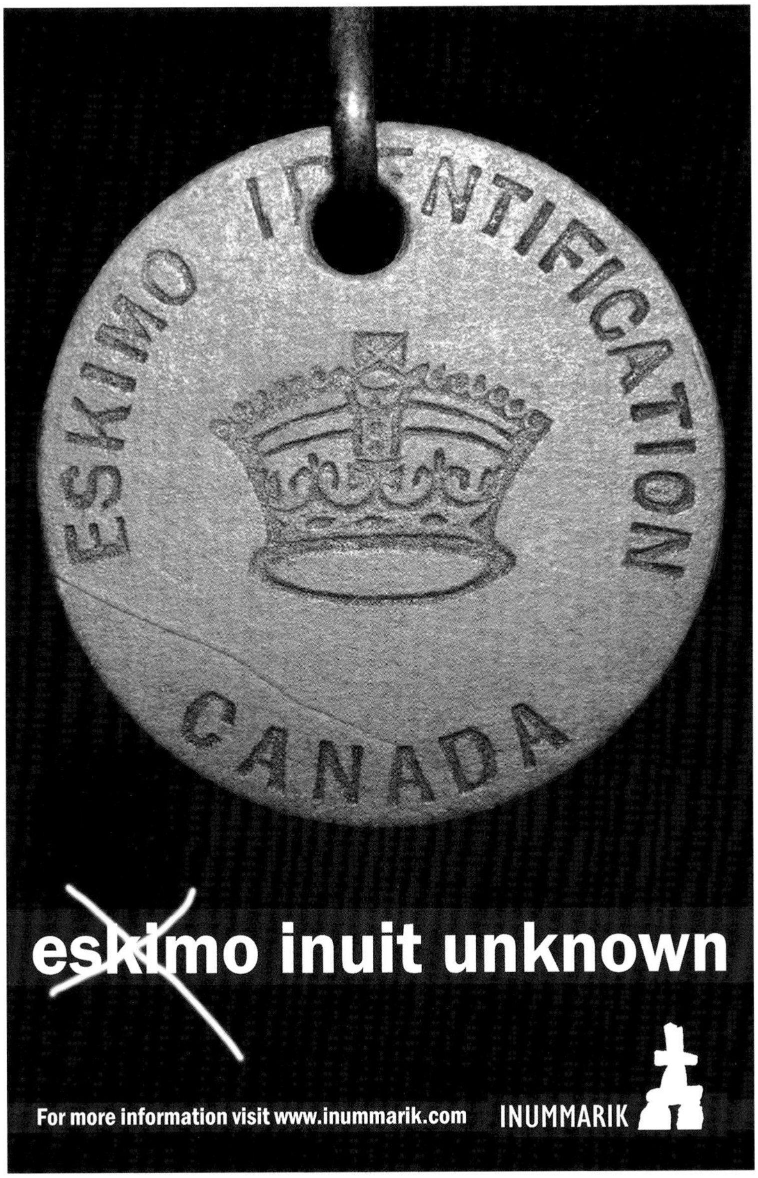

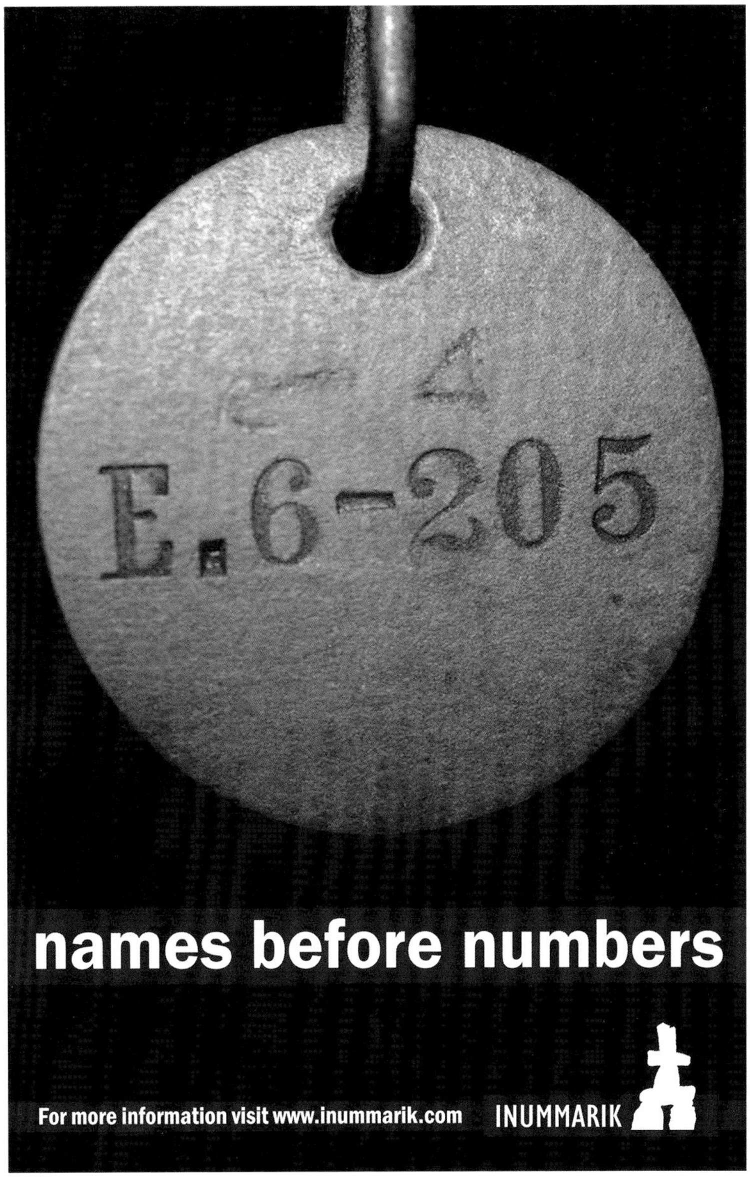

4.6a & b | *Surveillapocolypse*, 2014.

BP: The tags have owners, very specific owners, and the individuals who are photographed for the show have their own numbers. There was a difference there. I try to point that out to the individuals I talk to as well as institutions who automatically think that the individuals own these numbers … it's not the case at all. That's one of the things I have to keep reminding people and myself about is that the portraits and the disc numbers are two different situations.

You know, I've been very fortunate to have this [work] showcased in a number of venues. And Heather did a show called *Decolonize Me* where she had seven southern artists, Indigenous artists and I was included in that.[7] And it went across Canada. Now it's going to be shown in conjunction with some artwork over at the Art Gallery of Hamilton. Hamilton just acquired 133 works that were part of the TB sanatorium over there through an anonymous donor. The Art Gallery of Hamilton saw my works and a lot of those artworks were signed with E-numbers. So, they wanted to exhibit that topic using my work to show that aspect to the history of Inuit.

Surveillapocolypse Series

BP: These two images here (Figures 4.6a and b) were part of a show called *Surveillapocolypse*, which was developed with a group called "007." Barry Ace and Rosalie Favell and some other Indigenous artists here [in Ottawa] asked me if I would be interested in participating in a show they were putting together for Five Myle in Brooklyn. Leah Snyder actually designed these two posters for me. The whole point of the exhibition was to look at the government spying on individuals. The group asked me if I would be interested in contributing something to the show and I didn't really have anything that really reflected their main theme except this. I decided to develop work along these lines and as you look at it from an Inuk perspective.

Take the word "Eskimo": I've been told, and I think Piita Irniq and everybody else can agree, that we were always known as Inuit, not "Eskimo," right? I wanted to cross "Eskimo" out and put in "Inuit unknown." So, I put the element of facelessness into it. And on this side, I wanted to show that Inuit had names before numbers. Whether it's individual names, or community names, or whatever, but that Inuit did have those names. Heather talked about my name earlier on. I have a Christian name, Barry. My parents grew up through residential school experiences and through colonialism, so I have a Christian name, not an Inuk name. But that's because of the history so I find it fascinating on those lines: compare and contrast from an artistic standpoint that these things that have affected Inuit in general.

Foodland Security Series

BP: This project is called *Foodland Security: Access to Country Food in an Urban Setting by Inuit* (Figure 4.7). There are fifteen images in this series, all dealing with country food. We have a hard time getting country food at times here in Ottawa. So, I thought that collecting images of country food as a potential project to focus my energies on. These are from the Ottawa Inuit Children's Day event as well as Tunngasuvvingat Inuit community feast.

I also wanted to show that these are traditional delicacies as well. Sitting down and having a feast and sharing food: I wanted to show that aspect as well.

And the other one is called *Kanon-ized*! It's a soft political take. I developed a mock-up

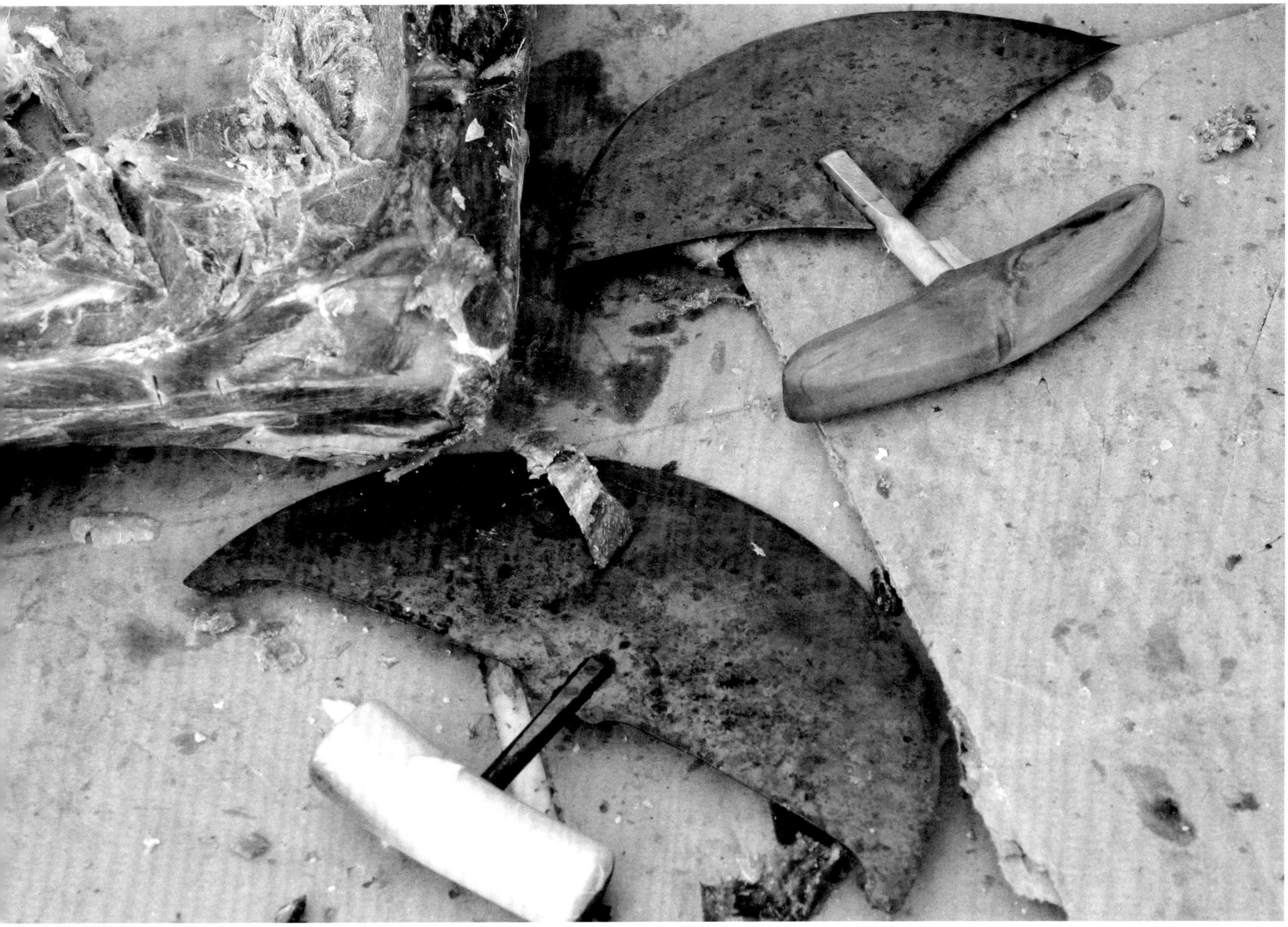

of a feast using cans and store-bought foods just to juxtapose the contemporary versus the traditional (Figure 4.8). My diet consists of cans and stuff from the store, things that are not very healthy for you. This is opposed to country food, which is very healthy for us, and it defines who we are. I wanted to show that aspect as well.

I find that if I compare and contrast First Nations, Métis, and Inuit in an urban centre, I find urban [Inuit] have not had the opportunity to be explored – to be visible within the mainstream society. That's what I'm trying to do as well, to bring that new variety, that topic to the fore as well.

4.7 | *Foodland Security*, 2012.

NOTES

1 Statistics Canada states that about 10,000, or 15 per cent of Inuit lived in urban centres outside of Inuit Nunangat in 2016.
2 Thomson, "80,000 Denied Eligibility."
3 Dunning, "Reflections of a Disk-Less Inuk."
4 E6 was the number used for Inuit from Pannirtuq.
5 E1 was the number used for Arviat.
6 E2 was the number used for Qamani'tuaq.
7 Igloliorte, *Decolonize Me / Decolonizer-Moi*.

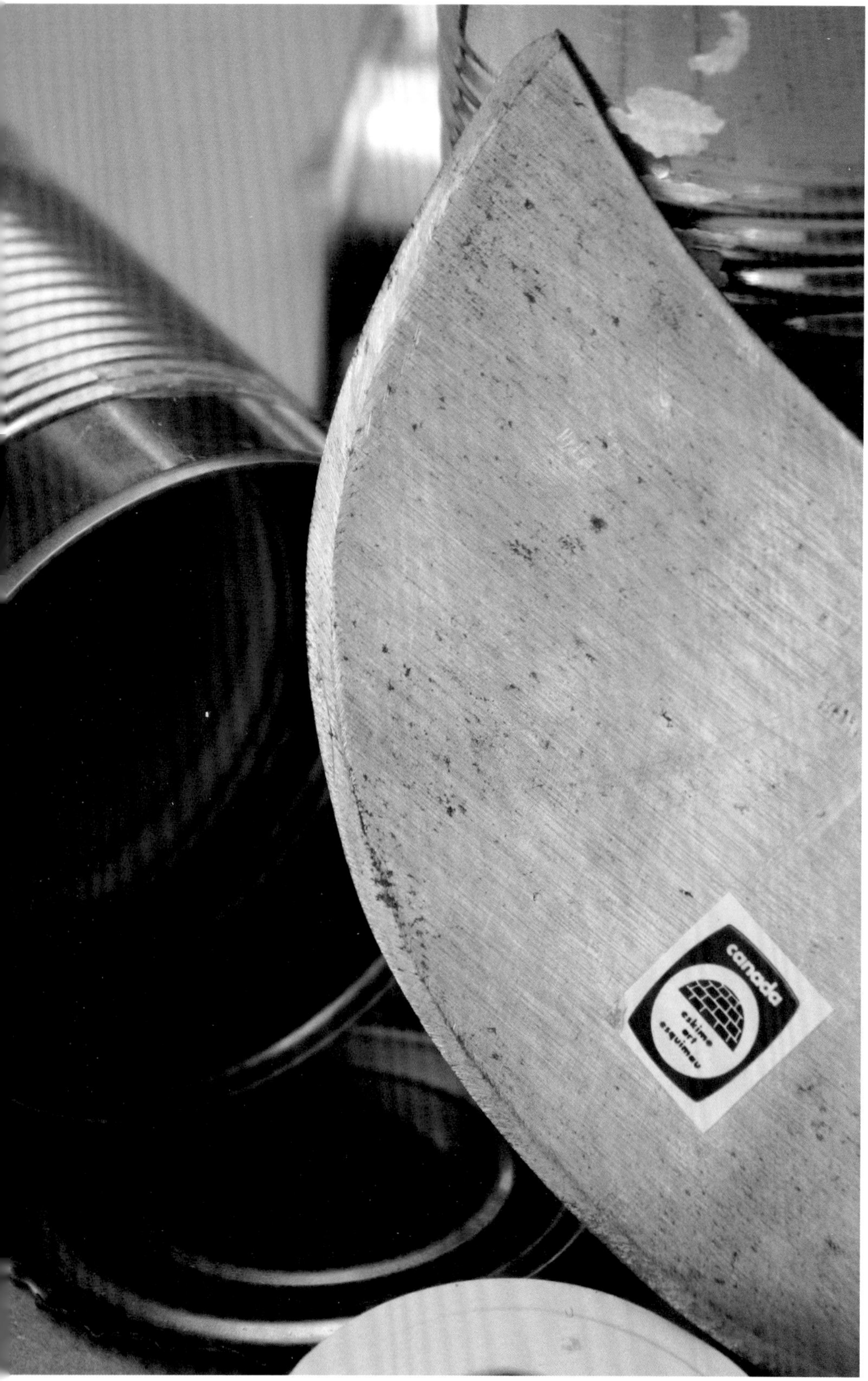

4.8 | *Kanon-ized* (From *Foodland Security* series), 2012.

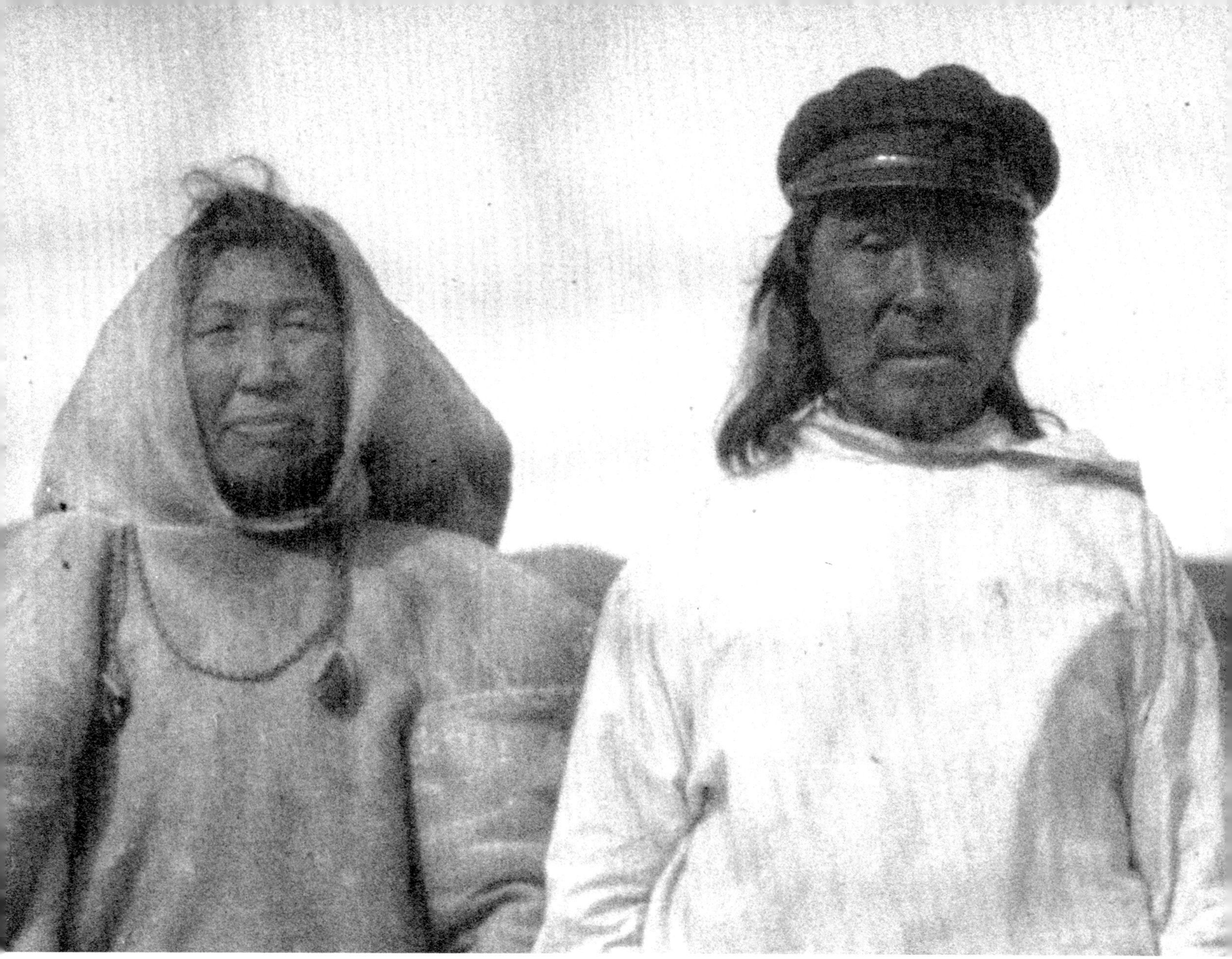

PART TWO

Atiqput: Inuit Elders Speak about Naming

INTRODUCTION

Christina Williamson and Deborah Kigjugalik Webster

One of the values of Project Naming is that it connects people to names after a long history of interventions in how Inuit have been named and renamed by southern society. It serves to humanize and indigenize an archival record that has long denied Inuit their basic right to their own names. Indigenous Peoples, scholars, and activists call for the indigenization and decolonization of Canada's federal archive, Library and Archives Canada (LAC). Gwich'in scholar Crystal Fraser and Métis scholar Zoe Todd argue that national archives' original intent was to legitimize the nation-state and that, "rather than decolonise the archives, the application of a decolonial sensibility is necessary to attend to the complex relationships between archives, and Indigenous peoples."[1] How do we apply a "decolonial sensibility" to the archives?

Embracing Indigenous research methodologies is one part of this answer.[2] In a 2018 discussion, scholar Sherry Farrell Racette offers her "Kitchen Table Theory" as one such methodology. This approach honours the reciprocal ways that knowledge and history are often shared around an Elder's kitchen table.[3] The kitchen table can be a site of knowledge reclamation and a hub for teaching and learning – through conversations over tea, beading, or sharing photographs. Many of the conversations in this section took place around the kitchen table, where Elders and youth meet and share stories over old pictures. Even if the discussions didn't always happen at the kitchen table, the spirit of that way of learning centres on an Inuit mode of telling stories through Inuit Knowledge and history.

The following chapters are all words from Elders who, as children, grew up "on the land." They tell stories of people they knew and know today, and, significantly, they name names. Atiqput – "our names" – offers a concept that centres Inuit naming and concomitant stories of that atiq or name-soul. For Sally Webster, this was in 1946 when she was a year old, and her family was at their summer camp at Schultz Lake, northwest of Qamani'tuaq. They were picked up by the RCMP who wanted to recruit Andrew Ooyoumut, her father, as a special constable based at the settlement of Qamani'tuaq.[4] In 1958, at age eleven, Piita Irniq was taken from his family, who were then living at an outpost camp in the Naujaat area, to attend residential school in Igluligaarjuk.[5] As a child, Manitok Thompson's family lived five miles outside of Salliq.[6] In 1963 or so, when she was about eight years old, her family was the last to relocate into the community.[7] Ann Meekitjuk Hanson was born in 1946 on the island of Qakutut, near Kimmirut. Following the death of her parents in the early 1950s, she was raised by relatives in Kimmirut, Iqaluit, and Qamani'tuaq. She later moved to Toronto where she attended high school and college.[8] David Serkoak was born on the northern part of Nueltin Lake, outside of Arviat where he lived with his family until they were forcibly relocated to Whale Cove and Arviat by the government on multiple occasions in the 1950s.[9]

Each of the Elders discusses having lived in changing times for Inuit, when colonial actions against Inuit brought relocation, settlement, residential schools, dog slaughter, and cultural adaptation, with all the positive and negative aspects that come with it. It was a shift that Irniq often describes as "from igloo to microwave." Each Elder recalled their personal experiences living through these upheavals. Webster explained that the laborious mudding of sled runners has been replaced by using Teflon plastic to make life easier.[10] Thompson said that she purchases Neet hair removal lotion to remove seal skin fur. "That's the new Inuit," she explained.

As Storytellers, the Elders share their knowledge and personal stories about relationships, family, and history. Project Naming is about identifying individuals in archival photographs, giving names and identities to those whose very humanity has been erased. But Project Naming also supports another goal. It prompts youth to ask their Elders about their lives, to listen to those stories, remember atiqput – our names – and hold their communities' histories in their hearts and minds. Having archival photographs in hand is a bit like teaching sealing by going out and hunting seals. Talking through pictures and sharing those stories helps prompt Elders not only to share their stories but also serves as a grounding for Inuit youth and non-Inuit to understand, a least a little, what living life full time on the land was like.

NOTES

1 Fraser and Todd, "Decolonial Sensibilities."

2 Price, "Tukisivallialiqtakka"; Kovach, *Indigenous Methodologies*.

3 Racette, Goodpipe, and Tootoosis, "Arts & Culture: Sakewewak Artists' Collective."

4 Personal communication, 2019.

5 Igloliorte, *We Were So Far Away*, 112.

6 Thompson, "Don't Just Think About It, Do It!," 139.

7 Thompson, personal communication, 2019.

8 Adams, McComber, Partridge, "The Honourable Ann Meekitjuk Hanson," 183–4; Hanson, "Women are Natural Leaders," 59–72.

9 Ahiarmiut who survived the relocations and their families received compensation and an apology on 22 January 2019. Laugrand, Oosten, and Serkoak, "'The Saddest Time of My Life'"; Bennett, "Statement of Apology for the Relocation of the Ahiarmiut."

10 During the 2017 Project Naming event, Sally Kate Webster began with the lighting of a qulliq (oil lamp) she purchased from a woman named Suzanne Mablick while she was in Naujaat. Mablick's father had made it. At first, Webster spoke in Inuktitut as if she shared a closeness with the audience in the room where everyone understood each other, and there was also this attentive silence when the qulliq was lit as the audience listened to her discussion about it. Webster explained that the qulliq serves as a candle for light and a stove to heat a pot. For fuel, she used canola oil in this case. For the wick, she used milkweed, readily available in southern Canada and a substitute for Arctic cotton. The silky, white milkweed fibres are collected in the fall, she said, and the seeds removed. She placed the wick at the front of the oil lamp, and by the gentle light of the qulliq, Webster talked about the qulliq's history, and use of it, as she tended to the lamp with a damper. While doing so, either time stood still or took us back in the past, or both, preparing the audience for the images and discussions to come.

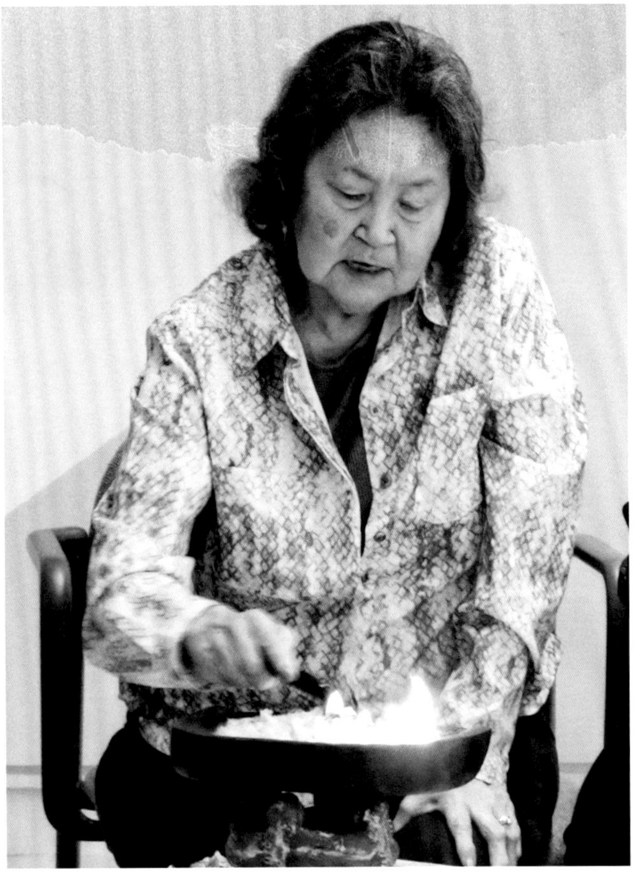

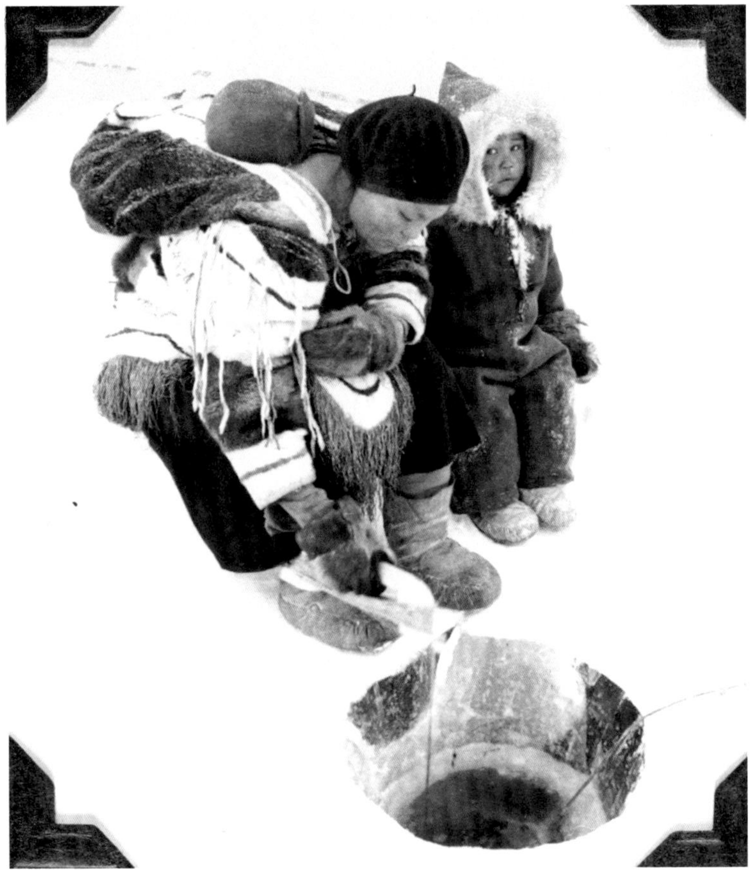

5.1 | Elder Sally Webster lighting a qulliq, Carleton University Art Gallery, Ottawa, 2017

5.2 | [Rhoda Qaqsauq with her daughters, Lucy Evo (in her amauti) and Janet Tagoona], Igluligaarjuk, 1952.

CHAPTER 5

"There was my mother!"

Sally Kate Webster

When I was coming home from Baker Lake (Qamani'tuaq) to Ottawa, I passed through Iqaluit and I had to stay overnight in a hotel there. I happened to pick up a magazine, *Nunavut News North*. And it asked, "Do you know your Elders?" I opened it, and there was my mother! (Figure 5.2.)

That's my mother, [and my sisters] Janet and Lucy. My father was a special constable, that means he was a helper for the RCMP. We used to travel back and forth between Chesterfield Inlet (Igluligaarjuk) with the RCMP in the winter by dog team, by boat in the summertime. My mother was ice fishing [in this picture]. See the hole? You don't use those modern ones [gas-powered ice augers] in those days. They used an ice chisel. We called it a tuuq. It's seven feet deep down. And you have an ilaut or a scoop to scoop the pieces of ice, [to] open it. Then you go ice fishing with a fishing jigger. She was fishing here. See this line here? I told my husband, "That's me," in here. He believes me! So, now he tells everybody every time visitors come [to our home]. Wow. I came home and told him that's my mother! You know, it says to call this number [if you recognize anyone in the photograph], so I called Debbie, "Can you call up there and tell them that's my mother?" She did and then she phoned back and even told me who the photographer was.

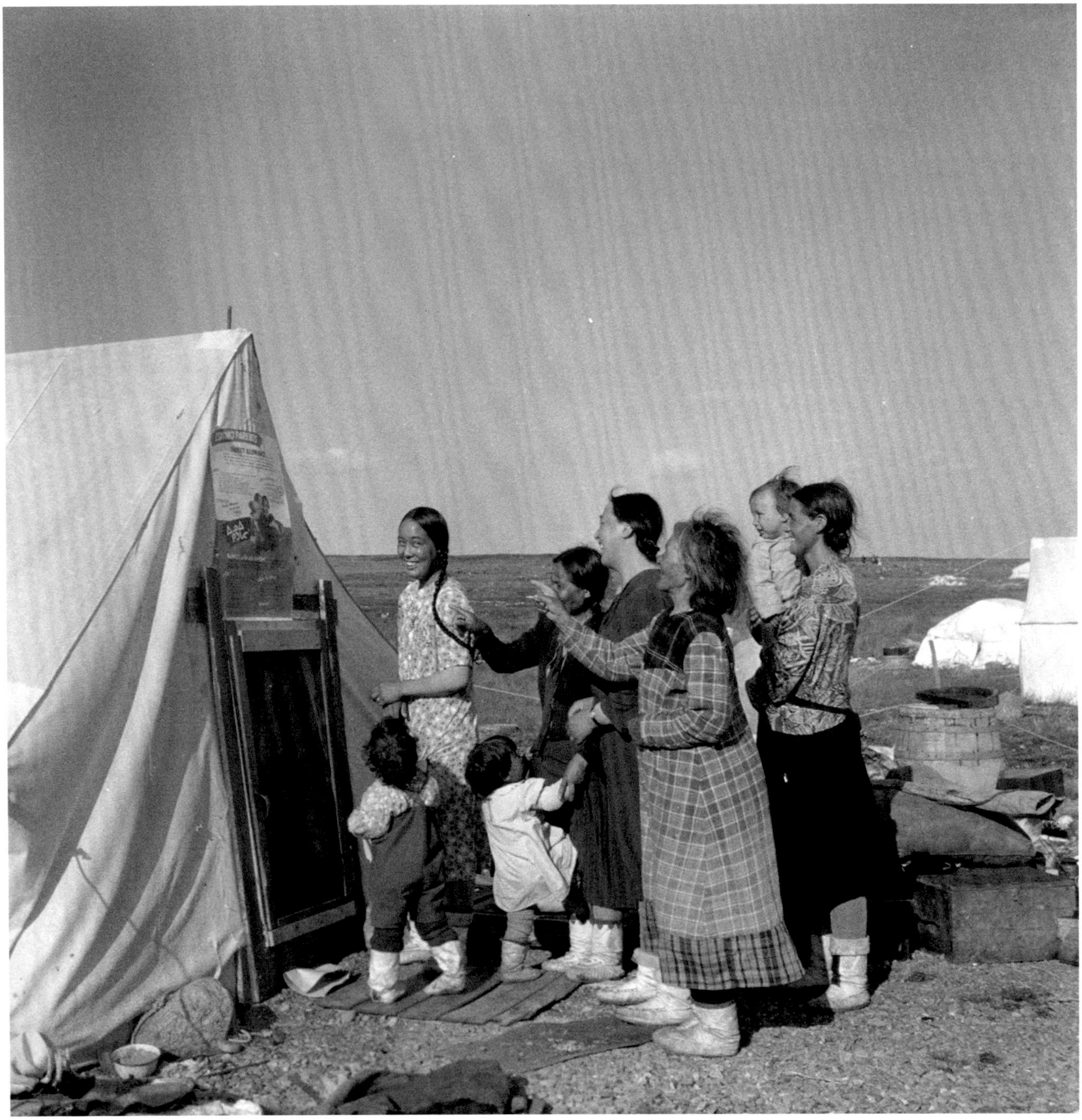

5.3 | [Winnie Attungala, Elizapie Ununniq (Thomas Tapatai's wife), Akumalik, and Lucy Tuupik (Francis Iyago's wife)], Qamani'tuaq, 1948. Original title: Eskimo family looking at Family Allowance poster, Baker Lake.

She quickly researched it. She's a researcher. So, what I had to do is ask her to call somebody and tell them that's my mother. Janet is two years younger than me and Lucy was two years younger than her. And that's when we were probably in Chesterfield Inlet (Igluligaarjuk) and we stopped and she was ice fishing.

They're looking at the picture when they were told, "Now your children can have family allowance": six dollars every month for one child. Then it went to seven dollars in 1968. It was 1969 when Deborah was born. That's when they're looking at the Canada allowance poster by the tent (Figure 5.3).

The tent is made of caribou skin ... I used to go with my mother in the springtime, like in the beginning of July, we put the whole caribou skin in the pond, put the skin with the fur down, the skin up. And soaked it in there, and, when it's soaked for a couple of days, we pull it up, put it [up] on the tundra and fold it from here to here [makes folding gesture], into three, and fold it again, and tie it with a rope. Let it sit there a couple days. In a couple of days, we go back and check it to see if the hair is coming off ... from the skin. [If] it's not ready yet, we fold it again and leave it for another couple of days. Then, we check it again ... I check with her and when we went back when all the hair is ready to come off, that's when it's ready. And that's how we have kamiks in the summertime without the hair ... That's what they would wear. And they had duffle socks inside ... Hudson Bay Company used to have duffle for sale ... They would have duffle socks inside because when you're walking on the tundra – well, on the rocks – you can really feel it, eh? ... [if] you don't have something inside your kamiks. We call it kamik miqquituq, caribou skin. In the wintertime, if you wear the kamik like that, what you do is put a piece of ... caribou skin, take the hair out so it, then it's warmer. That's it. Most people used to have braids all the time. When you see the old photograph, they have long hair and braided.

It's like the different types of kamiks. When you see them, you can tell ... from what area they are. As seamstresses, we can tell exactly who made that outfit or where ... it comes from. And [in the] same way, here they are made in Baker Lake, the gathering it's really, like a little gather and, [you] pull it, hold it close together and that's the way they make them. [You don't make them] flat.

Canon James was our missionary, Anglican missionary, in Baker Lake (Qamani'tuaq). They were 99 per cent Anglican in Baker, and maybe 1 per cent Catholic, because Anglican missionaries came to Baker Lake first. That's how a lot of Anglican people were in Baker. Canon James was teaching us. That was 1946. I was just one year old at that time. He's teaching Inuktitut syllabics and ... English. This is Ruth Annaqtuusi, Tulurialik's wife, when she was, younger. And, Isumataq was my step-father's first wife, Mary Tagoona's sister, younger sister. I don't know this little child (Figure 5.4).

See those [mitts] on the floor? They're made of caribou skin. The front legs of the caribou skin are mitts for women. The back legs of the caribou are for men's mitts. That's how they make them when they make caribou skin mitts. And that little fur, the white fur you see on the leg, it's always in the back, the bottom. Not the top. One day I went home to Baker Lake and Emily Alerk gave me a pair of pualuit (mitts) made out of caribou skin. I accepted. I looked at it. I noticed a mistake. I didn't say anything to her. She's an Elder. Then she looked at it. She said, "Oh, this is wrong. It's supposed to be at the bottom, not at the top." I didn't say anything to her but I noticed right away, she

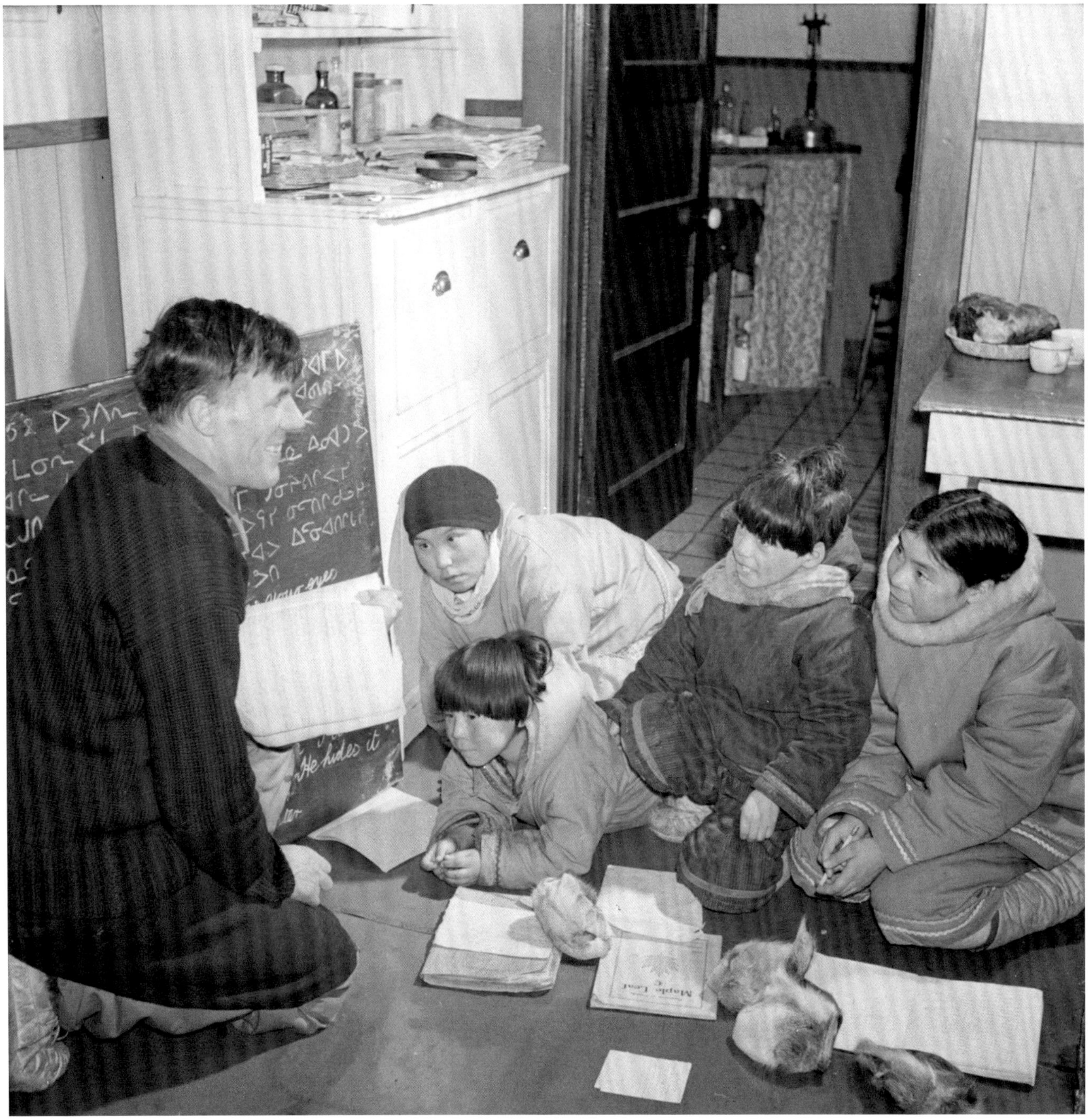

5.4 | Original title: Anglican Missionary Rev. W. James during catechism class with Eskimo children, Baker Lake Federal Hostel, Baker Lake, 1946.

made a mistake. But she carried on anyway. So, I accepted, I have them at home.

During the summer, my sister Janet and I would go to Canon James. He was a missionary there and he was teaching us Inuktitut syllabics, and also ABC English and arithmetic, to see how far we can go ... It's a space where you go to, if you're faster you go a little bit ahead, if you're slower ... he takes time to teach us. That was maybe '56, maybe '57 around there. And I know in 1958 there was starvation. That's when my uncle Peryouar talking on the CBC radio ... last week said, "In 1958, when there was a starvation in Baker Lake, the government started helping people. That's when the welfare started." And Peryouar asked Qiajuk, "You go with me to Sandy Lunan who was a Hudson Bay manager. And he never could understand me, you go to interpret for me, and tell him. All that stuff I got from the government ... all that whole year I trapped for fox skin; I will repay you back." And then Sandy Lunan would say, "Don't worry, you don't have to pay back. The government is paying for your groceries." That was when welfare first started 1958.

I remember when I was growing up, I used to put mud on the runners for the qamutik (Figure 5.5). Mudding. That's what they do. And once they mix it and put it there on the runners. They use the plane to smooth it and wet it. [You] use ... a piece of polar bear skin or caribou and then make it smooth. That's what he's doing on the qamutik so it runs smooth and faster. I just want to point that out. That's how men used to do it on the runners. But now it's Teflon. That's what they use now. But

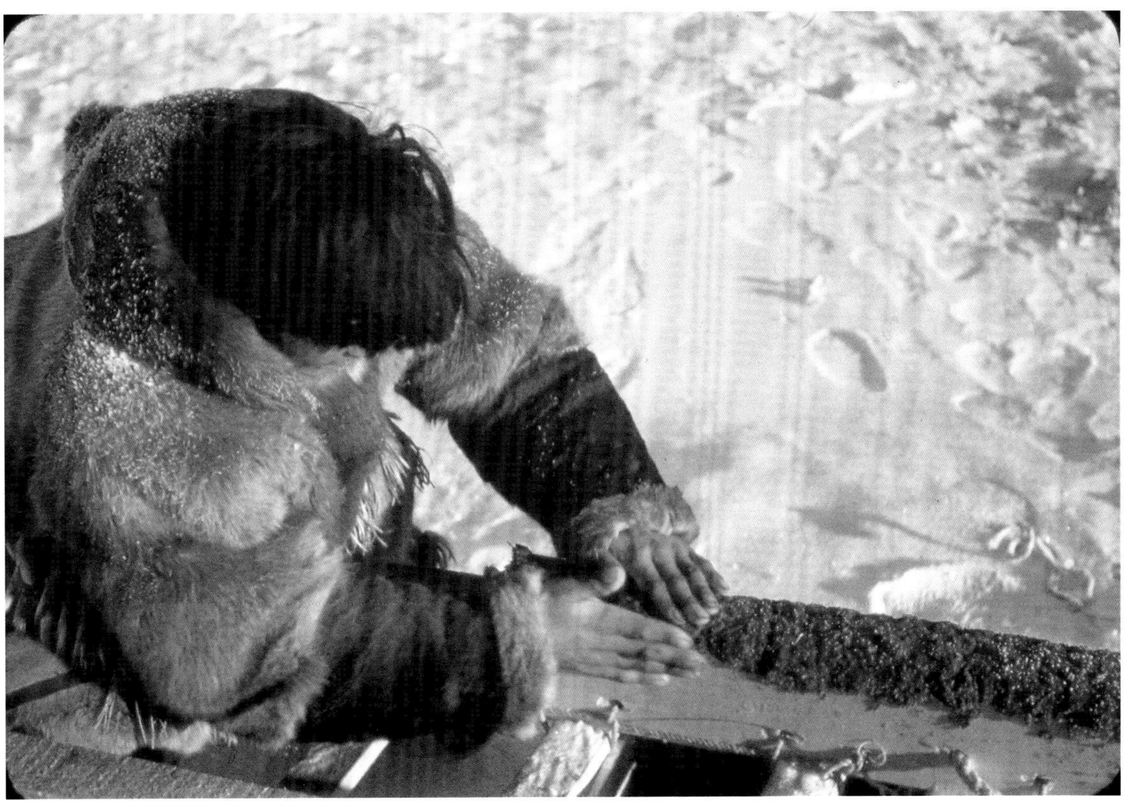

5.5 | [Unidentified man applying "mud" to the bare shoeing of his sled], Arviat, c. 1940.

they're dangerous. When your skidoo is running, you stop [and] it still goes. You have to be careful, you know? And that's why I just want to mention, when they have dog teams ... if they don't have a metal anchor to stop the sled, [they use a] caribou antler? It's an antler when it's on a caribou, but [when] it comes off it became everything ... they use it to stop the dog team or sled. When an antler is off, it can be anything. It can be a tool; it can be made into toys like ajagak. It became a lot of things. You can carve on it, a lot of Eskimo, in Eskimo Point (Arviat), they do a lot of carving on antler. And also in Baker Lake (Qamani'tuaq). Because if you don't have soapstone, you have to think of ways to make an income. Anything that's available, they use it. Antlers are everywhere, available. So, they make carvings out of that too.

Editors' Afterword

In these commentaries, recorded in 2017, Elder Sally Kate Webster's approach to archival photographs crystallizes the ways that Inuit Elders have participated in Project Naming as a whole. Her four succinct narratives are woven from a dynamic combination of the importance of naming, unikkaat (narratives told from personal experience), photographic promptings of specific memories, and the guiding principles of Inuit Qaujimajatuqangit (IQ).

Specifically, Elder Sally Kate Webster responds to four archival photographs depicting people and sites around her home community, Qamani'tuaq (Baker Lake), in the Kivalliq Region of Nunavut. Dating from the 1940s and 1950s, during her youth, the images elicit bursts of recognition from her. Indeed, she describes the feeling of being brought back in time unexpectedly by a 1952 image depicting her mother, Rhoda Qaqsauq, and sisters, Lucy Evo and Janet Tagoona. Elder Sally Kate Webster came across the image by chance as an adult in *Nunavut News North*'s regular feature, "Do You Know Your Elders?" (a collaboration with Project Naming). Opening the page, she recalled, "there was my mother!" We have borrowed that interjection for the title of these narratives to signal the affective power of photographs (and photographic reception) to transport Inuit over time and reconnect them with loved ones.

As with most Elders participating in Project Naming, Sally Kate Webster's recognitions result in identifications of people in the photographs; but through naming, they also extend beyond the frame of the photographs to reassert Inuit culture. Often, her stories depart from the assimilationist narratives that the (southern) photographer may have intended. An image promoting family welfare benefits and another depicting an English lesson taught by a missionary, for example, provide opportunities for Webster to talk about the skilful use of caribou skin to construct tents and clothing.

In this attention to family histories, rejection of assimilationist narratives, and assertion of Inuit skills and values, Elder Sally Kate Webster's narratives reflect the values of Inuit Qaujimajatuqangit (IQ). Perhaps more than any other IQ principle, she models Pilimmaksarniq, working together and the development of skills through mentoring and observation. Indeed, in narrating photographs and sharing her knowledge of sewing and life on the land, she participates in Project Naming by teaching, in an Inuit way.

CHAPTER 6

"Sometimes when you see the pictures, you come home"

Piita Irniq

Naming people is an extremely important aspect of Inuit culture. My name is Piita, Inuit call me Piita, English people call me Peter. When the Government of Canada came in 1940 ... they had ... disc numbers. So, for a long period of time, I was Peter E3–546. That was my identification under the colonialism of the Government of Canada ... That was one part of colonialism.

▸▸▸

I was born in an iglu and I lived in an iglu for the first eleven years of my life until I was taken by the church and the Canadian government to go to a residential school. That was in August of 1958. We got severely punished for speaking Inuktitut at the residential school and we had a loss of culture, loss of language, loss of Inuit shamanism, and loss of Inuit parenting skills. It's the kind of things that my generation are trying to get back in the name of healing and reconciliation. Retrieve what you've lost, reclaim what you've lost, take back our Inuit culture. And I think about my fellow Survivors at the residential school because we've been working on healing and reconciliation now for a good number of years.

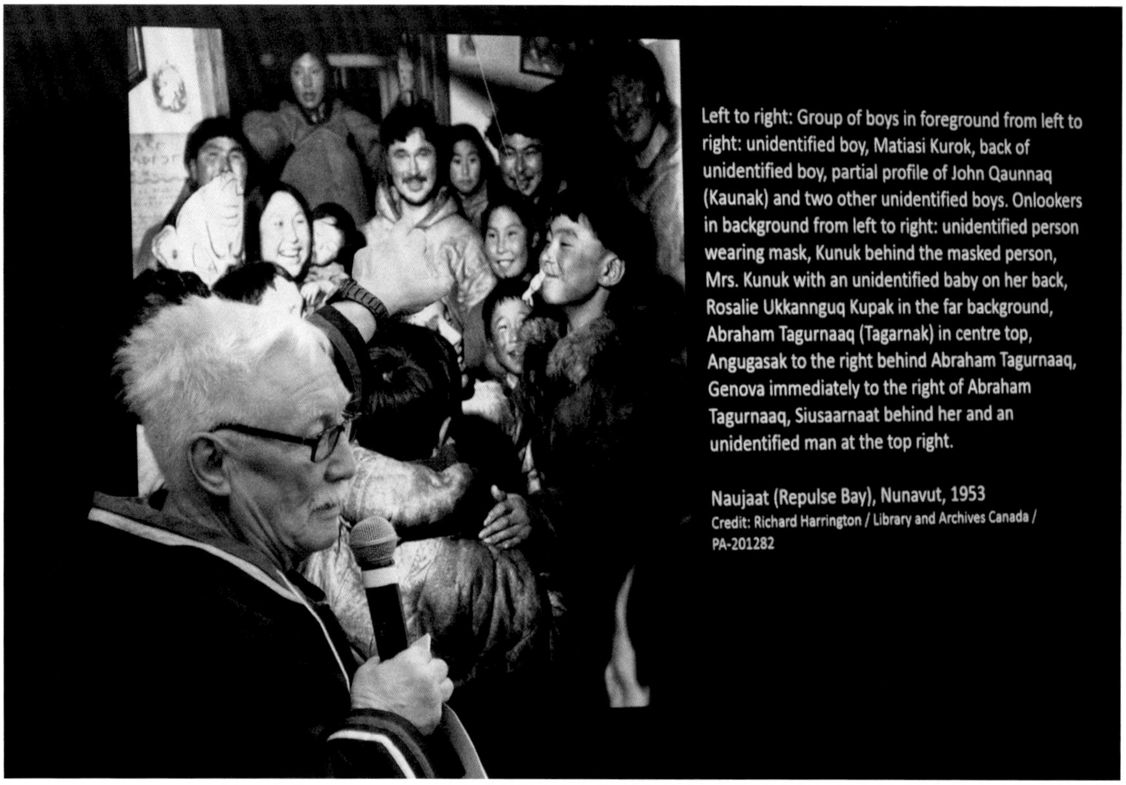

6.1 | Elder Piita Irniq speaking at the fifteenth anniversary of Project Naming event, Library and Archives Canada, Ottawa, 2017 [Irniq is discussing Figure 6.4].

▸▸▸

I still speak pretty good Inuktitut language. Some words I've forgotten, living in southern Canada and the business of doing things in English is a very powerful thing ... The reason why my generation still speaks Inuktitut is because when we would go home in the spring, in May, we would go back to our communities of Naajaut, Salliq, Qamani'tuaq, Kuugaarjuk, Gjoa Haven, Pond Inlet (Mittimatalik), Chesterfield Inlet (Igluligaarjuk). Yep, that's where the school was. We would speak to our parents only in Inuktitut. So, I know May, June, July, August Inuktitut language. But I completely forgot some of the winter language: formations of snow, winter weather forecasting, expressions of getting dark and cloudy, hunting words. We went from traditional Inuit legends to reading *Dick and Jane* at the residential school. So, what do I do? I go and call my uncle up in Gjoa Haven whose name is Uriash Puqiqnak. With Manitok Thompson, he was the first MLA in the Nunavut government on March 15, I think it was, 1999. I discuss traditional Inuit words with him, and I retrieve and I reclaim and take back what I've lost. I still speak pretty good English ... I still speak pretty good Inuktitut.

▸▸▸

I speak English to you although it's not my first language. I'm diabetic but I turned seventy the other day. I do a lot of exercise and I walk around a lot and I do exercises often. I said some time ago that there are two things that are in common: diabetes and residential school. They're both the same. They're lifetime healing. Forever. From here you can live a great life. I've lived a really great life in the last thirty years, forty years, because of my culture, my Inuit culture that always made me stronger than anything else. Just for your information, as a Survivor, I quit drinking twenty-two years ago. That has been my own healing journey from what happened to me at the residential school by the church. I quit smoking twenty-five years ago.

I've always worked to promote Inuit harvesting rights about sealing. I started back in 1977 when I was minister of economic development and tourism in the government of the Northwest Territories. That brought me all over the place, all over the world to speak about [the] Inuit sealing issue. So, that brought me to a convention on the international trade of endangered species in Buenos Aires. I had been speaking to about a thousand people at the conference. I have tried to make good speeches for most of my life. I don't try to make bad speeches, you know? I had been making what I thought was a fairly good speech about sealing by Inuit. There's lots of microphones and there's lots of TV cameras. And after I spoke about the Inuit right to harvest animals such as seals, an animal rights person got up and she took the microphone. She said, "Peter, you don't have to hunt seals to eat and to survive anymore. All you have to do is you go to the grocery store where meat and fish are made." I thought, I want to respond to that too, right? I said, "Mr Chairman, look, I am a seal hunter. I can wait for a seal at a seal hole on the ice at minus forty, or minus fifty, and wait patiently until I get one. That means I can, at most times, outlast government bureaucracy." And I thought to myself, "that's a good way of doing it." I repeat this [story] because Inuit survive by being patient. We outlasted those guys from a long time ago. I outlasted residential school. I can outlast anything. With Inuit, that's who we are.

▸▸▸

I want to say something about Project Naming … It's healing. What we're doing is moving healing and reconciliation together. For thirty-one years, I [have] worked on Inuit's experience at residential school. Now, today, we move towards healing and reconciliation. And I go to tell the stories of Inuit experience because I always feel that Canadians have a right, duty, and responsibility to know about what happened to us at the residential school. Because residential school is not only Inuit experience, residential school is not only Inuit history, it is Canadian history. That's why I always place an important emphasis on the fact that all Canadians have a right to know what happened to us. And we'll move healing and reconciliation together. We'll move healing and reconciliation as a team. We'll move Project Naming as a team. We'll work for the betterment of our people, as a team, our children, our grandchildren, and their children.

▸▸▸

The pictures we look at today and yesterday are heartfelt. They are also healing. Sometimes when you see the pictures, you come home. Sometimes you go right back to that living room in your tent, or in your igloo. What happened when I was taken away to go to a residential school in 1958 in August, I left a little "Eskimo" that morning and became a little white boy in the same day in the afternoon. I looked exactly like the pictures ... kamiik, tuktu clothing, Eskimo, isuma Inuit. But the same day I was reading *Dick and Jane*. So, you take back what belongs to you, reclaim, and you'll retrieve, and you help to revitalize the Inuktitut language as much as you can.

6.2 | Piita Irniq hunting on the floe edge.

Photograph Identifications

In this picture (Figure 6.2), Donat Milukuq and I were out hunting in the mid-1980s. Actually, this is at the ice floe. It was really cold that day when we were out seal hunting. It was minus forty or minus fifty and it was really windy. But here I am wearing caribou clothing, caribou parka, sealskin boots, and holding a harpoon ... holding the harpoon ... to test the thickness of the ice. You just go poke it like this and you make sure you don't fall in the water ... you don't want to go through ice that is too thin. That's the purpose of the harpoon at this point. I have a harpoon head on my qamutiik. You can see the marks of my qamutiik right there ...

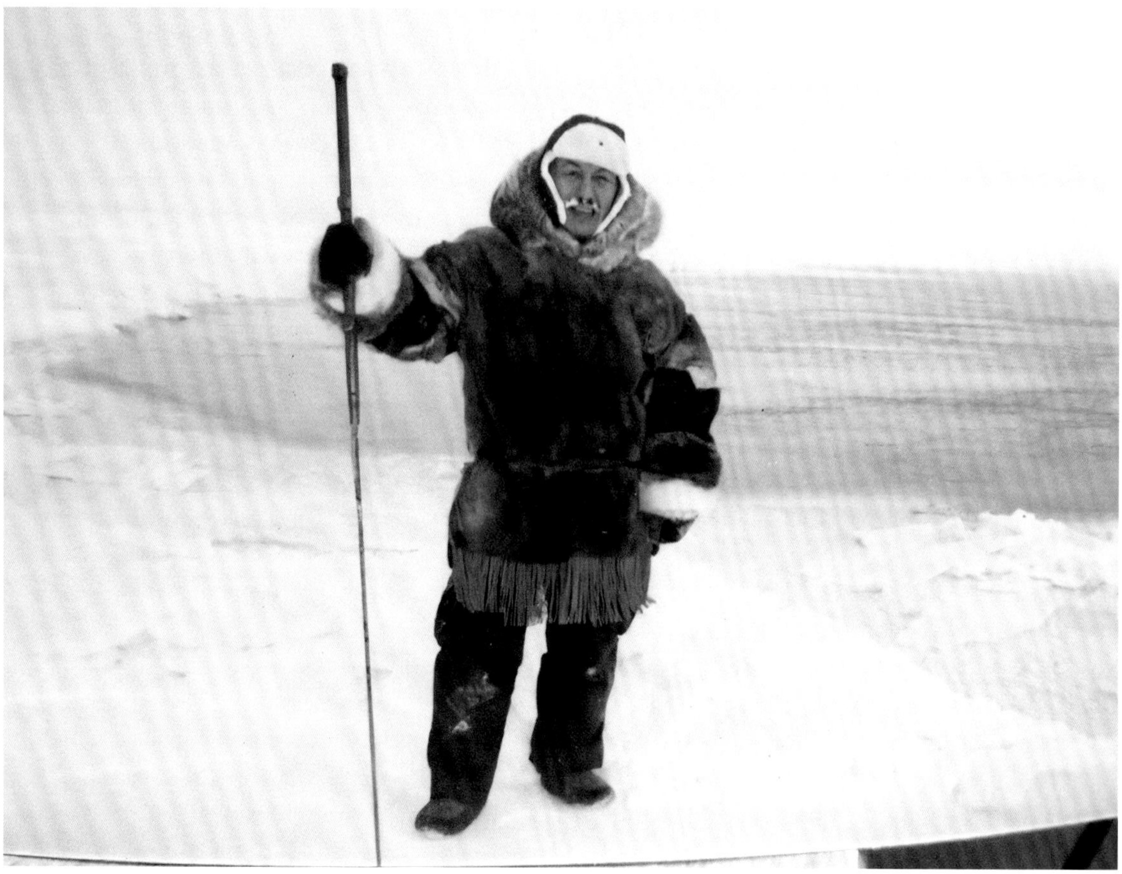

Seal hunting is part of survival. Seal hunting is having food on the floor. We Inuit always eat on the floor most of the time. Seal hunting meant making clothing for your mitts, for your boots, for your jacket, for your pants. And sometimes … to light the qulliq. The qulliq, it used to have sealskin fat. When we lived on the land, we used to have caribou fat. You know? Because it's from the inland. I'm from both the inland as well as coastal regions, we used to use both seal oil to light the qulliq and tunnuq (caribou fat) if you live on the land.

The Inuit have been seal hunting since time immemorial. It's not an easy job to hunt seal at the floe edge because sometimes you could be … broken away from the main ice because of the current, or because of strong winds, as it was that day. You would have been broken away. But, you know, as an Elder, as a hunter, an experienced hunter, you know what you're doing, as much as possible on the land, when you're out on the land. I enjoy going out seal hunting. And I enjoy going out on the land because it's healing. It's really, really healing when you go out on the land. You heal your mind, you heal your heart, you heal your body. So, when you hear people going out on the land, that's what it means.

This picture (Figure 6.3) was taken during Easter time in 1953 by the late Richard Harrington. We had Richard Harrington living in the adjoining room of the iglu for a little while. I have a mental picture of him. My mother made him caribou clothing. He had a little qulliq. I could see his picture, his mental picture still in my head. This is Aalu, Veronica Manilaq, Rosalie Kopak, Madeleine Isiqqut Krinayak, and Qaaq. They're playing a game at Easter time; the one who runs the fastest would win a prize. Maybe it could have been a bag of tea, it could have been a bag of flour, ten pounds. It could have been tobacco, too. Madeleine Isiqqut Krinayak became one of the best carvers in the 1960s. Her carvings are all over the place of various art galleries in southern Canada. The woman on the right is Qaaq, she later married a man named Ijakak.

There's an interesting story about this, too. Back in 1955, the Rankin Inlet nickel mine opened. A lot of people from Naujaat went to Rankin Inlet to go and work at the mine. If you take a look at my story, I went from iglu to microwave in less than fifty years. People like that, who went from iglu in the wintertime [and] tent in the summertime, went to work underground at Rankin Inlet mine. Wow, Inuit Ajunngi! It shows that Inuit are pretty adaptable.

Akkaq, means my uncle. Inuksuk. His first name was Isaiah. He used to live in Wager Bay, now Ukkusiksalik National Park. He used to live there for many, many years, and my family used to live there, too, for a number of years.

This picture (Figure 6.4) was also taken by Richard Harrington in 1953. I was six years old, and I remember all these things happening when this photo was taken. Inuit don't Google: we remember! We don't Google and we remember everything. In this picture, people are playing nukluktaq at Christmas time. He has something in his mouth, hanging on a string. I'm not sure exactly what game that is. But let me tell you who the people are … *Una*, this is late Mrs Rosalie Kupak [at the back, by the window]. When I was born in 1947, she was a traditional midwife to my mother in 1947. Paul Kunuk and his wife, Tulugaarjak [at left], who lives up in Naujaat and was originally from Igloolik. Paul Kunuk, father of Maria Tulugaarjuk. They called him Matiasi Kurok: that was his Inuktitut name. This is the late Abraham Tagurnaaq. He has lots of relatives up

6.3 | [Left to right: Aalu, Veronica Manilaq, Rosalie Kopak, Madeleine Isiqqut Krinayak, and Qaaq (married to Ijakak) during Christmas activities], Naujaat, 1953.

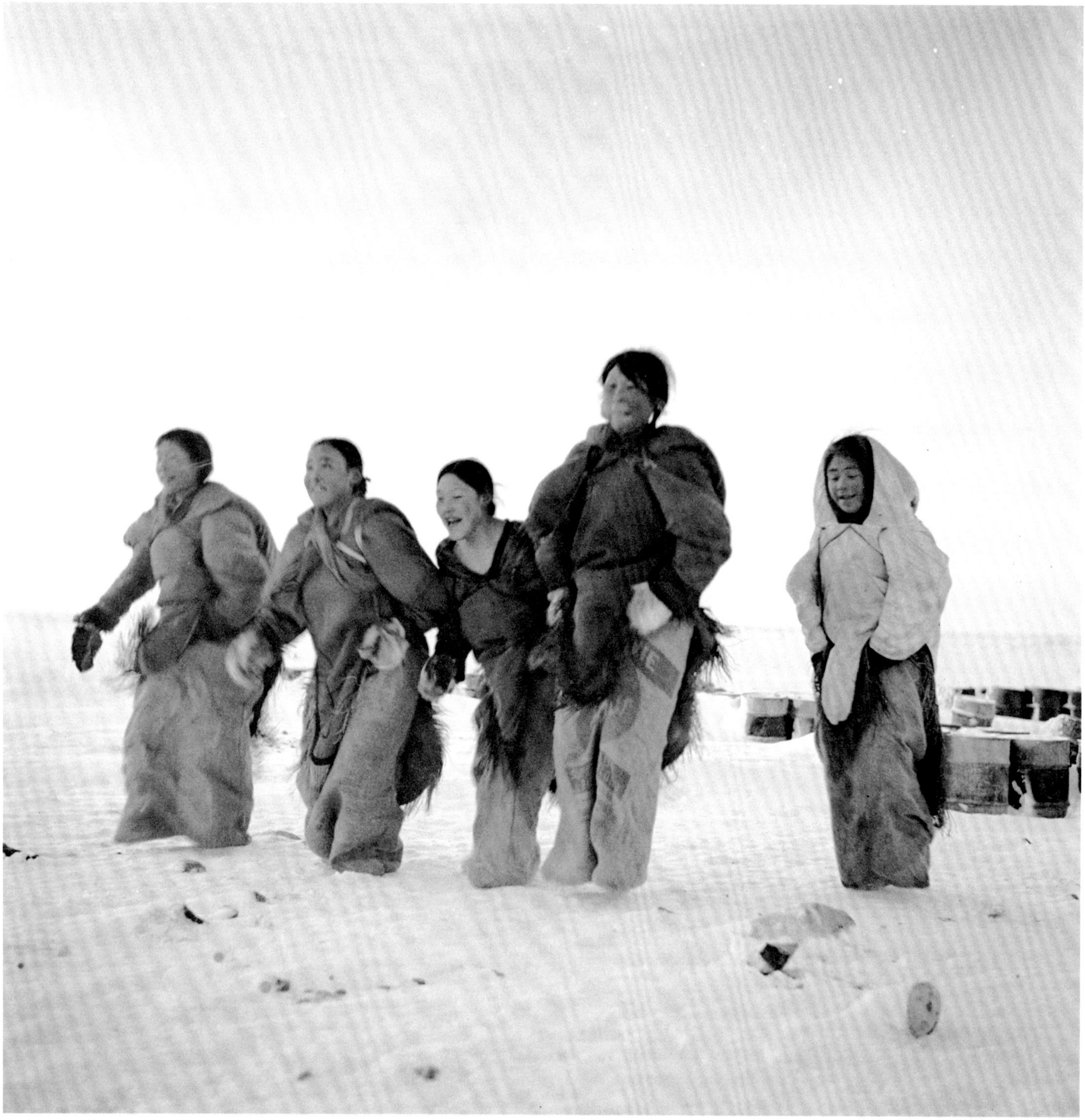

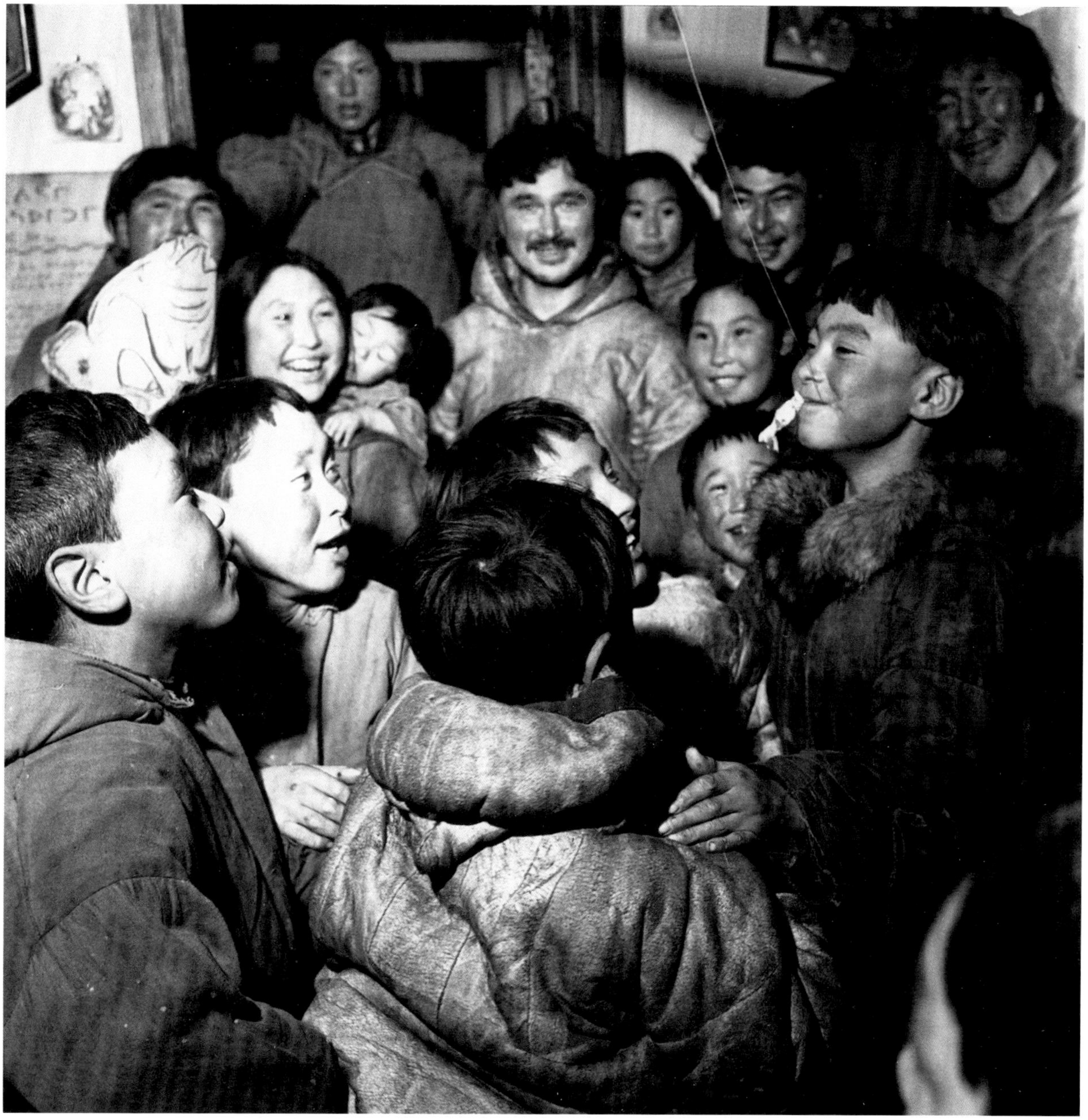

6.4 | [Group of boys in foreground from left to right: unidentified boy, Matiasi Kurok, back of unidentified boy, partial profile of John Qaunnaq (Kaunak) and two other unidentified boys. Onlookers in background from left to right: unidentified person wearing mask, Kunuk behind the masked person, Mrs. Kunuk with an unidentified baby in her amauti, Rosalie Ukkannguq Kupak in the far background, Abraham Tagurnaaq (Tagarnak) in centre top, Angugasak to the right behind Abraham Tagurnaaq, Genova immediately to the right of Abraham Tagurnaaq, Siusaarnaat behind her and an unidentified man at the top right], Naujaat, 1953.

in Igloolik as he does in Naujaat. Remember – I'm not sure if anybody remembers – Phillip Kripanik. Have you ever heard of that name? Okay, this is his younger brother, the late John Kaunak. His first wife. She's still alive, Angugasak. She lives up in Igloolik. Her name is now Angutimmarik. You know that young lady Lucy Tulugarjuk, the movie star in *Atanarjuat: The Fast Runner*? She is Angugasak's daughter, she still lives in Igloolik.

Editors' Afterword

For Elders like Piita Irniq, the commissioner of Nunavut from 2000 to 2005, speaking about archival photographs through Project Naming (as well as narrating more recent personal photographs) provides an opportunity to testify about Inuit culture.

Irniq's participation in Project Naming, over two decades, has involved the significant task of identifying people in images but it has also offered an opportunity to discuss the Inuktut languages, Inuit history, and his background. As such, his identifications are not straightforward and linear accounts of empirical information. Indeed, his discussion often departs from the literal scenes depicted in photographs to provide contextualizing information, particularly, about his history as a residential school survivor.[1] In short, the opportunity to speak through Project Naming becomes an opportunity for conveying historical experience and Inuit cultural values. Irniq, who has embraced the concept of reconciliation (more than some other Inuit), reflects on how photo-based memory work can aid the work of reconciliation and how this work requires the investment of Qallunaat, too.

Yet, while Irniq's conversation is wide-ranging, photographs nonetheless are crucial elements in his testimony. In this excerpt, for example, Irniq states poignantly that photographs "are healing. Sometimes when you see the pictures, you come home." Here, photographs function as what Marianne Hirsch and Leo Spitzer call "testimonial objects," remnants that "carry memory traces from the past ... [and] also embody the very process of its transmission."[2] When Irniq comes "home," through photographs, he reactivates the past and connects it to the present. They prompt him to recall individuals, ways of living, and connections and to tell of these details through a vivid, moving narrative. In this way, photographs – as testimonial objects – aid Inuit memory and transgenerational transmission.[3]

NOTES

1 Truth and Reconciliation Commission of Canada, *Canada's Residential Schools*, volume 2: *The Inuit and Northern Experience.*
2 Hirsch and Spitzer, "Testimonial Objects," 355.
3 For more on the connection between Project Naming and testimony, see Payne, "Disruption and Testimony."

CHAPTER 7

"I'm responsible for that name. If I lose that, I've cut off an Inuit encyclopedia"

Manitok Thompson

I'm Manitok Thompson. According to my tradition, when somebody died they named a newborn baby for the deceased a year after. In 1954, my aunt died, and a year later I was named. I am Manitok named after my aunt. I went to school not knowing a word of English. The teacher got me and my sister confused. Cathy Towtongie [my sister] was the president of Nunavut Land Claims for some time. She's actually not Cathy. I'm Cathy. Her real baptismal name is Louisa. I didn't have a clue what the teacher was saying. I said, "Manitok," and kept repeating it. She said, "Monica." She finally pronounced it "Man-ee-took." My baptismal name is Cathy, short for Catherine. But anyway, the teacher asked my sister, "What's your name?" And she said, "Qatanni," which is her Inuktitut name. Qatanni: sounds like Catherine. But I'm Catherine. I couldn't explain to the teacher in English that "*I'm* Catherine." So, my sister became Cathy because the teacher couldn't pronounce Qatanni.

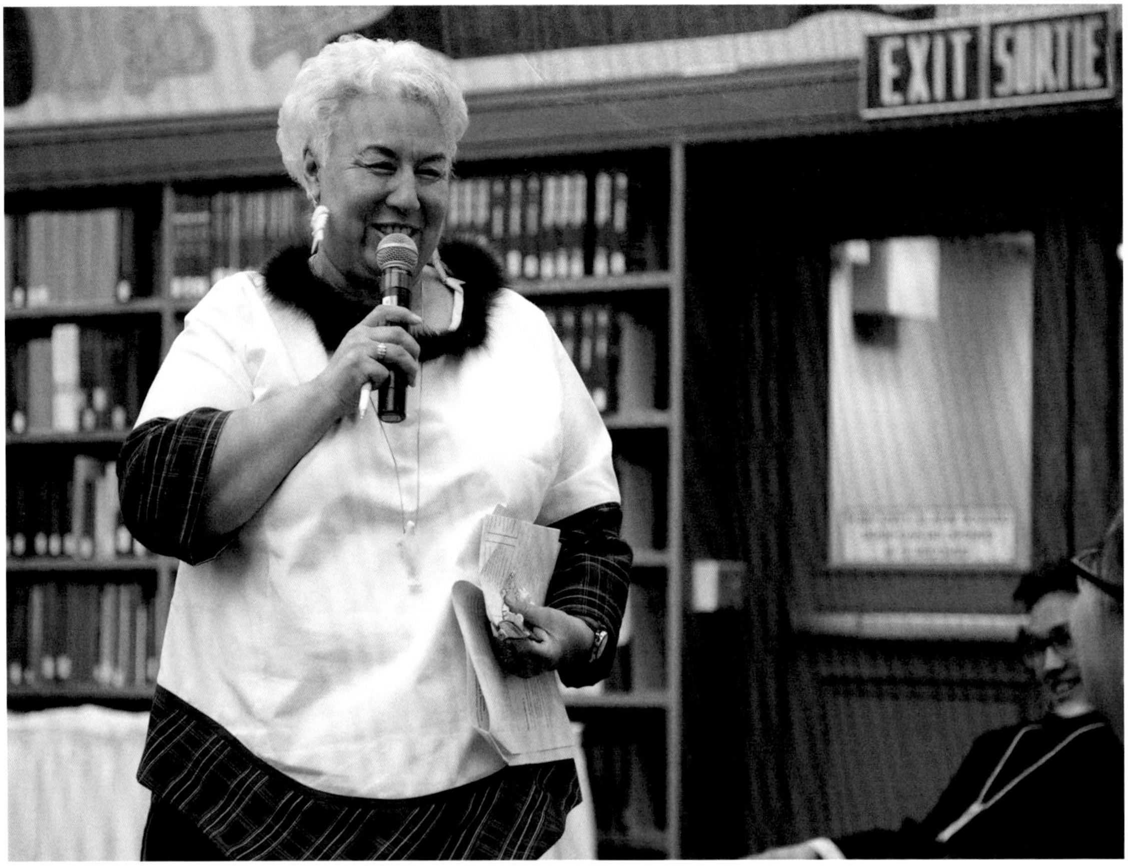

7.1 | Manitok Thompson speaking at the fifteenth anniversary of Project Naming event, Library and Archives Canada, Ottawa, 2017.

Before that, we were just numbers. And now, thanks to Project Naming, we're trying to find out who these people were.

How do you get those people up there to recognize these people and give you names? I work in archives at the Inuit Broadcasting Corporation (IBC). The best way to get the names is to post those pictures on the local swap and sell Facebook page. You get the answer in a few seconds: who they're related to, what the story is behind that photograph.

▸▸▸

I have a granddaughter whom we adopted. Her name is Tulugak, after my great-grandmother. I have a song for her. Inuit make up a baby song for each of their babies when they favour them. I know you have lullabies but this is different. My mom's mother, Toota, named my mother after her baby song Tweenaq.[1] She grew up with Tweenaq because she looked like a little doll. I have a song for Leanne, my adopted granddaughter. It goes like this:

Ajungitupaaluli
Nalinaartupaaluli

Piujupakulluli
Ajungilupakulluli

You are so capable
You are so lovable
You are so beautiful
You are so able to do anything

She has several songs:

Cutie patutie
Piujupaatuti
Ajungitupatuti
Nalinnatupatutie[2]

▸▸▸

This couple in Figure 7.2 are my great-grandparents. The lady is Tulugaq, my mother named my granddaughter after her. The man is Tassiuq. My grandfather, my mom's step-father, Dick Wager, was one hundred per cent Inuk. The whalers used to give names to Inuit that they met. His real name is Iqungajuq. My grandfather, Iqungajuq, was the first Inuk HBC trade post manager. He didn't know English, but he took over the trading post in Wager Bay (Ukkusiksalik). These are his parents. When the explorers came to find the Franklin ship, my great-grandparents were guides to those people searching for that ship – my maternal grand-parents and Dick Wager's parents.[3]

The British came to this area looking for the Franklin ship, with Dick Wager's parents and my grandmother Toota's parents, Maliki and Ujaralaaq. One group went that way; one group went this way. They guided those non-Aboriginals looking for the ship. In the summertime, they were walking on the tundra looking all over the place, Tassiuq said he could feel something under the ground. Something hidden, a treasure or whatever. He told his wife, "There's something under the ground." But he said, "I'm not going to tell these kabluunaq – white people – there's something under the ground. Because if I tell them, I'll be the one digging up that treasure while they sit and watch me dig it." So, they just pretended he never found anything. They did find an inuksuk with a note stuck in between the rocks. And the note said, "We're starving. We're eating each other now." And inside the big metal pot beside the inuksuk was a shoulder blade of a human being.[4] They both couldn't speak English, but the man ... seemed to be shouting, "Henry!" They remembered the name.[5]

▸▸▸

We lived in a little town outside Coral Harbour (Salliq), Snafu. It was called Snafu because the Americans came and brought this old ship filled with barrels and beached it. The old ship had a big sign with SNAFU on it (Figure 7.4). That's where my siblings and I grew up.[6] We lived outside of town, about four miles out of town. Maybe my parents didn't want us to be influenced by any other rearing practices. My father, Mikitok Bruce, worked for the Ministry of Transportation station, eleven miles from our house [Mikitok Bruce's grandparents are pictured in Figure 7.3]. I didn't go to a residential school. We were taught to survive and were able to survive in our environment. We never complained about having to walk to school.

My mom taught us the Bible and hymns. She made us memorize Bible verses in Inuktitut. My dad would walk eleven miles to go to work in the summer and by dog team in the winter. He would start at 5 o'clock in the morning to be there before 8 o'clock. He never wanted to be late for work. Sometimes the truck would come

7.2 | [Tulugaq and Tassiuq, Iqunagajuq's (Dick Wager's) parents and the great-grandparents of Manitok Thompson, Qatiktalik]. Original title: Eskimo couple, Cape Fullerton, 1904–05.

7.3 (*opposite*) | Nivisinaaq and Angutimmarik, Salliq. [Shoofly (left) was John Ell's mother. John Ell's daughter is Ookpik Patterk, Shoofly was the adoptive mother of Joe Curley Qayayuak and Pameolik], Salliq, 1926. Library and Archives Canada/Department of Indian and Northern Affairs collection/a099585. Credit: Lachlan T. Burwash

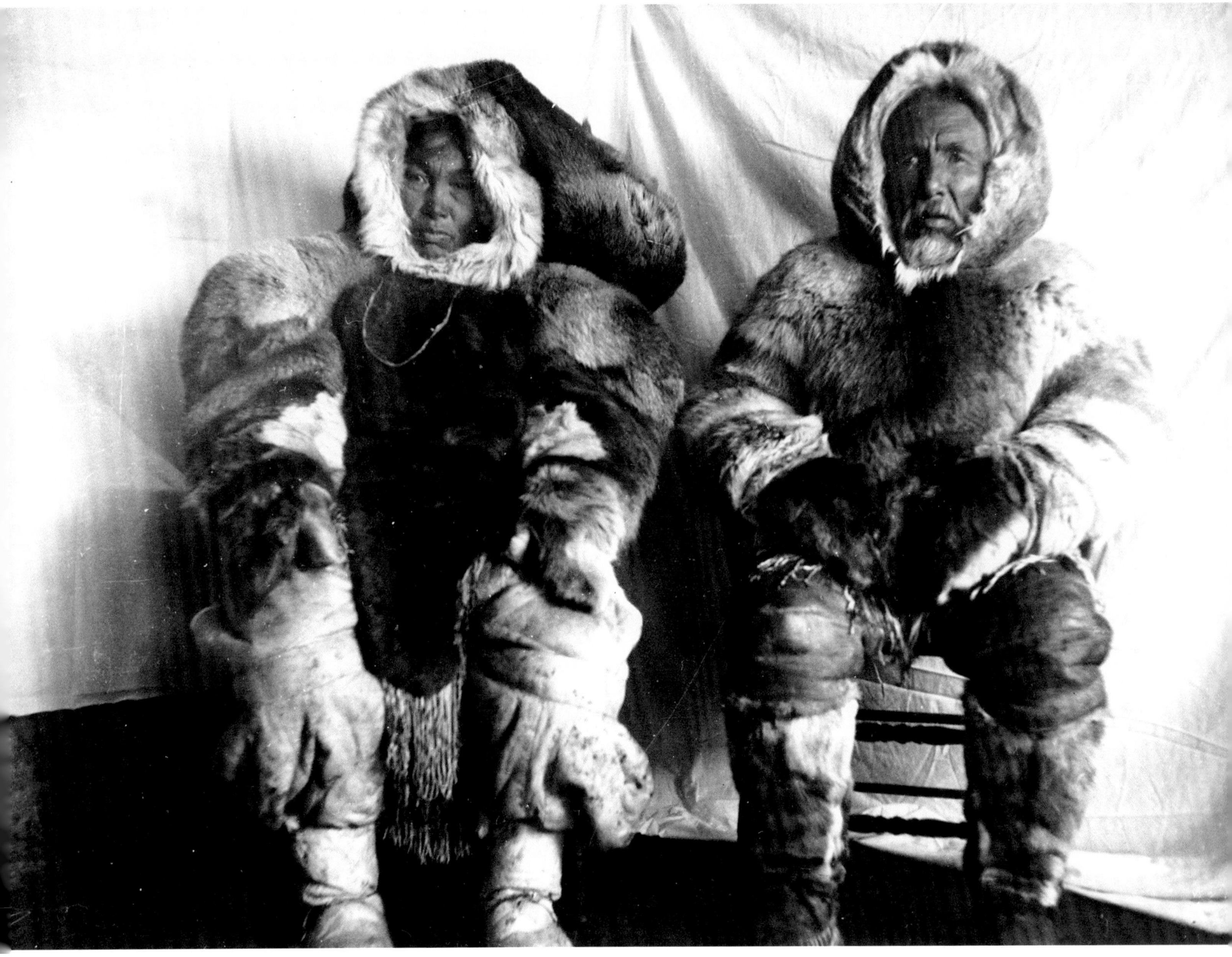

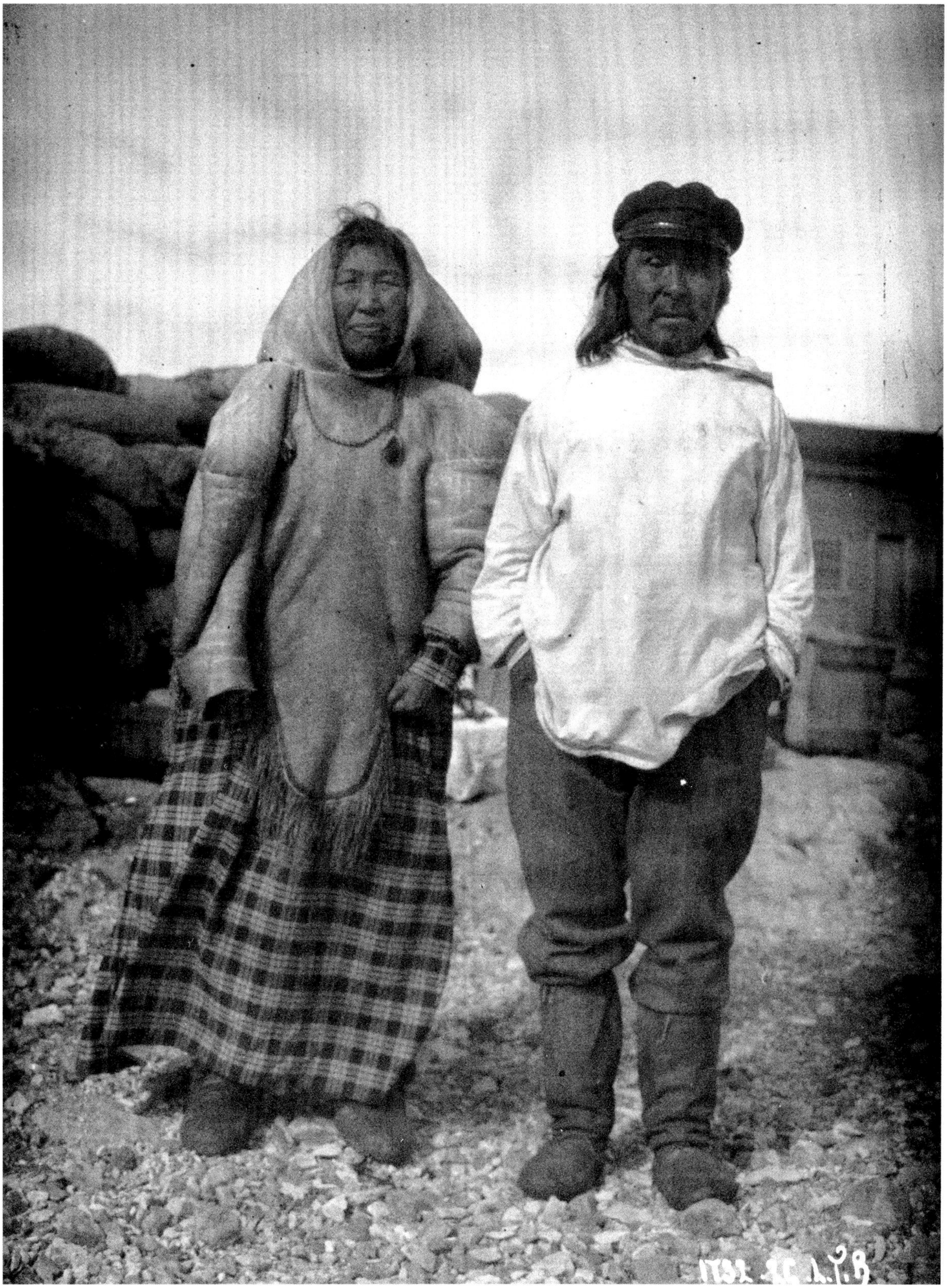

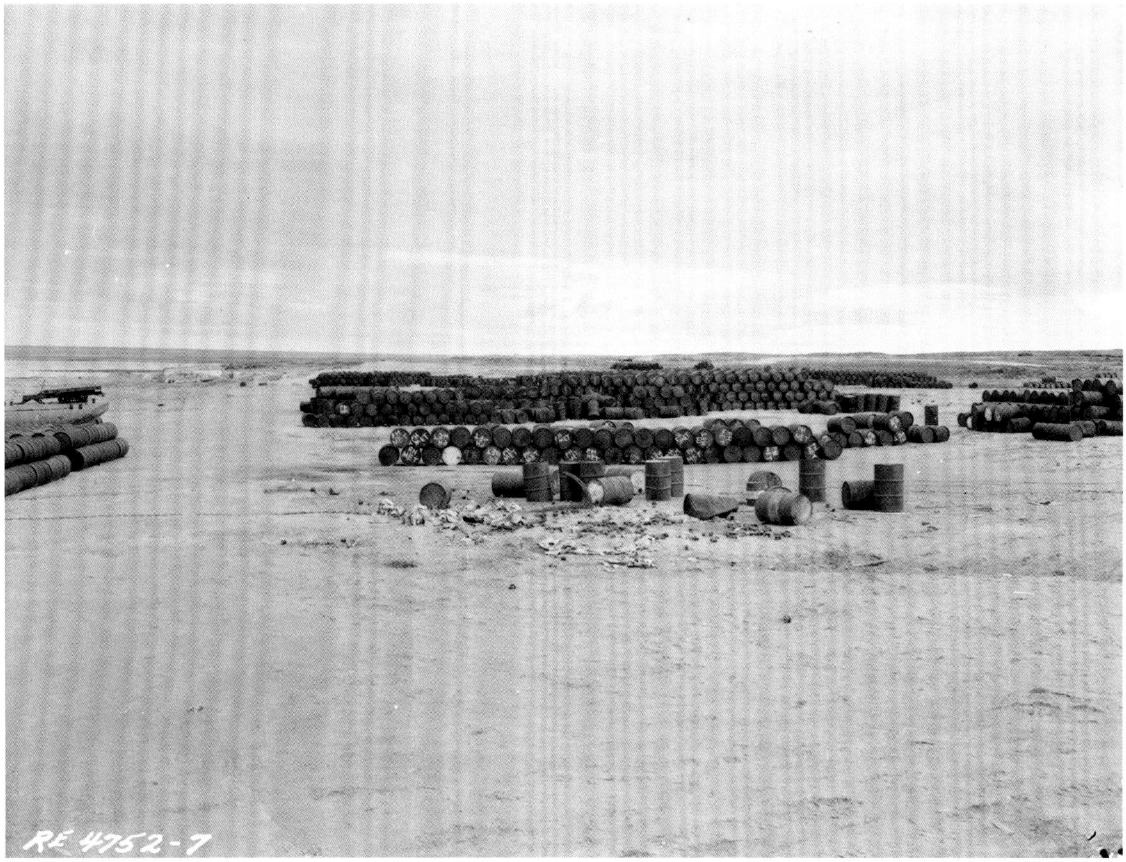

7.4 | Original title: Snafu Harbour, 3 miles from Coral Harbour, 1949.

down an old, dusty little road to pick him up. He didn't trust anybody to take him to work in case he was brought to work late.

My mother's biological father is Scottish. He was a trader in Wager Bay. His name is Jim Thom. He died in Ontario somewhere. She had blue eyes and light brown hair. But she was totally Inuk-minded, just her skin was non-aboriginal. We walked to school, we went by dog team, or we skated from one lake to the other to town. My father gave my aunt, Turaaluk, his sister, his account to buy our clothing or food if she needed to. My father did not believe in handouts or welfare from the government. My father often said welfare assistance has taken away the independence of a people. I believe the government wasn't aware we lived outside the town.

▸▸▸

Inuit lived in harmony with each other. The two churches – Anglicans and Catholics, the priest and ministers – caused divisions amongst Inuit and within families. You had to marry from the church you belonged to. In the 1960s, social housing started being constructed in Coral Harbour. It was about that time that my younger sister, Mona, had to start school. So, we moved into town. My dad said, "Now we'll have to go to a church." Up to that time when we were in town for school, we followed our aunts to the Catholic Church since they were all Catholics. Back at home in Snafu, we became non-denominational following my mother's study of the Bible.[7]

My father led the family. One day, he said, "Armand Tagoona is in town. He'll baptize the children. And he told us that we would be Anglicans. He gave us each a Bible and signed us up to the Anglican religion." Armand Tagoona kept saying to each of us children, "To the Church of England." We went home after the ceremony and my mom, who hardly ever argued with my dad, was furious. She told him, "My kids, they've been given to the Church of England when they should belong to Jesus and God." That really bothered her.

When I went to school, I didn't know any English at all. The whole education system was so foreign compared to what I was experiencing at home. Inuit education is one-on-one: observing and no asking questions. You don't dare ask questions. You just observe. Try again and again until you can do it properly, whatever you are being taught. In school you were graded, it is a totally different way of teaching. In the Kablunaaq system, you get better grades if you ask more questions. In the Inuit system, you did not ask questions. You were just told and listened. You had to address the teacher by their name. We wouldn't dare address any adults by their names as children. It was very impolite. It was either "my best uncle," "Judy's uncle," "my big uncle," or "my little uncle." You wouldn't dare say an adult's name, no not in my culture. Today, little children ask adults, "Kinauvit (what's your name)?" My parents thought that that was shocking, rude, and impolite.

At school, a teacher would tell strange stories, one of them being, three little pigs and the big bad wolf. And we wondered, "Did she make those things up or what are those animals? Where did that come from?" We would be encouraged to ask questions. We would be doing sign language. The teacher would have not a clue that we were actually answering by opening our eyes to say yes and moving our nose muscles to say no.

▸▸▸

I was minister in the NWT government in 1995 and a minister in the Nunavut government in 1999.[8] I was the first woman to be elected to the Nunavut government. I will give you a glimpse of what it was like going into Nunavut from NWT and starting a new territory.[9] I felt like being an adult and married to a teenager at times. The old government was well-oiled machinery for thirty years. The territory is now about eighteen years old [in 2017].

The first time I sat in my NWT cabinet office chair, I seemed to be having an out-of-body experience. I kept reminding myself, "I'm in charge of all the hamlets in the territory, my staff is majority non-aboriginal!" When you, or your people, have not had authority, it's a challenge to realize you have that authority. My mind had been brainwashed by the education system as a child to believe Inuit are less educated and that Inuit cannot hold one of the highest jobs in the country or any job in authority. The staff totally respected me as a minister and that helped me. But inside I had a lot of questions about authority and being in authority. After making decisions and having more experience, I understood authority and my authority as a minister. My survivor blood from my forefathers woke up and I understood where I stood as a leader.

I had two very good staff in my executive office, Brian Menton and Geela Qaqasiq as my secretary. Brian was my executive assistant whom my husband recommended. He worked for education and knew the Territory well. My first day as minister, my secretary Geela said, "Manitok, two staff members are here from your department. They're going to be briefing you." So, the two guys come in and sit right in front of me, introduce themselves.

"Minister Thompson?"

"Yes."

"My name is … from the division of community government. We need a decision on this."

I was nervous but I didn't show it. All I thought was, what if I don't comprehend the English words. As I was reading this paper, a fly flies on top of the page with my face behind the paper. I go like this [makes fly-swatting motion] put it down, and the two guys had disappeared. I went out, "Geela, where did the two guys go?" She said, "They just went running out my office. None of the ministers had ever done that to them before."

A fly taught me about authority that day.

After that incident it was a lot easier to get the bridge for my riding in Coral Harbour (Salliq).

▸▸▸

To some I might be called the Roadkill Lady. For people that didn't see CBC news story, I collect roadkill.[10] I skin them, I tan them, I make them into mitts, and I sell them. Right now, in my garage, I have three beaver skins, three coyote skins, two raccoons drying. I also have a deerskin.

I also skin couches near my office downtown Ottawa, if it's a leather couch. I always have a pocketknife in my purse; I recycle the leather into mitts. I have combined traditional practices and new ways of tanning with the skins I gather. Sometimes I use Neet to take the furs off. I also use the blender to make liquid oil from animal fat for my stone stove – Qulliq.

Our culture and customs have changed so much. We didn't have any birthday parties. We didn't have any Christmas with trees and presents. After Church service, the priests would organize candy throws and games. My family grew up without ever having a birthday party. We are Inuit with a different mindset. When I see a dog, I see a pair of mitts. When I see a leather couch, I see a pair of mitts. We just think differently. Different Elders have different opinions and different experiences from mine.

My beloved father, Mikitok Bruce, has passed on. Four years ago when he was about ninety years old, he was asked to go to school and talk about seals. He looked at me, "How can I talk about seal hunting in half an hour? Seal behaviour and seal hunting is a lifetime to me."

▸▸▸

When I'm given the microphone, I usually talk about the empowerment of the people, the independence of the people, and how equal we are with other races from different countries. I love to empower the youth.

I tell them that our brain is exactly the same size as everybody else's. Because that's what my dad would say. "Your brain is exactly the same size as anybody that you meet down the street anywhere in Canada." I've been in a lot of political situations. I've been trained by my parents to be a survivor. I'm bilingual, bicultural. I can pretty well live anywhere. Down here, I can drive my car and be free down south. I wish all grade twelve Inuit students could be like that. I know that a whole bunch of them at Nunavut Sivuniksavut are able. We're seeing those types of Inuit youth rise up to the challenge of being bilingual and bicultural.

I'm an Inuk. I'm from the People of the Walrus – Aivilingmiut.[11] I'm Inuit, First Canadian. That's who I am. My rights are protected in the human rights of Canada. We're called First Canadians because we were the first ones that landed here, but we are Inuit.

We have a certain way of dressing ourselves. Because a lot of the black and white photos don't have names and we have to give them the tools to know at least where those people come from by looking at their clothing style and also the stitches on the clothing. What we're trying to do is to get youth to talk with the Elders.

We need to get the youth to start talking about their culture. My questions are: What's your Inuktitut name? Who named you? Who is that person?

BRENDAN MANNIK: I'm Brendan Mannik from Baker Lake (Qamani'tuaq) (see Figure 7.5). I have three names. My first Inuktitut name is Uqaut. Uqaut is, I believe my granny's half-brother from my dad's side. Kadjut is my grandpa's name and Ipkarnark is from my mom's grandpa's brother from Chesterfield.

MANITOK THOMPSON: That's who you are. You're not just a no-name Aboriginal. You are not just a no-name Native. You are not just a no-name Indigenous.

SENNA OOLOOYUK: I'm Senna Ilaitutnaaq Oolooyuk from Rankin Inlet (Kangiqliniq).

MANITOK THOMPSON: You have an Inuktitut name? I knew you when you were a baby.

SENNA OOLOOYUK: So, my Inuktitut name, as I said before, is Ilaitutnaaq. I'm named after a very old lady who was known for her persistence. She survived through quite a few famines, shortages of caribou. She was really known for surviving through that starvation. She was also a great seamstress and fisherwoman. I was named after her. She's from the Whale Cove area, Tikiraqjuaq, and she wanted whoever was going to be named after her to be a boy, so I guess that's why.

CANDACE BARNABAS: I'm Candace Barnabas from Arctic Bay (Ikpiarjuk), my Inuktitut name is Qumangaapik, my grandma's sister.

MANITOK THOMPSON: So great.

CATHY PIKUYAK: I'm Cathy Kamuka Qamukkaaq Pikuyak from Hall Beach (Sanirajak). My Inuktitut name is Kamuka and I'm named after my father's brother who drowned in the sea back then, and my father named me after him. Yeah, Kamuka but my dad mostly calls me "Buddy."

JILLIAN KAVIOK: I'm Jillian Howmik Kaviok from Arviat. My Inuktitut name is Howmik and there was a lady named Howmik and my dad was brought to his adopted parents. My dad's adopted mom wanted to thank my dad's mom for giving her my dad, so I'm named after that girl who was a social worker or something. The person who I'm named after, she's living in Sanikiluaq.

DIONE ADAMS: My name's Dione Kijuarpik Adams. I'm from Rankin Inlet. My Inuktitut name is Kijuarpik. I'm named after my mom's uncle. I don't really know why.

MANITOK THOMPSON: I also knew you when you were a little boy. My grandmother is Toota, my grandfather was Jimmy Thom. This is on my mom's side. We're Aivilingmiut, People of the Walrus. My parents: my mom, Tweenaq Kanayuk Bruce, lived in Wager Bay. My father is Mikitok Bruce, from Coral Harbour.

Dick Wager is my step-grandfather. He's Inuk. Iqungajug is his name. He was the first

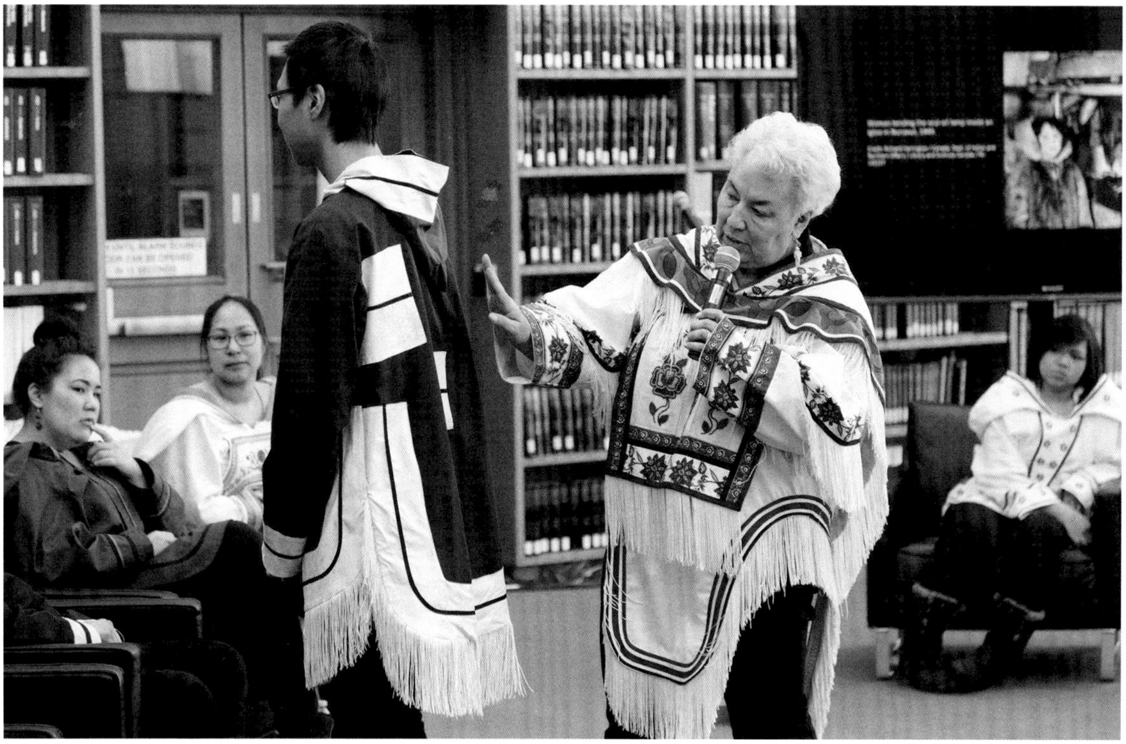

7.5 | Manitok Thompson discussing student Brendan Mannik's parka (Qamani'tuaq). Also present are students Jillian Kaviok of Arviat in red, Cathy Pikuyak of Sanirajak (Hall Beach), and Candace Barnabas of Ikpiarjuk (Arctic Bay). Fifteenth anniversary of Project Naming event, Library and Archives Canada, Ottawa, 2017.

unilingual Inuk manager in the 1940s at the Wager Bay trading post. My mom was born 1925. My grandmother, my mom's mother is Toota. Her father was Miliki. Her mother was Ujaralaaq. Iqungajug's (Dick Wager's) father was Tassiuq and his mother was Tulugaq. I can go to my father's side. Qavangat is his mother and Uppartuuq Tommy Bruce is his father. It's very important we know our family tree.

If you're named after somebody, you're a book of oral information. I'm named after Manitok. She died in 1954 during childbirth with her first baby. Her husband is Mike Bruce Tunalaaq, my dad's younger brother. They called me Manitok. My mom called me Nukaunguq, my sister-in-law. My airainnuk, my father, calls me sister-in-law. That's how I grew up. I was never called a daughter. My dad had a nickname for each of us siblings. He called me his little child, utaraaq. Our oldest sister was utarannaq, a beautiful child.

My mom would say to my father, instead of saying, "Manitok," she would say, "Airainuit (your sister-in-law), the person who you can't call by name, is coming in."

There's a lot more to a name in Inuit culture. That's why if you don't know who you are named after you have cut off a huge history, a family tree. You're responsible for that name.

Because this Manitok grew up, she knows exactly who her namesake was married to … Mike Bruce kept calling me "my wife." Tom Thompson, my husband, called me his wife.[12] But my uncle Mike Bruce called me his wife and I called him my husband since I was a baby. I'm responsible for that name. If I lose that, I've cut off an Inuit encyclopedia. You cannot say, as an Inuk, "I have an Inuktitut name but I don't know where that came from." You have to find out who you are through your namesake. You have to find out your Inuktitut name: who the husband was, who the father was, who the brothers and sisters were, at least. You have to. Because someday you will be standing here as an Elder, in Southern Canada, and probably doing a presentation on the naming system of Inuit. You don't want you to say, "I'm a no name brand."

You will talk about your clothing. What can you remember of that clothing? And where do you think it comes from? Now there's some parkas behind you, one of you guys can talk about them. And as a researcher you cannot say, "She's from Baffin." You cannot say, "that little kid is from Baffin." You have to know what their clothing styles are. Even the kamik.[13] The kamik stitches, very small little stitches. If you see a kamik and you look at the stitches, you would know what region they were stitched. There's a certain stitch you do on the kamik. One is amukattaq, which is a certain way of sewing it. That's a Baffin and Northern Quebec style.

The stitching that has a lot of lines typical of my people. It's called attungituinaaq. If you see their boots you can tell where they're coming from, what area. You can zero in on that area. Those are the people you ask about that photograph. That's what I'm trying to say. The Baffin and Northern Quebec kamik specialize in what we describe in Inuktitut as invisible stitching. No creases on their kamik. That was seen as beauty for them. For my people, a lot of little lines, that was the beauty.

We're going to give the floor to the students now. Who wants to be the first to take this mic and talk about their clothing? Where is your clothing from?

JILLIAN KAVIOK: This was made by Kathy Nateela from Baker Lake (Qamani'tuaq).

MANITOK THOMPSON: This is a Baffin style.[14] This is a happy hood point — we call it a happy thing. Happy hood point tail. Some of them look sad. You don't want a sad one when you're a seamstress. This has to be a happy hood point. This is a Baffin style. This part of the tail must be three fingers. The lady who sewed this knew what she was talking about. The sleeve of the seam is here. The cut of the arm, it starts from here and goes down. This is the original Baffin pattern. With the cut there to there. This is also original, but this is not as common anymore. The strength of the shoulder here is like a strap on a backpack.

BRENDAN MANNIK: This atigi was made from the school I went to, and I believe … that one of the Elders had made it for me for my graduation.

MANITOK THOMPSON: So, it's yours?

BRENDAN MANNIK: Yeah, I brought it from home in Baker [Lake]. I actually don't know the patterns, how it's made. But on the back, there's three different blocks.

MANITOK THOMPSON: This is also very common in the Igloolik area and Kivalliq

Region around Baker Lake. These blocks on the back of the parka have to be a certain length. This has to be here on this top. The middle one has to start here. A little bit down, about an inch. These are made [with] the white fur of the caribou's stomach (pukiq). That's a very traditional area for central Arctic around Kivalliq: Nattilingmiut, Pelly Bay (Arviliqjuaq), Igloolik, even Arctic Bay, Baker Lake, Arviat. Why do we have the fringes? The fringes are to keep the snow from coming in. They help with the snow.

DUSTIN JOANAS: And I'm Dustin Joanas from Kimmirut.

MANITOK THOMPSON: This is also a northern Quebec hood attached to central Inuit clothing style. See this is a traditional Kimmirut style. It's also worn in northern Quebec. It's actually worn just about anywhere now. But it originated from northern Quebec and Baffin, Kukukpaak.[15] There's a little bit of a curve to the hemline. It's not straight. Maybe a southerner, a touristy person, came into town and told the seamstress what to do.

Did you want to talk about your parka? What can you say about your parka?

AMBER NUKADLAAQ: My name is Amber Nukadlaaq from Arviat. My parka comes from the Inuvialuit region.[16]

MANITOK THOMPSON: Who made it for you?

AMBER NUKADLAAQ: I think one of the Elders at Nunavut Sivuniksavut made it.

MANITOK THOMPSON: This is much more common in storybooks and stuff. Because when you see that you know we're talking about Inuit. Look at the hood. If the back was made bigger the little babies would be able to put their little heads in here. The delta braid is cut up. It's from the western Arctic: Inuvik, Aklavik, Kugluktuk, Cambridge Bay (Iqaluktuuttiaq).

SURYA ANGATAJUAK: Hi. I'm Surya Angatajuak from Baker Lake. My tuilli was made by Aupaluktuq from Baker Lake.

MANITOK THOMPSON: Martha's mother.

SURYA ANGATAJUAK: Ii.

MANITOK THOMPSON: For you?

SURYA ANGATAJUAK: Yes.

MANITOK THOMPSON: Sally Webster wears this style. They call it now the Baker Lake tuilli but it's actually my style too.[17] Black and white, darker caribou skin, light caribou skin with some fringes and this is very well made. From traditional patterns. Did somebody make this for you? See the belt? Surya's tuilli's belt has buttons, like mine.[18] But Jillian's parka has a different style belt. Surya's amauti is a baby nursery, a naked baby inside here can go anywhere, even in sixty below. You can nurse it all inside this amauti because it has broad shoulders for your elbow to go up, grab your baby, breastfeed it, and put it back. Jillian's amauti is large enough for an older child. You can carry an older child up to two years old. The baby in Surya's tuilli better learn how to crawl and how to start walking sooner than Jillian's.

Editor's Afterword

Elder Manitok Thompson's contribution is a mixture of stories about her ancestors, stories about her own life, and advice to younger Inuit on how to tell their stories in the future. We see how genealogy is embedded within any story. Her stories are about her Elders, like her grandfather Tassiuq, about who is related to whom, and that knowledge is vital for understanding these tales and Thompson's connection to the stories. The stories she shares are always coloured with an element of resistance and refusal to engage with Qallunaat colonial incursions. Thompson's description of Tassiuq guiding members of the Schwatka expedition has a distinctly different focus from the stories written by the Qallunaat. Tassiuq's choice not to tell the expedition everything – because he would be the one forced to do the physical work – speaks to a moment of resistance where an Inuk made a choice to not support the expedition's mission.

Thompson's story of building a bridge when she was a Government of the Northwest Territories minister speaks to her own reclamation of power. The Inuit concept of ilira is useful here. According to Rosemarie Kuptanna:

> Inuit use ilira to refer to a great fear or awe, such as the awe a strong father inspires in his children or the fear of the Qallunaat [white people] previously held by Inuit ... This relationship, and the feeling of ilira to which it gave rise, meant that whatever the Qallunaat suggested or wanted was likely to be done ... In this cultural setting, a challenge to the authority of the Qallunaat or defiance of their requests was almost unthinkable.[19]

Elder Manitok Thompson's story of self-empowerment and a reversal of power roles is especially significant. After decades of Qallunaat undermining Inuit autonomy, and despite her private feelings of intimidation, she reversed the dynamic and created a feeling of ilira in the Qallunaat staff.

All these stories, told from an uncompromisingly Inuk perspective, finally leads to Thompson's conversation with Inuit youth from Nunavut Sivuniksavut. On one level, this portion of the conversation is a lesson in vestiary history of Inuit. In so doing, she is teaching students about who they are, why their Inuit names matter and why they need to understand their roots and foundation of their communities, which is expressed in the precise, small details of community parka designs. Thompson is compelling these youth to become the future leaders of Nunavut, but to be leaders in the future, they must understand their past.

NOTES

1 "Looks like a doll."

2 Manitok Thompson explained that this second song was a bilingual wordplay, using the English endearment "cutie patutie" and then Inuktizing it. Thompson in conversation with Payne, 2018.

3 Some of Thompson's ancestors' stories are "Qulittalik's Story" and her mother's recollections, which are recorded in Pelly, *Ukkusiksalik*, 141–52, 174–8, 202–12.

4 Tweenaq's story is about Iqungajuq assisting Lt Frederick Schwatka's 1878–80s search for the lost Franklin Expedition. Pelly, *Ukkusiksalik*, 155–65. See also, Schwatka, *The Search for Franklin.*

5 This is Heinrich Klutschak, who published a German-language account of the Schwatka expedition, *Als Eskimo under den Eskimos*. An English translation is Klutschak and Barr, *Overland to Starvation Cove.*

6 See also Thompson, "Don't Just Think About It, Do It!" in McComber and Partridge, *Arnait Nipingit*.

7 Father Duplain established a Catholic mission at Southampton Island in 1926. Luke Kidlapik, an Inuk Anglican catechist, was actively preaching in Salliq from 1924 until his death in 1954. He was trained by Rev. Edmund Peck and Bishop Flemming. Christianity is an important faith to many Inuit to this day and it, with the older Inuit beliefs and shamanism, has been integrated into Inuit culture and Traditional Knowledge. Harper, "Inuit Catechists at Blacklead Island – Part 2"; Laugrand and Oosten, *Inuit Shamanism and Christianity*.

8 Manitok Thompson was elected to the NWT Legislature for the riding of Aivilik where she held cabinet portfolios of minister of municipal and community affairs and was responsible for the Women's Directorate. Thompson was re-elected in 1999, the only woman elected in Nunavut's first election. She was the minister of community government and transportation and had held the portfolios of minister of education, human resources, and Arctic College.

9 Thompson, "Don't Just Think About It, Do It!"

10 Hwang, "Inuk Woman in Ottawa-Area Uses Traditional Know-How."

11 People from the area around Salliq on Southampton Island, Kivalliq Region.

12 As Manitok Thompson noted, naming a baby after a deceased person and seeing characteristics of the deceased in the child, "is a way to ease the pain when someone is lost, to see a baby named after that person enjoying the same things. It's a way of remembering that person and it helps ease the pain of missing that person. We say 'atiqsurtuq': like his/her namesake." Thompson in conversation with Payne, 2018.

13 For more on the importance of sewing, see Williamson, "Sewing in Arviat."

14 Though Kathy Nateela is from Baker Lake, the style of amauti she sewed has its origins on Baffin Island. The Baffin Island–style amautis are very popular in Kivalliq and frequently worn when packing a child, rather than the historical style worn by women in Kivalliq, called a tuilli.

15 The point of the hood.

16 Region in the western Arctic.

17 Amauti is a women's parka with a pouch in the back of the garment to carry a small child.

18 Tuilli is an amauti with broad, rounded shoulders that originated from the Kivalliq region; all tuillis are amautis, but not all amautis are tuillis. Williamson, "Attatsiaq," in *Uninvited*, 68–73.

19 Kuptana, "Ilira," 7.

CHAPTER 8

"A story about names"

Ann Meekitjuk Hanson

In conversation with Atsajuk Ituangat (Robert Joseph Flanagan), Jackson Meekitjuk Sagiatuq Hanson, and Robert Donald Malituq Hanson Comeau

Keemalu was perhaps one of the first Inuit women to receive a non-Inuit name in the early 1800s. Her new first name was Annie. The whaling captain could not remember her Inuit name, so he began to call her Annie. Thus, many of us Annies all over southern Baffin Island are named after her. Annie Keemalu was my great-great-grandmother.

This story is about names, Inuit names, non-Inuit names, how and why newborn babies were named by grandparents, Elders of importance, midwives, and close relatives. It's also about the meanings behind the names, keeping Oral History alive through names, *Inuktized* names, created names to get to Heaven, and why religious names were readily accepted. How Inuit created names for the newcomers, the Qallunaat.

We were straying away from so many Inuit cultural matters, Oral History, survival skills, the language, animal skin cleaning skills, sewing skills, storytelling, legends, throat singing, games, traditional songs, country food preparations, traditional recipes, and all

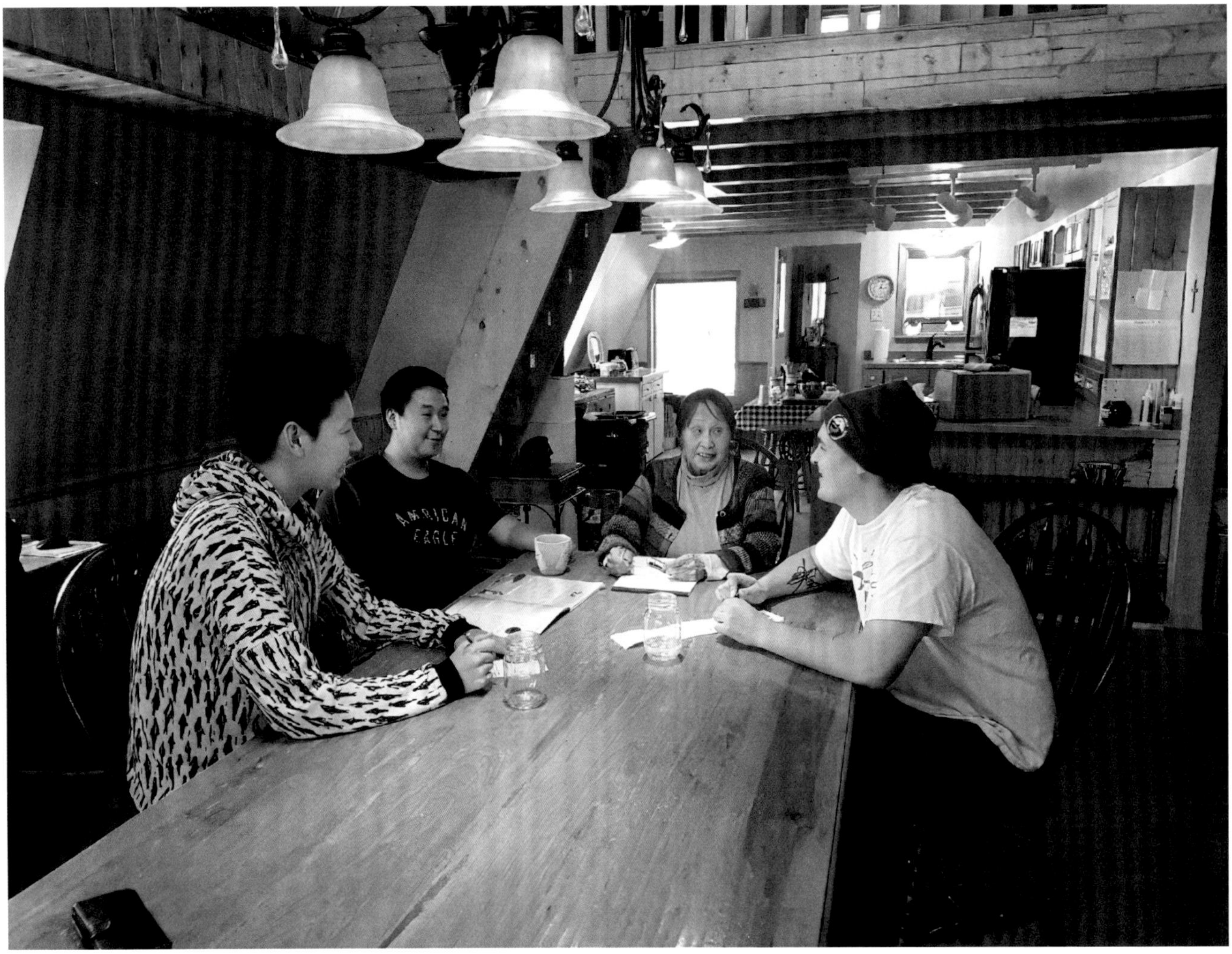

8.1 | Ann Meekitjuk Hanson in conversation with Atsajuk Ituangat (Robert Joseph Flanagan), Jackson Meekitjuk Sagiatuq Hanson, and Robert Donald Malituq Hanson Comeau, Apex, Nunavut, 2018.

things pertaining to Inuit way of life. We were in school all day learning another culture. When we learned to read and write English, it was very attractive and available. We had one book at home, *The Holy Bible,* in syllabics.[1] One element of our very own identity was in danger of being left behind, naming babies. This was a very sad time for our Elders, parents, and the Inuit community who didn't go to school. Some of us were even naming our newborn babies in English. Some of us even stopped consulting our people to name the babies. We picked names we liked, picked names from movies, books we had read, and soap operas once we had television programs. The foreign names we picked were impossible to pronounce or to remember by our people.

Fortunately, I was able to realize this dilemma before most Inuit names were overtaken by non-Inuit names. I interviewed an Elder, Leah Nutaraq, for CBC Inuktitut programs. She was more than delighted and grateful for the opportunity to express her concern. She talked about how names were picked after the baby was born. Leah said names were picked after deceased relatives, with great respect, good meaning, long life, good health, prosperity, history, and tradition in mind. Once the name or names were picked and agreed to, often the midwife named the baby. The midwife was considered to be one of the most important persons in the baby's life because while naming the baby, she made good wishes, predictions, high hopes, and wishes for a good life. For example, when she was naming the baby and if the baby was male, she said, "May you be a good hunter, good husband, great leader, generous, and wise." For the female baby, she said, "May you have beautiful long hair, may you be a good woman, good wife and mother. May you be generous and wise like your mother and grandmother." In the southern Baffin Island dialect, the midwife became the male baby's arnaaqutiga, meaning "my woman." When the boy becomes a hunter, his first harvested animal went to his arnaaqutiga. The midwife calls the baby boy she delivered her agusiaq: "the male I made." For the girl, the midwife becomes sanajiga, "my maker." When the girl became a good seamstress, the first garment went to her sanajiga, first fish, first ptarmigan, and anything worth giving. The midwife calls the baby girl she delivered arnaliara: "the girl I made."

Throughout our life, we are reminded of our names, several names. My names are Pilitaq, "the given one"; Palluq, my maternal grandmother's name; and Inusiq, "the life." I remember one Elder calling me "my grandmother." She was referring to the name Pilitaq. Apparently, her grandmother's name was Pilitaq. The Elder's name was Arnaquasaq, meaning "elderly woman." When I was named Annie, it was in reference to Keemalu, although the person naming me didn't say Keemalu. Everyone knew it was Annie Keemalu. When I was going to school in Toronto in the early 1960s, I was given yet another name, Ann, by my foster mom, Kathleen Cotterill. I liked it because there were too many girls named Annie in Baffin Island.

Throughout Inuit history, names were created to suit the times. For example, after Christianity was introduced and many Inuit were converting, names pertaining to belief and faith were aptly created: Aalutuq (looking up to the skies), Sagiatuq (converting), Majuriaq (way to go up), Gutiliaq (going to God), Qaumajuq (bright light), Qaumataq (being lit), Isuqangituq (eternity), and there are so many others that are being used today, too many to list. These names didn't exist before Christianity. Why did the Inuit create these names? Did they feel closer to God? To Heaven? Who did they want to please the most? God or the priest? We don't know.

In the early 1970s, I translated *People from Our Side*, a book by Peter Pitseolak with Dorothy Harley Eber. He talks about names in one section:

> When I was growing up I knew people who changed names as often as they felt like it – without being baptized. They were always looking for better names. When we started to be able to read the Bible, people would pick names from the Bible and say, "Maybe, if I have this name, God will save me." If people could not read the Bible, someone who would pick a name for them. It didn't

> always have to be Mosessee. They'd pick names that were related to the Bible. There was Kumwartok ("going up"), Kaka ("hills"), 'Gootilliaktuk ("going to God").[2] There was one family with a Namoonie ("where can I hide myself?"). He was married to Kumwartok ("up to God"). Their daughter was Samayo ("peacemaker"). One family had Nuna ("land"), Panni ("up"), and Tapanni. Together, their names could mean, "We will meet up there in a beautiful land." This all started in Frobisher Bay … the Frobisher Bay people were first.[3]

When Peter Pitseolak mentioned Mosessee, he meant Moses in the Bible. Biblical names were used as first names when people were baptized. James became Jaimisi; Paul, Paulusi; John, Joanasi; Abel, Aipilli; Cain, Kaini; Ruth, Uluti; Martha, Matta; Mary, Miali; Rebecca, Ulipika; Peter, Pita; Juda, Juta or Jutai; and so on. These names were readily accepted because they were given by the minister. The early Anglican ministers were given names, too. Uqamak, meaning "fluent in speech," was Rev. E.J. Peck. Ilataq; "new relative," was Rev. J.W. Bilby; Inutaqauq, "the new Inuk," was Rev. Archibald Fleming. There are many more examples of ministers with Inuit names across the Arctic.

The newcomers weren't the only ones giving names. The Inuit created new names for the Qallunaat, since we couldn't pronounce their names very well. The names were describing the looks or the mannerism of the person. For example, I remember Qingaluk, "big nose"; Qauraluk, "big forehead"; Ijiki, "small eyes." Ijiki was a famous translator for the Inuit and non-Inuit and his name was Leo Manning. Uqumiatujaq, "looks like he is eating something" or Pallualuk, "slanted eyes": this person was Henry Larsen in the RCMP. Natsili, "one who has a seal skin jacket"; Nalati, "person who listens to radios"; or Igaturalaq, "person with small eyeglasses": this person was Bernard Hantzsch, a German explorer who collected flowers and plants. Angijuqaruluk, "poor little boss," was Gordon Rennie, an HBC manager in Kimmirut in the 1950s, who still lives in Iqaluit. There are many more. Some knew their names in Inuktitut and appreciated them, some didn't because they didn't speak the language. In the earlier days, the newcomers always learned Inuktitut and became fluent, when they stayed for more than a year.

Inuit who are named after famous Inuit will keep our Oral History alive. Names like Tuqulituq (Tookoolito): she and her husband Ipibik (Ebierbing) sailed with Charles Francis Hall during his Arctic research expeditions in the 1800s. Hall probably named Tuqulituq; Hannah, and Ipibik; Joe, with endearment, since they are known as Hannah and Joe in the history books, as in *Life among the Esquimaux*.[4] These two people helped Hall a great deal, teaching him survival skills, how to eat our food to stay strong, navigating the unchartered Arctic waters, teaching him about the land, the islands, shallow areas of the seas, and clothed him with lifesaving garments. Names like Annie Keemalu and her husband Janibu (Johnnybow, from John Bull): these two people helped the whalers in the Cumberland Sound,[5] showing the whalers where there might be more whales, earning material items as payment from the whalers and sharing them with others to make life more comfortable in the harsh climate. Names of famous artists in the more modern times: Qinuajuaq, Kananginaq, Aksangajuq, Atsajuq Ituangat, Majuriaq, Okpik, Pisiulaq, Qajurajuk, Pautaq, and so many more. Some ancient names are gone now because they weren't used after the person died.

▸▸▸

Recently, I sat down with three young men, our grandsons. We talked about their Inuit and non-Inuit names and recorded them with their cell phones. Here is the edited version of the transcribed session:

ANN MEEKITJUK HANSON: I am writing a story about how we, Inuit, name our babies after they are born. The story is for Carleton University and for you, the youth so you may continue the tradition. The naming system is tradition, some of it is still in use. There are some that are no longer in use. I will answer all your questions. We will start with Joe on my right. Joe, who are you and who named you.

ROBERT JOSEPH ATSAJUK ITUANGAT FLANAGAN: My full name is Robert Joseph Flanagan. My Inuk name is Atsajuk Ituangat. My mother is Quvianatukuluk and my father Darrin. My father's middle name is Joseph, that's why my first name tends to be Joey.

ANN MEEKITJUK HANSON: Who named you Atsajuk Ituangat?

ROBERT JOSEPH ATSAJUK ITUANGAT FLANAGAN: My biological mother Helen in Panituuq (Pangnirtung) asked if one of my names could be Atsajuk Ituangat before giving me up to be adopted by Quvianatukuluk and Darrin Flanagan. It was already arranged that I'd be adopted. I was born in Panituuq. Helen's wish was granted and appreciated. So, that's my Inuk name, Ituangat. I only know that he, Ituangat, was an Inuk whaler.

ANN MEEKITJUK HANSON: He was more than that. Ituangat is very famous among us Inuit, the Elders, and the North. He was also a health care worker, working with Dr Otto Shaeffer in the 1930s, '40s, and '50s. He guided and helped Dr Shaeffer when he had to go on medical checkups along the coast of Cumberland Sound, visiting all the winter homes of Inuit. He taught Dr Shaeffer Inuktitut and he became fluent. They became friends for life. Yes, Ituangat was also known as an Inuk whaler. We used to interview him for CBC Inuktitut programs. One of his funny stories is about the time he was asked to be the cook for the whalers. He never cooked before but agreed to the job because he wanted to be one of the whalers. His first job was to make coffee. He had never seen coffee, let alone have it or make it! He was too embarrassed to ask anyone so he just went ahead and made coffee. It was so strong and no one drank it. He practised and practised when no one was looking. In time, the coffee became drinkable. He was in his early teens when he became one of the whalers. Ituangat is also known to be very kind. He is well remembered by those who met him and he received the Order of Canada in his later years.[6]

ROBERT JOSEPH ATSAJUK ITUANGAT FLANAGAN: He is my biological great-grandfather, my biological mother's grandfather.[7] I am very proud to have his name as my name. The only way to continue his name is to use it. The name connects me to his family, to my Inuk identity, to history and I feel connected to [the] tradition of naming. So good to know more about him. I didn't know he was also a health care worker or that he received [the] Order of Canada. Wow!

ANN MEEKITJUK HANSON: If you want to know more about Atsajuk Ituangat, talk to his relatives, friends, or Elders in Panituuq, they know so much about him. He did so much to teach, contribute, and inspire people in general.

Ituangat means "their Elder." It's a lovely name and very unforgettable. I will find out what Atsajuk means and let you know.

Jack, who are you and who named you?

JACKSON MEEKITJUK SAGIATUQ HANSON: My mother named me. Jackson was my grandfather Bob Hanson's uncle, we call him Pa. Meekitjuk was your father. Sagiatuq had just passed away before I was born so my mother picked this name. I don't know too much about Sagiatuq.

ANN MEEKITJUK HANSON: Yes, Jackson was your great uncle on your Pa's side. Your second name Meekitjuk was my father. Your other Inuk name Sagiatuq was a family relative, a relative but not close relative. He was known to be a natural comedian. He made people laugh. He used to play Santa Claus in the 1960s because he was jolly. He made a good Santa. Sagiatuq worked at a garage, and as a driver, a mechanic, a bus driver, and a heavy equipment driver. Since one of his co-workers could not pronounce his name properly, he called him Charlie, so he came to be known as Charlie Sagiatuq. Sagiatuq means "converting to Christianity." Meekitjuk means "tends to be humble." My father Meekitjuk was known to be very kind, feeding and clothing orphans, generous, always helping. He worked for the Americans during the Second World War. The Americans hired Inuit as guides to travel by dog teams, since the soldiers didn't know how to run dog teams, travelling on the land or sea ice, during their patrols.

JACKSON MEEKITJUK SAGIATUQ HANSON: I am also very proud to have an Inuk name. It makes me feel closer to the family of Sagiatuq. The family members are always happy to see me. Sometimes I wonder what would have happened if I didn't have an Inuk name. Maybe I wouldn't have as much connection to the family, the Inuit, the traditions, history, or Inuit way of life. Having an Inuk name connects me to Sagiatuq too, a person I've never met, connects me to community and its people, yet living in modern times.

ANN MEEKITJUK HANSON: Who are you and who named you?

ROBERT DONALD MALITUQ HANSON COMEAU: I was named after my Aunt Quvianatukuluk's firstborn Robert, who was named after our Pa, grandfather Robert Hanson, your husband. Quvianatukuluk's son Robert passed away, unfortunately, at birth. His name was to be Robert, had he lived. My parents named me and you named me Malituq. Donald was my grandfather, on my father's side. So, technically I am named after Robert Lyle Hanson, who we call Pa. I believe Malituq was your uncle.

ANN MEEKITJUK HANSON: Yes, one of them. There were many brothers and one sister. The eldest was Qapik, Meekitjuk, Yutai, Kutuq, Shuu, Malituq, and Ningiurapik. I was told these people were hard workers and productive. That's why you like making qajait (kayaks). They were very good in wood, they loved wood. They would scrounge around the shoreline after a big storm looking for driftwood. Your namesake Malituq had polio as a boy, that's why he couldn't walk very well all his life. Yet, he still worked hard. He never married. He was shy of his feet because they were deformed by polio. He would never take off his kamik (seal skin boots).

ROBERT DONALD MALITUQ HANSON COMEAU: It is always important to introduce myself as Malituq. When we were living in the South because my father got transferred, as an RCMP member, I used to introduce myself as Malituq and the Qallunaat would not understand that, so I had to say I am Robert. When I would introduce myself as Malituq, it reminded me of home, way up North. It connected me to the North, even though we were very far away from home. You taught me to introduce myself starting with my parents and grandparents. I've done this [a] few times at meetings. Twice, two people have come forward to tell me that he/she is my relative and that he/she knows my parents and grandparents! Works really well.

ANN MEEKITJUK HANSON: Thank you, Bob Don! I call you Bob Don from Robert Donald. Any questions from any of you?

JACKSON MEEKITJUK SAGIATUQ HANSON: Does using non-Inuit names hurt Inuit culture? Is using Inuit names as second names hurt?

ANN MEEKITJUK HANSON: Yes, it does hurt the Inuit culture, history too. It is disheartening and disappointing if we completely stop using Inuit names.

JACKSON MEEKITJUK SAGIATUQ HANSON: How about using names like Mary, making it into Miali and so on with many other names like Elizabeth, Elisapi, Martha, Matta …?

ANN MEEKITJUK HANSON: We call this Inutizing names from other cultures, like you said, Mary – Miali, Ruth – Uluti, Solomon – Salumuni, Mark – Makusi, Jessie – Siasi, and so on. This is all very fine with us Elders because it at least sounds like Inuktitut! This was started way back in my great-great-grandmother's time and it continues today.

▸▸▸

After learning more about their heritage names, the young men went away wanting to know more about Inuit names and their meanings.

I come from Keemalu, who had Kalajuk, Kalajuk's father was a Scottish whaling captain, John Burnet Walker. Kalajuk had Palluq, Palluq had Uqsiut, who was known as Josie, my mother. Our daughters are Kathleen Helen Josie, Mary Elizabeth, Quvianatukuluk Jennifer, Udloriak, and Neevee.

My absolute favourite Inuktitut name? Nitani, pronounced Neetanee. Nitani is just a name. There is no known meaning. It is so rare that I have known only one woman had this name. She was from Cape Dorset [Kinngait] and has died since. Every time we would meet over the years, I would tell Nitani "you have the best name in all the North!" and then we would break out in great laughter. If no one uses this as a first name, it will disappear and be nothing but a mere memory.

Editors' Afterword

In her contribution to this volume, Elder Ann Meekitjuk Hanson traces the meanings and histories of naming within Inuit culture that are central to Project Naming. Unlike most of the contributions to this volume and Project Naming as a whole, this essay does not explicitly use photographs as memory prompts or testimonial objects. Yet, Hanson's focus on Inuit names as generational connections reflects key precepts of Project Naming.

A writer, former broadcaster, and commissioner of Nunavut (from 2005 to 2010), Hanson is a vivid storyteller. Here she uses that narrative skill to tell a story about names that ranges from a discussion of the importance of family and midwives in naming to "the meanings behind the names, keeping Oral History alive through names, *Inuktized* names, created names to get to Heaven and why religious names were readily accepted." Hanson's narrative is in the tradition of "unikkaatuaq," which Louis-Jacques Dorais has defined as "narrating events that happened recently or in the not-too-distant past."[8] Although often described as strictly speaking from personal experience, Keavy Martin has argued that "unikkaatuat form a separate genre from life stories ... it is necessary and acceptable to speak of things beyond one's experience."[9] Indeed, here Hanson shows how every story is part of a longer chain of stories. For example, she narrates her discovery and reclamation of Inuit naming traditions by recounting stories she learned by interviewing Elder Leah Nutaraq and by translating the words of Peter Pitseolak.[10] Like those narratives within narratives, Inuit names are also stories within stories: each name speaking of a profound connection to another, across generations. In the final section of this contribution, Hanson explicitly demonstrates that intergenerational connection by speaking with her three grandsons about the histories of their names. Here she also provides a model of Inuit pedagogy, in which younger generations learn by observation and listening.

NOTES

1 Moravian missionary Friedrich Erdmann completed the first version of a Bible in roman orthography in Labradormiutut in 1869. John Horden and E.A. Watkins of the Church Missionary Society adapted the Cree Syllabarium in the 1850s at Fort George and Little Whale River. Rev. Edmund James Peck used this foundation to translate the New Testament starting in the late 1870s. Peck published the four gospels in 1912 and the Psalms in 1917. The book that Ann Hanson describes here is likely the New Testament translated by Rev. Peck. Erdmann, *Testamentetotak: Josuab Aglanginit*; Peck, *The Four Gospels*; Peck, *The New Testament*; Peck, *The Book of Psalms*; Harper, "Inuktitut Syllabic Orthography"; Nowak, "The 'Eskimo Language' of Labrador"; Bassler, *Vikings to U-Boats*, 44.

2 Ann Hanson explains that "Different spellings reflect changes in the way that names and words are spelled in Inuktitut. Gootiliak is a good example. Gootiliak is an old spelling when we didn't know how to spell properly at the time. Today we have changed the spelling on many Inuktitut words and names. Today we spell it Gutiliaq, to pronounce it better."

3 Pitseolak and Eber, *People from Our Side*, 61.

4 Hall, *Arctic Researches*.

5 John Bull is a personification of Englishness and British imperialism, similar to the Uncle Sam of the United States. The character was invented in 1712 by John Arbuthnot, the queen's physician. Taylor, "Bull, John."

6 Ituangat, Aksayook of Pangnituuq was appointed as a member of the Order of Canada in 1995.

7 After checking with Joey's biological parents in Panituuq, we have since learned that Joey's biological father, Jutani, says that his great uncle was Aksaajuq Etuangat, which I've been spelling Atsajuq Ituangat. It is not unusual to have different spellings in our names. But this is okay because the terms are the same for great-great-uncle and great-great-grandfather in Inuktitut, silapiruq. The same goes for great-great-grandmother and great-great-aunt.

8 The subtitle of this volume is derived from the root of this word, unikkaat. Dorais, *The Language of the Inuit*, 162–3.

9 Martin, *Stories in the New* Ski, 112.

10 Pitseolak and Eber, *People from Our Side*. Ann Meekitjuk Hanson translated Pitseolak's manuscript.

CHAPTER 9

"I have many names"

David Serkoak in conversation with Deborah Kigjugalik Webster

DAVID SERKOAK: I have many names. Our grandparents, and fathers, but even my age group just go by one name. All Inuit. It was very important to get that name. That's your only name for the rest of your life.

When my parents named me Hiquaq, I'm sure they were very careful. Who is Hiquaq? Who was Hiquaq? I was lucky. In 2007, when one of my Elders from Arviat, Mary Anowiak, visited Ottawa and said, "David, I want to record some songs for you. Your pihiq (song), your father's, your mother's, and your grandfather." Because of this, I was able to connect that song to my namesake. Hiqralaaq had a song, and that song is one that I inherited. Now it's mine. And I have a granddaughter, also named after me. She is also a co-owner of the song. And when I go away, then she will become the sole owner of the song. And that's how they pass on things.

Ataatavit
Pihiit nipiliulaulaka
Ataatatsiaqpillu
anaanavillu

During the course of growing up, we were moved towards the Hudson Bay coast. My name was also changing a lot at that time. My traditional name was replaced by E1–602. Then when we moved to the coast, probably in 1959, during a brief stay in Rankin [Inlet] (Kangiqliniq), just before we moved to Whale Cove (Tikirarjuq), that's when Armand Tagoona gave my family Christian names.[1] That's where my whole family was given "Andy," "Mary," "Silas," "Winnie," and "David."

And then after that, Project Surname came along towards the late sixties and early seventies when the government said that all the Inuit have to use a surname like they do in the South.[2] That's when the government-appointed Abraham Okpik who travelled in the Eastern Arctic in every Inuit community, visited every household, asked the same question. And "David Serkoak," "Silas," and "Andy Miki" came to be. One father, two brothers: we each have a different surname. When Abraham Okpik asked

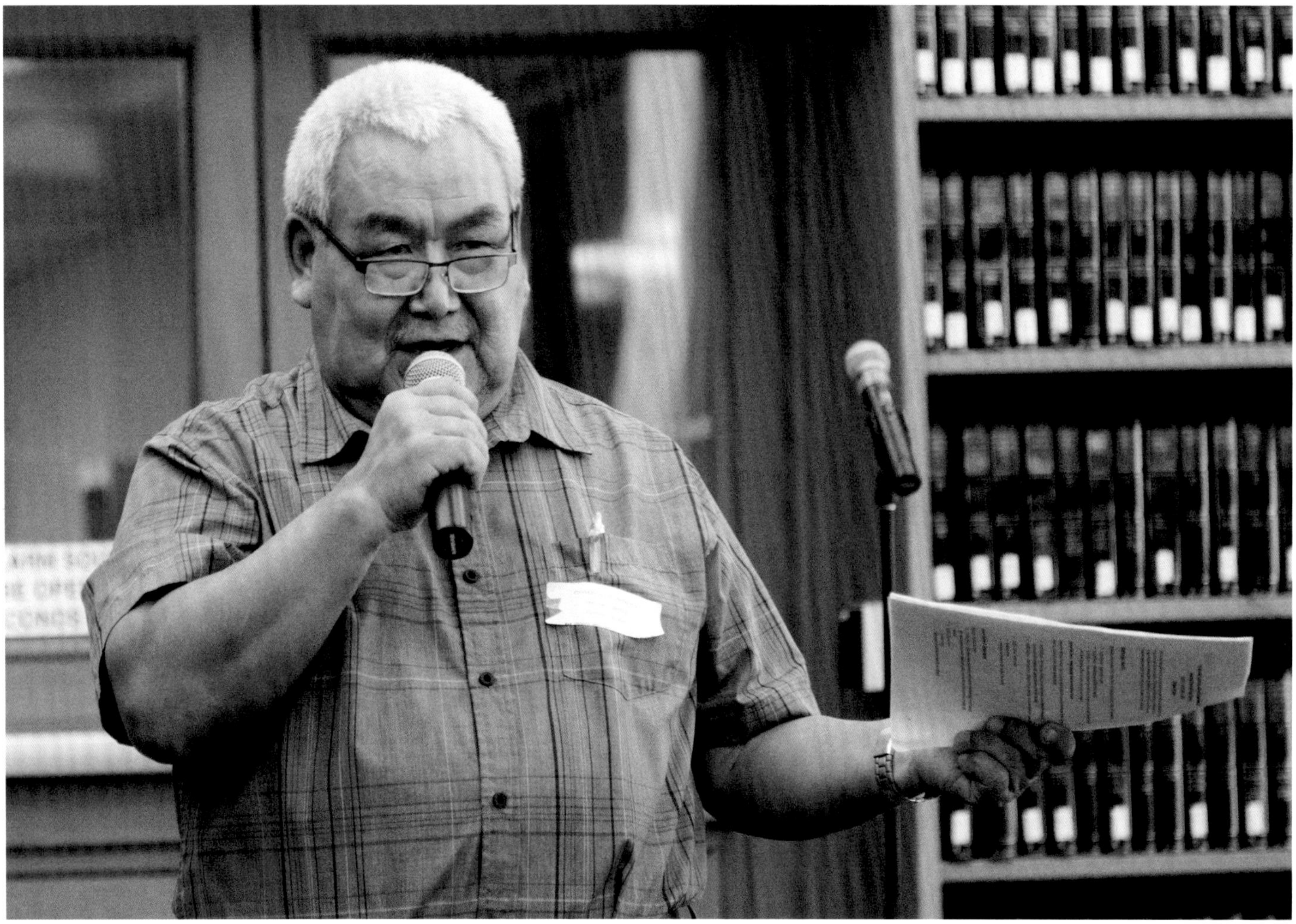

9.1 | David Serkoak speaking at the fifteenth anniversary of Project Naming event, Ottawa, 2017.

us [what names we chose], I guess my father wanted to go by "Miki" because that's his real name. Miki Andy. When my brother was asked the same question, now he became "Silas." He probably said, my name is "Silas Illungiayok," on the same day, I'm pretty sure. Then it was my turn to pronounce my name "Hiquaq." I didn't want to go by "Miki." Miki is my father's name, not mine. So, I was known as David Serkoak. This was in mid-1960s in Whale Cove. And it's still my name today. Verbally, you pronounce it "Hiquaq." My teachers at the time kind of pronounced "H,"[3] so, my name was written "Serkoak" today but orally everyone back in Arviat calls me Hiquaq.

Just before I got married, all of my documents were sort of mixed up all the time: "David," "Miki," "David Serkoak." Just before I got married or soon after, we hired a lawyer [and] got all of my government documents under the name "David Serkoak."

DEBORAH KIGJUGALIK WEBSTER: You know, this is funny how today in 2019 we are here talking about your name. Because when I was a kid, the first time I met you, my dad told me ... we are going to meet my friend, David Serkoak. And I said, but your name is David, too. He said, yes. And I said, well, what if we are going to get mixed up? And he said, well, you can give him another name. So, I called you "David X."

DAVID SERKOAK: I still call myself "David X" today.

DEBORAH KIGJUGALIK WEBSTER: It sticks!

DAVID SERKOAK: Right up to today. I have lots of funny names. Being a teacher, sometimes they call me "David the Great," "David X," and "Super Dave." All those kinds of things. I don't mind. Some people have called me worse names before.

avaaq

DAVID SERKOAK: Everyone was encouraged to go to church on Sundays. I don't know who told me that but I think either Armand Tagoona was trying to get Hiquaq to go to church. They probably made a few visits to Hiquaq. Someone told me that one of the church officials was telling him how God and Jesus made everything. Everything you see. Not knowing this, Hiquaq said, Boy, he's good!

DEBORAH KIGJUGALIK WEBSTER: Was Hiquaq a shaman?

DAVID SERKOAK: I don't know. But we had a shaman in the group, but he died en route from Ennadai Lake.[4] He was one of the first people to die. Starved, maybe, maybe not. But that's my own theory. It's almost like he lost his power due ... That's my own thinking. Now, he's nobody maybe. Maybe he did starve. I don't know. People were starving. But at the time, we were short of food all the time. Usually, he would, in that situation ... other men or families still managed to share food. I am sure that they would have shared with him, but I don't know. Maybe, he starved. I always think, maybe he did but also sort of gave up. I don't know. But if ... I was reading about other relocations to the High Arctic, some person died in the same way. I am not sure if he starved, too, or ... it's almost giving up life ...

DEBORAH KIGJUGALIK WEBSTER: Like your avaaq, do you go to church?

DAVID SERKOAK: No. Occasionally, if I have to or with friends. And I am not sure when we became Christianized, whether we liked it or not. At first, growing up, I really believed in going to church and stuff. I really believed what I heard at church. A second coming and all that stuff. I gave money at the end of the service. Be nice on Sundays. Don't sin. I really believed that growing up. But during my adolescent years … those beliefs sort of faded away and I guess that's the time I was getting towards I was not sure where to go on my own life … at a crossroads. Until I got myself educated through adult education like your dad [to Deborah]. My math and English started to climb up and after testing where I am at, that gave me some sort of education in my pocket. Then I lived life on my own. And from there on, although all my age group, my friends, become good Christians. I never did. And I find it hard to find an answer why.

Before we moved, we were just Inuit and I guess I am partly that. I am not sure if I would be a good Christian. I don't know. And I am comfortable enough like what I am today. After my adolescence, I didn't go to church every Sunday … and I am still the same. Maybe my name has a connection [to this].

DEBORAH KIGJUGALIK WEBSTER: That's what I think … The traits or the things that your namesakes share and how we inherit them.

DAVID SERKOAK: I am most comfortable when I am away on the land. [It is] more comforting than being in church, for me. I find peace. I find quietness when I am out there. That is why, in all my teaching years, it's almost like counselling for me, being on the land. Sometimes, I would pack on Thursday. After the bell on Friday, I am on the trail for a day or two. Then when I am out there, I don't think about the schools, grumpy teachers, all those things. I forget about home problems. I think that's how I was right up to today.

DEBORAH KIGJUGALIK WEBSTER: Do you take after your avaaq in other ways?

DAVID SERKOAK: Sometimes, I think at the time, he is planting stuff for me … what I should be like when I'm an adult, kind of thing. I also have another avaaq. She's a lady. She also plays a role in how I should be like as an adult. A combination of the two. You should make sure that you share food, be friendly … but they always tell me, you should be better than me. You should be more outgoing; you should look after yourself. All those things.

DEBORAH KIGJUGALIK WEBSTER: When we name, we always want the person being named to be better, right?

DAVID SERKOAK: Be more outgoing, do the right thing, do the right thing for others. Those kinds of encouragements.

DEBORAH KIGJUGALIK WEBSTER: To have strengths that the namer did not have. To be stronger.

DAVID SERKOAK: Those things always come back … not unknowingly, they are a part of me.

▸▸▸

DAVID SERKOAK: Name-searching is very important. My three daughters. They are adults. They were in the age frame where they don't know where their names came from. They just know that they each have an Inuk name.

I took my three grandsons to Arviat. First two asked, "Are we going hunting?" Basically, this trip was to get them to see my late parents' graves and to learn where their names come from. Both of my grandsons were named after my late father: Miki and Ulaayok. So, we visited and they connected.

I also took my three oldest granddaughters back to Arviat … and visited the graveyard where their great-grandparents, grandmother and … Qahuq, my late mother. I think my granddaughter visited her grave, seven or eight years earlier but at fourteen, it was more meaningful. It was the granddaughters' turn to visit Arviat and hunt and fish. They have many cousins. My brother has lots of kids and all of their daughters have lots of kids. I think close to fifty. They met their cousins for the first time. I am sure that the Arviat cousins were quite curious about these urban cousins coming from Ottawa. What they look like, how they talk, and that sort of thing … a fun week.

I try to do this because when I was young, I never had a chance to make … all the connections with my history and important stuff like naming. So, I try to make sure my grandchildren have a better experience.

Editors' Afterword

In "'I have many names,'" Inuk Elder and educator David Serkoak talks about the history of his name. A southern reader might expect such a narrative to be very brief and straightforward. For example, we might imagine a Qallunaaq simply saying, "This is what I am called. Here is who I am called after." But for Inuit, naming is rarely so linear.[5] A name and the act of naming cut to the core of Inuit cultural identity and generational connections. At the same time, the names of Elders also often trace the difficult histories of interactions with southern institutions. In these ways, Inuit names speak of community connections, transcultural contacts, and multiple identities. Identifying these connections – reinforcing Inuit bonds even while testifying to southern-led cultural disruptions – is particularly important for Serkoak. Since the 1980s, he has used his skills as an educator, speaker, and activist to draw attention to the history of the Ahiarmiut people and their forced relocations between 1950 and 1960.[6] The history of David Serkoak's name is also a history of that struggle.

He was named at birth for Hiquaq or Hiqralaaq, developing characteristics associated with that Elder, his avaaq/atiq. Hiquaq and another avaaq guided him, planning for their namesake's adulthood. Soon after, a government-issued disc number became a kind of name by which he was known in governmental records. Later still, the Biblical name David was added. Under Project Surname, Abraham Okpik visited his family, and each family member chose a last name. Once in school, the spelling of Hiquaq, now his surname, changed, again, to reflect the teachers' pronunciation of Hiquaq as Serkoak. And to avoid confusion in governmental paperwork, all of these identities became legalized as "David Serkoak." All of these names, all of these identities, remain with him today as he tells the stories of the names and seeks out his grandchildren's names to animate those histories and strengthen those bonds. At the same time, these stories illuminate the history of the Ahiarmiut. As David Serkoak eloquently summarizes, "I have many names."

NOTES

1 Armand Tagoona (1926–1991) was born in Naujaat to Hannah Aaluluuq Siksik and a Qallunnaq father. He was born a Catholic and converted to the Anglican faith. In 1969, he founded a new religious group in Qamani'tuaq, the Arctic Christian Fellowship. This was arguably the first Inuit church he established. Tagoona, "Our Move to Qamanittuaq in 1938"; Tagoona, *Shadows*; Laugrand and Laneuville, "Armand Tagoona and the Arctic Christian Fellowship."

2 Alia, *Names, Numbers, and Northern Policy*.

3 The dialect in David Serkoak's community uses the "h" sound in place of the "s" sound found in other eastern Inuktitut dialects such as North and South Qikiqtaaluk. So, the word for sun, for example, is hiqiniq in David Serkoak's dialect and siqiniq in the Qikiqtaaluk dialects.

4 Laugrand, Oosten, and Serkoak, "The Saddest Time of My Life."

5 For detailed histories of Inuit naming practices and assimilationist policies, see Alia, *Names and Nunavut*; Alia, *Names, Numbers and Northern Policy*.

6 Duhamel and Bernauer, "Ahiarmiut Relocations and the Search for Justice."

CHAPTER 10

Pictorial Essay II: Naming

asinnajaq

My mother Carol Rowan made my body, with the nutrients her body received. She made my body with fish, wild fish from the waters of the Ungava. She made my body with flesh, blood and marrow of animals from the beautiful lands of Nunavik. She made my body with history; I am a single pause in an infinite story. Carol, my mother, treated me so lovingly as a womb dweller. As a result of her love, I began my relationship with her and the foods of my homelands long before my naked and bloody debut into the world writ large. After those nine months of transformation, my mother entered into labour and my father Jobie Weetaluktuk fulfilled the role of a midwife. He too helped me in my shifting of forms. With a sharp blade, he cut my umbilical cord, releasing me into the world. In this action, and so many before and after, we are bonded. Both my parents gave me gifts; that of this very life and a sprawling extended family. With my naming, they invited further connections with my loved ones. Upon my birth, my parents gave me a carefully crafted name.

Lovingly, my parents named me Isabella Rose Mary Rowan-Weetaluktuk and looked forward to calling me little Rosie. Isabella, for the aunt of my grandmother. Isabel Caldwell lived with her sister, my great-grandmother, while she worked as a teacher during the depression. At

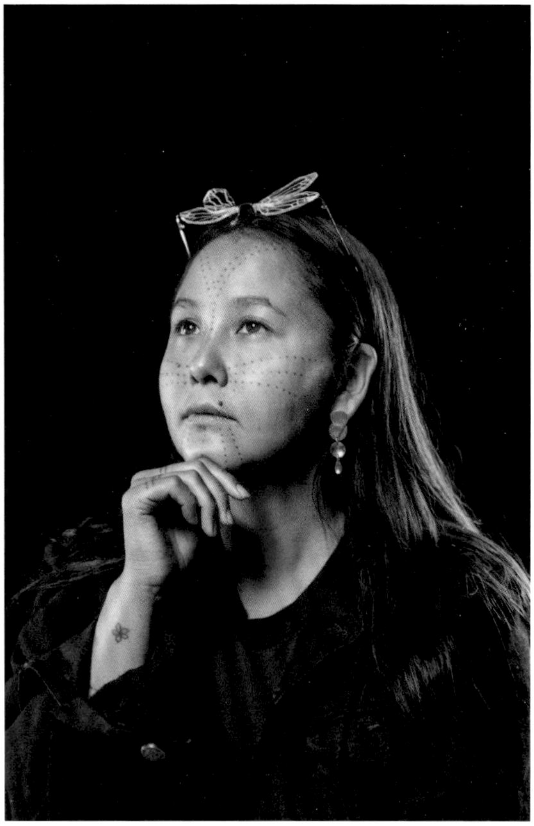

this time, Isabel used her wages to help support her sister, brother-in-law, and their four children. Without Isabel, my grandmother's life would have been immensely more difficult during those times of hardship. I'm named Mary for my maternal grandmother, Mary Hains Rowan, who taught kindergarten and has spoken out against nuclear arms and environmental damages for all of the time that I remember, and probably before that. Rowan, for the family of my mother's father. Weetaluktuk for all my wide-eyed learners from my father's side of the family. Finally, I'm named Asinnajaq for my aunt Mary Asinnaijaq Weetaluktuk who is an incredible seamstress, fisher, and lover of eating her food right down to the bone. In different ways, these names hold me in the family.

10.1 | asinnajaq.

10.2 | Still from the film *Three Thousand* (2017).

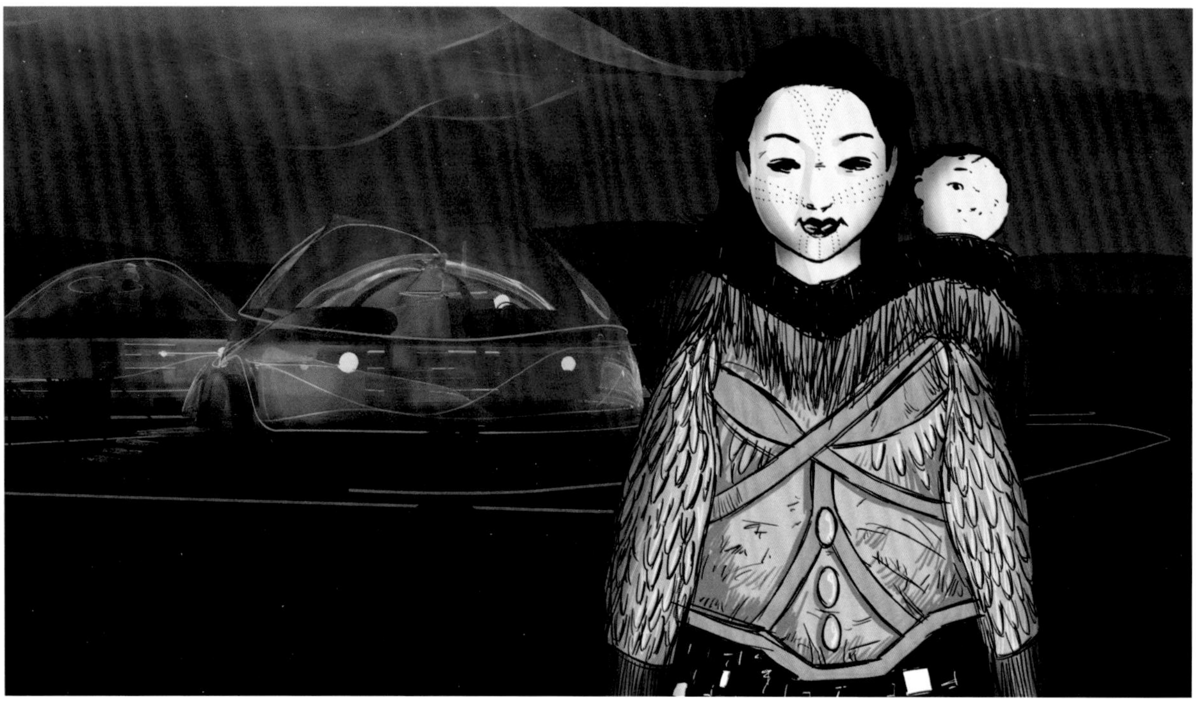

As things go, I was never really called Rosie. Even though I may try, I can't even imagine who Rosie is. That body was never mine to inhabit, and that name has never called to me. Some names fit and others slip right off, so it seems right to me when I hear stories that our Inuit ancestors didn't name a child until after they were born. How do you know for sure who someone is until you meet them? Eventually, Bella is the name that stuck instead. I know exactly who Bella is. She is full of energy, wants to have adventures, and be creative. She can make a home and family out of an old worn-out pair of sneakers if need be. Bella was a wonderful name for a tiny little Inuk girl growing up around a whole lot of non-Inuit, Bella was a familiar name that helped me fit into my surroundings. The name served me fairly well, I did have to get used to sharing a name with family dogs. I didn't love it but it was really okay until the moment when *Twilight* came out and my identity became entwined with that of Bella Swan. This is a special kind of punishment, I'm not sure exactly how I earned it, but trust that I have suffered.

I am constantly learning and growing as I experience the world. One day, the feeling of connection to the name Bella became severed. One way to explain it is like a root that is still there but dehydrates slowly and so though it's still there it doesn't sustain you anymore. At university, I began finding out what was most important to me. Since graduating I have been making my best efforts to shape and live a life that is in line with my values. During the making of *Three Thousand* (2017), I did extensive research. I began to feel strongly that it was important to receive my Tunniit. I travelled to Denmark to work on my Tunniit with a trained Inuk tattoo artist, Maya Sialuk. Following this experience, my heart changed, and I lost the connection to the name of my life prior to that moment. At this point in my life, even though some people still call me Isabella or Bella I don't really feel like they are talking to me at all. I feel like they are talking to someone else. My name that calls to me that I can understand as myself is asinnajaq. asinnajaq is a name that connects me to my family more than two generations before. asinnajaq has seen multiple generations live and die and is entwined in the glimmering network of family ties.

The names given to me by my parents are important to me, I think they have served me well and I am thankful for that. I am also thankful to my parents for so quickly being on my team when it came to moving along from Bella to asinnajaq. Their unwavering support in my decisions is a most encouraging presence in my life.

I know my life is full of movement and growth. I see that those around me are changing as well, as people are full of the potential to be changed. Some changes are so profound that they shift our core as people, this must be reflected in the exterior world. In my understanding, it isn't unusual at all for a person to have a name change. After a life-threatening sickness or a traumatic event perhaps. I've seen it happen when people decide, as I have, that it's important to assert cultural connection and pride. I've also seen it happen when someone goes through a change in their gender expression. Names, like this life, are not stuck or in a stagnant state. As people change and the world moves a new name might come calling.

Names are a gift that provide memory and connections, and sometimes they change.

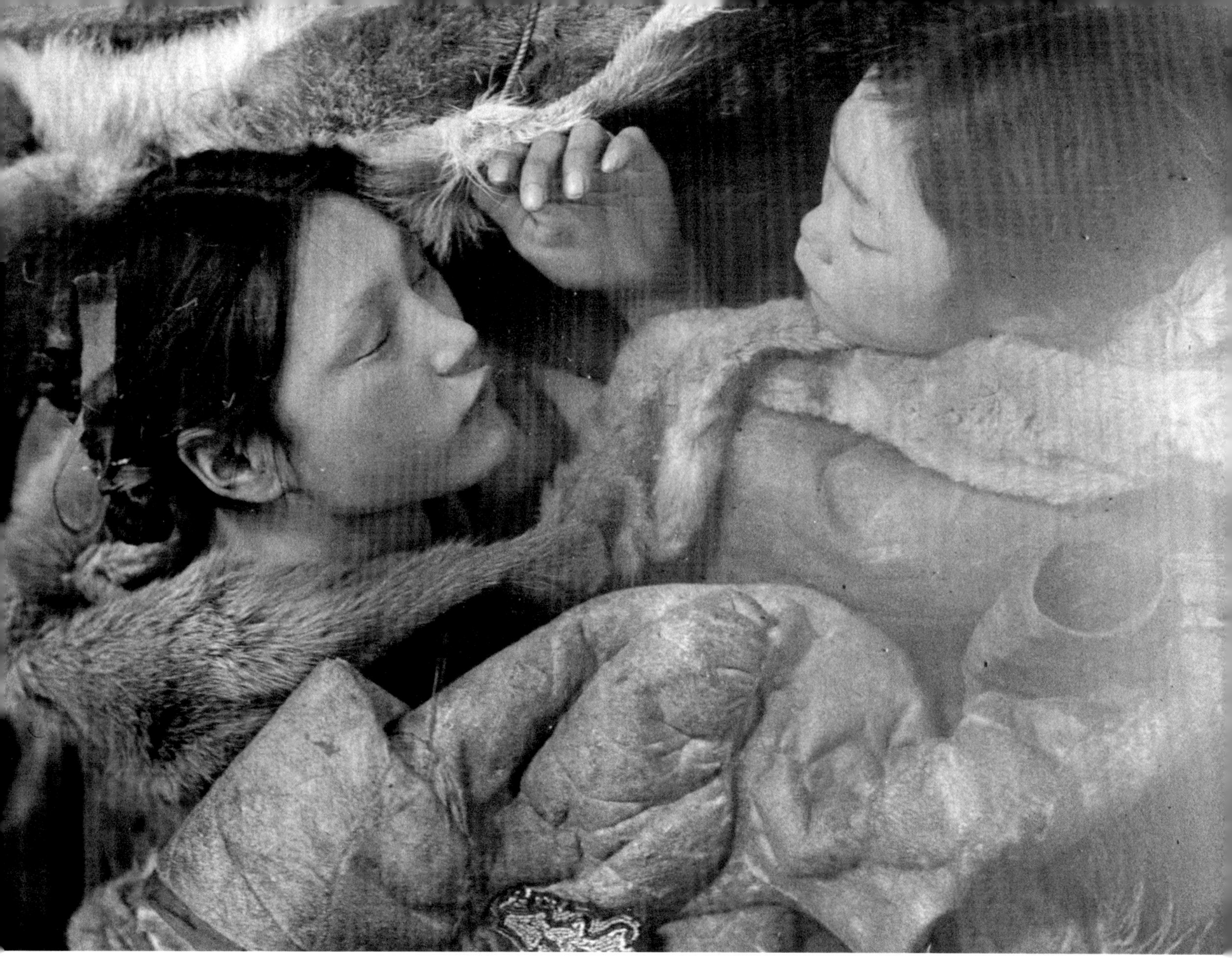

PART THREE

Extending Project Naming

INTRODUCTION

Carol Payne

Through Project Naming, Inuit Elders working with faculty and students at Nunavut Sivuniksavut (NS), along with staff at Library and Archives Canada (LAC), started a conversation. It began with atiqput. Elders identified Inuit depicted in archival photographs from LAC's collection during naming sessions. Through those meaningful names, it has touched on many aspects of Inuit history and culture: family and ancestry, pre-contact life, the Inuktut languages, and the detrimental effects of southern interventions in the North.

Project Naming also proposes new ways to think about historical photographs of Inuit and other Indigenous Peoples and new models for Indigenous-settler collaborations. In this respect, Project Naming is a part of global conversations about reframing the colonial archive (including its photographic archive) from Indigenous subject positions as well as the place of collaborations between Indigenous Peoples and European or settler institutions.[1] These interventions include the influential work of Indigenous photo-based artists such as Jeff Thomas (Onondaga), Hulleah Tsinhnahjinnie (Seminole-Muscogee-Navajo), and Michael Aird (Australian Aboriginal);[2] the work of such Indigenous scholars and writers as Amy Lonetree, Paul Seesquasis, Michelle Raheja, and Celeste Pedri-Spade;[3] and such collaborations between Indigenous groups and colonial archives as those undertaken jointly by the Kainai Nation (of southern Alberta) and Oxford University's Pitt Rivers Museum, as well as the international database project Returning Photos: Australian Aboriginal Photographs from European Collections.[4] Project Naming has contributed to this global interrogation of the colonial photographic archive by fostering knowledge of Inuit history through Elders' wisdom, maintaining a long-standing research collaboration, and by dramatically changing the way a major settler institution (LAC) undertakes research.

Here in Canada, various Indigenous communities, museums, and archives have also restoried photographic archives with Indigenous histories and knowledge. Among others, recent research programs include Recognizing Relations, a collaboration between the Stoney Nakoda and the Whyte Museum of the Rockies; the Qatiktalik (Fullerton Harbour) Photo Narrative Project at the Glenbow Museum; the Names and Knowledge Initiative of the Hudson's Bay Archives; Krista Ulujuk Zawadski's recent exhibition and research project *Nuivisi: Threading Our Beads at Qatiktalik*; and Tuhallruuqtut, Ancestral Sounds, an initiative of the Inuit Heritage Centre in Qamani'tuaq (Baker Lake, Nunavut) available through the Virtual Museum of Canada.[5]

The four essays in this section demonstrate how the conversations and uses of photographic archives initiated by Project Naming have continued, grown, and taken many different forms. They each describe research programs that have developed directly in affiliation with Project Naming while also engaging in those broader challenges to the colonial archive. Similarly, the authors demonstrate how the methodologies established by Elders working with NS and LAC for Project Naming have the pliancy and cultural relevance to grow and take extended forms. In short, these contributions show how the Project Naming conversation has made deep impacts on Inuit culture and innovations into historical research involving archival photographic collections.

In Chapter 11, "Naming Names: Image Captions of Inuit RCMP Special Constables," Inuk anthropologist, author, and co-editor of this volume Deborah Kigjugalik Webster discusses photographic identifications in the research she is conducting for a book on Inuit RCMP special constables from what is now Nunavut. Inuit special constables played important roles in recent Inuit history but Webster also discovered that they were often erased from the historical record. As she states, "I want to remove them from the shadows of anonymity and highlight their contributions to policing in the North." Research into photographs from collections at LAC along with Oral History interviews have been central to Webster's efforts to identify special constables. Her ongoing research has both aided information on the Project Naming database and, in turn, been aided by the database. Indeed, this is an example of reciprocal research at work. In this essay, Webster provides a glimpse into her research by narrating a series of photographs of special constables and discussing her findings. By "naming names" in this way, Deborah Kigjugalik Webster is rewriting recent Inuit history.

Frank Tester and Curtis Kuunuaq Konek introduce their work as part of a team of Inuit youth, Elders, and University of British Columbia faculty in the Nanisiniq Arviat History Project and Nanivara History Project in Chapter 12. Both were titled by Elder Piita Irniq, who is a contributor and gave the title to this volume. Nanisiniq means "Journey of Discovery" while Nanivara translates from the Inuktitut as "I found it!" The Nanisiniq Arviat History Project[6] was established in 2010 as a multimedia history research project engaging Inuit youth and Elders in Arviat. The Nanisiniq team collaborated closely with Project Naming, which supplied photographs for their video interviews with Elders. Photographs, as Frank Tester reminds us in this essay, "tell incomplete stories." Photographs are employed in the Nanisiniq and Nanivara Projects in interviews between youth and Elders as "invitation[s] to explore what is suggested, but hidden from view." As Curtis Kuunuaq Konek writes in the essay, "the Nanisiniq History Project has helped me to gain more knowledge about what my ancestors – especially my grandparents – went through. This project has helped me to express my feelings and my grandparents' or ancestors' hardships." Following the success of the Nanisiniq project, the team initiated the Nanivara History Project in Uqsuqtuuq (Gjoa Haven) and Naujaat (Repulse Bay) in 2015.[7] It also engages Inuit youth to learn their own history through interviews with Elders and the use of visual media.

Chapter 13, by Carol Payne and Sheena Ellison, introduces Views from the North, a photo-based Oral History project developed as a collaboration between Project Naming and Carleton University from 2005 to 2014. It adopts Project Naming's central methodology: using archival photographs of Inuit made by southerners to reconnect Inuit to their past and reshape the southern archival record in Inuit terms through identifications or naming. Views from the North extends that protocol to include photo-based Oral History. For the project, NS students conduct interviews with Elders over photographs from their home communities. The resulting interviews – along with archival photographs, follow-up interviews with students, and new images made by the students – are accessible across Nunavut through a cyber cartographic atlas developed by Carleton University's Geomatics and Cartographic Research Centre.[8] In adapting Project Naming to longer format interviews, Views from the North stresses both the importance of intergenerational learning as well as Oral Tradition and storytelling within Inuit culture. The essay concludes with a discussion of three broad themes that emerged in these intergenerational discussions: the animation of specific stories of the past, the assertion of intergenerational connections, and powerful affective tones across the discussions.

This section on extensions to Project Naming closes with Chapter 14, "Looking for Kenojuak," by Sandra Dyck, director of the Carleton University Art Gallery. Here, Dyck explores how photographs have contributed to the circulation of and knowledge about Inuit art. Specifically, she reviews how the renowned Kinngait-based artist Kenojuak Ashevak (1927–2013) was represented in photography and film from the 1940s through the 1960s. While Project Naming has been devoted to identifying hundreds of previously anonymous Inuit public records, Kenojuak, in contrast, was one of the most celebrated and recognizable Inuit of her time. But, as Dyck argues, "the project of 'naming' also encompasses identifying the contexts for their production, use and circulation." Studying images of Kenojuak illuminates the environment in which this celebrated artist produced her work and negotiated with her many audiences.

NOTES

1 Among this literature is Edwards, "Talking Visual Histories," in Peers and Brown, *Museums and Source Communities*, 83–99; Geismar and Herle, *Moving Images*; Lydon, "Technologies of Indigenous Memory," 173–87; Peers and Brown with members of the Kainai Nation, *Pictures Bring Us Messages*; Poignant with Poignant, *Encounter at Nagalarramba*; Wright, *The Echo of Things*.

2 "Jeff Thomas" https://jeff-thomas.ca/; Tsinhnahjinnie, "Photograph Worth a Thousand Words?" in Pinney and Peterson, *Photography's Other Histories*, 40–51; Aird, "Growing Up with Aborigines," in Pinney and Peterson, *Photography's Other Histories*, 23–39.

3 Among others, see Lonetree, "A Heritage of Resilience"; Seesequasis, *Blanket Toss Under Midnight Sun*; Pedri-Spade, "'Never Only the Master's Tools'"; and Raheja, "Reading Nanook's Smile."

4 Peers et al., *Pictures Bring Us Messages*; Returning Photos: Australian Aboriginal Photographs from European Collections website, accessed 25 January 2022, https://ipp.arts.uwa.edu.au/; Lydon, *Calling the Shots*.

5 Dubois, "Histories in Relation"; Glenbow Museum, "Qatiktalik Photo Narrative Project"; HBC Archives, "Names and Knowledge Initiative"; Zawadski, Nuvisi; Inuit Heritage Centre, "Tuhaalruuqtut, Ancestral Sounds."

6 Tester, *Nanisiniq: Arviat History Project* (blog), accessed 25 January 2022, http://nanisiniq-blog-blog.tumblr.com/.

7 Tester, "Nanivara Project."

8 Payne, Views from the North website, accessed 25 January 2022, http://viewsfromthenorth.ca/index.html.

CHAPTER 11

Naming Names: Image Captions of Inuit RCMP Special Constables

Deborah Kigjugalik Webster

The Royal North-West Mounted Police (RNWMP, 1904–20) and the Royal Canadian Mounted Police (RCMP, 1920 to present) together have a long history in the Canadian Arctic and they could not have performed their duties without the assistance of local special constables. With some exceptions, literature written by former Mounties or others about policing the Canadian Arctic often indicates the ranks and names of the white settlers while the names of Inuit special constables are rarely mentioned. If identified, it is either with the nicknames whalers gave them, their first name only (even after family names were used), or they are referred to as "Eskimo guide" or "employed native." These terms are also frequently used in the original captions of archival images and reflect the period when they were created and the biased attitude of the photographer.

As a researcher working on a project about Inuit RCMP special constables from what is now Nunavut, I want to remove them from the shadows of anonymity and highlight their contributions to policing in the North. The book I am presently writing will include a comprehensive list of Inuit members, their biographies with some of their stories collected from interviews, and each member's photograph. In this essay, I present a few examples of problematic captions ascribed to archival images of some members and discuss my mission to name names. Where this information becomes available, I notify the manager of Project Naming.

Not Named

The first image (Figure 11.1) depicts five individuals and its original caption reads "July 15–16, 1944 – Eastern Arctic Patrol (July 01 to Oct 02) – aboard RCMP Peterhead boat *Lake Harbour*, Lake Harbour, NWT. From Left to Right: RCMP Special Constables (3) with RCMP Cst. McLaughlin and RCMP Cst. Marchbank."

As part of my research project, I manage a Facebook page, @InuitSpecialConstables, to acknowledge the contributions of, and pay tribute to, Inuit RCMP "Specials" from Nunavut. I posted this image asking if anyone could identify the three Inuit RCMP specials and the Inuk man in the middle was possibly identified as Muusa by two people. Recommendations about whom to ask for identifications were also provided.

Nicknames from Whalers

In the early 1900s, some Inuit special constables working for the RNWMP at Qatiktalik (Cape Fullerton) were given nicknames by American and Scottish whalers because Inuktitut names were too difficult for them to pronounce. One such name was "Bye & Bye" (also Bye Bye or By-and-By) with the original caption "Bye and Bye (Iwilingment native)." How that name was chosen, we might never know. Through my research, I discovered that Bye and Bye's Inuktitut name was Siattiaq.[1] Unfortunately little archival information is available about Siattiaq but we do know that he was hired on 1 December 1916, by Inspector French, making him one of the earliest Inuit special constables (Figure 11.2). He assisted in the now-famous Bathurst Inlet Patrol, the longest patrol of any police force in the world, to investigate the alleged murder of Harry Radford and George Street. His term with the Canadian police likely carried on after 1920, when the RCMP was established.

First Names Only

When missionaries baptized or christened Inuit, they were given first names and some were called only by those names and not their Inuktitut name. This RNWMP image (Figure 11.3) includes two Inuit identified as Akular and "Joe." In 1916, at the time this photograph was taken, the rank of special constables, especially for Indigenous people, were not generally provided. The back of the image contained the caption, "Akular, Cpl. Conway, Cst. Kennedy, Cst. Pasley and Joe. Insp. Beyts and S/M Caulkin. Baker Lake, July 1916."

Even in a service file, his name was recorded simply as "Joe." RNWMP records show that "Joe [was] a native Eskimo with the RNWMP and RCMP at Churchill, Man., Fullerton, Chesterfield Inlet, and Baker Lake, NWT from 1936 to 1938 at Eskimo Point." While details in his service file are sketchy, they indicate that he served on the Bathurst Inlet Patrol (c. 1916–18) and was mentioned in an RCMP Annual Report.

There were a few Inuit men named Joe including Joe Akular, Joseph Kangnijuaq or "Pork," as the whalers nicknamed him, and Joe

Gibbons who worked for the RNWMP in the same general area and time period. I hope that interviews with his descendants will provide more information as to Joe's Inuktitut name.

"Employed Native"

Early Indigenous Peoples who assisted the RCMP on a temporary basis were also referred to as "employed natives." LAC has a photograph in its collection (Figure 11.4) taken by David L. McKeand with the caption "RCMP employed native and family returned from Craig Harbour to Pond Inlet. 19th September, 1934." Killiktee (back row, right) was likely temporarily

11.1 | "July 15–16, 1944 – Eastern Arctic Patrol (July 01 to Oct 02) – aboard RCMP Peterhead boat *Lake Harbour*, Lake Harbour, NWT. From Left to Right: RCMP special constables (3) with RCMP Cst. McLaughlin and RCMP Cst. Marchbank." Inuk man in the middle has been identified as Muusa.

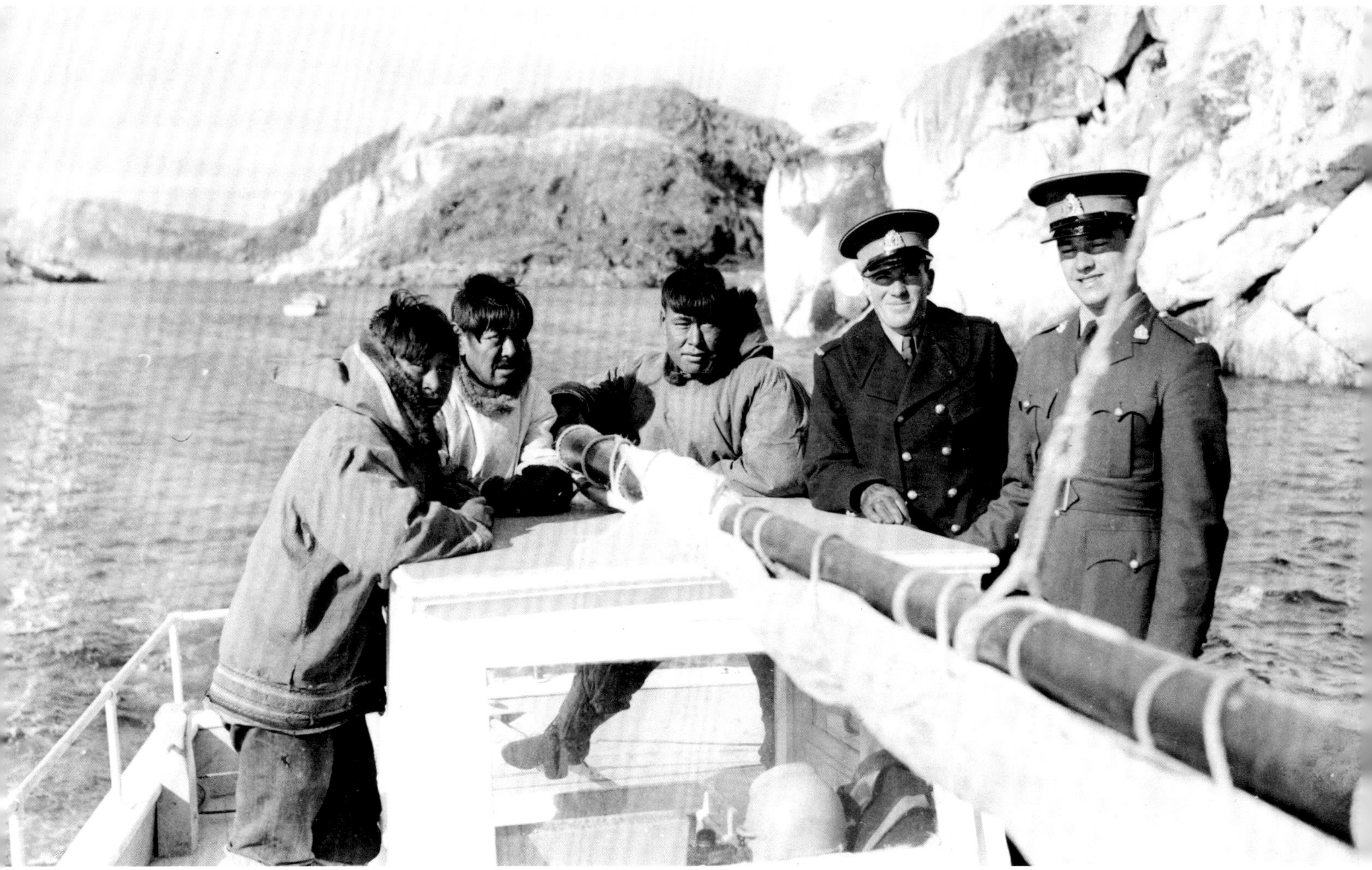

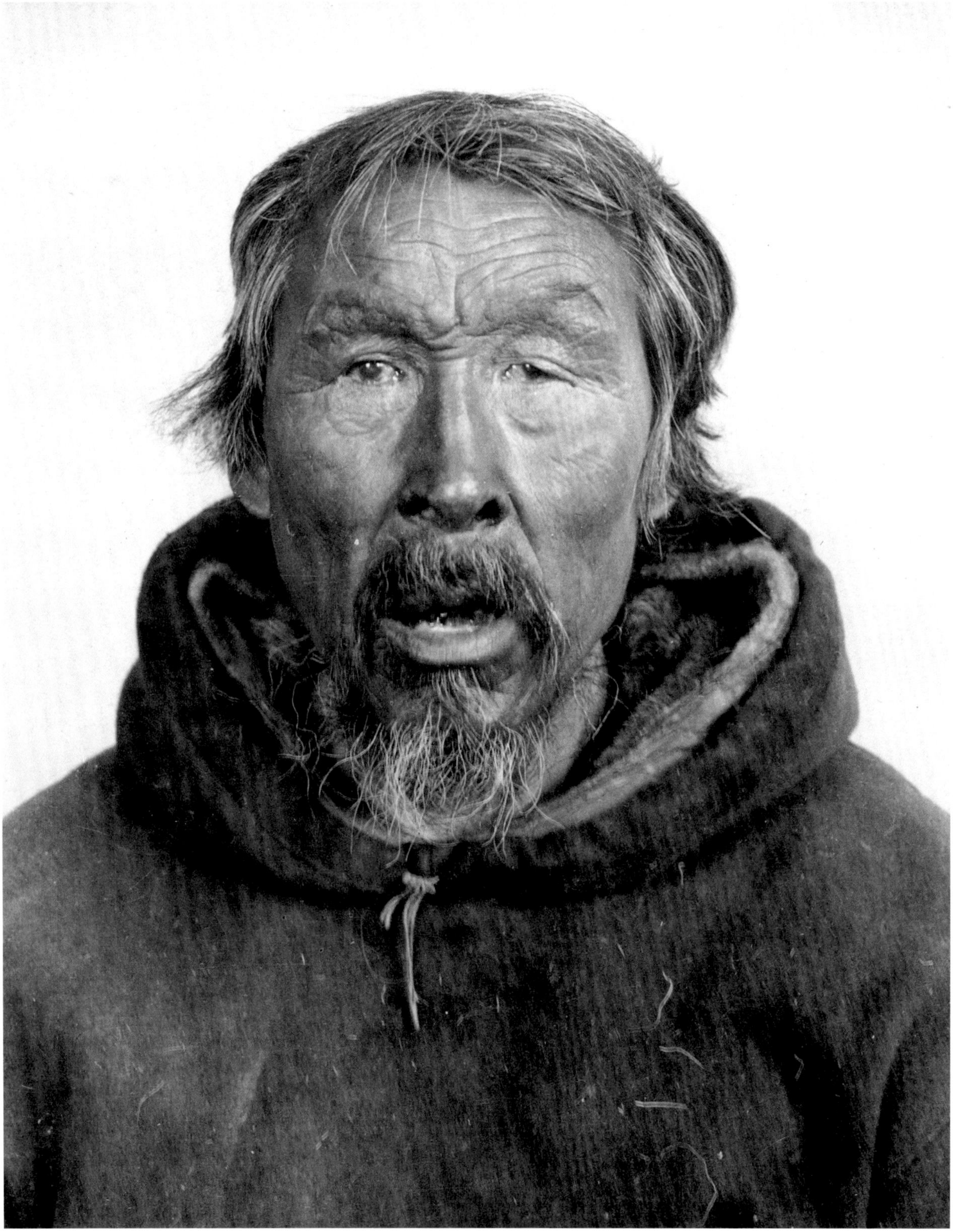

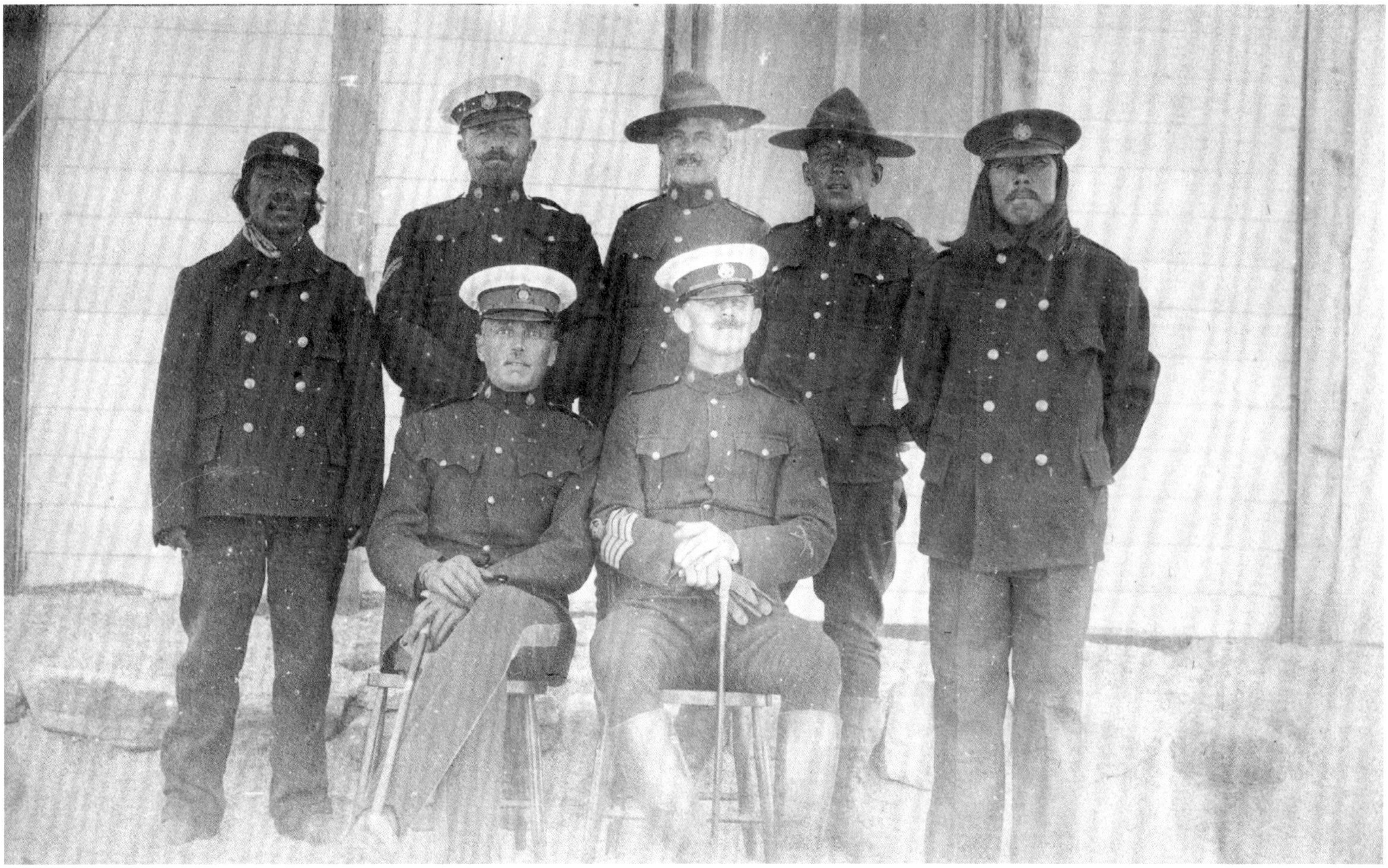

employed by the RCMP because his service file could not be located in an ATIP request, but his son Ningyou Killiktee became a special constable in 1948. Through Project Naming, the individuals were subsequently identified as, from left to right, Inuguk Panikpak, Kunualu Qiliqti, Marsi Qiliqti, and Qaumajuq.

Project Naming has been updating image captions so that Indigenous people can be properly identified. While researching the above-mentioned images, it became evident that Inuit Oral History is still very strong.

11.2 (*opposite*) | Special Constable Siattiaq, Naujaat [Original title: "Bye and Bye (Iwilingment native)"], 1926.

11.3 | Akular, Cpl. Conway, Cst. Kennedy, Cst. Pasley, and Joe. Insp. Beyts and S/M Caulkin. Baker Lake, July 1916.

Through Oral History interviews, archival research, and other forms of information sharing such as social media, naming names is essential to put at the forefront of history Indigenous individuals from archival images.

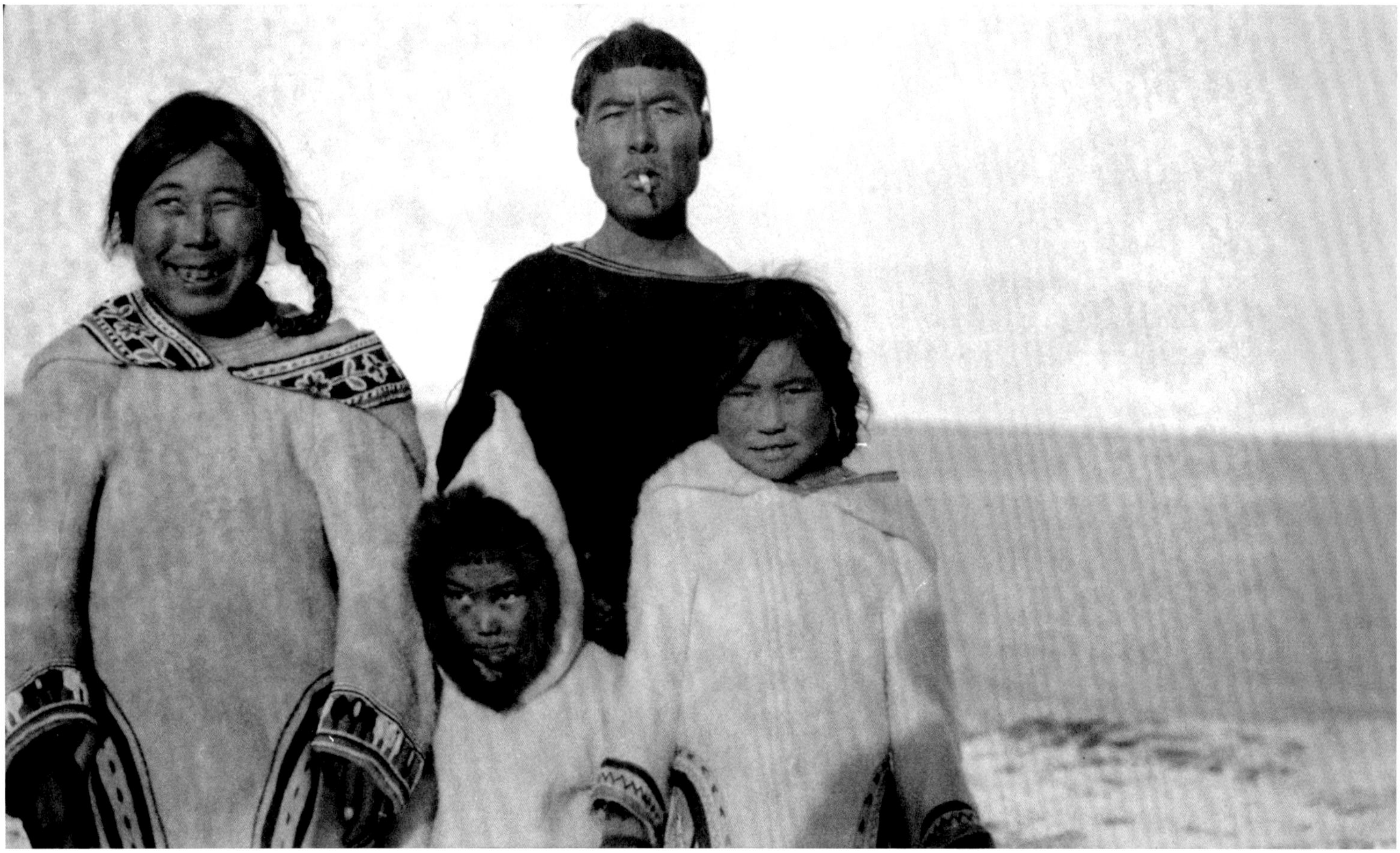

11.4 | Royal Canadian Mounted Police (RCMP) employed native and family returned from Craig Harbour. [Left to right: Inuguk Panikpak, Kunualu Qiliqti, Marsi Qiliqti, and Qaumajuq. They worked for the RCMP] Mittimatalik (Pond Inlet) 19 September 1934.

After my book is published, it will be possible to include more information regarding the identity of Inuit special constables. In the future, when someone searches the keyword "special constable" while consulting Library and Archives Canada, they will find the proper rank and name of the Inuit RCMP members.

NOTE

1 Eber, *Whalers*, 162.

CHAPTER 12

Picture This: Self-Esteem, Project Naming, and the Nanisiniq/Nanivara History Projects

Frank Tester and Curtis Kuunuaq Konek

Frank Tester

Among the thousands of Arctic photographs I have looked at in Library and Archives Canada (LAC) in my research and collaborative work on the Nanisiniq and Nanivara History Projects, the photo in Figure 12.1 stands out. It is among my favourites, speaking symbolically and directly to the central role of children in Inuit life, pamiqsainirmik (things done in the "making of an able human being"), as well as the iglu and its place in Inuit culture and survival. There is more. Caribou meat (a reference to a hunting and gathering culture), the fur trade and the basic necessities it afforded (pots, pans, and kettles among them), and the mark of colonial history: the photographer's foot(print).

The picture was framed by Donald Marsh. In the mid-1920s, Marsh was a missionary to Arviat, called Eskimo Point at the time. Later he became bishop of the Arctic. He was one of the first people in the Canadian Arctic to use Ektachrome colour film to record Inuit life. Ektachrome was first introduced by Kodak in 1935, and Marsh apparently started using it in the late 1930s and early 1940s. The colour, contrast,

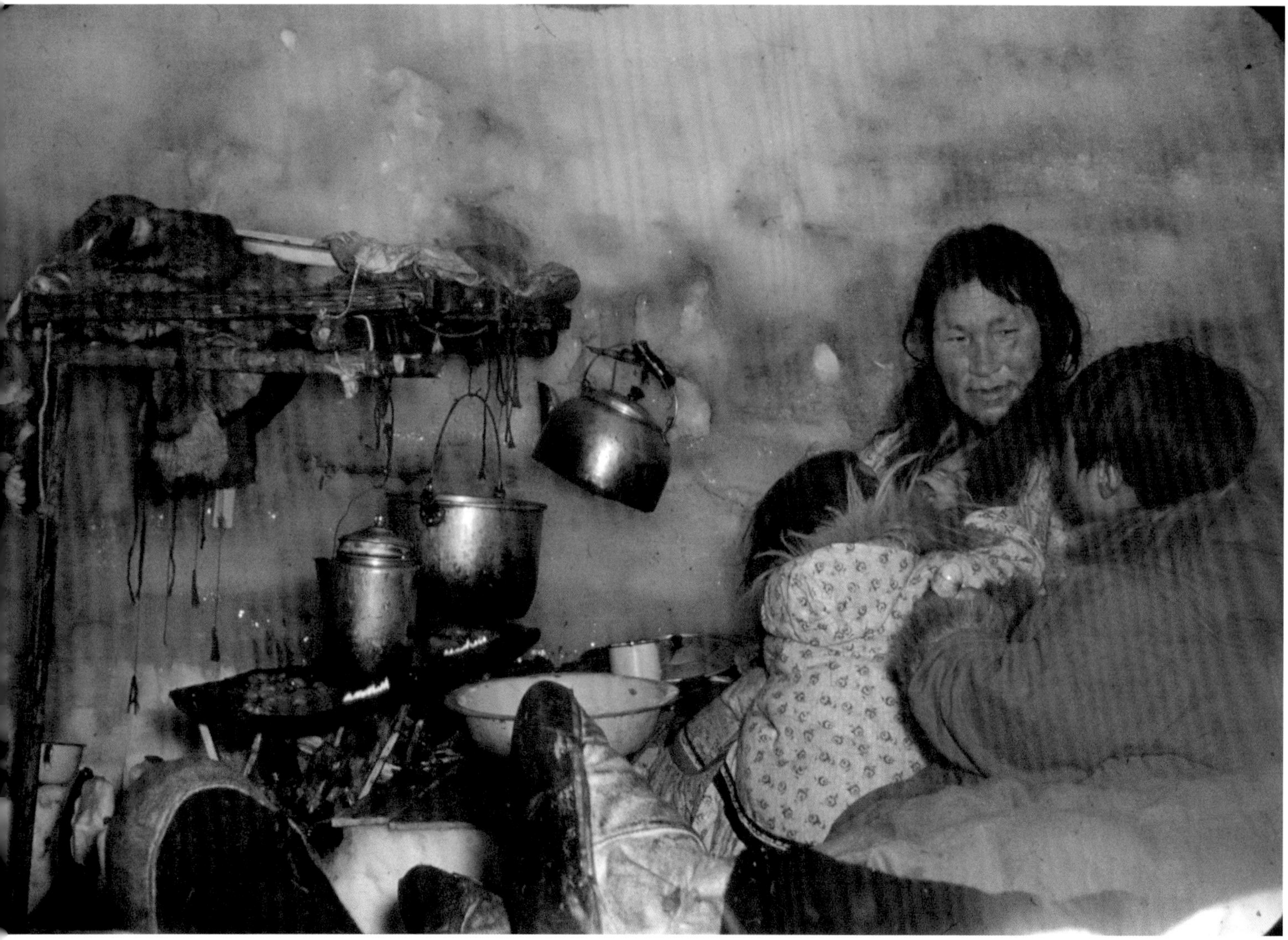

12.1 | Unidentified woman and children inside an iglu, unknown location, 1944. In the early phase of Project Naming, LAC staff received an email stating that the woman in this photograph was Flossie Pappiklok with her children near Ulukhaktok (Holman) in the western Arctic. However, the file containing this image is labelled Arviat, in the Kivalliq region of Nunavut. LAC is still working on the identity and the location.

and composition of the original picture are impressive.

This photograph says a lot about what is suggested but not present in the picture.

Theoretical Considerations

What do photographs tell us about history? How and why are they made (taken)? What purposes do they, and can they, serve? What can we learn from the history of photography? What meaning(s) and purposes were associated with the historical photographs we have of places, events, and people from the Canadian Arctic? These pictures are overwhelmingly the product of Qallunaat photographers. Theory is helpful in making sense of their motives, the content of their work, and the different ways that Inuit have re-interpreted and re-purposed these pictures. The observations of Curtis Kuunuaq Konek that follow are illustrative.

The literature on these topics is extensive, involving a long list of well-known philosophers, art historians, and theorists. Contributions include Roland Barthes's *Camera Lucida*, a challenging and evocative work, published in 1980 just before his death. It was preceded by Susan Sontag's *On Photography* (1977), an award-winning look at the history, role, and politics of photography in capitalist culture. Focusing on the emotional content of photography, the work of Sontag and Barthes triggered a wealth of writing on the meaning and significance of photography in a modern world, including a major contribution by John Tagg, building on a long list of other theorists.[1] These theoretical ideas are relevant to making sense of tens of thousands of photos in collections of Library and Archives of Canada, which document Inuit culture, state interventions, and the consequences of Canada's presence and response to changing conditions for which it was largely responsible.

In *The Disciplinary Frame,* Tagg explores the documentary tradition of photography, the work of John Grierson, and the photography of Walker Evans, well-known for his evocative photos of Americans suffering through the Depression. Much of the Arctic collection of the LAC can be understood with reference to this tradition while questioning an essentialist interpretation of the material. James Elkins's *What Photography Is* (2011) challenges claims made by Barthes. Geoffrey Batchen's *Burning with Desire: The Conception of Photography* (1997) explores modern and postmodern sensibilities and the meaning given to photographs. What, if anything, is essential about "the picture," or are we to understand it in relation to the culture of its origins? An examination of the work of Inuk photographer Peter Pitseolak (1902–1973), *People from Our Side: A Life Story with Photographs and Oral Biography*, brings life to these questions.[2]

The brilliance of Barthes's text is not just what he says but how he expresses himself; poetic language that doesn't necessarily lead one to agree or disagree with what has been stated or implied. His text, like the subjects of photography, invites personal reflection; an emotional response not only to what is in the image, but what lies beyond. What lies beyond is captured nicely by Tagg, quoting Lacan:

> The picture, Lacan tells us, is a trap. It captures and it tames the viewer's gaze. It gives the voracious eye something to feed on but invites the viewer to whom it is presented to lay down and abandon their gaze, "as one lays down one's weapons." Like animal mimicry, void of any instigative intersubjectivity, the picture is a lure, a function whose exercise grasps the viewer and into which the subject is inserted. At the same time, it is also an incitement, an "appearance that says it is that which gives the appearance," driving the viewer to pursue what is behind it, to hang on the question of the thing "beyond appearance."[3]

One can react to a picture in ways that might lean on significant elements of one's lived experience. Pictures tell stories. They suggest the unknown. Figure 12.1, taken by Marsh, tells a story, much of it left to the imagination. How did the photographer gain access to this iglu? Was the photographer intrusive? The Inuk mother is breastfeeding. Was it staged? Does it matter? Why are the photographer's feet showing? Where was this picture taken? What clues does it offer about life and cross-cultural relations at the time?

In working with Inuit youth researchers in the Nanivara (I found it!) and the Nanisiniq (Journey of Discovery) Projects, our exploration of photography, and our production of a photographic and filmic record, does precisely this. It raises questions. These resources are evocative of what is difficult to record; an emotional response to kin and ancestors working as an invitation to indulge Inuit social history and culture. The value of Project Naming lies in what waits beyond the image held in hand. Meaning and the photograph, or meaning and the cascading images of a film, experienced or made in the Nanivara and Nanisiniq Projects, are foundations for these exploratory initiatives.

It is impossible to identify the ship in Figure 12.2 by looking at the life ring hanging in the top right-hand corner. The name of the ship is on the top, the port is on the bottom. But even when enlarged, one can't make out either the name or the port. This is a problem commonly encountered in working with archival photos. Fortunately, this picture came with a caption and was taken on board the *C.D. Howe*. Project Naming is about putting names to otherwise unidentified faces. Sometimes the context helps. The *C.D. Howe* was used in the 1950s and 1960s to transport Inuit TB patients to southern Canada for treatment, and this picture, is of women boarding the ship, something made obvious from the direction in which they are walking. Knowing other relevant information, even without a caption, would allow for further interpretation.

Given the way they are dressed and knowing the difference between what Inuit were typically wearing when they went south, compared to what they were given to return home, they are likely boarding the ship at its home port of Quebec City, something one could reasonably conclude without a caption. They are most likely returning home after being treated for tuberculosis. One of the women either has a cold or is crying. What's going on here? Who are the formally dressed white folk at the bottom of the ramp? When was it taken?

I have some clues because I am familiar with the archival record related to trips made north by the *C.D. Howe*. The photo may have been taken by S.J. Bailey, a prolific photographer and public servant sent north in the late 1940s and early 1950s to document the impact of the federal Family Allowance Program on Inuit families and children. It is also possible that it was taken by Wilfred Doucet, a photographer with the National Film Board. He was present on the 1951 trip north made by the *C.D. Howe* and was there to photograph the opening of the RCMP post at Craig Harbour.[4] The tears may be tears of joy.

There are mysteries associated with photographs that invite investigation and exploration. They tell incomplete stories. The detective work and the challenges posed by a photograph – as Curtis Kuunuaq Konek makes clear in what follows – contribute to the interest that Inuit youth subsequently develop in an exploration of their history and culture.

There are also stories within stories. There's a story behind one photograph that I acquired

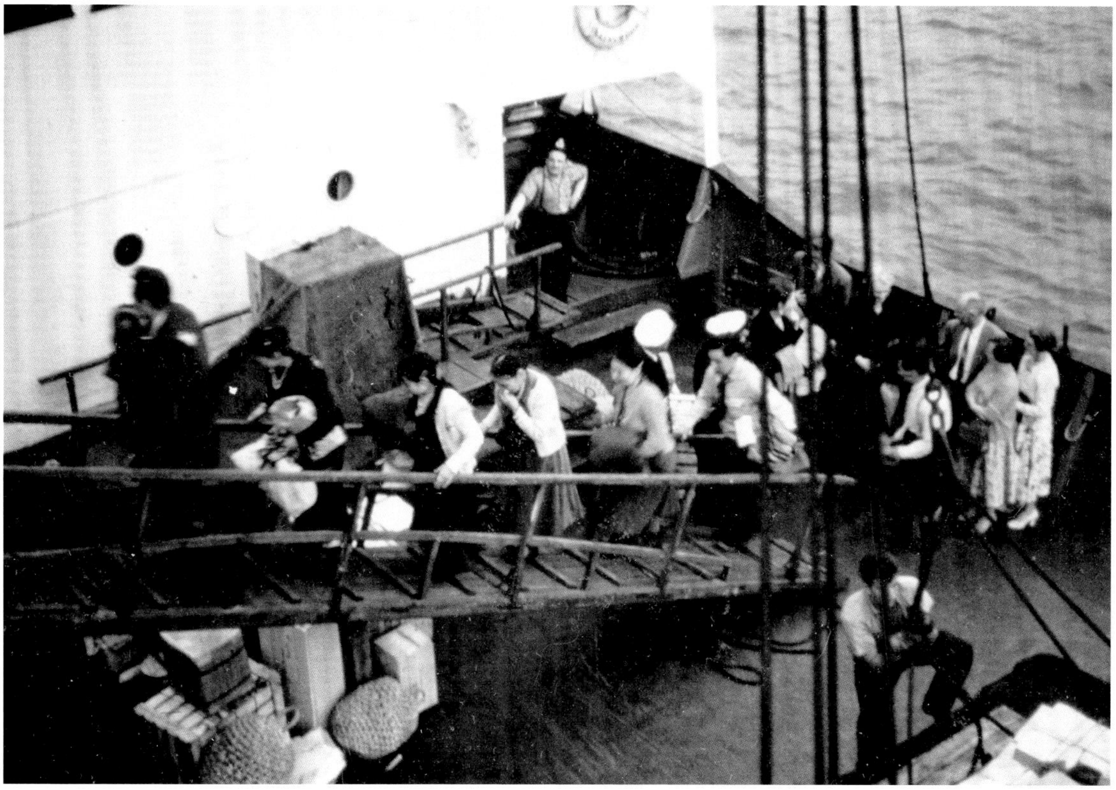

in a most unusual way. It was in the back of a copy of a book, *My Life with the Eskimo*, written by the well-known Arctic explorer, Vilhjálmur Stefánsson. I had loaned a copy to someone who didn't return it, so I went to buy another one at a used bookstore in Vancouver. Knowing the content, I didn't bother looking through the book. I took it home. When I got home, I flipped through it. Two photographs fell out. Figure 12.3 is one of them. With the help of Piita Irniq and André Tautuk, we have since gone about identifying the year and the location, and have named everyone in the picture, with one exception. Pictures like this have been part of Project Naming and, as happened here, they serve to bring Inuit together and engage family and community in an exploration. Who

12.2 | Inuit on board the *C.D. Howe* on their way home from the sanatorium, Quebec City, 1955. [Frank Tester has attributed this to S.J. Bailey]

are these people, and what was going on at the time?

Pictures also generate a wide range of feelings. They can be sources of considerable joy and feelings of respect, appreciation, and sorrow. If you are an Inuk student, you see relatives you've never met. You may experience laughter and sadness, all at the same time.

Photographs can ground us. They tell us not only who we are, they tell us about where we have been. They may suggest something that's not shown in the picture but is inspired by it. A picture may suggest the opposite of what is

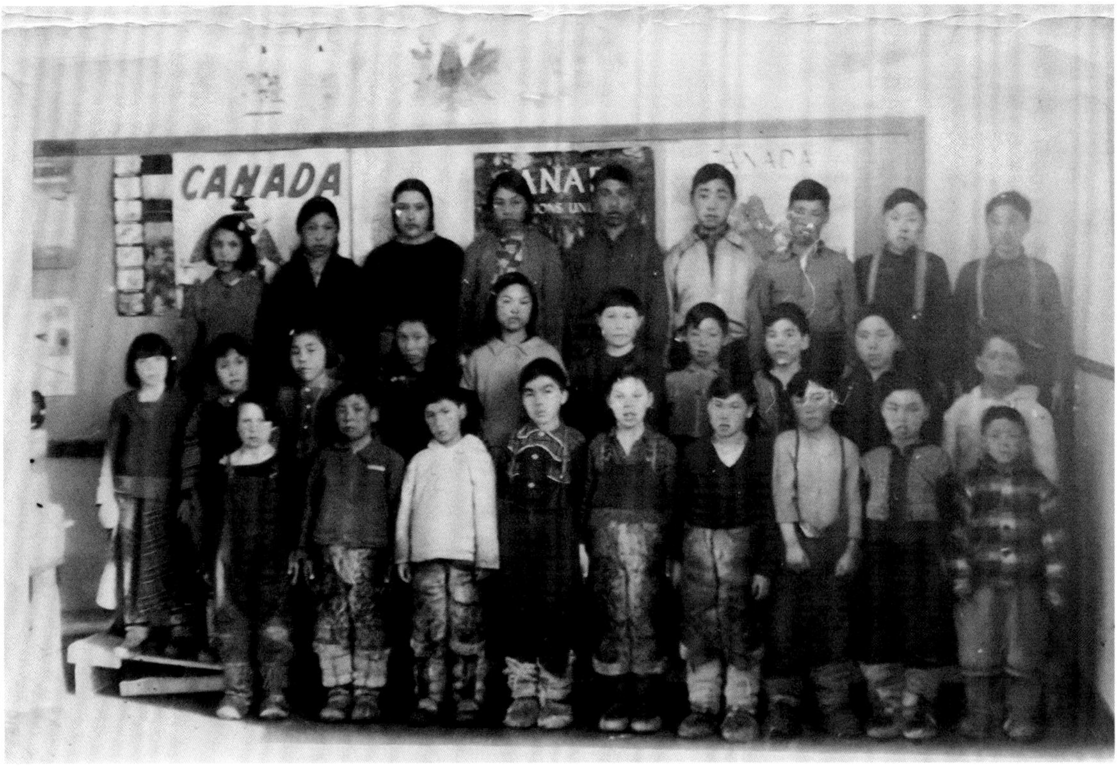
CANADA

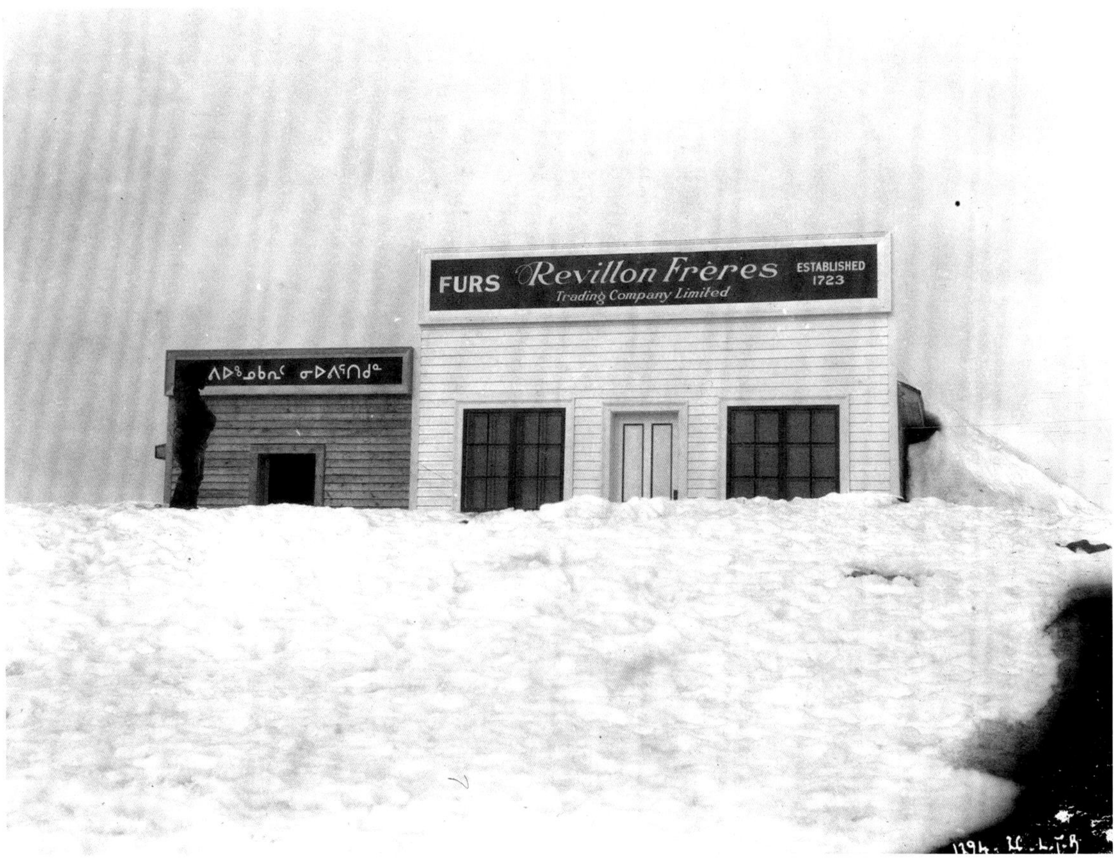
FURS
Revillon Frères
Trading Company Limited
ESTABLISHED
1723

shown: who it is we would like to become, and where we would like to go – "not there!"

Not only photographs of people are important. So are pictures of buildings, places, and events. Figure 12.4 is a picture of the Revillon Frères fur trading post in Naujaat (Repulse Bay), taken in 1926. What was the Revillon Frères fur trading company? Who was involved in this company? How did it get started? What was a company based in France doing in Inuit Nunangat? The picture invites an exploration of history. The answer to one question can lead to another. Why and how did the Hudson's Bay Company come to be part owners of this company? What does this say about the fur trade and what happened to Inuit in the Depression of the 1930s, when fox fur trapping was the only source of Inuit income? How did the fur trade affect Inuit culture and life on the land?

A photo is an invitation to explore what is suggested but hidden from view. A single image can, for Inuit youth, open the door to an experience and generate a passion that lasts a lifetime. Pictures and the historical record help ground all of us – Inuit youth being no exception – in who we are, where we have come from, and what our parents, grandparents, and ancestors did to get us here. Even when these stories involve pain and conflict, they can be grounding. They invite an exploration of places, times, and circumstances that help create an identity; something that is a struggle for many Inuit youth, dealing with the realities of a different world and culture than the one from which they came, and the experience of parents and Elders. Rather than a crisis, I refer to this as "an identity challenge."

12.3 (*opposite top*) | Federal Day School, Igluligaarjuk, 1951 [Front row: Emma Ford, Luke Isaluk, André Tautuk, Mark Kalluak, David Aglukkark, Cyril Nanauq, Anthyme Kadjuk, Casmir Kreterdluk, and Armand Kolit. Second row: Mary-Jane Ford, Sabine Kautak, Melanie Lilok Amarok, (unidentified girl), Leonie Putuluk, George Tanujak, Bernie Suluraajuq, Timotee Taliriktuq, Simionie Iyerak, Camille Cimik. Back row: Eva Alainngaq Tanujaq, Monica Ayaruak Bruce, Rosalie Iguttaq Sammurtuq, Madeline Tartuk, Tommy Tullik, Simionie Aklunark, Charlie Kingmiaqtuq, Celestino Makpah.] (Identifications by André Tautuk and Piita Irniq.)

12.4 (*opposite bottom*) | Revillon Frères Trading Company Limited, Naujaat, 1926.

The Nanisiniq and Nanivara History Projects

With funding from the Social Sciences and Humanities Research Council of Canada, we put together the Nanisiniq History Project (2010–13, Figure 12.5) and the Nanivara Project (2014–17). These projects were named by Piita Irniq, Elder and former commissioner of Nunavut (see Chapter 5), during meetings with the youth researchers and Elders who undertook this work. The Nanisiniq Project had nine youth researchers from Arviat. The Nanivara Project involved seventeen youth researchers from Gjoa Haven and twenty-two from Naujaat. Some participants drifted in and out of the project, accommodated by recognizing that participants have different material and social circumstances, responsibilities that may change from day to day, and other interests and distractions. In all cases, however, projects had a core of committed Inuit youth researchers. They also had a committed and energetic team of university-based student research assistants working alongside them.

Approach

Theoretical considerations, with which I introduced this chapter, give some clue as to the methodological sensibilities informing these initiatives. Experiential learning and participatory action research guided both projects. There are many definitions of experiential learning. James Saddington offers the following straightforward definition. It fits well with what we attempted in working with Inuit student researchers. "Experiential learning is a process in which an experience is reflected upon and then translated into concepts which in turn become guidelines for new experiences."[5]

Archival and photographic records formed the basis of both projects, archival records being a cause for reflection that is hard to avoid. As a project participant said to me in looking at colonial records: "This stuff kind of hits you in the face, and then sticks in your mind for a long time." Or on another occasion when a participant, studying a letter written by a missionary writing in the early 1950s and then looking into space, asked out loud a question of herself: "I wonder why they called us 'primitive' …?"

> [This project] reminded me [of] what my grandmother used to say to me, and my grandfather. So it brought back a lot of memories. – Dorianna Malikki, Naujaat

The historical and colonial record, as well as the experience of listening to and recording on film the accounts given by Elders of their historical and cultural experiences and knowledge, combined with the archival record, evoked, for some, strong feelings. Learning, or becoming capable by acquiring knowledge and skills – pilimmaksarniq – is not only a focus on *what* is learned but *how*. Unlike many ideas about how Qallunaat[6] should learn – separating knowledge and fact from values and valuing – Inuit learning includes the acquisition of the values important to both learning from and working with others. The assumption is that most important tasks involving what one has learned will, sooner or later, require participation by others. "By showing that you have a helping spirit, you are building a relationship that will bring others to your aid when you need it."[7] This is profoundly different than an orientation to "independence" and "original (personal) thinking," and a long list of values and objectives characteristic of most Qallunaat educational experience.

Another dimension important to learning is the relationship between feeling and meaning; what inevitably happens when Inuit encounter in the LAC collection, pictures of relatives they have never seen. The theme of meaning runs through Jennifer Moon's thorough examination of reflexive and experiential learning. How is one to know what constitutes, for Inuit participants, a meaningful experience?

Feelings – emotional responses to documents, photographs, or encounters – provide those of us concerned with the design of research and experiential learning with clues as to what works, and what counts. The experience with the Nanisiniq Project thus informed the design of the subsequent Nanivara Project. The response of Inuit youth to photographs, especially of family, and to historically important artifacts, is profound. It engages youth and

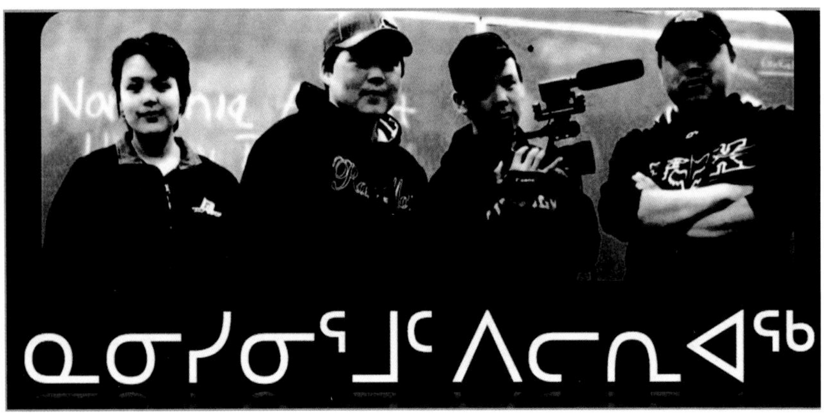

12.5 | Amy Owingayak, Curtis Kuunuaq Konek, Jordan Konek, and Patrick Pingushat. Screenshot of Ninisniniq: Arviat History Project, Tumblr page, 2011.

Elders alike in intense searches for records that speak to history, culture, and family. This was evidenced by the emotional response of one youth to a carving made by his grandfather. He stumbled upon it in the basement storage for Inuit carvings held by the National Gallery of Canada. In tears, he asked that we leave him alone for a while with the piece in hand. A photograph brings, evokes, and creates meaning. It is attention to the meaning of the photograph, or the artifact, that directed both projects. What this looks like in practice is best illustrated by what Curtis Kuunuaq Konek has to say later in this chapter.

Resources

Photography and film were used to bring Elders and young people together – the Internet, Facebook, and other social media platforms – to communicate what we were doing in making history and culture come alive. In the Arviat Nanisiniq History Project, we were inspired by Elders to set up a Tumblr site.[8] In the years I have spent in Nunavut, I have heard Elders often say: "You know, we need to find a way to talk to young people. We need to find a way to communicate what it is we know to young people." Modern means serve well, the interests and concerns of Elders.

The work done by Inuit student researchers owes its existence not only to the photographic collections of LAC but also to an extensive archival database, now housed at the University of Manitoba Archives and Special Collections.[9] The database, compiled over about twenty-five years, contains copies of or links to about twelve thousand documents detailing the social and colonial history of Inuit from the early 1880s to the 1990s. The original documents are scattered in the archival collections at LAC and other collections across the country. Compiling these records involved working through hundreds of cases of material in the records of the northern administration and government departments responsible for the administration of the former Northwest Territories. It includes material from collections found at the Prince of Wales Northern Heritage Centre, Yellowknife, as well as church archives and other archival collections across the country. These records also consist of material given to me by different actors in the making of Inuit social and colonial history; former public servants, teachers, administrators, etc.

The photographic record found in Arctic archival holdings contains pictures of people, places, and things. These detail a modern colonial history, to be distinguished from what happened in the nineteenth century to Indigenous Peoples elsewhere in Canada, and internationally. The record is unique. It reflects a colonial history, much of which unfolded after the Second World War during a period of Canadian liberal welfarism. It was driven in large measure by what were seen to be at the time, liberal and progressive humanitarian values. These are reflected, for example, in the creation of the United Nations Declaration of Human Rights and in Canada, policies like Family Allowances and Medicare. The record – textual and photographic – asks many questions. What, if anything, was different about colonial experiences in the Canadian Arctic? What, if anything, distinguishes them from the way Indigenous Peoples were treated in the period before the Second World War, given the attention to human rights and social justice that some claim emerged during the post-war era?

There are interesting problems posed by many of these photographs; not just what's there, but what's missing. This is particularly

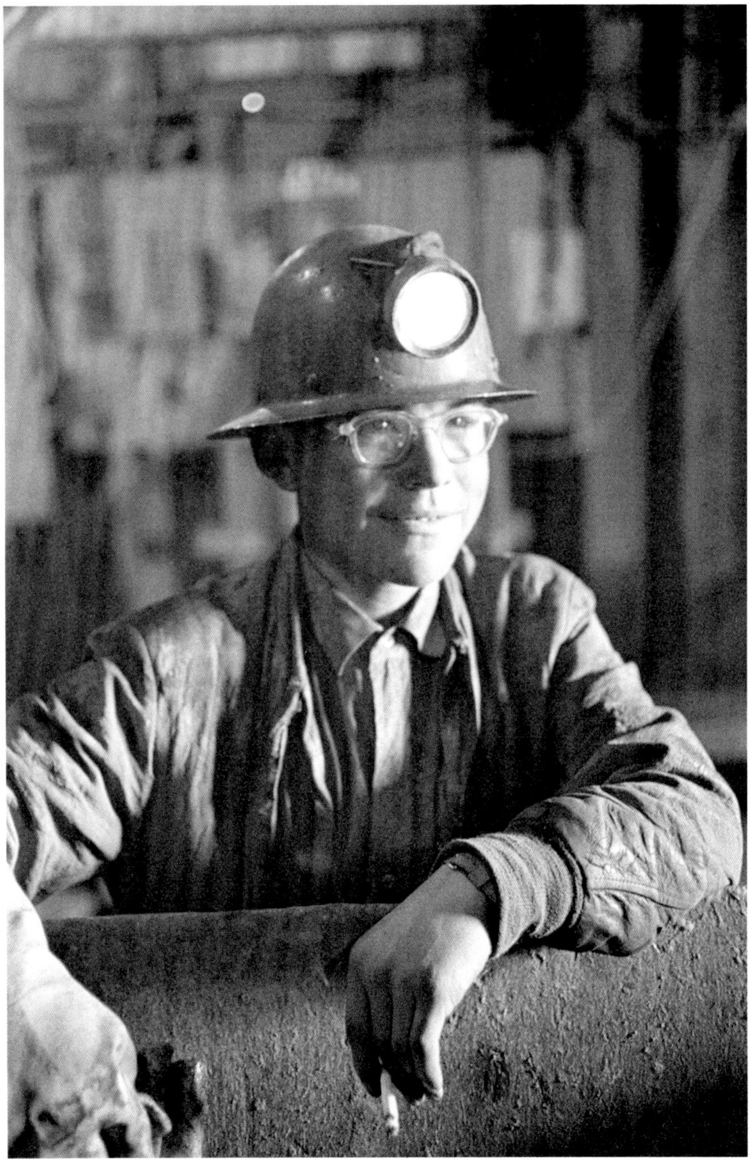

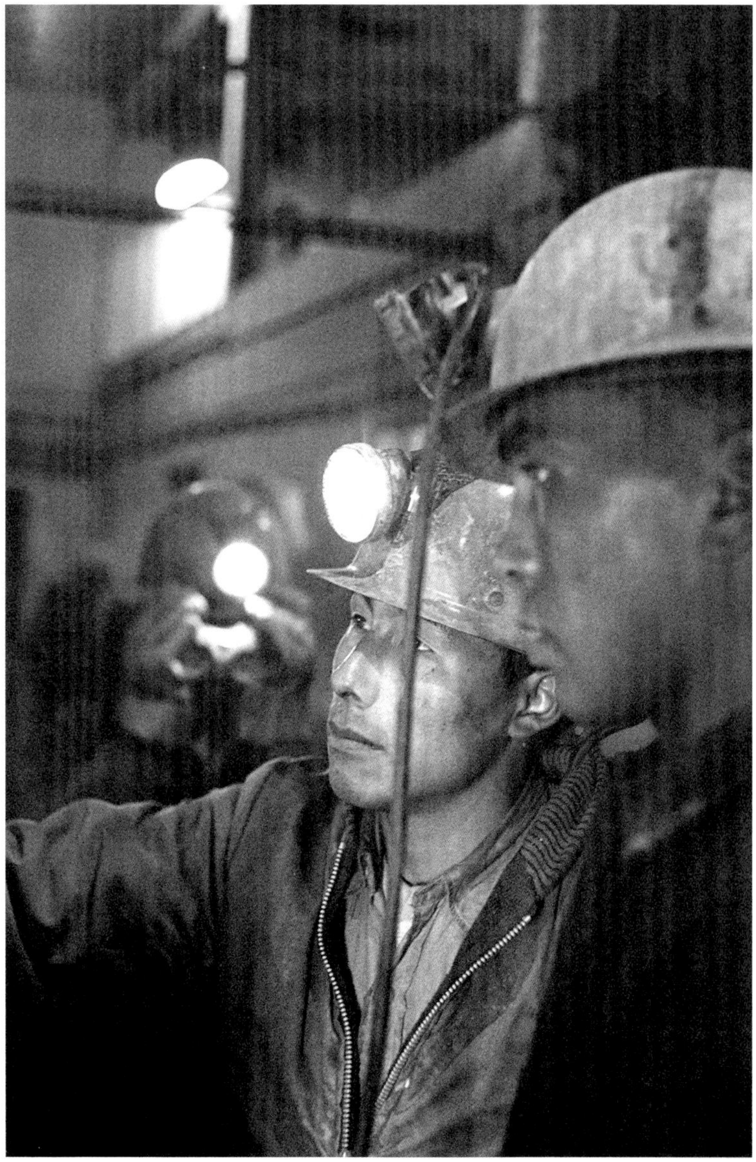

12.6 | [Timothy Taleriktok], Rankin Inlet Mine, Naujaat, c. 1960.

12.7 | [Peter Karlak (left) and unidentified], Rankin Inlet Mine, Naujaat, c. 1960.

true, for example, in the case of Kangiqliniq (Rankin Inlet), and the history of the North Rankin Nickel Mine (1957–62), where a series of photos (Figures 12.6 and 12.7) by Kryn Taconis, a professional photographer, show an exemplary mining camp and Inuit having successfully adjusted to what was regarded at the time as a "modern" industrial setting. What wasn't captured is significant: a Canadian equivalent of the kind of segregation found, at the time, in the southern United States.

In contrast to the photographs, the textual archival record is revealing. For the first few years of operation, Inuit lived separately from the white population in an "Eskimo village." They experienced overcrowded and underserviced plywood "homes" with no facilities, a bare lightbulb in the ceiling of a home with no running water or sanitary facilities. They were paid a fraction of what white miners were paid for doing the same job; realities obscured by photos of happy, smiling faces. Understanding the photographic record is greatly facilitated by the textual record, and the textual record, in turn, is enriched by the photographic record. The one without the other – something true of the many "coffee table" productions of Arctic photographs originating in the 1960s and 1970s – has left many Canadians with a badly distorted view of what Arctic experience and history was all about.

Challenges

One of the biggest problems faced by Inuit is the impact of this colonial history on self-esteem, an intergenerational issue, for well-known historical reasons. Not knowing who you are, where you belong, and not feeling good about yourself gives rise to a long list of personal problems and struggles. Lack of self-esteem gets in the way of holding down a job. It gets in the way of achieving at school. It gets in the way of talking about, exploring, and doing things,-including engaging that which brings meaning and purpose to one's life. Suicide among young Inuit is a much talked about problem in the Canadian Arctic. It has origins in being made to feel that your culture is deficient, that your ways of thinking and living were "primitive," that your beliefs were "pagan," and that to succeed, you need to adopt ways of thinking and doing characteristic of a colonizing culture. These are all features of federal day schools and residential schools and have left intergenerational scars on all Indigenous Peoples in this country.

Once you know something – once you've learned and felt something that affects *all* of you – what do you do with it? Is it just interesting "stuff" that changes one's life – how one understands and feels about oneself? Is there something else to be done?

Elders worked on both projects (Figure 12.8). Their participation was an active one, essential to the role of Inuit Qaujimajatuqangit (IQ) (Inuit wisdom and knowledge), in how these projects unfolded. Student facilitators from the University of British Columbia worked with Inuit student researchers. What everyone accomplished, working together, was impressive.

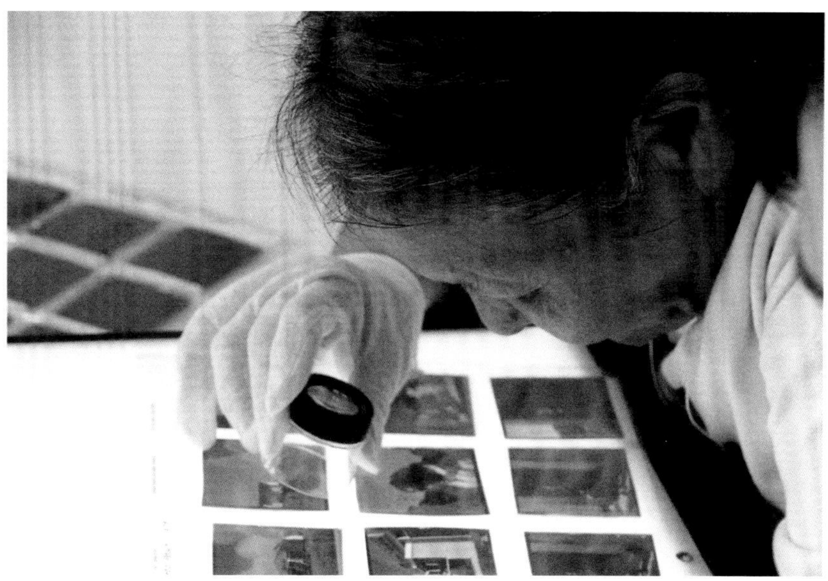

12.8 | Elder Martha Otokala, working at Library and Archives Canada, Ottawa, 2011.

What They Accomplished

Experiences were worked into the fabric of these projects. They included interviewing and learning to record Elders on film, visiting and learning to use archival collections, and visiting museums in Yellowknife, the Maritime Museum in Vancouver, LAC, Ottawa, and the National Archives of Norway in Oslo (Figure 12.9).

Students acted on what they learned, presenting at conferences in Vancouver, Ottawa, Montreal, Washington, DC, and the Arctic Indigenous Education Conference held in 2016 at the Sami University College, Kautokeino, Norway.

> My experience in Norway was unforgettable. I had a lot of fun and learned quite a few things. My favourite memory was when we went to go visit some of the students in the Sami High School. Meeting with the youth from Norway was pretty interesting because I found out that they weren't that different from us, they were also struggling with keeping their culture alive. – Renee Angotialuk, Naujaat

Students with the Nanisiniq Project used what they had learned about climate change from interviews with Elders for presentations at the

12.9 | Student researchers with a statue of Henry Larsen, Maritime Museum, Vancouver. *From left*: Jason Uttak, Simon Alaralak (Naujaat), and Peter Jayko (Gjoa Haven).

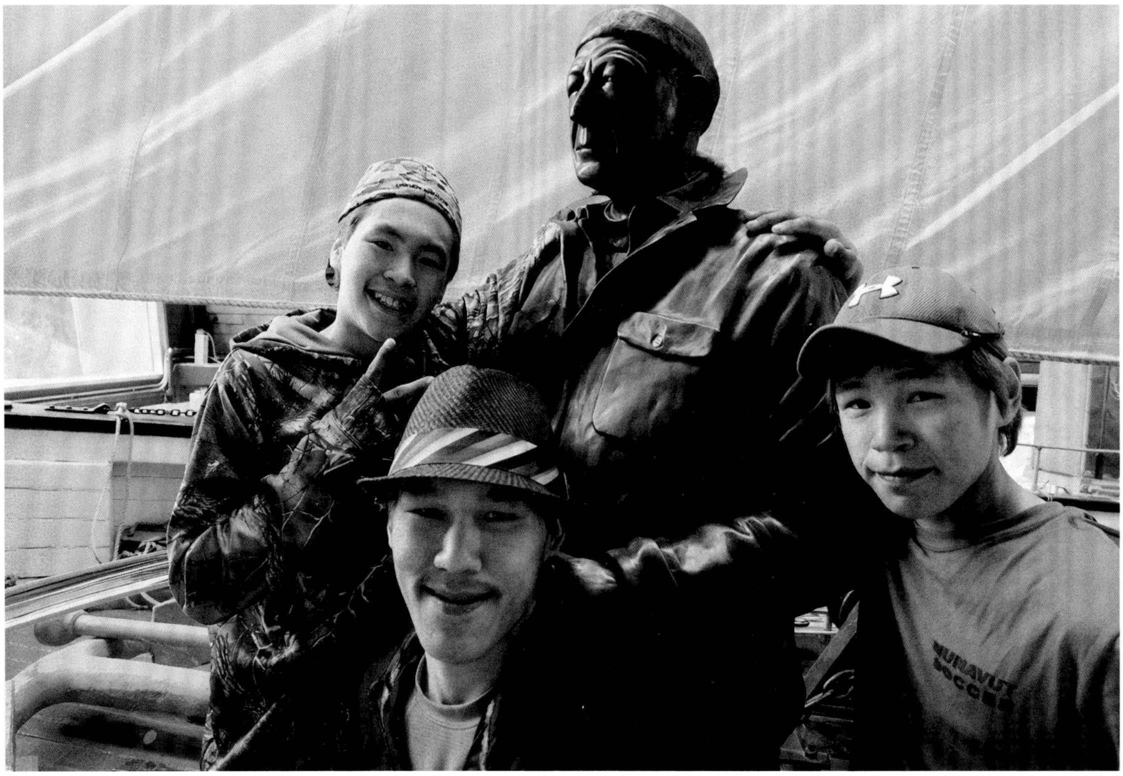

United Nations COP17 international conference held in Durham South Africa in November 2011. A press conference they held got international attention.

A colonial history, poorly understood by most Canadians and one with which Inuit youth are not overly familiar, combined, as noted, with incredibly rapid social change have contributed to a significant intergenerational gap between Inuit youth and Elders.[10] This disjunction is related to effects an assimilative, post-war colonial agenda had on Inuit Elders and parents, and an education system that replaced the role of Elders in making able human beings. Inuit culture has undergone incredible change since the 1950s when most Inuit moved from land-based camps into coastal settlements.[11] The work of Inuit student researchers brought Elders and youth together.

We hoped that Inuit youth would discover, in examining the photographic and written historical records, the considerable skills they could bring to researching their history and culture. As a result, they would better understand events, especially those unfolding after the Second World War, and the strength and resilience of parents and Elders. We read, viewed pictures, talked, and explored and they filmed discussions with Elders from Arviat, Uqsuqtuuq (Gjoa Haven), Naujaat, Arviat, and Rankin Inlet. They produced a valuable and important historical record, recording many Elders who are no longer with us. Youth researchers contributed significantly to two project films, *Nanisiniq: A Journey of Discovery*, and *Beneath the Surface: Inuit Miners at Rankin Inlet, 1957–1962*.[12] Students working with the Nanivara Project contributed to documenting artifacts from Amundsen's 1903–05 stay at Gjoa Haven, on his trip through the Northwest Passage. They contributed interviews with Gjoa Haven Elders to the Nattilik Heritage Centre.

After the projects ended, student researchers went on to work in their communities on social, cultural, and related issues, working for government and non-governmental institutions. Jordan Konek, a student researcher, went on to become a video journalist with CBC. Jennifer Ullulaq, a student researcher from Gjoa Haven is now manager of the community's Nattilik Heritage Centre and in 2017, Barbara Opik founded the Gjoa Haven Film Society.

What we attempted in the Nanivara and Nanisiniq Projects addressed the personal and social challenges grounded in this history, without talking about them directly. Rather, for Inuit student researchers, it was a "journey of discovery."

Curtis Kuunuaq Konek speaks eloquently to this in what follows.

Curtis Kuunuaq Konek

My name is Curtis Kuunuaq Konek. I live in Arviat, Nunavut. I just wanted to say my Inuktitut name. My Inuktitut name is Kuunuaq, meaning "something about a river." I was named after my grandma's cousin. She wanted to use her name because they were good friends and good cousins, just like me and my cousin, Jordan Kunni.

I just wanted to say something about the Nanisiniq History Project and being a part of it.[13] I have gained a lot of knowledge about our Elders and their knowledge and experiences about living in the land. I have learned about experiencing the difference between living in an iglu and living in a house. In the Nanisiniq Project, we worked a lot with youth and Elders from our community, Arviat. We talked a lot about relocations, climate change, and starvation. The project has helped me to gain more knowledge about what my ancestors – especially my grandparents – went through.

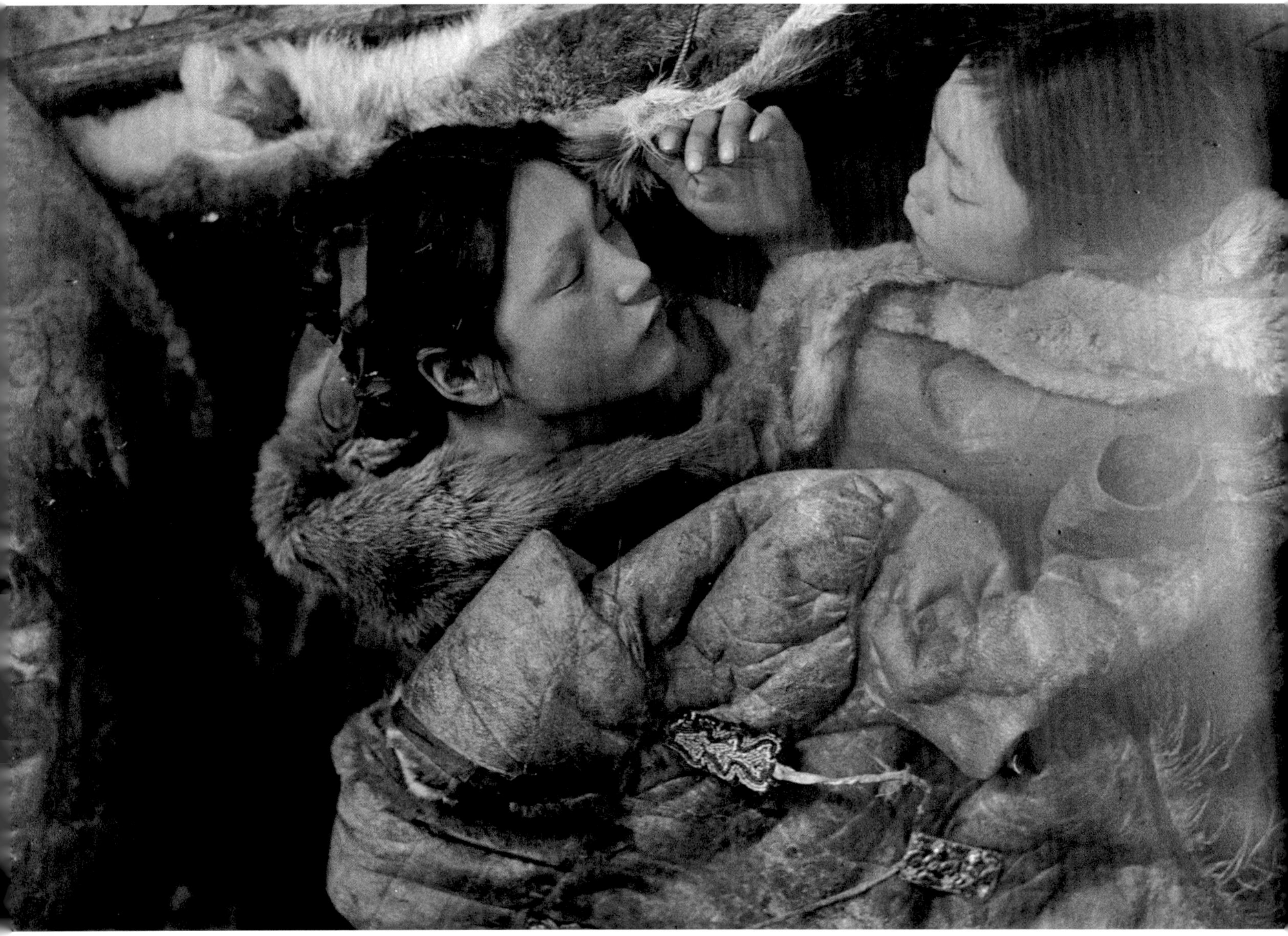

12.10 | [Helen Aagatok Konek (left) and May Kinaalik Haqpi (right)], Saningayuaq, near Padlei, 1950.

12.11 (*opposite*) | [Pallak plays a string game with her daughter May Kinaalik Haqpi. Pallak was also the mother of Helen Aagatok Konek], Saningayuaq, near Padlei, 1950.

It has also helped me to express my feelings and talk about my grandparents' and ancestors' hardships.

We can do it ourselves, and others can help to get it out there and get Inuit known and get a better knowledge about our own history. With the Nanisiniq History Project, we did a lot of our presentations in different provinces and countries. It has helped me to overcome my fears and speak to people about our experiences and history.

I want to talk about how we connect to Project Naming. We came to LAC to look at the history of our ancestors through photographs. In 2013, our Nanisiniq team came to Ottawa, and we were interviewed about the Rankin Inlet Nickel Mine. Along the way, we went to the National Gallery of Canada and saw my grandmother's wall hanging. We didn't know that she was making wall hangings at the time and had sold it to a Qallunaat. We found it at the National Gallery. That was a good experience for Martha Otokala, the Elder who was with us to see it.

These are my family (Figures 12.10–12.14). This is my grandmother, Helen Aagatok Konek, and the other is my grandmother's sister, May Kinaalik Haqpi with her mother, who is on the right playing string games (Figure 12.11). Her name is Pallak. I would have never seen these before until I went to LAC. That made me feel like ... I could know them and their way of living in the past.

I want to talk about how, in the past, Inuit were living in isolated areas within different places in the Arctic. My family were living with missionaries back then. They had access to small things that missionaries brought with them. My grandmother, Aagatok, is still alive and she is eighty-seven years old, and my grandfather died recently. I really like this

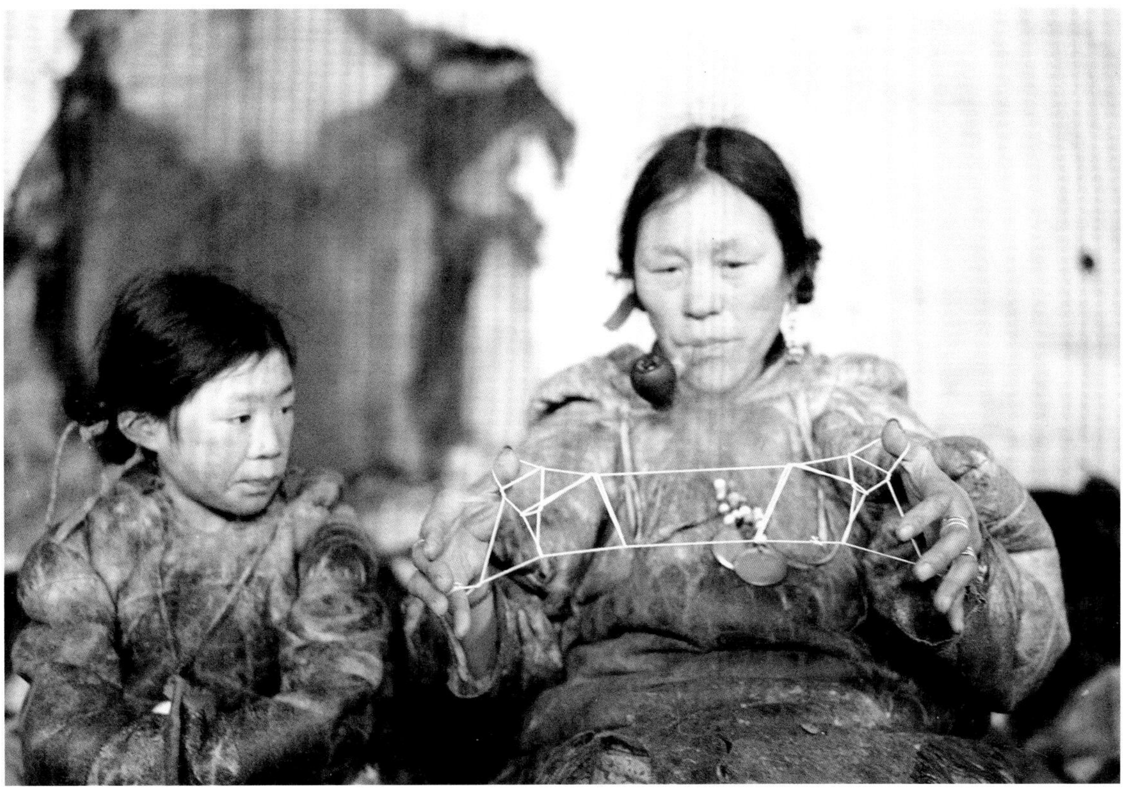

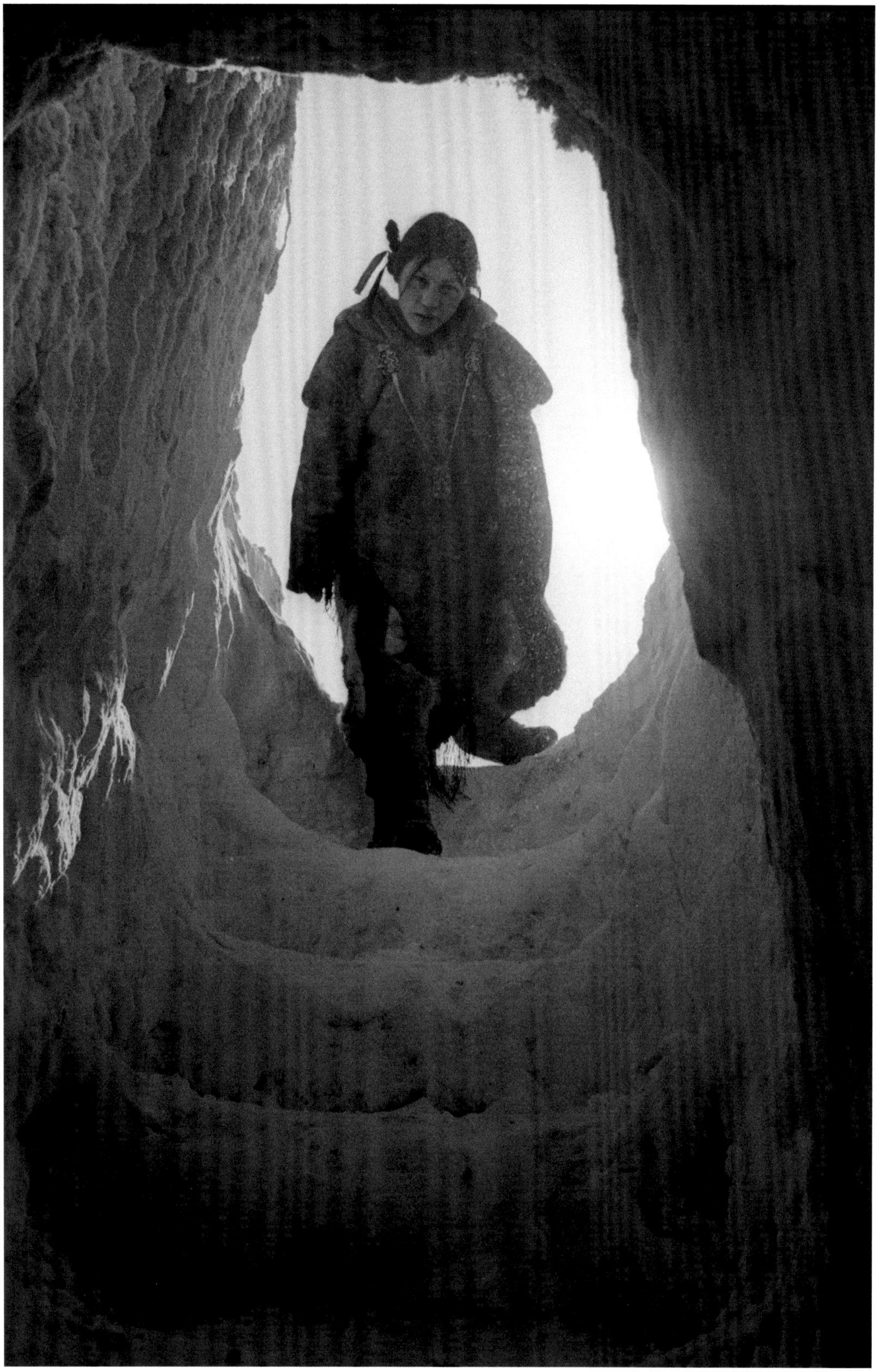

12.12 | [Helen Aagatok Konek going into the iglu], Saningayuaq, near Padlei, 1950.

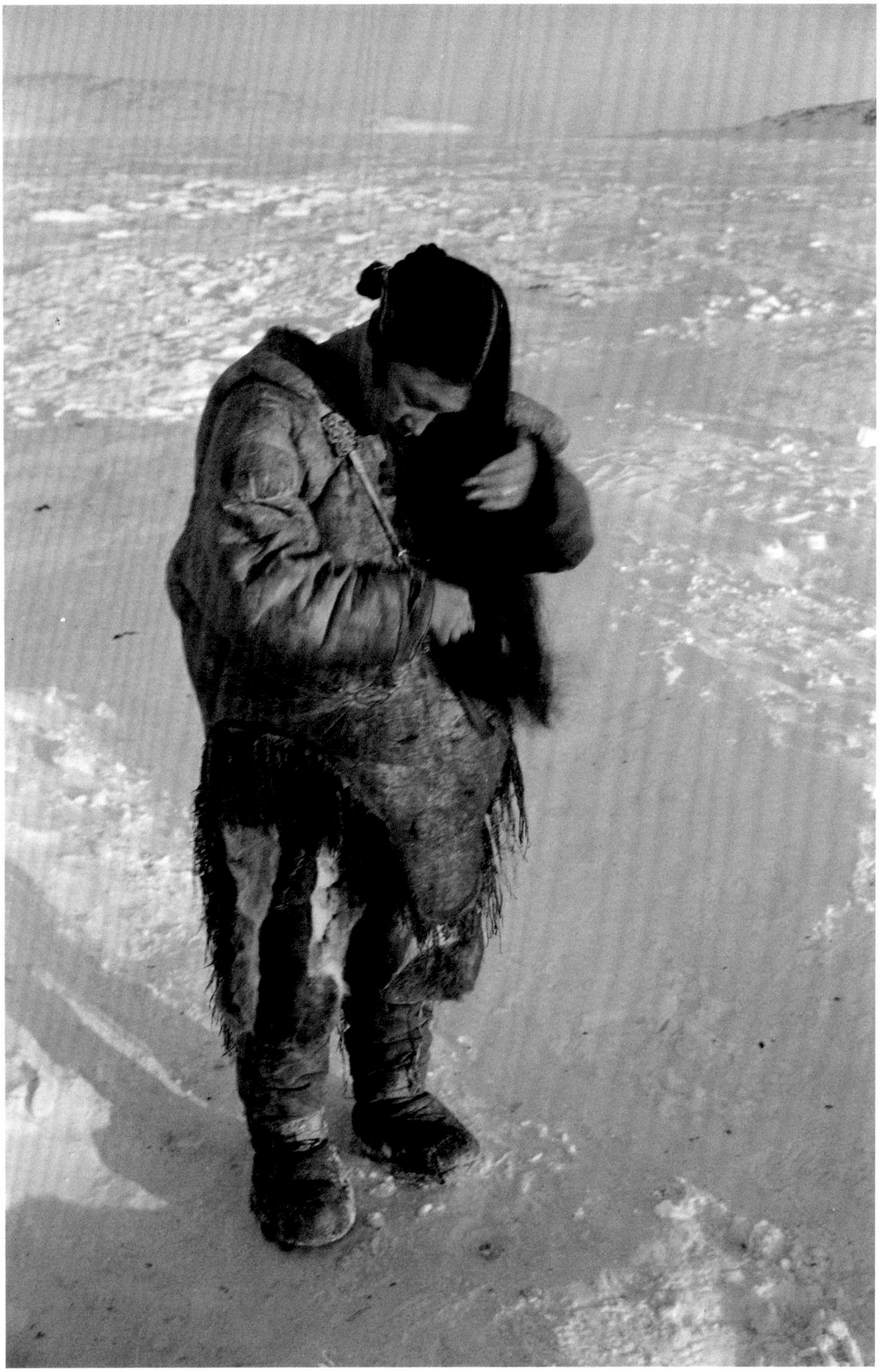

12.13 | [Helen Aagatok Konek], Saningayuaq, near Padlei, Nunavut, 1950.

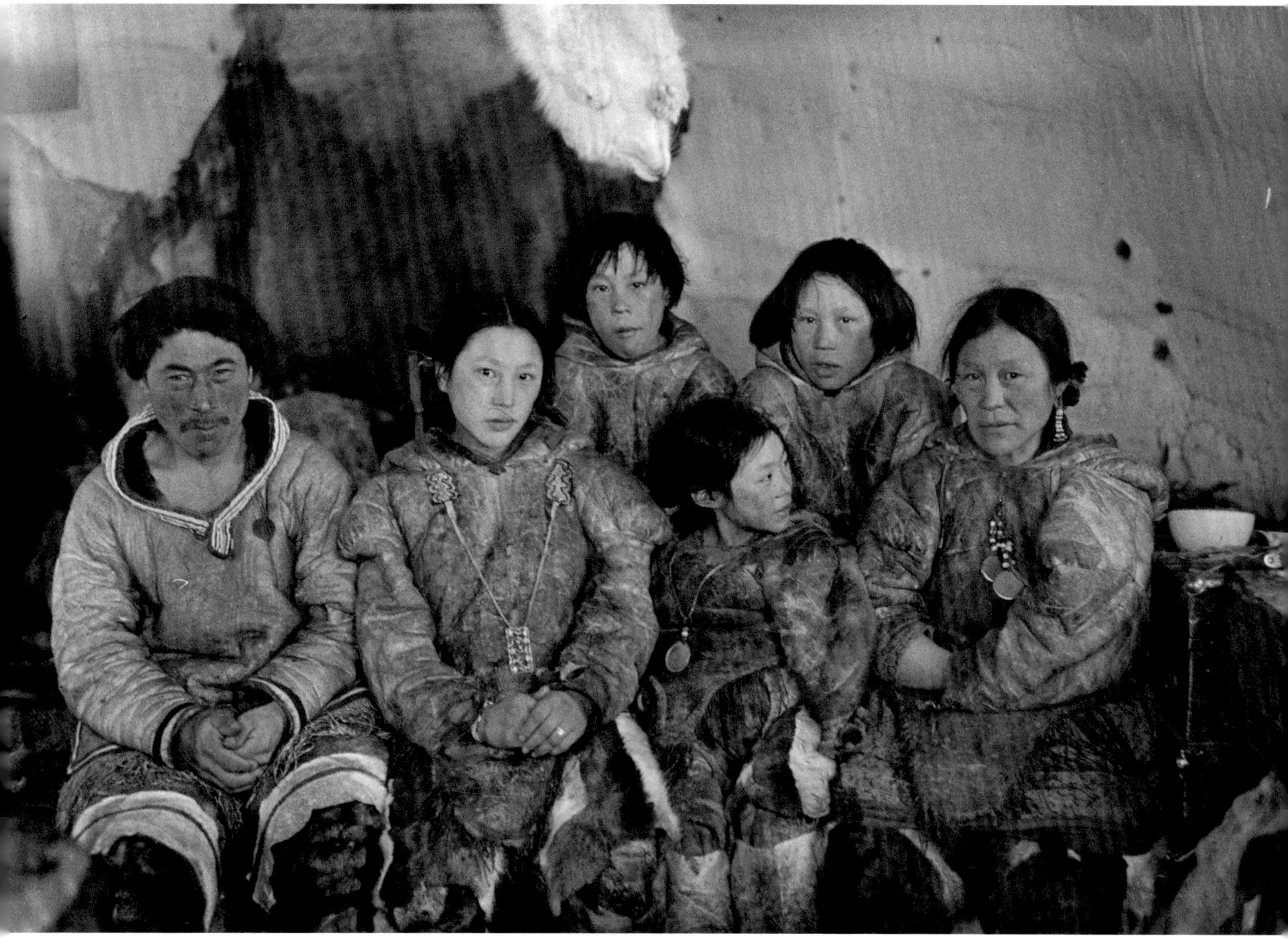

12.14 | [Front row, left to right: Piqqanaaq, Helen Aagatok Konek, Nanauq, and Pallak. Back row, left to right: Pukiluk and May Kinaalik Haqpi], Saningayuaq, near Padlei, 1950.

photo because it tells me about how they lived, what they wore, and what type of iglus they lived in. This picture (Figure 12.12) surprised me because Arviat is pretty flat, and in this one, she seems to go downhill into the iglu. This was an incredibly big iglu buried deep in the snow.

That I didn't know. In this image (Figure 12.13), my grandma is brushing her hair. She probably got the brush from the missionaries.

I want to talk about my family. My grandmother lived through hardships during her time. My grandparents experienced starvation and relocation. These photographs tell me that they were strong people living on the land. I want to talk about my family because I saw these pictures at LAC. These were taken by Richard Harrington who camped with my grandparents in 1950.[14] And my grandparents: my grandmother sometimes tells me stories about what this person was like, what he was doing and, and how they were interacting with each other. I want to also talk about my great-grandfather, Piqqanaaq (see Figure 3.4). He was a great person, as my grandmother tells me. He was a caring person and cared for his family.

I also want to talk a bit more about my experience with the Nanisiniq History Project and working with Inuit and Inuit Elders and youth. We really got to start talking with our Elders about their history, their knowledge, their experience of living on the land. This is important because within thirty years there's going to be few Inuit left who were born on the land. Many spent five or ten years [on] the land and then moved to settlements and heated housing. Without talking to them, we're going to lose a lot of information about our own history and our own heritage in our region. So, what we need to do is create more projects about these old images that say a lot about the history of Inuit. Mutna.

NOTES

1 Tagg, *The Disciplinary Frame*.
2 Pitseolak and Eber, *People from Our Side*.
3 Tagg, *The Disciplinary Frame*, 75.
4 The *C.D. Howe* was built by the federal government as a hospital ship and as a means of supplying the newly forming settlements along the coast of the eastern Arctic. Launched in 1950, it made its first trip to the eastern Arctic in 1951. On board were social workers, doctors, dentists, nurses, and other health-care professionals. It is known primarily for its role in transporting Inuit south for the treatment of tuberculosis. It served communities of the eastern Arctic until 1969.
5 Saddington, "Learner Experience," 41.
6 Qallunaat is, generally, the Inuktitut word for white people. Not unlike Inuit names, it carries with it playful references, in this case, to people with bushy eyebrows (qablu) and a belly (naaq). Scottish whalers were among the first white people with whom Inuit had significant contact so the term is likely an apt description of those they first encountered.
7 Angalik, "We Inuit Call Our Children Qiturngat," 87.
8 "Nanisiniq: Arviat History Project," Tumblr.
9 University of Manitoba Archives & Special Collections, "Social History of the Eastern Arctic Database."
10 Tester and Kulchyski, *Tammarniit (Mistakes)*.
11 Baker Lake (Qamani'tuaq) is the only inland community in Nunavut Territory. Relocation was driven by the collapse of the fox fur trade that had supported Inuit in their land-based camps since the end of Arctic whaling, just before the First World War. The spread of communicable diseases, a TB epidemic, and the location of nursing stations and schools in settlements further contributed to the move to settlements and a very different way of living.
12 Tester, *Beneath the Surface*.
13 "Nanisiniq: Arviat History Project," Tumblr.
14 Harrington, "Padlei Trip: January – April 1950."

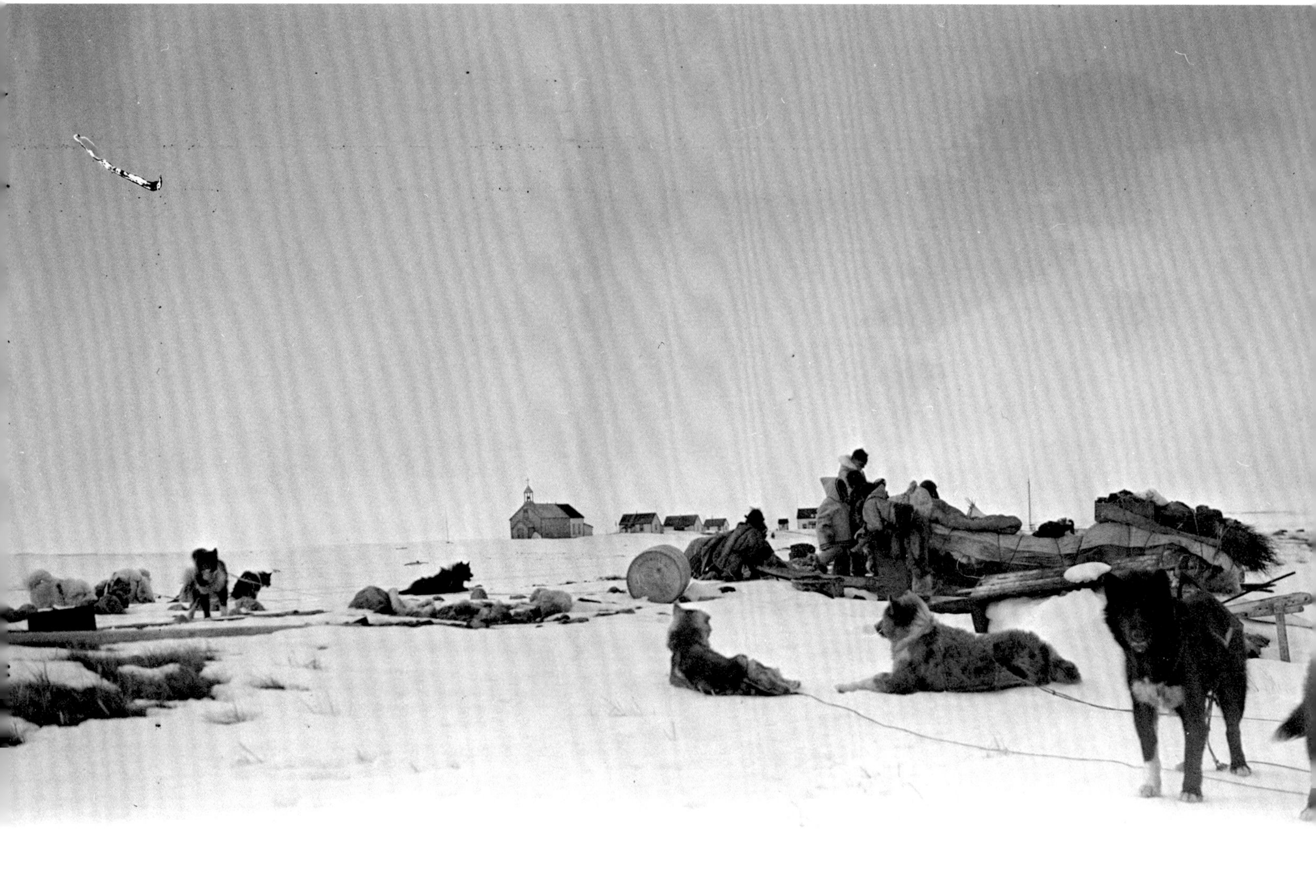

13.1 | Inuit family loading a komatik (sled) with their dog team [Arviat when it was little more than the Anglican mission beside a cluster of HBC buildings] between 1926 and 1943 [the people in the photograph have not been identified yet].

CHAPTER 13

Views from the North: Photographs, Generations, and Inuit Cultural Memory

Carol Payne and Sheena Ellison

In late December 2005, Sharon Angnakak and Corenna Nuyalia (then both Nunavut Sivuniksavut students) interviewed Inuk Elder Akeeshook Joamie and British-born Christian missionary Mike Gardner, who is also Sharon Angnakak's grandfather, in Iqaluit. Gardner helped to translate for the young women as Elder Akeeshook Joamie looked at archival photographs dating from the 1950s through the 1960s depicting the southern Qikiqtaaluk region. The photographs prompted both men's memory and the enthusiasm of the two young women reinforced the importance of passing on knowledge. Looking at old photographs of a dog team, Akeeshook Joamie explained in detail how important dogs were in hunting, while he also introduced Inuktut language, and took delight in describing the teams.

> AKEESHOOK JOAMIE: In spring and summer seasons, the dogs would pack our food and supplies. The people would go out on the land using dogs for our catch … The dogs are very strong when packing

caribou, they can carry caribou hinds and full front. A dog had been a most valuable support system. The dog can carry the heavy pieces of forefront and back while the body and other parts are carried by a person. When packing the meat, we just tie it around the dog with rope ... We make the harness and secure it around the neck area because their head is very useful. It is very tiring to use the head when it is too tight around here and keep the weight off. There is this thick piece that goes through here to protect the head, and it can be secured here and tied around here.

MIKE GARDNER: Yes, to keep the weight off and too tiring and it wasn't shared, in other words, this head has a support so he knows as well as to pack.

AKEESHOOK JOAMIE: Yes, it was rope. This is known as "Ikayuuti" (support) to support the head and it is also tied to the back and it is a long piece. And this piece here is thick so that it slaps into here ... but the other part here are the ropes ... With the dogs, the things that they can pack have individual names. Some dogs are very strong packers, so that would mean the dog is big enough for male caribou pieces packed by one dog. But some, most, dogs can pack let's say certain fore piece of the caribou and only those pieces. They cannot add on certain pieces to carry. There are some dogs that will only pack certain items as some are weaker than the other dogs.[1]

Then the conversation took a more sombre turn as the two elderly men reflected on governmental efforts to destroy dogs at that time. As Akeeshook Joamie reflected, "The dogs were their main thing in life as they were their dog team and they were the transporters of food supplies ... They were strong. The people had suffered hardship when their dogs were killed."

The two young women listened quietly throughout most of the photo-based conversation. It was an opportunity to witness Elders' memories and learn more about recent Inuit history and their Elders' lives. Through images and conversation, the past – ranging from traditional life to assimilationist policies – was reactivated and shared.

This conversation took place as part of Views from the North, a research program that partnered with Project Naming. In collaboration with Nunavut Sivuniksavut and Library and Archives Canada, this research program was active from 2005 to 2014. Over the course of its eight years of active research, eighty youth, Elders, and other community members participated. It extended Project Naming's emphasis on photograph identifications to include photo-based Oral History interviews conducted by NS students with Elders in their home communities. As such, Views from the North is a series of conversations between different generations of Inuit with the concept of unikkaat central to them all. And, indeed, it was designed to enhance youths' experiences as much as it was devoted to capturing Elders' recollections for posterity. At the same time, like Project Naming as a whole, Views from the North involves a collaboration between Inuit and Qallunaat that aims to use the straightforward technologies of photo elicitation to record Elders' stories and engage youth in their own community and family histories.

This chapter introduces Views from the North, as a research partner of Project Naming. In what follows, we recount Views from the

North's methodology, its emphasis on orality, and provide an overview of the interviews. We will close with a discussion of three recurrent themes that appeared in Elders' conversations and follow-up interviews with students: the animation of specific stories of the past, the assertion of intergenerational connections, and powerful affective tones across the discussions.

Methodology

Through SSHRC funding, Views from the North attempted to bridge Project Naming's approach to identifications, Inuit cultural protocols, the pedagogy at Nunavut Sivuniksavut (NS), and Oral History.[2] It involved post-secondary students at Nunavut Sivuniksavut who chose to participate. All were paid to conduct research over the New Year's break while visiting their families and home communities in Nunavut. Each student or group of students was given a photo album filled with archival photographs of their community and asked to interview Elders about these images. Like the students, Elders were compensated as paid researchers for participating in the project. Often another family or community member also participated, usually as a translator; they, too, were paid as researchers. By design, the Qallunaat researchers involved in the research program – including the authors of this chapter and Carleton University research assistants – did not directly interview Elders. Instead, those conversations were within and between Inuit, although interviews in which Elders gave permission for recording were accessible more widely on the web.

Prior to the interviews, students attended workshops organized by Carleton University faculty and graduate students, including the authors. The workshops principally addressed Oral History interview practices, uses of technology, and connections to the NS curriculum. For the first few years, Métis photo-based artist Rosalie Favell also participated in the workshops teaching photographic techniques.

The workshops were a forum for students to offer feedback and contribute to the development of the methodology. Indeed, Views from the North's approach to Oral History was developed in conversation with students. During the first workshop session, students suggested an approach based on the Inuit Qaujimajatuqangit (IQ) principle of Pilimmaksarniq, the practice of learning by listening to and observing Elders. This approach reflects the traditional Inuit transfer of knowledge and relations between generations. Rather than a strict question-and-answer interview format typical to southern Oral History approaches, in this model, students showed the photographic albums to Elders, allowing the conversations to unfold in a more organic fashion. In short, the photographs "asked the questions" and participating youth engaged in active listening. We also worked with the Carleton University Office of Research Ethics to develop an Inuit-appropriate protocol for oral consent agreements, rather than requiring a signed consent waiver.

We compiled photo albums of archival images depicting the home communities of participating students. The photographs, dating from the 1950s and 1960s, were primarily from LAC collections, with some used from the holdings of the National Gallery of Canada (NGC). Initially, Views from the North exclusively used National Film Board of Canada Still Photography Division images (NFB) from both LAC and NGC, an archive that Payne had worked with previously. But as the research project continued with increasing numbers of students and, at times, with students from hamlets not represented in the NFB fonds, we extended the source photographs to holdings from across the LAC's photographic collections. In all cases, extra photographs were printed so that Elders could keep any prints that were meaningful to them.

The conversations between youth and Elders often took place in the Elders' homes. Working on their own or in small groups, youth would approach grandparents, other family friends, and neighbours to show their pictures and learn about the past. As noted above, many students chose to invite parents, aunts, uncles, or neighbours to assist with language translation and to help mitigate generational gaps.

In addition to the photo albums, students were given audio recorders and digital cameras to record their interviews and take photographs of their communities, allowing them to create their own "views from the North." As the project progressed, students increasingly began to prefer to use their own personal technology to record their interviews. With this, we began to collect video interviews that captured different aspects of the conversations between youth and Elders: facial expressions, songs performed, and warm glances.

When students returned to Ottawa following their break, we conducted follow-up interviews to discuss their participation in the project. Students shared their experiences and reflections and often recounted that they heard new stories about family and specific details about the history of colonization in their community. They also enjoyed learning about changes to the physical landscape of their communities, noting when Elders have pointed out the development of familiar stores, schools, or other buildings at places that do not appear in the older photographs. Students often commented that prior to attending NS, they were intimidated to talk to Elders but their experiences at NS helped foster those relationships.

All the data collected and used in the project – archival photographs, interviews with Elders, students' photographs, and follow-up interviews – were made publicly available on the website. Interviews appeared as digital media files and as transcriptions. Whenever possible, information was in both English and Inuktut, with translations provided by translator Rhoda Kayakjuak.

The website was developed by Carleton University's Geomatics and Cartographic Research Centre (GCRC), which also co-hosts the Great Lakes Research Alliance for the Study of Aboriginal Arts and Culture. The cybercartographic platform is part of Dr D.R. Fraser Taylor's Nunaliit Cybercartographic Atlas Framework, which provides adaptable cartographic technology for storytelling. Designed by Amos Hayes (GCRC research and development manager) and supported by Jean-Pierre Fiset using Nunaliit software, the Views from the North site joined other cybercartographic atlases aimed at sharing northern and Indigenous Knowledge.[3] Users could search the atlas using text such as participant names and communities or browse information by scrolling over comminutes on the atlas interface.

Towards the end of the project, we developed a Facebook page to help further user engagement in the North and continue the conversations that began between Elders and youth as part of Views from the North. Archival photographs have been posted as community albums and users continue to tag one another and identify individuals in the photographs, as well as share stories and memories that the photos prompt. As photographs continue to be shared among Facebook users, new conversations are launched.

An Emphasis on Orality

Views from the North contributed to the broader goals of Project Naming by emphasizing the importance of orality to Inuit culture and pedagogy. And in addition to modifying southern Oral History protocols to reflect Inuit culture, it also incorporates photographs as prompts for longer narratives.[4]

Views from the North, largely based on participating students' experiences, emphasized the ways that Inuit Knowledge is traditionally understood to be passed on orally from Elder to youth through stories. In this, the research program also attempted to complement NS's pedagogy. As Louis-Jacques Dorais has demonstrated, the oral literature of present-day Nunavut includes unikkaaq (stories about myths and legends), which in turn include either unikkaatuaq (a story that tells of recent or relatively recent events), or unikkausiq, (a legend or myth from long ago); songs and magic formulas; and contemporary oral literature.[5] The stories that Elders shared with youth and recorded for Views from the North largely comprise contemporary Oral History or inuusirmingnik unikkaat, which, as defined by Keavy Martin and discussed elsewhere in this volume, are life stories told from direct experience.[6] Indeed, as discussed in the introductory chapter to this volume, unikkaat informs Project Naming and all of its affiliated research programs.

Today, in Nunavut and other areas of the North, there is a sense of urgency to preserve Inuit Elders' stories through Oral History. Inuit groups and affiliated scholars have coordinated and drawn on Oral Histories to maintain those memories and to advocate for Inuit cultural and language retention.[7] Among the most influential of these projects are the volume *Uqalurait: An Oral History of Nunavut* and *Listening to Our Past*, which comprise a series of Oral Histories published by Nunavut Arctic College in collaboration with various Inuit Elders and southern scholars initiated in 1994.[8] As Frédéric Laugrand, one of the founders of Nunavut Arctic College's Oral History projects, and scholar Keavy Martin have pointed out, the emphasis on Oral History – and, particularly, the retention of Elders' Traditional Knowledges, especially naming practices – is political.[9] It reflects an emphasis on IQ, which in turn forms the guiding set of principles for the governance of Nunavut and is a means of privileging Inuit epistemologies over those of the South.[10]

Views from the North built on the achievements of Inuit Oral History projects like *Uqalurait* and *Listening to Our Past*. But it also augmented Oral History with the use of photographs.[11] In a methodology known as photo elicitation, anthropologists have long used images to prompt recollections and stimulate discussion among subjects in interviews. But photo elicitation has also been criticized as an extractionist practice: one that takes information away from the communities it involves. Views from the North – like Project Naming as a whole and like the Inuit Oral History initiatives described above – aimed at a more dialogic and collaborative practice. In this way, Views from the North, Project Naming, and the other partnered research programs discussed in this volume contribute to a wide range of dialogic Indigenous-settler photographic "returns" projects from around the globe.[12] In Views from the North, Inuit youth interviewed their Elders in their own communities over photographs and the resulting interviews were made accessible across Nunavut on the web. The photographs themselves function, in scholar Elizabeth Edwards's words, as relational or "social objects"[13] resulting in a "relational view

… in which photographs become entities acting and mediating between people."[14]

Views from the North, with its emphasis on intergenerational learning through unikkaat, also reflects the values of IQ. Young people learn from Elders through stories, which reframe southern archival photographs from Inuit perspectives. In the wake of the Truth and Reconciliation Commission of Canada (into the history of residential schools) and the Qikiqtani Truth Commission (into the enforced assimilation of Inuit in the Qikiqtaaluk region of Nunavut from 1950–75), the interviews conducted as part of Views from the North are a testament to Inuit cultural autonomy and resilience.[15]

Photo-Based Conversations across Nunavut

The conversations that NS students had with Elders reflected the local and specific concerns of family relations, community life, local traditions, and changes seen firsthand. They also shared a sense of pride in Inuit culture more broadly. Although not every community in Nunavut was represented, the interviews took place across all three regions: Kitikmeot, Qikiqtaaluk, and Kivalliq. The cybercartographic atlas developed by the GCRC used a map interface, which allows visitors to listen to interviews from across Nunavut and shows the wide reach of the project. A few examples from each of Nunavut's three regions give a fuller sense of these photo-based conversations. All were available on the Views from the North website and several of those interviews are included in images reproduced here.

Interviews were conducted in Qikiqtaaluk communities, including Sanikiluaq (Belcher Islands), Kinngait, Iqaluit, Pangniqtuuq (Pangnirtung), Mittimatalik (Pond Inlet), and Iglulik (Igloolik). In early 2012 in Sanikiluaq, the late musician Kelly Fraser conducted three photo-based interviews. She spoke with Nunavut member of the Legislative Assembly Moses Appaquq; the oldest woman in the community, Sarah Kittosuk; and Fraser's own mom. All three recognized people in the archival photographs and told Kelly about the changes they had witnessed. On 7 January 2010, NS student Andrea Flaherty interviewed Franny Flaherty in Iqaluit with the help of her aunt Lavinia Flaherty. Prompted by photographs, Franny Flaherty talked about her life in Aujuittuq (Grise Fiord) in the Qikiqtaaluk region (see Figure 13.2). During the next year (2011) in Aujuittuq itself, NS students Pauline Akeeagok and Arqnarulunnguaq (Arna) Audlaluk spoke with Elders Minnie Killiktee and Larry Audlaluk. Audlaluk dated the photographs exactly, talking about the arrival of the medical ship the *C.D. Howe* and changes in buildings and sealskin clothing.[16] The same photographs in the same communities often prompted different conversations and recollections. In 2011, NS student Janet Evic interviewed Jarloo Akulujuk, her brother-in-law's father, from Pangniqtuuq. From him, she learned about whaling in the area. Following the interview, Evic created a video showing the collection of family photographs in her home. In 2009, student Natasha Mablick of Mittimatalik interviewed her father, learning how her parents met and about hunting and trade in northern Baffin decades ago.

Students from the Kivalliq region also learned about local history and tradition in the communities of Naujaat (Repulse Bay), Salliq, Igluligaarjuk (Chesterfield Inlet), Qamani'tuaq (Baker Lake), Kangiqliniq (Rankin Inlet), Takirarjuaq (Whale Cove), and Arviat (Eskimo

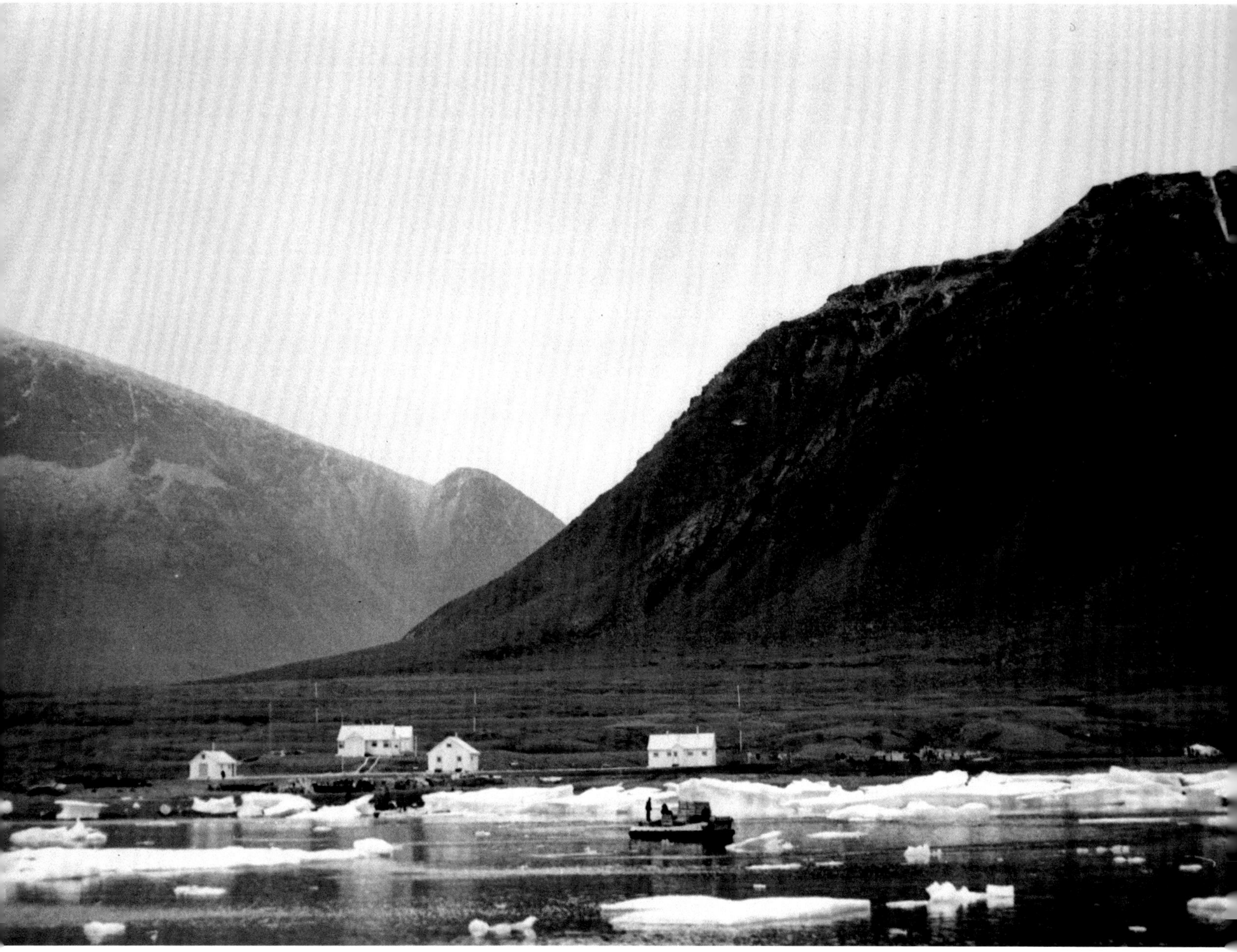

13.2 | *View of Grise Fiord*, n.d.

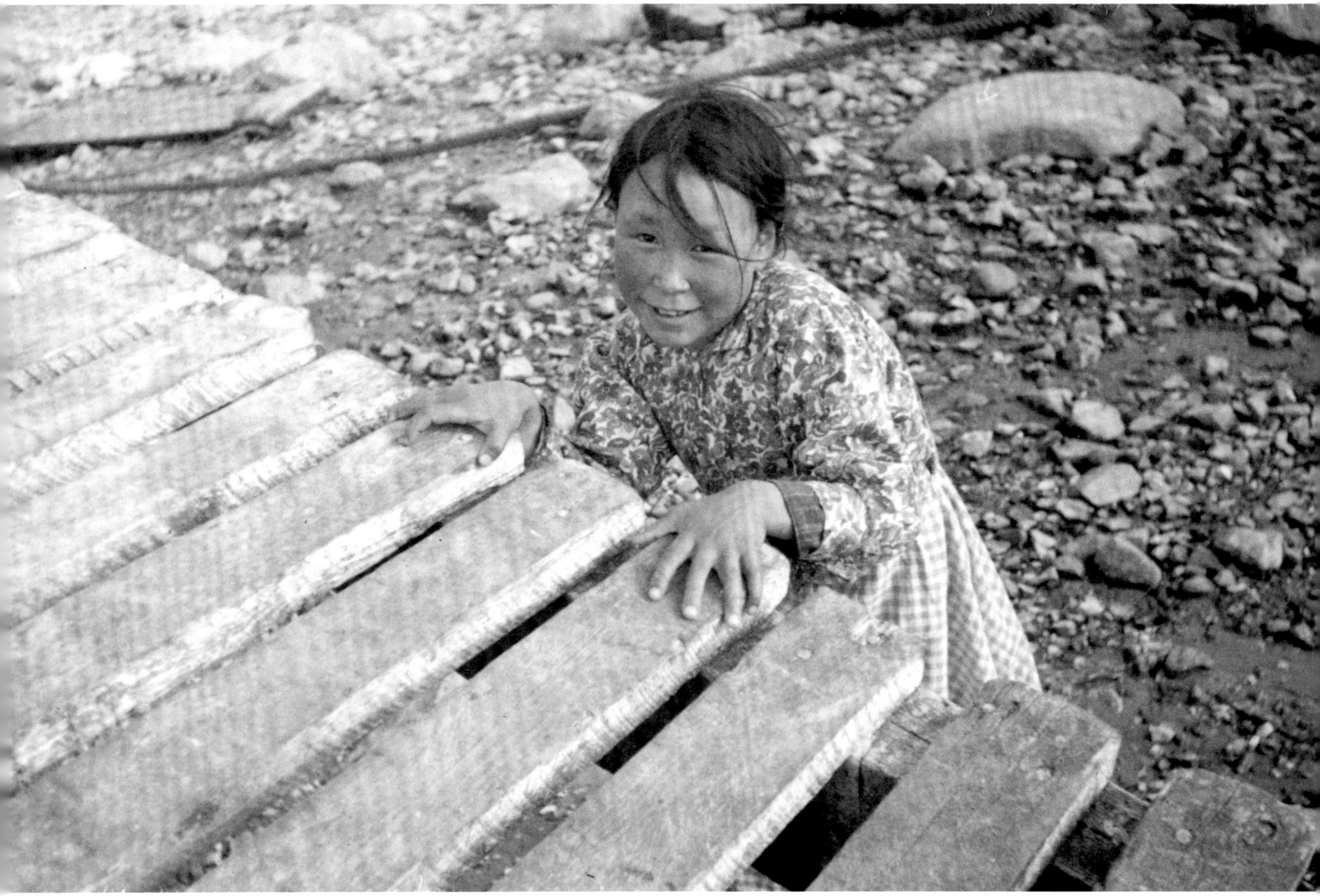

13.3 | [Maryann Tattuinee. This photograph was probably taken at Salliq. Ms Tattuinee now lives in Kangiqliniq], c. 1945–46.

13.4 (*opposite*) | [Mona Tigitkok with baby Adam Katiek], Kugluktuk, 1949–50.

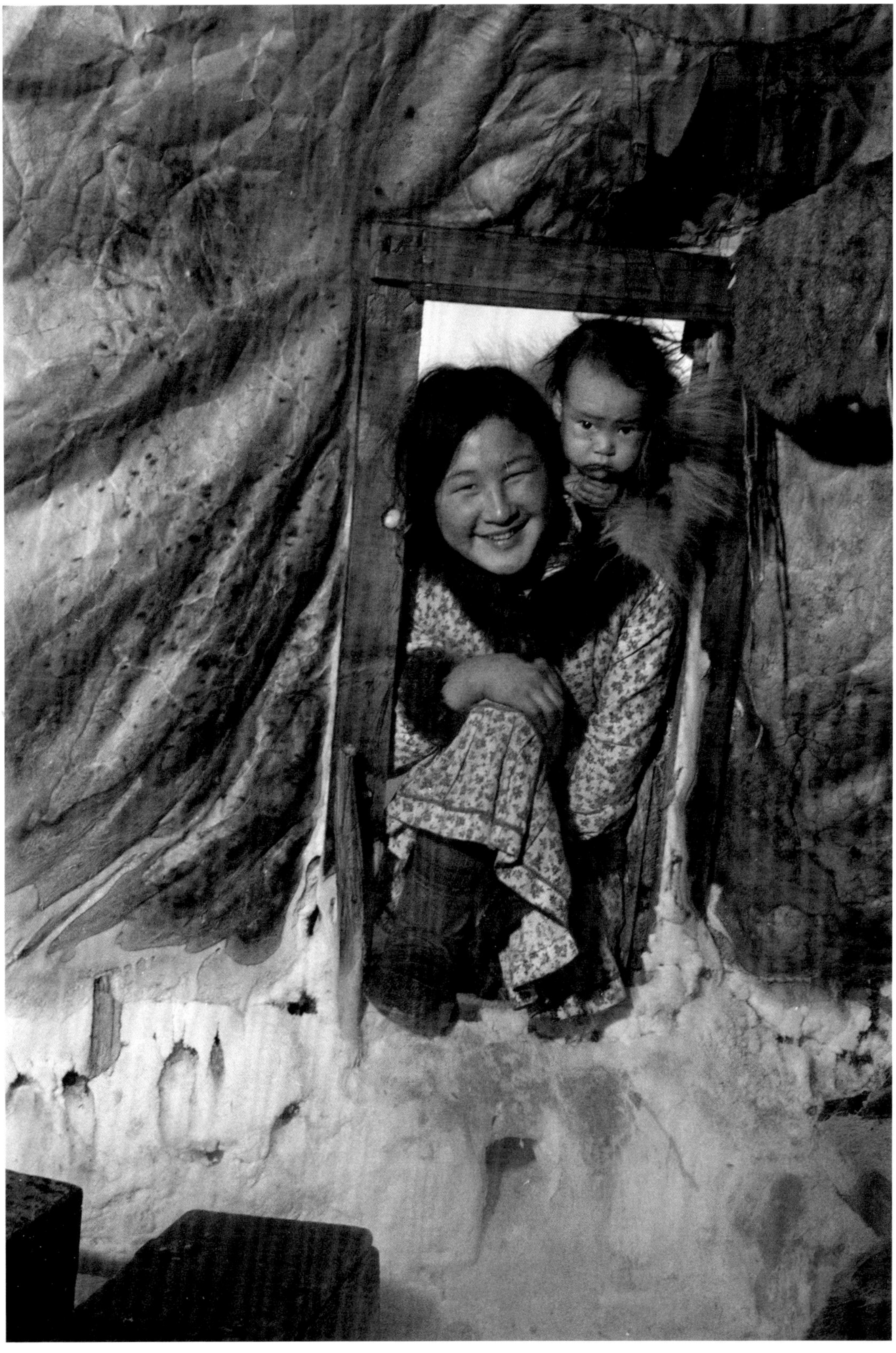

Point). Student Rebecca Sammurtok of Igluligaarjuk organized a community gathering with several Elders at the local community centre where they identified people in the photos, including Sammurtok's own grandfather.

However, most of the interviews were more intimate. Then-student Kerri Tattuinie interviewed her grandmother Marianne Tattuinie in Kangiqliniq, who described the changes that had occurred over the decades in the hamlet and its people (Figure 13.3). In Arviat, students Kukik Karetak and Amy Owingayak interviewed four Elders: Eva Muyunaganiak, Henry Isuanik, and Rhoda and Johnny Karetak. (Amy also participated in the Nanisiniq Arviat History Project discussed by Frank Tester and Curtis Konek in Chapter 12.) Owingayak and Kukik Karetak later recalled their favourite part of the interview with CU student Spencer Stuart: "We actually got to do games, like a game with the Elder. She was trying to show us how to [play] this game and we didn't even know how. The one that, you know, we had to learn a traditional song, and she explained that well, and that's always my favourite, and I never knew what that was and she told a story about what it translates into."[17]

Photo-based interviews were also conducted by NS students with Elders in the Kitikmeot Region in the communities of Kugluktuk, Arviliqjuaq, and Uqsuqtuuq (Figure 13.4). In 2005, student Tolok Havioyak interviewed Elder Ahmie Anahanak who talked about family life and the passing down of names. And, as described in the introductory chapter to this collected volume, Elder Bernadette Elgok saw herself in photographs during a conversation in Kugluktuk with then student Katrina Hatogina (see Figure 1.2). Moreover, the interviews have contributed to the students' ongoing research. During the summer of 2018, for example, former NS student Jennifer Ullulaq co-organized the first annual Gjoa Haven Umiyaqtutt Festival and drew on her experience interviewing Elders at NS and for Views from the North.[18]

What Was Learned

Many things were learned through these photo-based conversations that took place across Nunavut that were organized by Views from the North in affiliation with Project Naming. But in surveying those conversations and in follow-up interviews with participating NS students, a few key themes recurred. First, the specific content of these photo-based encounters tended to emphasize local knowledges, including familial and community identifications as well as Inuit Traditional Knowledge. Secondly, youth and Elders reflected on the experience of meeting across generations itself, emphasizing the importance of connection. Finally, most of the interviews revealed a heightened affective tone that enhanced that connectivity.

In all the photo-based interviews conducted under the auspices of Views from the North, Elders were keen to share Traditional and local Knowledge. In the young students, they had enthusiastic audiences, young Inuit who were eager to engage with tradition and community. Following the goals of Project Naming as a whole, atiqput, reclaiming Inuit names, was central. Elders identified people in the photographs to ensure that their names were known. These identifications were important to the Elders and are, perhaps, a testament to the popularity of Project Naming's "Do You Know Your Elders?" newspaper feature across Nunavut. Elders were poised to name sitters in the images. But these interviews also showed that atiqput introduced other knowledges.

Indeed, it often seemed that the photographs were a mere pretext for other conversations. For example, Elders often took the photographs as points of departure for conversations about local communities and traditional Inuit life. They discussed living on the land, hunting, and sewing, among other topics. While the photographs that prompted these discussions usually depict traditional life from a colonialist perspective, picturing Inuit as primitivized others; Elders' narration reframes the same images from Inuit perspectives, reclaiming pre-contact life and participating in Inuit resurgence. As we have described above, the Elders were intent on teaching their young interlocutors and the students were eager to learn.

An interview conducted in Kangiqliniq in 2006 by then student Faith Kakuktinniq with Elder Lizzie Putulik provides a rich example of that sharing of specific, local knowledge. In the conversation, Elder Lizzie Putulik talked at length about life on the land and her specific experiences sewing:

> LIZZIE PUTULIK: There were no clothing stores so we had to make our own garments. That is how we lived. Even if we don't know how to make kamiks, we participated in other task[s] such as making the hide into leather. Once we got it in softer, we would get help making kamik patterns and we tried hard to piece them together by sewing them. I remember when I quit when [my mother] was not looking and they would find out that I did not do it right so they took the stitches off and I had to try again from the top. Even when I was not very happy about my certain task, we had to listen to what we are told to do and do it. We cannot disobey. That is how we were taught.
>
> FAITH KAKUKTINNIQ: How old were you when you started sewing?
>
> LIZZIE PUTULIK: I was about nine years old. I was trying to do a lot of things and even on my own, I tried to do things because I was so envious. I was even working on fox fur at that age.
>
> FAITH KAKUKTINNIQ: Some people now cannot work with fox fur.
>
> LIZZIE PUTULIK: I learned how to work with it very well. I was even eight years old when I learned to work with fox fur. I learned how to dry them helping my mother drying the fur and cleaning the dried fur.
>
> FAITH KAKUKTINNIQ: You were able to do that on your own at that age?
>
> LIZZIE PUTULIK: I helped my mother in drying and cleaning it. We would put it on a board and nail it on the wooden board for drying. Once I learned that I would do it, they would encourage us to see who finishes first. I think that is how they were training us. They would say that the one who finishes first will get an item. We would race.
>
> FAITH KAKUKTINNIQ: When you work really fast with your sewing do your garments come out perfectly?
>
> LIZZIE PUTULIK: I was always told that even if I don't have evenly perfect stitching, it doesn't matter as long as it doesn't twist. Kamiks can be uneven or sideways if you don't sew it properly. They can look like two different boots. They can look very

warped and uneven. It is that it is sewn sort of twisted. The body part of the boot would slide onto the sole part. That is how. You have to sew it evenly [to avoid] Qipigayuq [twisting]. It is ok if you don't have very fine stitching as long as it secures it that would be fine and that is how they taught us. If it is sewn so tight and evenly also it would come apart so even if you don't sew it then it would be more secure. If the stitching is secure and the sewing is not flipping the sole then they would say it is very well sewn.

FAITH KAKUKTINNIQ: What kind of sinew did you use?

LIZZIE PUTULIK: Caribou and whale.

FAITH KAKUKTINNIQ: Are they strong?

LIZZIE PUTULIK: Yes, they are very strong sinew even the muscles of whales.[19]

In addition to specific local knowledge, a sense of connection was experienced throughout the encounters. As Payne has discussed elsewhere, in follow-up interviews, participating students consistently talked about renewed bonds with Elders through their experiences at NS. Views from the North was a very small part of that pedagogical experience, but it contributed to that reconnection with Elders and Inuit culture as a whole. Many students were initially intimidated to speak with Elders, often because of a language barrier. The photographs and the act of sitting down with Elders to discuss them provided new points of connection. But the Elders also reinforced that sense of connection. For example, they regularly used conversation to place the youth within the images by talking about how their young interviewers were related to the people in the photographs. In this way, through these connections, the photographs were not only narrated as part of the past but reframed as the future. A conversation in Kugluktuk with student Tolok Havioyak and Elder Ahmie Anahanak stressed the importance of transgenerational learning:

AHMIE ANAHANAK: Young people, why can't they go listen to the Elders and maybe they might even have an education ... an interesting time and interesting person to learn about Elders ... What the education ... or the public education should have a strong word for pushing the youths to go to the Elders so they could learn and understand.[20]

Finally, throughout the photo-based conversations and in follow-up interviews with students, there was a heightened affective tone. As they rekindled familial and community connections, youths and Elders alike *felt* the experience of connection. Often, there were emotional moments of recognition as Elders saw themselves as young people or long-gone loved ones. They also faced difficult histories. In a 2010 interview conducted in Iqaluit by then NS student Andrea Flaherty, Elder Franny Flaherty recalled her life in Grise Fiord as one of the Inuit relocated to the High Arctic. Elder Franny Flaherty had some fond memories of her life there but also told Andrea Flaherty that "we went through hardship. We were starving when we first moved there. We were thirsty and there was no water. I would melt water from the sea ice. We would really have to look everywhere for ice."[21]

Views from the North (2005–14) grew out of, and was inspired by, the approach of Project

Naming. Working in collaboration with LAC and NS, the project played a small part in the students' overall NS experience. Nonetheless, it attempted to complement the Inuit-centred pedagogy developed at the school, as discussed earlier in this volume. By adding recorded photo-based Oral History interviews, Views from the North emphasized the importance of Oral Tradition and unikkaat in Inuit culture. In this way, it also built on the important Oral History projects undertaken across Nunavut. Adding a photographic component to Oral History interviews served as an accessible and engaging way to spark Elders' memories and through those memories to reframe federal colonial images within Inuit remembrance and storytelling.

Acknowledgments

We acknowledge the Social Sciences and Humanities Research Council's support. Many thanks to the students, Elders, and others who have participated in Views for the North. We also thank former NS faculty Murray Angus and Morley Hanson for facilitating student involvement in the project, and helping to draw connections between their work on Views from the North and their school curriculum. We are also grateful to Beth Greenhorn and Library and Archives Canada for their support in allowing us to build upon the important work of Project Naming and providing access to archival materials as well as support using their collections. Artist Rosalie Favell's photographic workshops with students for the project enhanced the experience of the research. The team at the Carleton University Geomatics and Cartographic Research Centre – particularly Fraser Taylor, Amos Hayes, and Jean-Pierre Fiset – is owed a big thanks for bringing the research to even more people in Nunavut through the cybercartographic atlas. Rhoda Kayakjuak's translations contributed to the project's accessibility. Finally, we would like to extend our gratitude towards the students – Hellin Alariaq, Suzanne Crowdis, Claire Mackenzie, Spencer Stuart, and Laura Schneider – who, like Sheena Ellison, worked as research assistants helping to collect, catalogue, transcribe, and upload interviews over the course of the project. Unfortunately, at press time the Views from the North site is not up. We hope the material will be accessible soon.

NOTES

1 Photo-based Oral History interview with Elder Akeeshook Joamie conducted by Sharon Angnakak and Corenna Nuyalia with the assistance of Mike Gardner, 30 December 2005. Translation: Mike Gardner and Rhoda Kayakjuak. (This is an excerpt of the full interview. For the full interview in Inuktitut and English, see the Iqaluit page on Views from the North website, accessed 26 January 2022, http://viewsfromthenorth.ca/index.html.)

2 Payne, "Culture, Memory and Community."

3 "Views from the North." Other GCRC sites include the Arctic Bay Atlas, the Cybercartographic Atlas of Antarctica, the Indigenous Perspectives and Knowledge Atlas, the Gwich'in Atlas, the Lake Huron Treaty Atlas, the Pan Inuit Trails Atlas, the Siku Atlas Kitikmeot Place Name Atlas, and the Fifth Thule Expedition Atlas.

4 For more on photo-based Oral History in general, see Freund and Thomson, *Oral History and Photography*.

5 Dorais, *The Language of the Inuit*, 162–71.

6 Martin, *Stories in a New Skin*, 98–120, 139.

7 McGrath, "Isumaksaqsiurutigijakka"; Collignon, Therrien, and Duchemin-Pelletier, *Orality*; Dorais,

The Language of the Inuit; Laugrand and Oosten, *Inuit Shamanism and Christianity*; Nakasuk, Ootoova, and Angmalik, *Interviewing Elders: Introduction*.

8 Bennett and Rowley, *Uqalurait*; Kublu, Laugrand, and Oosten, "Listening to Our Past"; Nakasuk, Ootoova, and Angmalik, *Interviewing Elders: Introduction*.

9 Laugrand, "Écrire Pour Prendre La Parol"; Martin, "Are We Also Here for That?"

10 Igloliorte, "Arctic Culture / Global Indigeneity"; Tester and Irniq, "Inuit Qaujimajatuqangit."

11 Freund and Thomson, eds, *Oral History and Photography*.

12 Clifford, *Returns*; Edwards, "Talking Visual Histories"; Edwards and Hart, *Photographs Objects Histories*; Geismar et al., *Moving Images*; Lydon, "'Behold the Tears'"; Lydon, *Calling the Shots*; Peers et al., *Pictures Bring Us Messages*; Poignant and Poignant, *Encounter at Nagalarramba*.

13 Edwards, "Photographs and the Sound of History"; Edwards, "Exchanging Photographs"; Edwards, "Material Beings"; Edwards, "Objects of Affect."

14 Edwards, "Photographs and the Sound of History."

15 Their Oral Histories call to mind Gerald Vizenor's neologism "survivance": Indigenous resilience and survival. Vizenor, *Survivance*.

16 Inuk leader Larry Audlaluk has also written movingly about his experiences as a High Arctic Exile. Audlaluk, "What I Remember."

17 Karetak and Owin in conversation with Stuart, 2012.

18 Ullulaq email correspondence with Payne, 2018. "Umiyaqtutt Festival."

19 Photo-based Oral History interview with Elder Lizzie Putulik conducted by then Nunavut Sivuniksavut student Faith Kakuktinniq. Kangiqliniq, December 2006. Translation: Rhoda Kayakjuak. (This is an excerpt. For the full interview in Inuktitut, see Kangiqliniq page on the Views from the North website, accessed 26 January 2022, http://viewsfromthenorth.ca/index.html.)

20 Photo-based Oral History interview with Elder Ahmie Anahanak conducted by then Nunavut Sivuniksavut student Tolok Havioyak. Kugluktuk, 30 December 2005. Interview recorded in English. (For a full recording of the interview see the Kugluktuk page on the Views from the North website, accessed 26 January 2022, http://viewsfromthenorth.ca/index.html.)

21 Photo-based Oral History interview with Elder Franny Flaherty conducted by then Nunavut Sivuniksavut student Andrea Flaherty. Iqaluit, 7 January 2010. Translation: Rhoda Kayakjuak and Lavinia Flaherty. (For the full interview in Inuktitut and English, see the the Iqaluit page on the Views from the North website, accessed 26 January 2022, http://viewsfromthenorth.ca/index.html.)

CHAPTER 14

Looking for Kenojuak

Sandra Dyck

It is something of a paradox to be writing about photographs of Kenojuak Ashevak (1927–2013) in a book on Project Naming. She was the only woman whose work was featured in Kinngait's inaugural print collection (1959), produced by the community's new cooperative (today, Kinngait Studios).[1] In 1960, the cooperative released her now-iconic stonecut, *The Enchanted Owl*. The National Film Board of Canada's film *Eskimo Artist: Kenojuak* (1963) made her a star. In Kinngait's 1964–65 print catalogue, the first to include biographical information, she was described as "probably the best-known" of Inuit artists.[2] Kenojuak went on to receive an inaugural Order of Canada medal (1967) and co-produce an imposing mural for the Canadian Pavilion at Expo '70 in Osaka, Japan. Then, as now, she is known in the English-speaking south by the mononym Kenojuak and her face is instantly recognizable.[3] When you start looking for her in photographs, she's hard to miss.

Kenojuak was among the artists and printmakers whose portraits were reproduced in the 1960 print catalogue, designed by Norman Hallendy, an industrial designer employed by the Department of Northern Affairs and National Resources (DNANR). The Ottawa-based freelance photographer Rosemary Gilliat shot these portraits in the fall of 1960, while on a trip largely financed by the DNANR and including stops in Iqaluit, Kuujjuaq, and Kinngait.[4] Later catalogues regularly included photographs of the artists, often shot by visiting Qallunaat and published to satisfy the curiosity of the Qallunaat buyers of the prints who, as Jimmy Manning has observed, always wanted to know what the artists looked like.[5]

Gilliat's photographs are part of a vast archive of visual culture, amassed since the mid-nineteenth century and comprised of photographs made by Qallunaat visiting Inuit Nunangat, many on state-sponsored trips. "The first time I saw a white man, he had a camera," John Amagoalik has said, "and it seems that whenever government officials or tourists came North, they always had cameras."[6] These photographs, shot of and with (but usually not for) Inuit and largely circulated in the South, are not neutral. They are the products and records of personal encounters sometimes marked by asymmetrical power relations, promoting and disseminating specific images of Inuit that are caught up in the colonization of Inuit Nunangat. As Natan Obed, president of Inuit Tapiriit Kanatami, has said, Qallunaat photographs have "served as the building blocks for persistent stereotypes and generalizations about our people and our experiences that continue today."[7]

This essay surveys photographs of and a film about Kenojuak Ashevak, made from the late 1940s through the late 1960s. Colonizing forces intensified radically in the Qikiqtaaluk Region, where Kinngait is located, during this period.[8] To take just one measure of the impact of those forces, culturally: the proportion of Kinngait's total income from hunting and trapping fell from 36 per cent in 1950–51 to less than 1 per cent in 1966–67, while income from "handicrafts" increased from nil to 40 per cent of the local economy.[9] Some Inuit navigated these intensely destabilizing decades by forging new roles as artists. As the artist Pitseolak Ashoona said in 1968, "I am making my living on paper – paper that tears, and I depend so much on it."[10]

Project Naming consolidates and circulates historic photographs of Inuit taken by Qallunaat, bringing them to public attention and facilitating the naming of people they depict. How such photographs are viewed and experienced, as Paul Seesequasis has written, depends of course on who is doing the looking and where they come from, literally and figuratively.[11] It is also contingent on the particular context in which each image was created, as the Qikiqtani Inuit Association cautioned in a prefatory note to its recent collection of community histories, which is mostly illustrated with photographs of Inuit taken by outsiders.[12]

The relational, cumulative, and revelatory processes of viewing, experiencing and naming connect diverse individuals in and across images, over time, traverse boundaries of geography, language, kin, and culture. Kenojuak Ashevak, however, rarely needs to be identified in photographs because over the course of her half-century career, she became the face – and the name – of Kinngarmiut art.[13] The production and circulation of named images of the artist were in fact fundamental to her renown. Kenojuak may not have controlled the myriad ways in which photographs of her were reproduced, editorialized, or received, but she collaborated in their creation. She can also be understood, as Aaron Glass and Brad Evans have argued in a different context, as an agent in the dissemination of these images and "party in unique ways to their consumption."[14]

When it comes to photographs of Kenojuak Ashevak, then, the project of "naming" also encompasses identifying the contexts for their production, use, and circulation. Such activities underscore the status of these photographs as representations, characterized by the inherent capacity to navigate the circumstances of their making and the intentions of their creators.

Eastern Arctic Patrol

Beginning in 2013, the Qikiqtani Inuit Association (QIA) published landmark histories of the thirteen communities in the Qikiqtaaluk Region, including Kinngait, based on testimonies that Qikiqtaalungmiut made to the Qikiqtani Truth Commission (QTC) between 2007 and 2010. Each history is organized according to three periods, which successively chart the dire changes wrought by colonial incursions in the region.

During the first period, Taissumani Nunamiutautilluta (when we lived on the land), most Kinngarmiut lived at ilagiit nunagivaktangit (places used regularly for hunting, harvesting, and gathering) located along the south coast of Baffin Island, east and west of Kinngait.[15] Families visited Kinngait on occasion, typically at Christmas and in summer when supply ships arrived. The *Nascopie*, the *Regina Polaris*, and the *C.D. Howe* were among the ships that carried missionaries, traders, scientists, tourists, and photographers to the region. Filmmaker and photographer Robert Flaherty and ornithologist J. Dewey Soper were among the early visitors who made photographs in the area, in 1913–14 and 1929, respectively.

From 1922 to 1968, the ships also brought members of the Eastern Arctic Patrol (EAP), a sustained effort by the Canadian government to assert its sovereignty over the Arctic.[16] The EAP prioritized the visual documentation of its yearly voyages. Photographs shot by Qallunaat amateurs and professionals were collected into albums, today found at Library and Archives Canada (LAC), in the Department of Indian Affairs and Northern Development (DIAND) fonds.[17] All sixty-nine of these "departmental albums" have been digitized and many individuals depicted within their pages, including Kenojuak, have been identified through Project Naming.[18]

Two early Qallunaat images of a youthful Kenojuak are included in the EAP's 1948 album, which features photographs made by patrol commander S.J. Bailey (Figures 14.1–14.2). His typewritten captions, cut and pasted into the album, indicate that the *Regina Polaris* departed from Quebec City and made its first stop at Kinngait.[19] Bailey occasionally named the subjects of his photographs, as in an image he shot at Kinngait of Udluriak (the eldest daughter of Peter Pitseolak) standing aboard the *Regina Polaris* with crew members.[20] Participants in Project Naming paid attention to an adjacent photograph on that album page, affirming Bailey's naming of Udluriak and identifying her companion as Kenojuak Ashevak.[21] With this information in hand, both women can easily be identified in a group photograph elsewhere in the album, where they stand on the ship's deck with other Kinngarmiut, none of whom are named by Bailey[22] (see Figure 1.1).

Family Photographs

The arrival of increasing numbers of Qallunaat in the Qikiqtaaluk Region coincided with the arrival of photographic technology. Kinngait's renowned photographer Peter Pitseolak acquired a 122 box camera through a Roman Catholic missionary, in the 1940s.[23] Pauta Saila, Paulassie Pootoogook, Sakiassie Ragee, and Salomonie Pootoogook are other Kinngarmiut photographic pioneers of this period. By

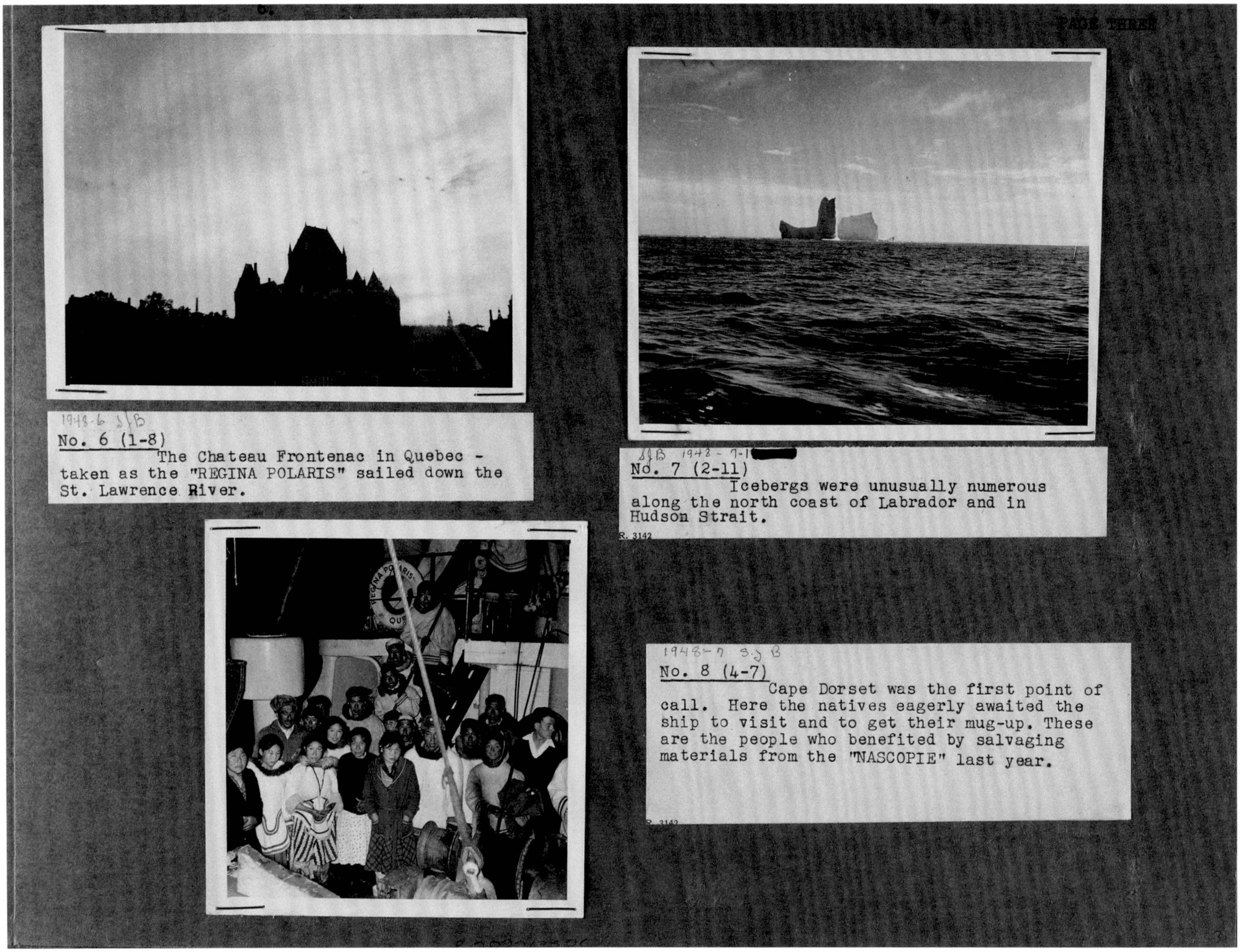

14.1 | [Album 38, page 3 with photographs of the Chateau Frontenac in Quebec City, icebergs off the coast of Labrador, and group of Inuit on board the Eastern Arctic Patrol ship MV *Regina Polaris* in Kinngait, Eastern Arctic Patrol], 1948.

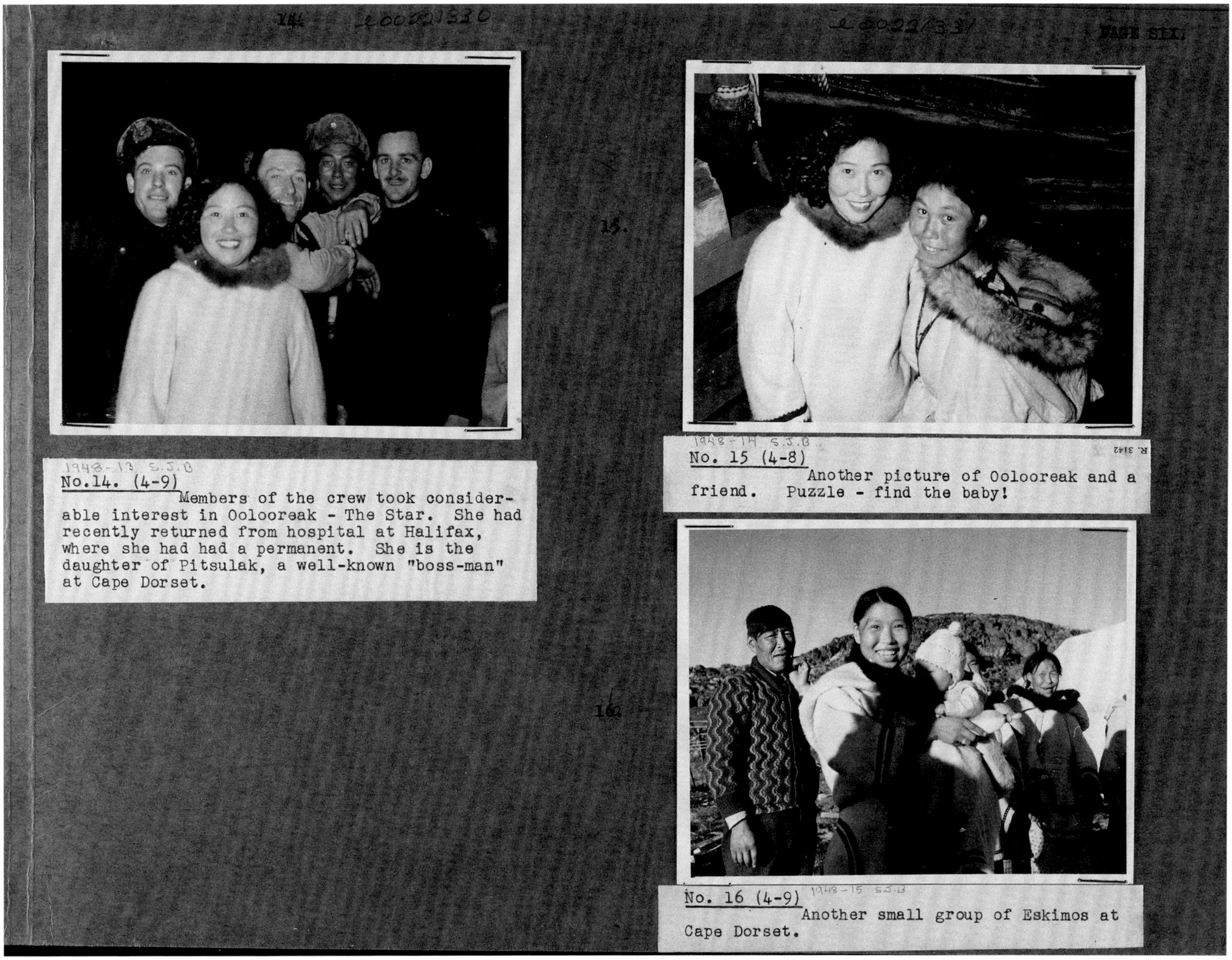

14.2 | [Album 38, page 6 with photographs of Udluriak with the crew of the Eastern Arctic Patrol ship MV *Regina Polaris*, Udluriak and Kenojuak Ashevak, and a group of Inuit. In the photograph at lower right, Timothy Ottochie is seen on the left and his wife Aukshuali is in the centre holding their baby, Kinngait], 1948.

the 1950s, cameras were "not unusual" on Baffin Island.[24]

Kinngarmiut began making photographs of that most familiar of subjects – each other. The rise locally of family photography – images taken by, of, and for family members and viewed and circulated privately – is often associated with Peter Pitseolak because his work has been exhibited, published, and collected in the South.[25] Pitseolak took the first such pictures of Kenojuak, who joined his extended family in 1946 when she married his brother-in-law, Johnniebo. The young couple lived at several ilagiit nunagivaktangit in the late 1940s, including Kiattuuq, where Pitseolak was leader.

Peter Pitseolak was interested in the evidentiary value of his photographs – he staged photos of particular hunting and fishing activities to "show how for the future" and made a point of photographing people in caribou skin clothing at a time when it was becoming less common.[26] He made many other images of Kiattuuq residents of all ages, engaged in everyday activities, inside and outside. Some smile for Pitseolak's camera, willing participants in his documentary enterprise; others appear tolerant or disinterested. These are, in other words, typical family photographs.

Peter Pitseolak's Kiattuuq photographs of Kenojuak and Johnniebo mostly take the form of casual portraits, shot individually or with friends and relatives (see Figures 14.3 and 14.4). What his images of the young couple do not show is the increasing presence and impact of colonizing forces. Johnniebo and Kenojuak were wed a second time – in "the Christian way" – by an Anglican clergyman in Pitseolak's wood house at Kiattuuq and issued alphanumeric identification tags (ujamiit) by the Royal Canadian Mounted Police (RCMP). They also began negotiating the difficult transition to an unstable wage economy; Johnniebo found work in construction, including the building of a school in Kinngait.

Rabbit Eating Seaweed

The EAP ships that visited Kinngait annually brought diseases, even as they imported another form of photographic technology – the X-ray. Kenojuak was X-rayed for tuberculosis aboard the *C.D. Howe* and eventually evacuated to Quebec City, not long after the birth of Qiqituk, her son. In a photograph of Kenojuak taken at Parc Savard Hospital by fellow patient Peter Pitseolak, she sits beside her bed, clad in a bathrobe, face impassive. While away from her home and family for three years of treatment (1952–55), she experienced an indescribable tragedy – the deaths of her three children. Although Kenojuak had been cleared to return home, she became very ill after receiving this devastating news, conveyed in a letter to another patient. Speaking of this period, nearly forty years later, she said, "At that time, I did not care whether I lived or died."[27]

Kenojuak's time in hospital occurred during the years described by the QTC as Sangussaqtauliqtilluta (1950–65), which means "the time when we started to be actively persuaded (or made) to detour (or switch modes)."[28] During this time of intensifying centralization, the agents of government, trade, and the church were increasingly present in the lives of Kinngarmiut. Families were under pressure to leave the ilagiit nunagivaktangit and move to Kinngait, where such government services as health care and education were being consolidated.[29]

The Canadian government was meanwhile encouraging the production of art for southern markets to create new sources of income for

14.3 | *Johnniebo Ashevak at Kiattuuq*, c. late 1940s. [Canadian Museum of History caption: "Portrait of Johnniebo, photo by Peter Pitseolak, 1940–1960."]

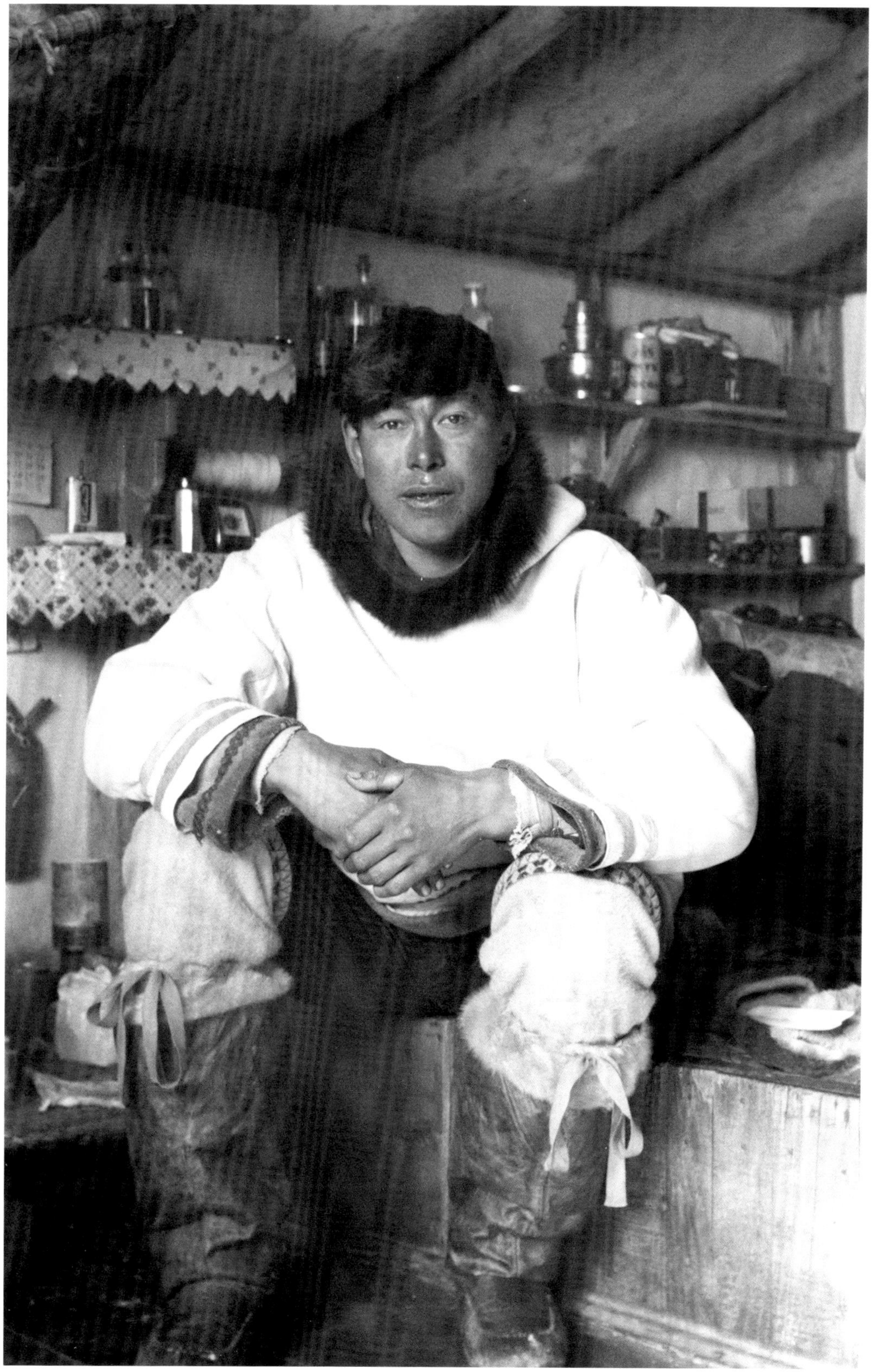

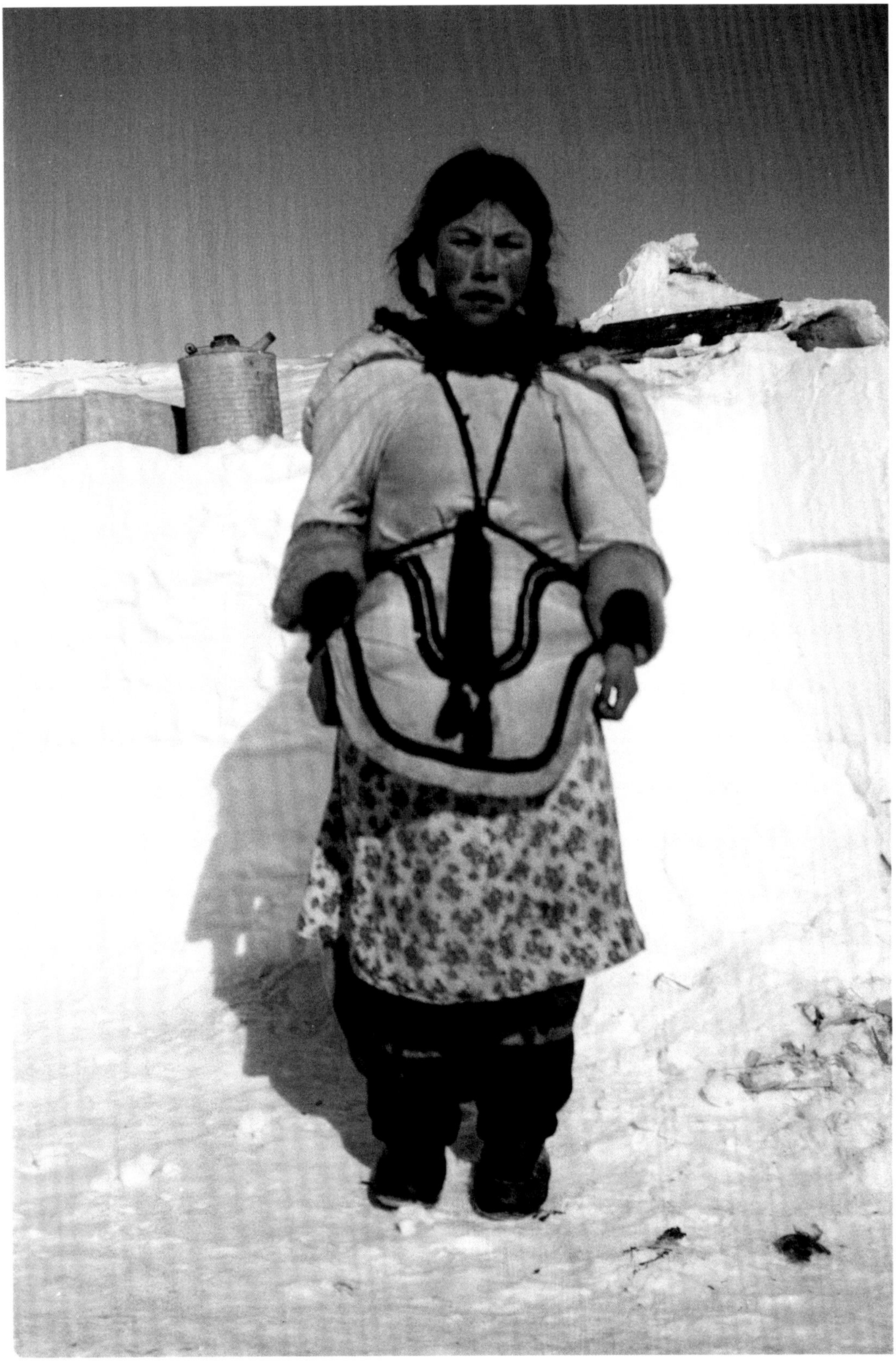

14.4 | *Kenojuak Ashevak at Kiattuuq*, c. late 1940s. [Canadian Museum of History caption: "Kenojuak wearing a dress and amauti, photo by Peter Pitseolak, 1940–1949."]

hunters and their families who had relocated to Kinngait and other communities. In 1956, the year after Kenojuak returned home, James Houston moved with his family to Kinngait, where he worked as the DNANR's newly appointed Northern Services Officer. Houston and his wife, Alma, were active in the community and nearby ilagiit nunagivaktangit and Kenojuak was soon persuaded to try her hand at the various forms of artistic production they were facilitating, including crafts, drawing, and sculpture.[30] Houston collaborated with Kananginak Pootoogook, Iyola Kingwatsiak, Lukta Qiatsuq, and Eegyvudluk Pootoogook on the experiments that led ultimately to the establishment of Kinngait's printmaking enterprise.[31] Kenojuak was represented in the community's inaugural print collection with *Rabbit Eating Seaweed* (1959), a stencil print produced by Iyola Kingwatsiak and inspired by a sealskin bag of her design, now known only through a photograph.[32]

"Poet of the Arctic"

Increasing numbers of camera-carrying Qallunaat ventured northward before and during Sangussaqtauliqtilluta. Prominent among them were photographers and filmmakers on assignment from the National Film Board of Canada (NFB). Such photographers included Bud Glunz, Jean Roy, Wilfrid Doucette, Gar Lunney, Ted Grant, Rosemary Gilliat, Benny Korda, and Roloff Beny.[33] Laura Boulton's *Eskimo Arts and Crafts* (1943), Douglas Wilkinson's *Land of the Long Day* (1952), and John Feeney's *The Living Stone* (1958) and *Pangnirtung* (1959) are among the NFB films shot in Inuit Nunangat during this period. The intensity of southern fascination with "the North" cannot be underestimated. Already by 1960, Kinngait resident Andrew Kingwatsiak told Gilliat and Alma Houston that "so many people had taken his photo that he had no more pictures left in him."[34]

Photographs and texts produced by the NFB and disseminated and consumed in the South were central to the development of Kenojuak's public persona as an artist. The 1960s began auspiciously for her, with *The Enchanted Owl* (1960). A stonecut printed by Lukta Qiatsuq and Eegyvudluk Pootoogook from a drawing by Kenojuak, it remains the most famous and valuable print made in Canada.[35]

Rosemary Gilliat's 1960 photographs of Kenojuak, Lukta Qiatsuq, and *The Enchanted Owl* feature prominently in "Kenojuak – Poet of the Arctic," a photo story issued by the NFB in the summer of 1961 (see Figures 14.5 and 14.6).[36] Photo stories are narrative pictorials on particular subjects, produced as ready-to-use files that were widely circulated in Canada and abroad, principally through publication in newspapers and magazines.[37] They inevitably portrayed Canada in "glowing, jingoistic terms" and supported the NFB's mandate to visually promote and naturalize Canada's national identity.[38]

"Kenojuak – Poet of the Arctic" is an early manifestation of the tensions inherent to Qallunaat representations of the artist. Gilliat's photographs depict Kenojuak as a young, working mother at home in her canvas tent, cigarette in hand, making a large drawing while caring for Adamie, her toddler son. This visual context is barely acknowledged in the accompanying texts, in which the NFB writers characterize the artist's work as beginning "in ordinary life" but soon taking flight into the "rhythmic world of imagination," where it existed as a "flowing fantasia." This is an early example of the fantastical meaning-making

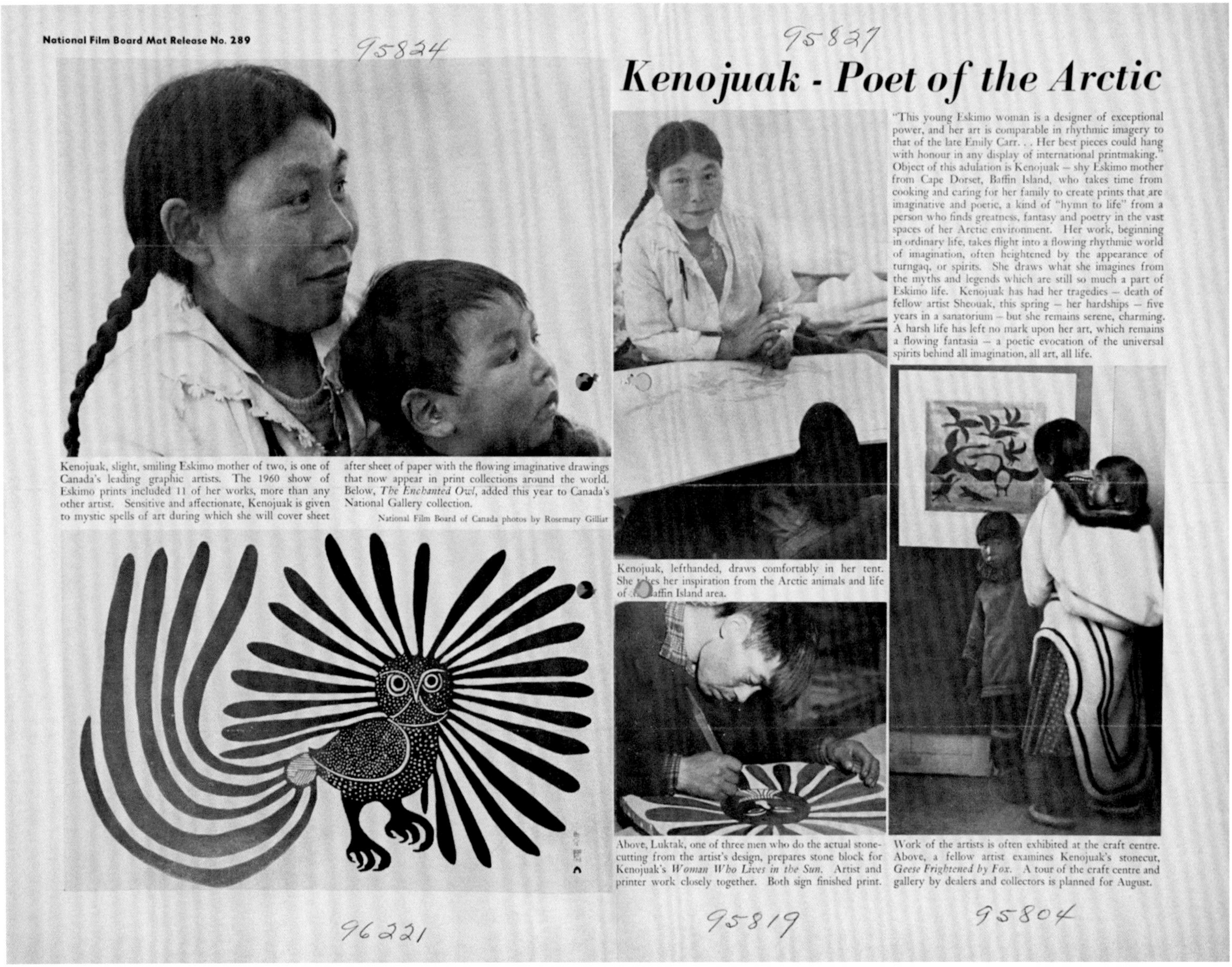
National Film Board Mat Release No. 289

Kenojuak - Poet of the Arctic

"This young Eskimo woman is a designer of exceptional power, and her art is comparable in rhythmic imagery to that of the late Emily Carr. . . Her best pieces could hang with honour in any display of international printmaking." Object of this adulation is Kenojuak – shy Eskimo mother from Cape Dorset, Baffin Island, who takes time from cooking and caring for her family to create prints that are imaginative and poetic, a kind of "hymn to life" from a person who finds greatness, fantasy and poetry in the vast spaces of her Arctic environment. Her work, beginning in ordinary life, takes flight into a flowing rhythmic world of imagination, often heightened by the appearance of turngaq, or spirits. She draws what she imagines from the myths and legends which are still so much a part of Eskimo life. Kenojuak has had her tragedies – death of fellow artist Sheouak, this spring – her hardships – five years in a sanatorium – but she remains serene, charming. A harsh life has left no mark upon her art, which remains a flowing fantasia – a poetic evocation of the universal spirits behind all imagination, all art, all life.

Kenojuak, slight, smiling Eskimo mother of two, is one of Canada's leading graphic artists. The 1960 show of Eskimo prints included 11 of her works, more than any other artist. Sensitive and affectionate, Kenojuak is given to mystic spells of art during which she will cover sheet after sheet of paper with the flowing imaginative drawings that now appear in print collections around the world. Below, *The Enchanted Owl*, added this year to Canada's National Gallery collection.

National Film Board of Canada photos by Rosemary Gilliat

Kenojuak, lefthanded, draws comfortably in her tent. She [illegible]s her inspiration from the Arctic animals and life of [illegible]affin Island area.

Above, Luktak, one of three men who do the actual stone-cutting from the artist's design, prepares stone block for Kenojuak's *Woman Who Lives in the Sun*. Artist and printer work closely together. Both sign finished print.

Work of the artists is often exhibited at the craft centre. Above, a fellow artist examines Kenojuak's stonecut, *Geese Frightened by Fox*. A tour of the craft centre and gallery by dealers and collectors is planned for August.

14.5 | National Film Board of Canada, Still Photography Division, Photo story 289. "Kenojuak – Poet of the Arctic," 11 July 1961.

14.6 (*opposite*) | [Kenojuak Ashevak, her husband Johnniebo Ashevak, and their two children], Kinngait, 1960.

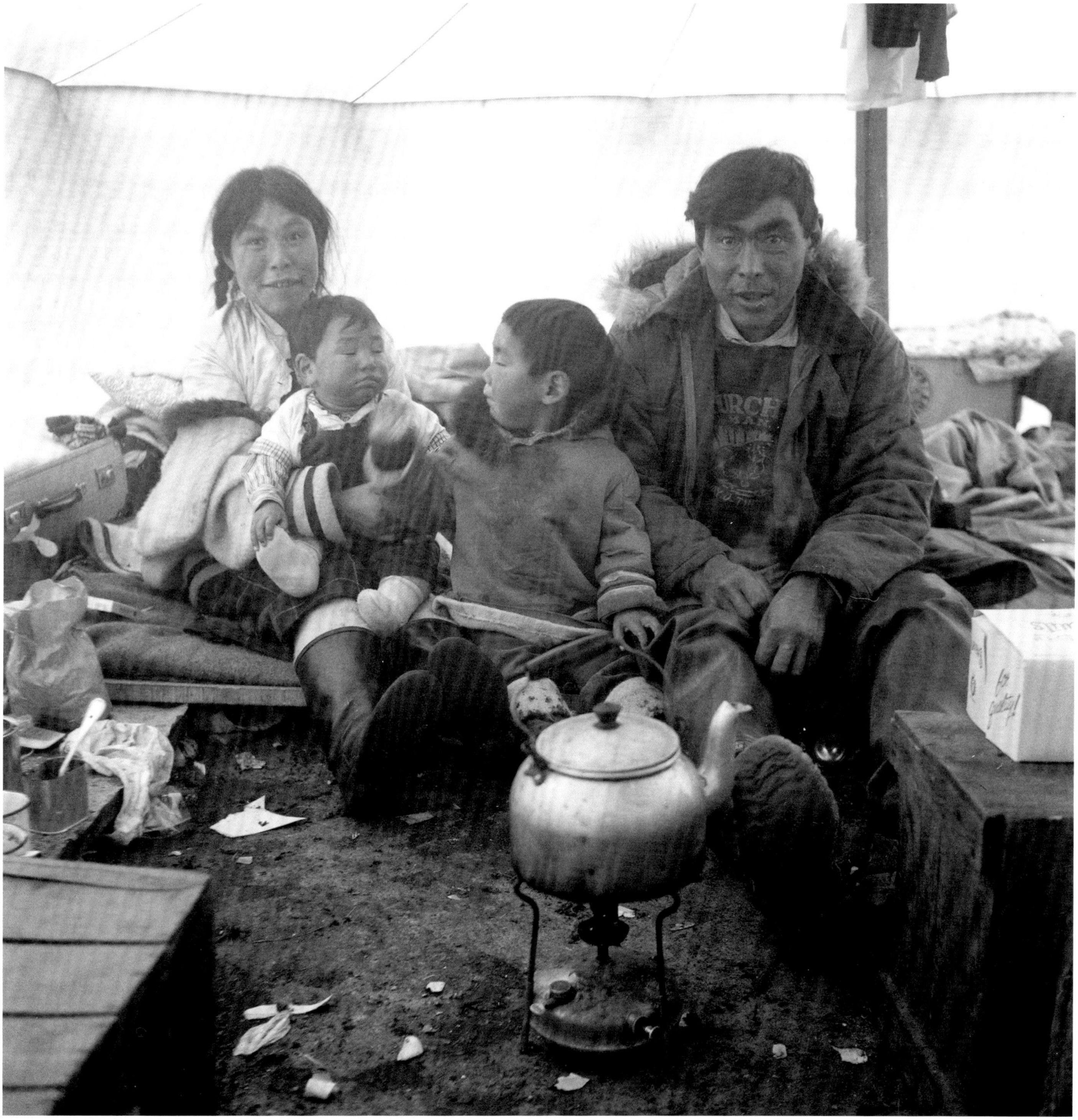

that often pervaded Qallunaat discourse on Kenojuak Ashevak and her work. She sometimes spoke back to it, and these responses are occasionally documented in the public record.

"You Missed the Eye"

Qallunaat mythologizing reached an apogee in *Eskimo Artist: Kenojuak*, directed by John Feeney (with James Houston as a consultant) and produced with the DNANR's cooperation. Shot in the spring of 1962 and released the following year, the NFB film is voiced by Alma Houston, who narrates Feeney's script, written and performed in the first person as if to express the artist's thoughts.

Eskimo Artist: Kenojuak is structured around several narrative arcs: the Ashevak family's journey by qamutiq from Itilliarjuk to Kinngait, the making of Kenojuak's stonecut *The Arrival of the Sun* (1962), and the dawning of "modernity" in Kinngait. It includes footage of Feeney's local screening of the famed NFB film *Universe* (1960). Kenojuak and others are shown watching the projection, apparently rapt, they learn that the earth is round and that the sun is further away than the moon. Houston, speaking for "Kenojuak," says of *Universe*, "These people who make the sun and moon's picture, they know the whole world and more. I know the world between here and our camp, that is all I know." These words Feeney puts in Kenojuak Ashevak's mouth underscore his portrayal of her – and Kinngarmiut, by extension – as the passive recipient of Qallunaat knowledge, visualized in the film by contemporary Kinngait, with its wood houses, snowmobiles, X-ray machine, and English-language schooling.

The ever-present gap between images of Inuit and the purposes they are made to serve is epitomized by a scene in *Eskimo Artist: Kenojuak*. This sequence, one of the few instances in the film where Kenojuak's Inuktitut speech is not obscured by Alma Houston's voice-over, takes place in the print shop. Johnniebo and Kenojuak stand with art advisor Terry Ryan, watching as a fresh impression of *The Arrival of the Sun* – printed, as Houston informs us, on "a piece of paper from the outside world, as thin as the shell of a snowbird's egg" – is pulled from the stone matrix. Houston intones that Ryan is asking Kenojuak why she chose this topic, and she replies that she doesn't know, but Johnniebo thought "the spirits must have whispered in my ear." A translation of Kenojuak's Inuktitut commentary reveals that Ryan is actually asking her if the print looks nice and she responds by pointing out an error made in interpreting her drawing: "There was supposed to be an eye here, but you missed the eye," she says.[39]

Eskimo Artist: Kenojuak was nominated for an Academy Award in 1965, the same year it was named best short film by the British Academy of Film and Television Arts.[40] It made Kenojuak a star and her work "famous to people in Canada and abroad," as the 1966 Kinngait print catalogue declared.[41] In one of the few substantive interviews with Kenojuak, published in 1983, the artist acknowledged the film's positive impact on her career, observing that it had helped to make her work popular.[42] She also described the tedium and labour of the film shoot, remembering that she "used to get so mad" at Feeney, especially one day when her sons Arnaquq and Adamie fell off the qamutiq during filming. She "just felt like walking out on the whole thing," but Feeney would not let her quit (see Figure 14.7).[43]

For Kenojuak, financial autonomy was the film's most important benefit. The income allowed Johnniebo to buy a canoe, supporting

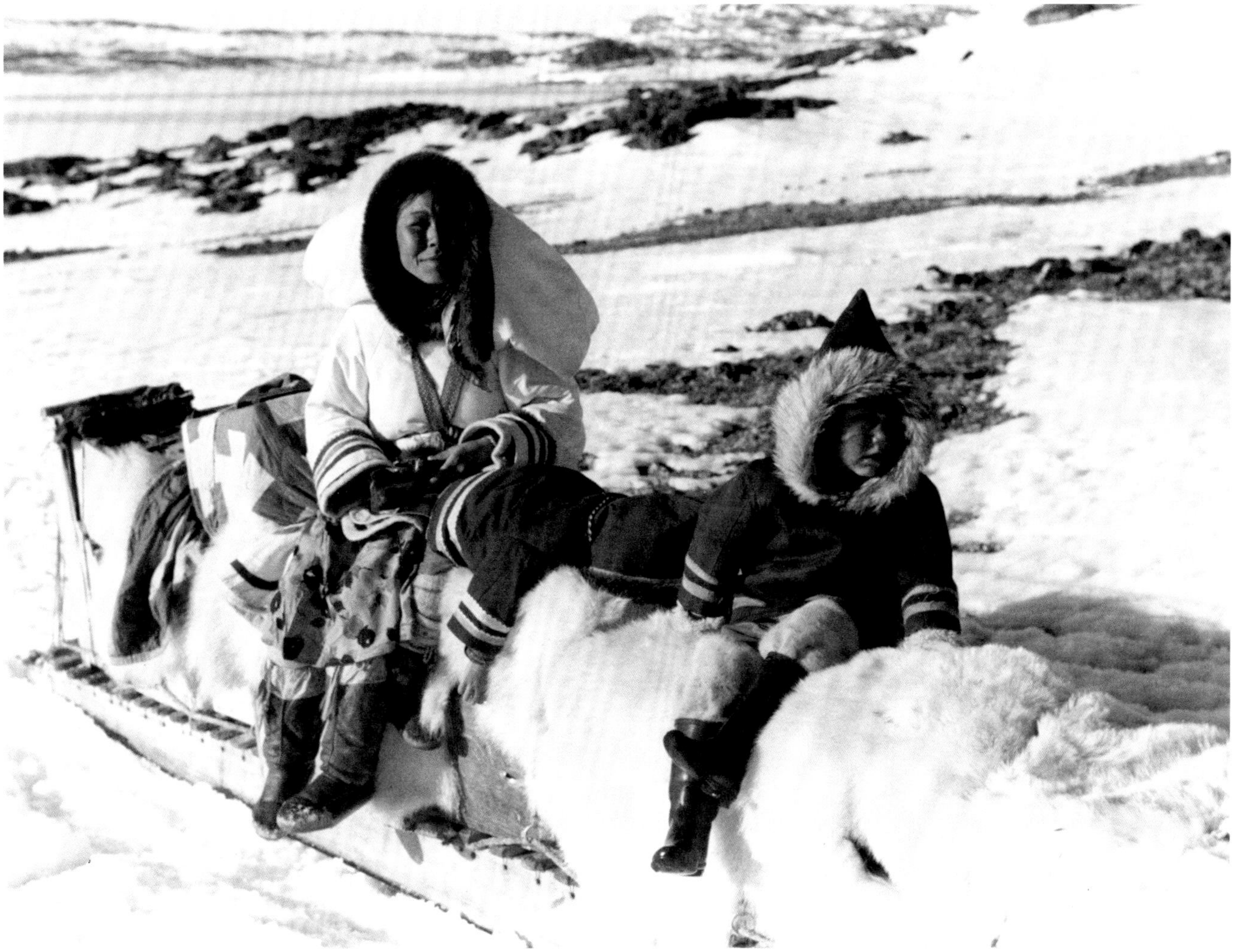

his work as an independent hunter and mitigating the family's reliance on the wage economy. "It seemed like a new beginning for us," she later said.[44]

14.7 | [Kenojuak Ashevak with her sons Ashevak (in amauti hood), Adamie (sleeping), and Arnaqu (sitting up) during the filming of *Eskimo Artist: Kenojuak*], location?, 1963. Original title: The famous artist Kenojuak with her two children on an Eskimo sled, 1963.

Engraving on Copper

The visual impact of *Eskimo Artist: Kenojuak* was immediately felt in *Eskimo Graphic Art,* the distinctive publication documenting Kinngait's 1963 print release. This was the third catalogue produced for the co-op in the 1960s by the Ottawa studio of Paul Arthur, managing editor and designer at *Canadian Art* magazine, director of publications at the National Gallery of Canada (NGC), and a member of the recently established Canadian Eskimo Arts Council (CEAC).[45] Designed by Fritz Gottschalk, who worked for Arthur, it exemplifies the clean, modernist International Style then in vogue in Canada (Figure 14.8).[46]

The catalogue is illustrated with photographs shot by cinematographer François Séguillon, today held in the NFB archives. It opens with a reproduction of Kenojuak's *Bird Dream* on a vellum sheet, the translucency of which affords a glimpse of the next page: an image of Lukta Qiatsuq printing *The Arrival of the Sun*. Next follows an arresting two-page spread in which large Inuktitut syllabics (Our art) are positioned above Séguillon's photograph of Kenojuak drawing in the Styrofoam igloo Feeney had built for the film. A second two-page spread, at the centre of the catalogue, features Séguillon's

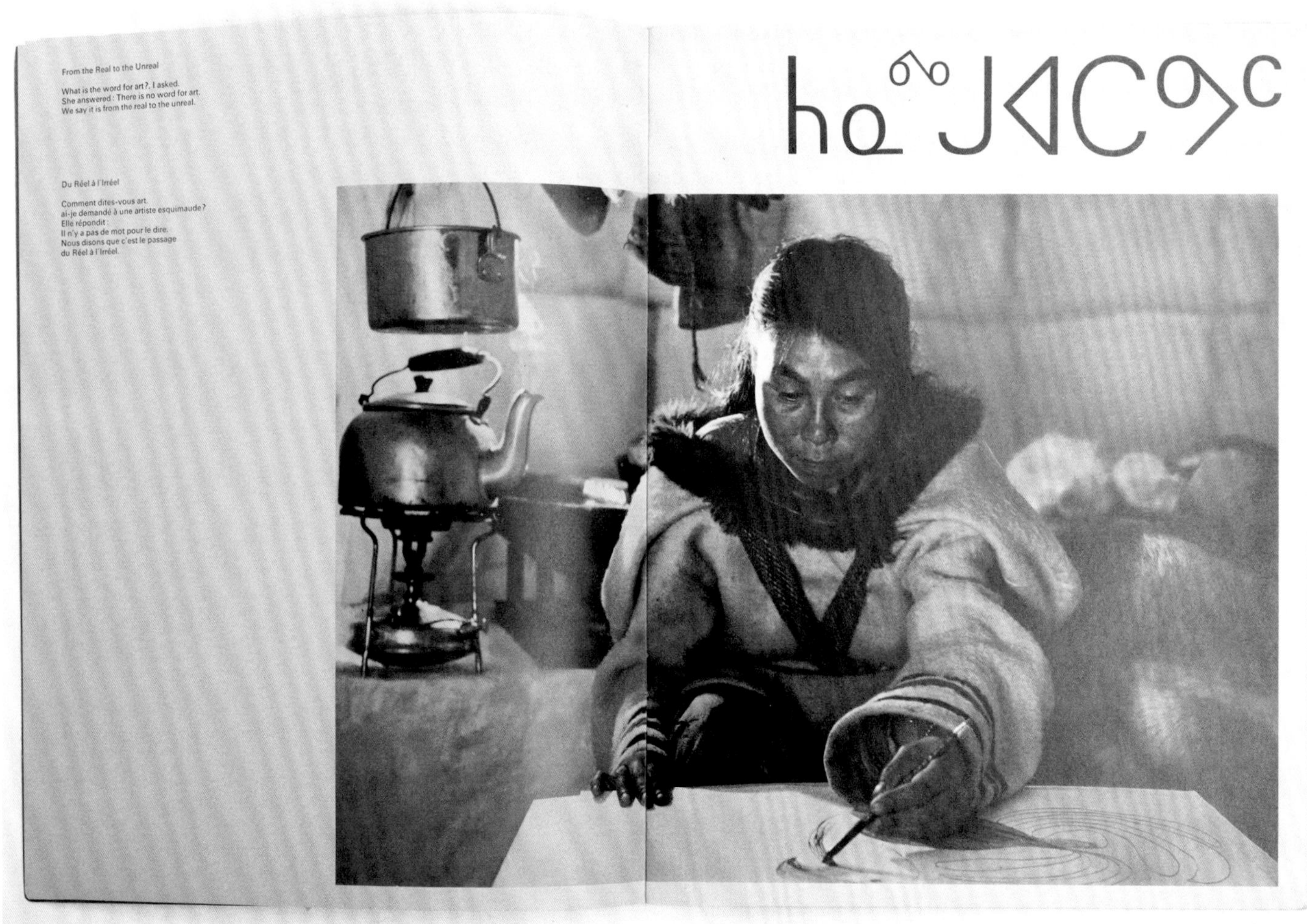

14.8 | *Eskimo Graphic Art*, the catalogue of Kinngait's 1963 print release, designed by Fritz Gottschalk of Paul Arthur and Associates, Ottawa. The opening pages feature a photograph of Kenojuak Ashevak by Francois Séguillon, shot on the set of the National Film Board of Canada film *Eskimo Artist: Kenojuak*.

close-cropped portrait of Kenojuak, her face encircled by the fur of her amauti hood and lit dramatically by the sun. Gottschalk deploys NFB photographs to make a strong visual argument for "Our art" and to make Kenojuak its face, literally and symbolically.[47]

The 1963 catalogue also marshals its communicative powers to raise the profile of copper engraving, closing with a full-page Séguillon photograph of the artist Kiakshuk working on an engraving plate. Engraving was introduced in Kinngait in 1962 at Norman Hallendy's suggestion, in response to southern criticism of stonecuts as the compromised products of a collaborative process.[48] The medium, as Terry Ryan explained, allowed "the creative artist to draw directly onto the plate instead of his drawing being transferred by a printer."[49]

Fifty-eight engravings (accounting for 85 per cent of the collection) were released in 1962, a risky move for a fledgling studio that had built its reputation on stonecut and stencil. Engravings made up only 58 per cent of the collection the following year, in a possible corrective measure to the market's lukewarm response.[50] Engravings were consistently priced at and sold for lower prices than stonecuts and ultimately phased out in the 1970s, as lithography took hold in Kinngait.

Moving to Kinngait

The evolution of copper engraving manifested in Kenojuak Ashevak's work – her first engraving was released in 1962 and her last in 1976 – parallels the development of Kinngait during Nunalinnguqtitauliqtilluta. This period, defined by the QTC as the "time when we were actively (by outside force) formed into communities," occurred from 1965 to 1975.[51] When this process of centralization was largely complete in the Qikiqtaaluk Region, by 1970, one hundred smaller communities had been merged into thirteen larger ones.[52]

When Kenojuak and Johnniebo first started working on copper plates, in 1962, they lived at Itilliarjuk and visited Kinngait periodically. That spring, they stayed in Kinngait for three months while filming *Eskimo Artist: Kenojuak*. Although they subsequently lived at Itilliarjuk for several years, the family moved permanently to Kinngait in late 1966, when local nurses urged a pregnant Kenojuak to stay in the settlement because of her fragile health.

When Johnniebo and Kenojuak Ashevak left Itilliarjuk, only fifty-five Kinngarmiut lived at three ilagiit nunagivaktangit.[53] Johnniebo continued to hunt but Kenojuak recalled that "it was the end of a way of life for us," as it was for other Kinngarmiut who gravitated to the settlement for such reasons as education, housing, employment, and health care.[54] It was a traumatic period across Inuit Nunangat, as the authors of the *National Inuit Strategy on Research* have recently written: "In settlements, stressors such as household crowding, infectious diseases, and the adverse effects of residential schooling converged on many families against a backdrop of rapid social, spiritual, and economic upheaval."[55]

Kenojuak's increasing proficiency in copper engraving is evident in the transformation from her tentative (untitled) works in the 1962 collection to the astonishing complexity and delicacy of *The Gathering*, released in 1971. Her production of engravings peaked at eighteen in 1967, including six that constituted a special portfolio of her work issued to commemorate the one-hundredth anniversary of the Canadian confederation (Figure 14.9).

Nineteen sixty-seven was an extraordinary year for Kenojuak, who was in the first group

14.9 | Kenojuak Ashevak, *Two Spirits*, 1967. This engraving was featured in the special portfolio of Kenojuak Ashevak's work issued to commemorate the one hundredth anniversary of the Canadian confederation.

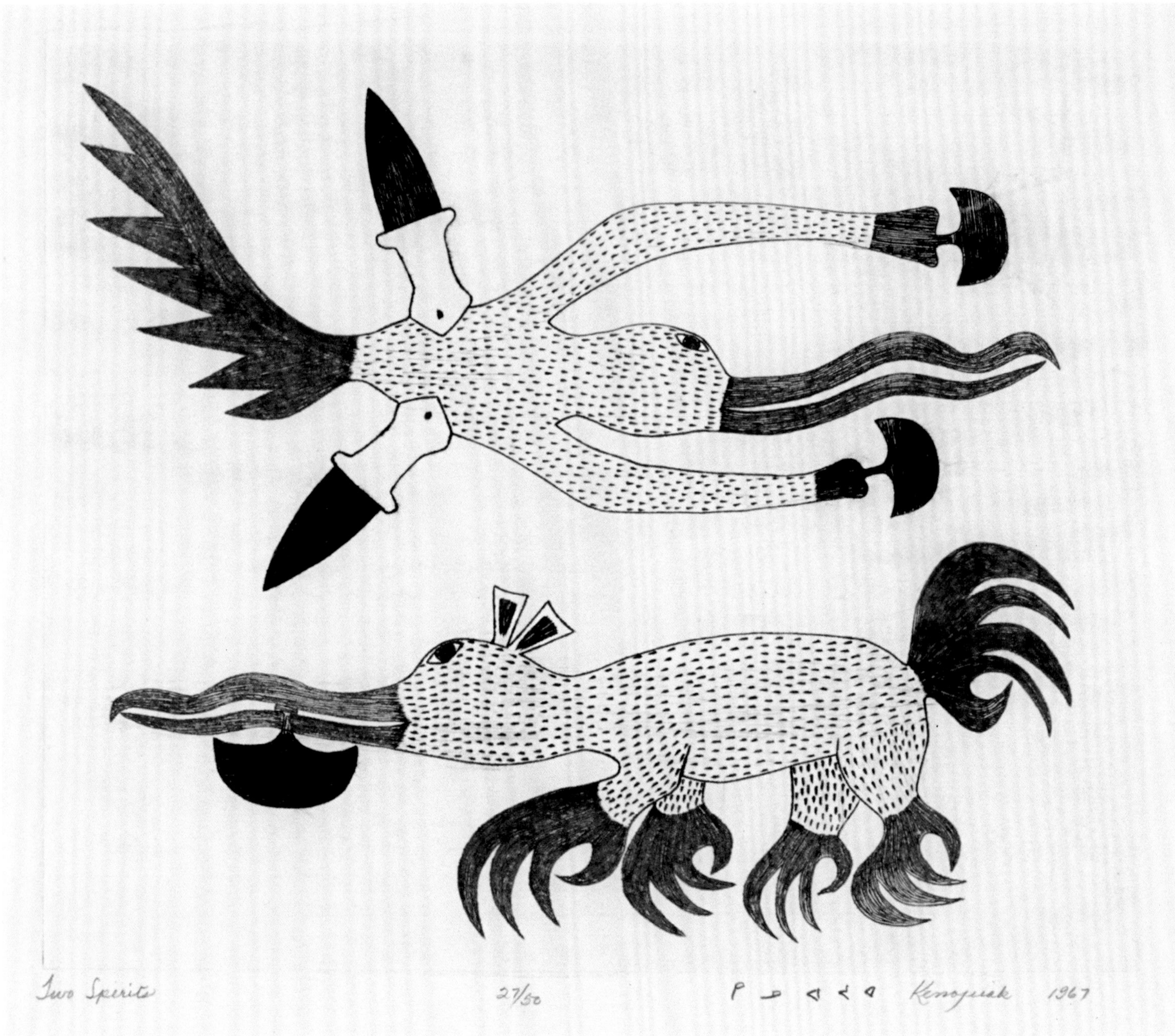

appointed to the newly established Order of Canada. Late in the year, she and Johnniebo travelled south, where they went to the medal ceremony at Rideau Hall, opened an exhibition of their graphic work at the National Library, and visited Queen's University, in Kingston, where the Agnes Etherington Art Centre was presenting the exhibition *Eskimo Graphic Art*.[56] Montreal art critic Robert Ayre reported that when he asked Kenojuak what impressed her most about her time in the South, "she didn't say anything about the streets and the crowds and the skyscrapers. 'The medal,' she replied, smiling as she brought it out of her purse."[57]

It is never difficult to identify Kenojuak Ashevak in photographs, but sometimes the photographs themselves prove elusive. Such is the case with an image of Kenojuak's investiture into the Order of Canada, which took place in the Rideau Hall ballroom on 24 November 1967. As recently as 2019, visitors to Rideau Hall could access a laminated copy of a black-and-white photograph that depicts Kenojuak with Governor General Roland Michener just before he pins a medal to her floor-length white gown. The original image has yet to be located at Library and Archives Canada. Fifteen years later, when Kenojuak was promoted from officer to companion of the Order of Canada, the prominent Ottawa studio photographer John Evans captured an equivalent likeness of the artist. She stands at the same spot in the ballroom, this time with Governor General Edward Schreyer, as he affixes a medal to her sky-blue dress (Figure 14.10). Interviewed by *Inuktitut* magazine the day before the ceremony, Kenojuak said that the honour impelled her to think not just of herself, but of her children: "When I am no longer around, my children will always remember me by it."[58]

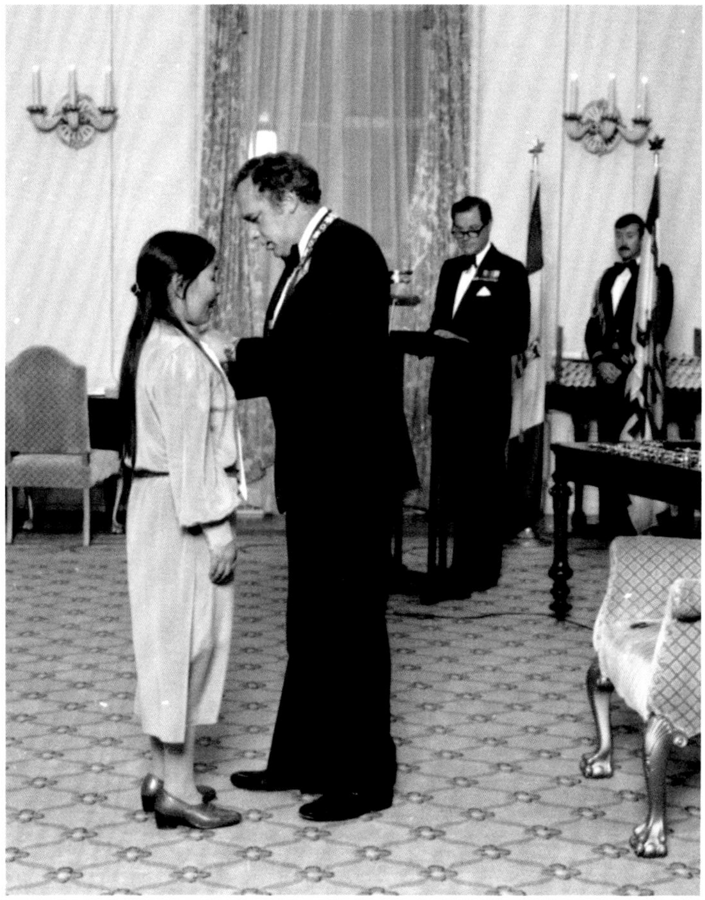

14.10 | Kenojuak Ashevak receiving the companion of the Order of Canada from Governor General Edward Schreyer, Rideau Hall, Ottawa, 20 October 1982.

Kenojuak at Work

In the spring of 1968, just a few months after Johnniebo and Kenojuak Ashevak returned home, Norman Hallendy arrived in Kinngait. In the early 1960s, Hallendy joined the NFB's Still Photography Division, where he designed and curated exhibitions, produced publications, selected images by freelance photographers for acquisition and reorganized the Division's vast and growing collection.[59]

Hallendy was a self-taught photographer and frequent visitor to Kinngait before and long after 1968.[60] Like the freelance photographers commissioned by the NFB without a "specific shooting script" for assignments, Hallendy had considerable freedom while working in Kinngait that spring.[61] He shot the local terrain and the building of an igloo but was particularly keen to photograph artists. Today, his negatives from the 1968 trip are divided between the Canadian Photography Institute at the NGC and the McMichael Canadian Art Collection, where Hallendy donated his archives.[62] Some are also held privately as Hallendy made a practice of tacking up photographs from his previous year's trip in the Kinngait printshop so artists and others could take them home.

The majority of Hallendy's 1968 photographs depicting artists are similar in approach; they are black-and-white, head-and-shoulders portraits shot against mostly empty backdrops of varied tone and texture.[63] He carried his Pauxette 35mm camera around the community and upon encountering an artist, "asked" (using gestures, as he could not yet communicate in Inuktitut) to take their picture.[64] The portraits were typically shot inside the artist's house, against a curtain or empty wall and using available light. A sitter sometimes donned his or her amauti, at Hallendy's request.

From 1968 through 1973, Hallendy's portraits were prominently featured in the Kinngait print catalogues, designed by NFB staff member Sharon van Raalte (with Hallendy as co-designer in 1968 and 1969).[65] The small, often close-cropped, reproductions were laid out in grids in keeping with International Style design conventions. Other Hallendy photographs were occasionally given prominence in the catalogues, when used as an opener or frontispiece, or to mark a section break. Such is the case with his photograph of Kenojuak, a large reproduction of which announces the engravings in the 1968 catalogue (Figure 14.11).

As with his other portraits, Hallendy photographed Kenojuak indoors, against a blank wall. Wearing a plain, buttoned-up cardigan, her hair in loose pigtails, Kenojuak sits near the corner of a table that is covered with a piece of pristine white fabric. She leans over a copper engraving plate, touching its shiny surface with a burin held in her left hand. A concentrated source of raking light from her right side illuminates the highly reflective plate, leaving much of her face in shadow. In Hallendy's similarly staged image of Ningeeuga Osuitok, probably made during the same shoot, he depicts the artist sitting at a fabric-covered table, attired in an amauti, and touching the tip of her pen to a drawing that appears finished.[66]

Hallendy's carefully posed photograph of Kenojuak was likely shot with its future editorial use in mind.[67] Strictly speaking, it is not a documentary image of "an artist at work." It indexes Kenojuak's appearance and the tools of her profession at a particular moment in time but reveals little about the actual work of making an engraving or the context in which that work occurred. It has the neutral, placeless appearance of a studio photograph and could have been shot anywhere.

It turns out that apart from Séguillon's 1962 photograph of Kiakshuk, Hallendy's 1968 photograph of Kenojuak is one of the few published images bearing witness to the existence (if not the practice) of copper engraving in Kinngait. Editorial photographs of engraving rarely featured in the 1960s and 1970s print catalogues, which, not surprisingly, privileged the stonecut.[68] The chiaroscuro surfaces of the carved stone blocks, laboriously achieved; the bold and simplified compositions; the theatric

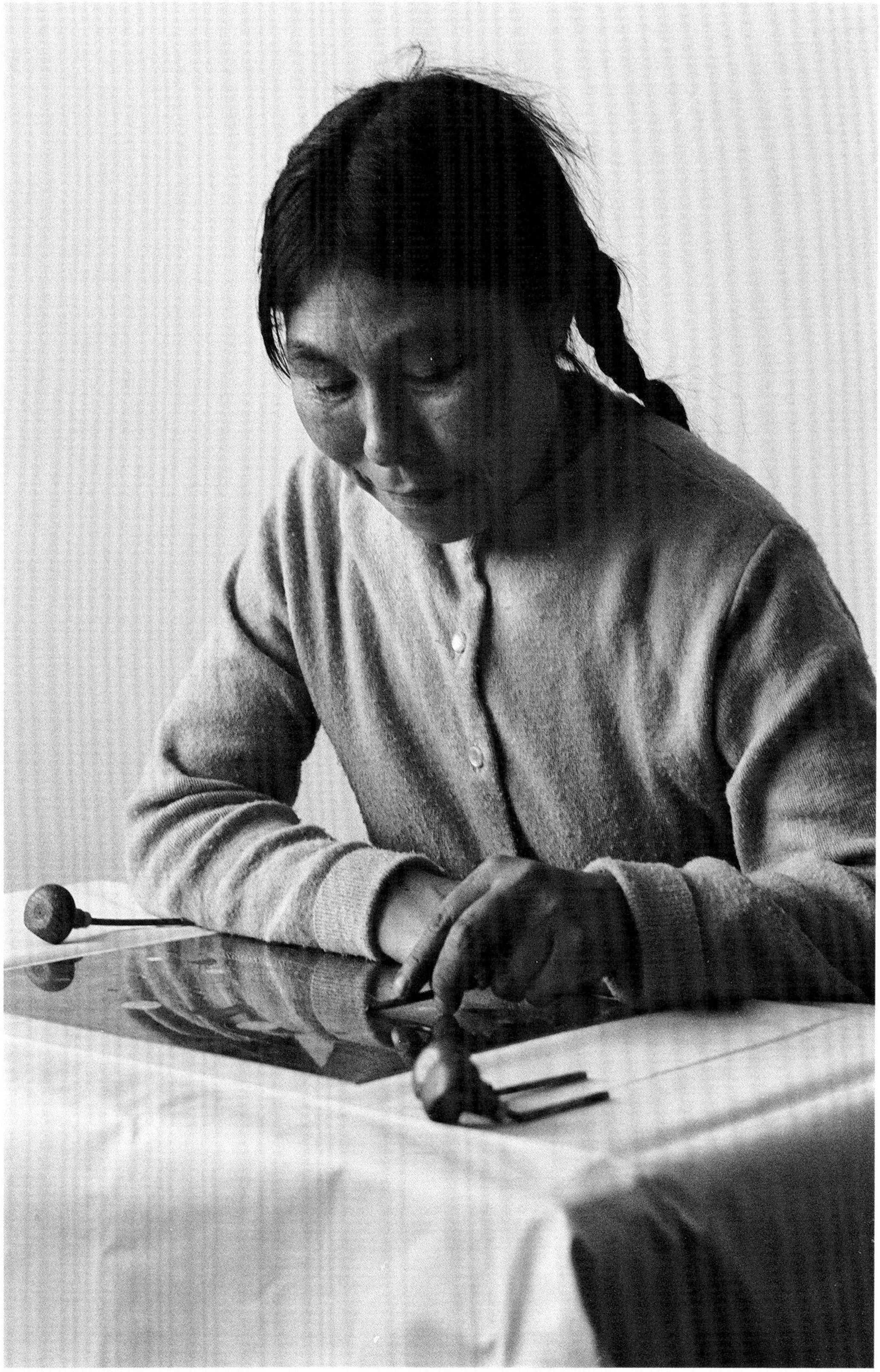

14.11 | *Kenojuak Ashevak*, April 1968.

pull of a fresh print from the inked stone – these aspects of stonecutting made for dramatic photographs, which illustrated Qallunaat stories of an iconic and lucrative art form, invented in Kinngait.

▸▸▸

In the ten years following the Kinngait co-op's 1959 release of its inaugural print collection, Kenojuak was the focus of much Qallunaat mythmaking. She often tempered the hyperbole when interviewed. In 1969, the Montreal writer Dorothy Eber visited Kenojuak in Kinngait and reported on her trip for the *Globe and Mail*. The artist received Eber at her prefab home, "friendly but somewhat amused" and clearly accustomed to meeting the press. Eber asked Kenojuak whether her "enchanted and magical" prints represented birds with "special powers." The artist laughed and, speaking through an interpreter, replied, "Not really, I make them out of my mind." When Eber questioned Kenojuak about such prints as *Two Spirits* or *Bird with Spirits* (both of 1967), the artist said that she didn't know "why the white man is giving them these names," but understood that "the white man likes to hear about such things."[69]

That summer, Kenojuak and Johnniebo Ashevak lived in Ottawa for two months while they carved a massive plaster mural commissioned for the Canadian Pavilion at Expo '70 in Osaka, Japan. The composition was dominated by a central, stylized owl with radiating plumage – a signature Kenojuak motif. Just before the couple's return to Kinngait, Eber attended the mural's press preview in Ottawa. She reported in the *Montreal Star* that Kenojuak gave interviews, and all afternoon engaged in "make-believe carving" with Johnniebo for a film crew documenting the commission. When Eber asked the artist how she liked the film work, she replied immediately, "It is boring."[70] Kenojuak nonetheless cooperated, no stranger to the artifice of image-making and well aware of its power.

NOTES

1 The cooperative was first incorporated as the West Baffin Sports Fishing Co-operative and was later renamed the West Baffin Eskimo Co-operative. Boyd Ryan, *Cape Dorset Prints, A Retrospective*, 29–32.
2 West Baffin Eskimo Co-operative, *Cape Dorset Eskimo Graphic Art 1964–65*, 16.
3 Kenojuak is the English transliteration of the artist's Inuktitut name that is most often used in the English-speaking south. It has also been spelled Qinngnuajuak, by Jimmy Manning, in "Reflection"; and Qinnuajuaq, by Taqralik Partridge and Laakkuluk Williamson Bathory, in Hudson, Piirainen, and Uhlyarik, *Tunirrusiangit: Kenojuak Ashevak and Tim Pitsiulak*.
4 Siemens, "Photographic Encounters in the North," 9–10.
5 Adams, "Interview with Photographer Jimmy Manning," 28.
6 Geller, *Northern Exposures*, 14.
7 Obed, "How to Overcome the Erasure of Inuit Identity in Archival Photos."
8 The Qikiqtaaluk (formerly Baffin) Region is the easternmost administrative region in Nunavut.
9 Qikiqtani Inuit Association, "Cape Dorset," *Qikiqtani Truth Commission Community Histories 1950–1975*, 30.
10 West Baffin Eskimo Co-operative, *Eskimo Graphic Art*, frontispiece.
11 Seesequasis, *Blanket Toss under the Midnight Sun*, 3.

12 Qikiqtani Inuit Association, "About the Photographs," 6–7.
13 People of the region around Kinngait call themselves Kinngarmiut. Qikiqtani Inuit Association, "Cape Dorset," *Qikiqtani Truth Commission Community Histories 1950–1975*, 9.
14 Evans and Glass, *Return to the Land*, 9–10.
15 Qikiqtani Inuit Association, "Cape Dorset," 14.
16 Geller, *Northern Exposures*, 4.
17 From the 1930s onward, EAP commanders and other ship personnel documented the ships' voyages, in contrast to previous decades, where professional photographers and filmmakers were employed for this purpose. See Geller, *Northern Exposures*, 39, 42, 47.
18 In a photograph in Greenhorn's article, "Project Naming / Un Visage, Un Nom," 4, Elder Abraham Ulayuruluk and Joanna Quassa are shown examining a departmental album.
19 This was the first year that the EAP travelled aboard the *Regina Polaris*. The *Nascopie*, the EAP's previous vessel, was wrecked on a reef near Kinngait on 21 July 1947.
20 The photograph of Udluriak with members of the ship's crew (LAC e00221330) is one of three on the sixth page of Bailey's album (LAC, e010983683).
21 Bailey's caption for this photograph (LAC, e002213331) hints that Kenojuak is carrying a baby in her amauti. This is Jamasie, first child of Kenojuak and Johnniebo, born in 1947; the top of his head is just visible in Bailey's photograph.
22 This group photograph (LAC, e002213326) is one of three on the third page of Bailey's album (LAC, e010983680). Kenojuak stands in the front row at left, hands clasped and wearing a chevron-patterned skirt. Udluriak stands immediately behind Kenojuak's left shoulder. Bailey identifies this group as those who salvaged materials from the wreck of the *Nascopie* in 1947. Peter Pitseolak tells the story of the wreck and salvaging in Pitseolak and Eber, *People from Our Side*, 133–41.
23 Pitseolak and Eber, *People from Our Side*, 12.
24 Eber, "Peter Pitseolak, An Historian for Seekooseelak," 13–15, 20.
25 *Peter Pitseolak (1902–1973), Inuit Historian of Seekooseelak* is the catalogue of a 1980 exhibition at the McCord Museum. See also Pitseolak and Eber, *People from Our Side*.
26 See Eber, "Peter Pitseolak, An Historian for Seekooseelak," 19–21. Some of Pitseolak's models borrowed caribou skin clothing from Eleeshushee, the photographer's older half-sister, in which to be photographed.
27 Ashevak, "Kenojuak's Memories," 98. See also Blodgett, *Kenojuak*, 18.
28 Qikiqtani Inuit Association, *Guide to the Community Histories and Special Studies of the Qikiqtani Truth Commission*, 20.
29 Qikiqtani Inuit Association, "Cape Dorset," 18–25.
30 While a patient at Parc Savard Hospital, Kenojuak made beautiful fabric dolls under the encouragement of the sculptor Harold Pfeiffer, the brother of Walter Pfeiffer, one of her doctors. Blodgett, "The Art of Kenojuak," in Blodgett, *Kenojuak*, 31–2.
31 Qikiqtani Inuit Association, "Cape Dorset," 25.
32 Blodgett, "The Art of Kenojuak," 34.
33 Seesequasis writes eloquently about Gilliat's Kinngait photographs in *Blanket Toss*, 10–34.
34 Siemens, "Photographic Encounters in the North," 75.
35 *The Enchanted Owl* sold for $216,000 hammer price at Waddington's Inuit Art Auction in Toronto on 20 November 2018. See Sandals, "Records Broken at Canada's Fall Art Auctions," *Canadian Art* online.
36 "Kenojuak – Poet of the Arctic" is NFB photo story number 289, dated 11 July 1961. The mat release is in the National Gallery of Canada's collection.
37 Payne, *The Official Picture*, 37–45.
38 Ibid., 43.
39 Rhoda Kayakjuak's translation of the Inuktitut dialogue in this scene is Ryan to Kenojuak: "Does it look nice?" Kenojuak to Ryan: "This part right here. You separate the colour right on the knee. There was supposed to be an eye here, but you missed the eye." Rhoda Kayakjuak, email to the author, 25 November 2018.
40 The Oscar nomination was in the category of documentary (short subject).
41 *Eskimo Graphic Art*, unpaginated.
42 "Inuktitut Asks Kenoajuak," *Inuktitut*, 11.
43 Ibid., 11–12. See also Blodgett, "Kenojuak Ashevak," 22.

44 Blodgett, "Kenojuak Ashevak," 22.
45 Donnelly, *Mass Modernism*, 81–4; and Gustavison, *Arctic Expressions*, 88.
46 See Donnelly, *Mass Modernism*, 65–88.
47 The 1963 catalogue is organized by artist for the first time and Kenojuak's work appears first.
48 Hallendy's role in introducing engraving is discussed in Gustavison, *Arctic Expressions*, 15. For an early commentary on engraving in Kinngait, see Eber, "The History of Graphics in Dorset," 29–31.
49 Ryan, "Some Notes on the Cape Dorset Prints," unpaginated.
50 Crandall, *Inuit Art*, 161.
51 Qikiqtani Inuit Association, *Guide to the Community Histories and Special Studies of the Qikiqtani Truth Commission,* 20.
52 Qikiqtani Inuit Association, "The Official Mind of Canadian Colonialism," *Qikiqtani Truth Commission Thematic Reports and Special Studies 1950–1975*, 29.
53 Only the previous year (1965), 155 individuals were living in five ilagiit nunagivaktangit. Qikiqtani Inuit Association, "Cape Dorset," in *Qikiqtani Truth Commission Community Histories 1950–1975*, 27.
54 Blodgett, "Kenojuak Ashevak," 23.
55 Inuit Tapiriit Kanatami, *National Inuit Strategy on Research*, 9.
56 Alma Houston accompanied Kenojuak and Johnniebo on the trip. The December 1967 edition of the Agnes Etherington Art Centre's *Bulletin* indicates that the exhibition also included sculptures by Kenojuak.
57 Ayre, "Kenojuak Just Loves That Medal," *The Star*, Montreal, 6 December 1967.
58 "Inuktitut Asks Kenoajuak," *Inuktitut*, 18.
59 Payne, *The Official Picture*, 47, 50–1; author's telephone interview of Hallendy, 22 October 2018.
60 Author's interview of Hallendy. He recalls his first visit to Kinngait as occurring in the late 1950s or early 1960s and, thereafter, made annual visits through 2004. The research he conducted with Kinngarmiut over decades resulted in such books as *Inuksuit: Silent Messengers*; *Tukiliit: The Stone People, An Introduction to Inuksuit*; and *An Intimate Wilderness*.
61 Payne, *The Official Picture*, 40; author's interview of Hallendy.
62 The NFB's photography collection is divided between Library and Archives Canada (photographs up to 1962) and the National Gallery of Canada (photographs after 1962).
63 The information in this section is from the author's telephone interview of Hallendy. A selection of these portraits is reproduced in Hallendy, *An Intimate Wilderness*, 320–3.
64 Hallendy said that, with the exception of Pudlo Pudlat, who was wary of Qallunaat, the artists were open to having their photographs taken.
65 Sharon van Raalte worked as a designer for the NFB's Still Photography Division from 1966 to 1970, during which she designed several Kinngait print catalogues. Her connection to the West Baffin Eskimo Co-operative was through Norman Hallendy. Sharon van Raalte, email to the author, 14 January 2019.
66 This Hallendy photograph of Ningeeuga Osuitok is reproduced at the back of the 1968 print catalogue. A related (unpublished) Hallendy photograph of Jamasie Teevee, in the National Gallery of Canada's collection (NFB grey card 68-6537), depicts him sitting at a fabric-covered table and touching a gouge to the surface of a lino block.
67 A contact sheet in the McMichael's archives (ARC-NH 1991.1) demonstrates that Hallendy tested many poses and angles in his photoshoot with Kenojuak.
68 One exception is Macintosh's photograph of Lukta and Ningushiak at the engraving press, reproduced in *Dorset 76*, 47.
69 Eber, "Art Centre ... For How Long?", *Globe and Mail*.
70 Eber, "'It's not magic, it's from my mind,'" *The Star*.

GLOSSARY

Note that the plural designation only denotes the Inuktut plural form for three or more things and not the plural denoting two things.

agusiaq The boy I made. A term in the South Qikiqtaaluk dialect used by a midwife to refer to a boy she delivered.

Ahiarmiut "The people from away." A group of Inuit who lived around Ennadai and Nueltin Lakes in the south-west portion of Nunavut, most descendants live in Arviat.

airainnuk Sister-in-law.

Aivilingmiut "The people of the walrus." A group of Inuit who originated around the Igloolik area and moved south in the nineteenth century along the west coast of the Hudson Bay.

ajagak A cup and pin game, typically made with bone and sinew.

akkaq Paternal uncle (all dialects of Inuktut).

amauti A women's parka with a pouch on the back to carry a child.

amukattaq A style of stitching typical of Baffin Island Inuit.

arnaaqutiga My woman. A term in the South Qikiqtaaluk dialect used by a boy to refer to the midwife who delivered him.

arnaliara The girl I made. A term in the South Qikiqtaaluk dialect used by a midwife to refer to a girl she delivered.

arnaquasaq Elderly woman.

atiq/avaaq A name-soul.

atiqput Our names.

aqiqaqpuguttauq We also have names.

atigi A general term for parka with fur facing inwards against the body.

atiqsurtuq Like his/her namesake.

attungilattaaq A style of stitching typical of Inuit of Nunavik.

attungituinaaq A style of stitching typical of Aivilingmiut.

Honda A catch-all term to describe an all-terrain vehicle (ATV).

ii Yes.

ilagiit nunagivaktangit Camps; "places used regularly for hunting, harvesting, and gathering" (from the Qikiqtani Truth Commission).

ilaut Scoop for removing ice from an ice hole used for fishing.

ilira A strong sense of awe or fear.

Inuinnaqun Language of Inuinnait of the western Canadian Arctic, especially in Iqaluktuuttiaq, Kugluktuk, and Uluhaktok.

Inuit Qaujimajatuaqangit That which has long been known to Inuit. A phrase used to describe Principles of Inuit Traditional Knowledge, a living, breathing body of knowledge, abbreviated as IQ.

inuksuk (singular) Cairns to mark a place. Cairns serve many purposes including navigational aids, to indicate good hunting and fishing areas, or where a food cache is located.

Inuktitut Language of Inuit in the eastern Canadian Arctic, it encompasses many dialects: Natsilingmiutut, Kivallirmiutut, Aivilingmmiutut, Qikiqtaaluk uannangani, Qikiqtalluk nigiani, Nunavimmiutitut, and Nunatsiavummiuitut.

Inuktut Describes Inuit languages including Inuktitut, Inuttitut, and Inuinnaqtun among others.

inuusirmingnik unikkaat Life stories told from direct experience.

isuma/ihuma To think. A term that describes the state being capable of good reasoning, decision-making, and being a rational, competent person.

kamik Traditional footwear of Inuit, made of animal skin, called mukluks in the western Arctic and in southern Canada.

kamik miqquituq Dehaired caribou skin kamik.

kigju A specific small tattoo with a horizontal line and three vertical lines underneath, located on the nasal bridge.

kinaugavit May I have your name?

kinauvit What is your name?

kukukpaak Sewing term. The point of a hood.

matna Thank you in the Kivalliq region (alternatively spelt Ma'na).

nakurmiik Thank you in the South Qikiqtaaluk and Nunavik dialects.

nanisiniq Journey of discovery.

nanivara I found it.

nukluktaq A target game; players try to spike through a hole in a suspended piece of ivory or caribou antler.

Nunavummiut Inuit from/residing in Nunavut.

pamiqsainirmik Things done in the "making of an able human being."

panik/utaraaq Daughter.

pilimmaksarniq IQ principle of skills and knowledge acquisition.

piliriqatigiingniq IQ principle of the development of collaborative relationships or working together for a common purpose.

qajaq (singular), **qajait** (plural) Kayak. A covered, highly maneuverable boat.

qallu/qablu Eyebrow.

Qallunaat/Qablunaat Non-Inuit of European descent (singular Qallunaq/Qablunaaq).

qamutiq/kamutik Dog sled.

qarmaq Sod hut.

qimuksiqtuq Dog team with one driver.

qipigayuqu Twisted sewing stitches.

qulliq A long, shallow oil lamp. Also spelled qudliq/kudliq.
qujannamiik Thank you in the North Qikiqtaaluk dialect.
sanajiga A term used by a girl to refer to the midwife who delivered her meaning "my maker" in the South Qikiqtaaluk dialect.
suqaa Why not?
tuilli An amauti historically worn by Inuit women in the Kivalliq region; it has exaggerated shoulders and a long, narrow hood.
tuktu (singular), **tuktuit** (plural) One caribou, tuktuit for three or more caribou.
tunniit (plural) Tattoos.
tunnuq Caribou fat found along the back.
tuuq Ice chisel.
ujamik (singular), **ujamiit** (plural) Necklaces. A term used to describe the dog tags used in the Eskimo Identification Disc system.
una This.
unikkaaq A myth or legend.
unikkaat/unikkaatuaq/quliaqtuat Story about something that happened relatively recently, life stories.
unikkausiq/unipkaat Story about something that happened long ago.

INUKTUT PLACE NAMES

Agvituk Hopedale, "place of the whales."
Aklavik "Barren ground grizzly place."
Akulivik "Central prong of a kakivak [three-pronged fishing spear]."
Arviat "Bowhead whale," formerly Eskimo Point.
Arviliqjuaq "Place with lots of bowhead whales," officially known as Kugaaruk, "little stream," formerly Pelly Bay.
Aujuittuq Grise Fiord, "place that never thaws."
Aupauluk "Where the earth is red."
Igluligaarjuk Chesterfield Inlet, "place with a few houses."
Iglulik Igloolik, "place of houses."
Ikahuak Sachs Harbour, "where you go across to."
Ikpiarjuk Arctic Bay, "the pocket."
Inuit Nunangat A term to describe the Inuit homeland in Canada that comprises the land, water, and ice of this region, which includes Inuvialuit, Nunavut, Nunavik, and Nunatsiavut.
Inukjuak Translates to "the giant," but the name is a misnomer of Inurjuak, meaning "many people," formerly Port Harrison.
Inuvialuit Either refers to the people of the Inuvialuit Settlement region, or it may be a shortened form of the Inuvialuit Settlement Region located in the Northwest Territory and Yukon.
Inuvik Headquarters of the Inuvik region.
Iqaluit "Place of many fish," formerly Frobisher Bay.
Iqaluktuuttiaq Cambridge Bay, "a good place with lots of fish."
Ivujivik "Place where ice accumulates because of strong currents."
Kangiqliniq Rankin Inlet, "deep bay/inlet," also spelled Kangiq&ugaapik/Kangiqtiniq.
Kangiqsualujjuaq "The very large bay," formerly known as George River or Fort George.
Kangiqsujuaq "The large bay," formerly Wakeham Bay
Kangiqtugaapik Clyde River, "nice little inlet."
Kangirsuk "The bay," formerly known as Payne Bay and Bellin.
Kativik An administrative region that includes all of Nunavik except some Cree reserve land.
Kikiaq Rigolet, "carpenter's nail, coin."
Kimmirut "Looks like a heel," formerly Lake Harbour.

Kinngait Cape Dorset, "high mountain."
Kitikmeot North-west administrative region of Nunavut including Victoria Island.
Kivalliq Southern mainland administrative region of Nunavut.
Kugaaruk See Arviliqjuaq.
Kugluktuk "Place of moving water," formerly Coppermine, also spelt Qurluqtuq.
Kuujjuaq A mispronunciation of Saimuuq, "let's shake hands," formerly Fort Chimo.
Kuujjuarapik "Small great river."
Maquuvik Makkovik.
Mittimatalik Pond Inlet, "place where Mittiima is buried."
Nanisivik "Place where people find things," company town for a lead-zinc mining operation near Ikpiarjuk.
Naujaat "Nesting place for seagulls," formerly Repulse Bay.
Nunatsiavut "Our Beautiful Land" in Inuttut. It is the settlement region located in Labrador claimed by Inuit of Newfoundland and Labrador.
Nunavik "Great Land." This is the homeland of Inuit in Quebec and encompasses the northern third of Quebec.
Nunavut "Our Land." Nunavut is a territory of Canada.
Pangniqtuuq Pangnirtung, "place of the bull caribou."
Paulatuk "Place of coal," Paulatuqq (alternative spelling).
Puvirnituq "Place where there is a smell of rotten meat."
Qamani'tuaq Baker Lake, "big lake joined by a river on both ends."
Qatiktalik Cape Fullerton.
Qauqtaq "Tapeworm."
Qausuittuq "Place with no dawn," Resolute, or Resolute Bay.
Qikiqtarjuaq "Big island," formerly Broughton Island.
Qikiqtaaluk Easternmost administrative region of Nunavut. It includes Baffin Island, Melville Peninsula, and most of the Arctic Archipelago.
Qingaut Bathurst Inlet, "the nose."
Qipuqqaq Postville, "Sperm whale."
Salliq Formerly Coral Habour, "a large, flat island in front of the mainland."
Salluit "The thin ones," formerly known as Sugluk.
Sanikiluaq Named for a man known to be a fast runner, located on the Belcher Islands.
Saningayuaq Near Padlei.
Sanirajak Hall Beach, "one that is along the coast."
Takirarjuaq Whale Cove, "long point."
Taloyoak "Large stone caribou blind," formerly Spence Bay, also spelt Talurjuaq.
Tasiujaq "Which resembles a lake."
Tuktoyaktuk "It looks like a caribou." (Tuktuyaaqtuuq, alternative spelling.) Formerly called Port Brabant.
Ukkusiksalik National Park "Where there is material for the stone pot," located around Wager Bay, an area occupied by Inuit from the eleventh century until settlement.
Ulukhaktoq "The place where ulu parts are found." (Ulukhaqtuuq, alternative spelling.) Formerly Holman Island.
Umingmaktoq "Where s/he caught a muskox," formerly Bay Chimo, also spelt Umingmakttuq.
Umingmakttuq "S/he caught a muskox."
Umiujaq "That which resembles a boat."
Uqsuqtuuq Gjoa Haven, "place of plenty of fat."

FIGURES

Note: Titles of archival photographs in square brackets are based on information provided through *Project Naming*.

BIBLIOGRAPHY

"The 37th Academy Awards | 1965." Oscars, n.d. https://www.oscars.org/oscars/ceremonies/1965.

Adams, Amy. "Arctic and Inuit Photography, Part One: An Accurate Representation of the World?" *Inuit Art Quarterly* 15, no. 2 (Summer 2000): 5–10.

– "Arctic and Inuit Photography: Part Two: Through the Looking-Glass: The Photographs of Robert J. Flaherty and Peter Pitseolak." *Inuit Art Quarterly* 15, no. 3 (Fall 2000): 4–15.

– "Interview with Photographer Jimmy Manning." *Inuit Art Quarterly* 15, no. 4 (Winter 2000): 20–9.

Aird, Michael. "Growing Up with Aborigines." In *Photography's Other Histories*, edited by Christopher Pinney, Nicolas Peterson, and Nicholas Thomas, 23–39. Durham, NC: Duke University Press, 2003. https://doi.org/10.1215/9780822384717-003.

Alia, Valerie. *Names, Numbers, and Northern Policy: Inuit, Project Surname, and the Politics of Identity*. Halifax, NS: Fernwood Publishing, 1994.

– *Names and Nunavut: Culture and Identity in Arctic Canada*. New York: Berghahn Books, 2009.

Anahanak, Ahmie, in conversation with Tolok Havioyak. Kugluktuk, 30 December 2005. http://viewsfromthenorth.ca/index.html.

Angalik, Louis. "We Inuit Call Our Children Qiturngat." In *Inuit Qaujimajatuqangit: What Inuit Have Always Known to Be True*, edited by Joe Karetak, Frank Tester, and Shirley Tagalik, 83–8. Black Point, NS: Fernwood Publishing, 2017.

Angus, Murray, and Morley Hanson. "The New Three R's." *Our Schools/Our Selves* 20 (Summer 2011): 31–52.

Aporta, Claudio. "The Power of Maps: Inuit Land Use and Occupancy Project (1976) as a Landmark in Inuit Land Use Studies." In *Early Inuit Studies: Themes and Transitions, 1850s–1980s*, edited by Igor Krupnik, 354–73. Washington, DC: Smithsonian Institution Press, 2016.

Arnaquq-Baril, Alethea. *Tunniit: Retracing the Lines of Inuit Tattoos*. Documentary. Unikkaat Studios, Inc., 2011.

– *Angry Inuk*. Digital, Documentary. National Film Board of Canada, 2016. https://www.nfb.ca/film/angry_inuk/.

Ashevak, Kenojuak. "Kenojuak's Memories." In *Inuit Women Artists: Voices from Cape Dorset*, edited by Minnie Aodla Freeman, Marion E. Jackson, and Odette Leroux, 93–111. Vancouver: Douglas & McIntyre, 1995.

Ashevak, Mathewsie. "Voices from Nunavut: Personal Account of Mathewsie Ashevak." Library and Archives Canada, February 2004. http://www.collectionscanada.gc.ca/inuit/020018-1101-e.html.

Audlaluk, Larry. *What I Remember, What I Know: The Life of a High Arctic Exile*. Iqaluit: Inhabit Media, 2020.

Awa, Apphia Agalakti. "The Old Culture: Stories Since a Long, Long Time Ago." In *Saqiyuq Stories from the Lives of Three Inuit Women*, edited by Nancy Wachowich in collaboration with Apphia Agalakti Awa, Rhoda Kaukjak Katsak, and Sandra Pikujak Katsak. Montreal: McGill-Queen's University Press, 2001.

Ayre, Robert. "Kenojuak Just Loves That Medal." *The Star*, 6 December 1967.

– "Foreword." In *Eskimo Graphic Art*. Cape Dorset: West Baffin Eskimo Co-operative, 1967.

Azoulay, Ariella. *The Civil Contract of Photography*. Trans. Rela Mazali and Ruvik Danieli. New York: Zone Books, 2008.

– "What Is a Photograph? What Is Photography?" *Philosophy of Photography* 1, no. 1 (2010): 9–13.

Barthes, Roland. *Camera Lucida*. Translated by Richard Howard. New York: Hill and Wang, 1981.

Bassler, Gerhard P. *Vikings to U-Boats: The German Experience in Newfoundland and Labrador*. Montreal: McGill-Queen's University Press, 2006.

Batchen, Geoffrey. *Burning with Desire: The Conception of Photography*. Cambridge, MA: MIT Press, 1997.

Bennett, Carolyn. "Statement of Apology for the Relocation of the Ahiarmiut." 22 January 2019. https://www.rcaanc-cirnac.gc.ca/eng/1548170252259/1548170273272.

Bennett, John, and Susan Diana Mary Rowley, eds. *Uqalurait: An Oral History of Nunavut*. Montreal: McGill-Queen's University Press, 2004.

Best, George. "A True Reporte of Such Things as Hapned in the Second Voyage of Captayne Frobysher, Pretended for the Discouerie of a New Passage to Cataya, China, and the East India, by the North-west. Anno. Do. 1577." In *A True Discourse of the Late Voyages of Discouerie, for the Finding of a Passage to Cathaya, by the Northvveast, Vnder the Conduct of Martin Frobisher Generall* [...]. Early English Books Online Text Creation Partnership. London: Imprinted by Henry Bynnyman, seruant to the right Honourable Sir Christopher Hatton Vizchamberlaine, 1578. http://name.umdl.umich.edu/A09429.0001.001.

Billson, Janet Mancini, and Kyra Mancini. *Inuit Women: Their Powerful Spirit in a Century of Change*. Lanham: Rowman & Littlefield, 2007.

Bird, Hilary. "Baby Named Sahaiʔa Prompts Changes to Vital Statistics Act." *CBC News*, 13 June 2016. https://www.cbc.ca/news/canada/north/nwt-aboriginal-font-official-id-1.3630353.

Blodgett, Jean. "The Autobiography of Kenojuak Ashevak, as Told to Patricia Ryan." In *Kenojuak*. Toronto: Firefly Books, 1985.

Boyd Ryan, Leslie, ed. *Cape Dorset Prints, a Retrospective*. San Francisco: Pomegranate, 2007.

Brown, Alison, and Laura Peers. *Pictures Bring Us Messages: Photographs and Histories from the Kainai Nation: Sinaakssiiksi Aohtsimaahpihkookiyaawa*. Toronto: University of Toronto Press, 2006.

Budach, Gabriele, Donna Patrick, and Teevi Mackay. "'Talk Around Objects': Designing Trajectories of Belonging in an Urban Inuit Community." *Social Semiotics* 25, no. 4 (8 August 2015): 446–64. https://doi.org/10.1080/10350330.2015.1059575.

Campbell, Heather. "A.P. Low and the Many Words of Love in Inuit Culture." *Library and Archives Canada Blog* (blog), 14 February 2019. https://thediscoverblog.com/2019/02/14/a-p-low-and-the-many-words-of-love-in-inuit-culture/.

– "Introduction to Inuktut." In *Nations to Nations: Indigenous Voices at Library and Archives Canada* edited by Library and Archives Canada, 6. Ottawa: Library and Archives Canada, 2021. eBook. https://www.bac-lac.gc.ca/eng/discover/

aboriginal-heritage/initiatives/Pages/nations-to-nations-indigenous-voices-at-LAC.aspx
– "Reclaiming Our Names." *Inuit Art Quarterly* 27 November 2020. https://www.inuitartfoundation.org/inuit-art-quarterly/iaq-read/iaq-feature.
Canadian Women Artists History Initiative. "Moodie, Geraldine." Montreal: Concordia University. Accessed 9 October 2018. https://cwahi.concordia.ca/sources/artists/displayArtist.php?ID_artist=5611.
Cape Dorset Eskimo Graphic Art 1964–65. Cape Dorset: West Baffin Eskimo Co-operative, 1965.
Christopher, Robert J. "Through Canada's Northland: The Arctic Photography of Robert J. Flaherty." In *Imaging the Arctic*, edited by J.C.H. King and Henrietta Lidchi, 181–9. Seattle: University of Washington Press, 1998.
Clifford, James. "On Ethnographic Allegory." In *Writing Culture: The Poetics and Politics of Ethnography*, edited by James Clifford and George E. Marcus, 98–121. Berkeley: University of California Press, 2010.
– *Returns: Becoming Indigenous in the Twenty-First Century*. Cambridge, MA: Harvard University Press, 2013.
Close, Susan. "Geraldine Moodie's Arctic Photographs." In *Framing Identity: Social Practices of Photography in Canada, 1880–1920*, 49–73. Winnipeg: Arbeiter Ring Publishers, 2007.
Collignon, Béatrice, Michele Therrien, and Florence Duchemin-Pelletier, eds. *Orality in the 21st Century: Inuit Discourse and Practices: Proceedings of the 15th Inuit Studies Conference*. Paris: INALCO-CERLOM, 2009. www.inuitoralityconference.com.
Comeau, Robert, and Geneviève Morin. "Healing Journey: Project Naming at Fifteen." Mp3. Library and Archives Canada's Discover Podcast, 6 July 2017. http://www.bac-lac.gc.ca/eng/news/podcasts/Pages/project-naming-at-15.aspx.
Condon, Richard G. "The History and Development of Arctic Photography." *Arctic Anthropology* 26, no. 1 (1989): 46–87.
Cook, Terry. "Archival Science and Postmodernism." *Archival Science* 1 (March 2001): 3–24.
Crandall, Richard C. *Inuit Art: A History*. Jefferson: McFarland, 2005.
Curriculum and School Services Division, Government of Nunavut. "Inuit Qaujimajatuqangit Education Framework For Nunavut Curriculum." Nunavut Department of Education, 2007. https://www.gov.nu.ca/sites/default/files/files/Inuit%20Qaujimajatuqangit%20ENG.pdf.
Distard, Merrill. "Frobisher, Sir Martin." In *Encyclopedia of the Arctic*, edited by Mark Nuttall, 684–6. New York: Routledge, 2005.
Donnelly, Brian. "Mass Modernism: Graphic Design in Central Canada, 1955–1965, and the Changing Definition of Modernism." MA thesis, Carleton University, 1997.
Dorais, Louis-Jacques. *The Language of the Inuit: Syntax, Semantics, and Society in the Arctic*. McGill-Queen's Native and Northern Series 58. Montreal: McGill-Queen's University Press, 2010.
Dorset 76: Cape Dorset Annual Graphics Collection, 1976 / Dorset 76 : Collection Annuelle Des Gravures de Cap Dorset, 1976. Toronto: M.F. Feheley Publishers, 1976.
Dubois, Dagny. "Histories in Relation: Viewing Archival Photographs of Banff Indian Days with Stoney Nakoda Elders." MA thesis, Athabasca University, 2018. http://dtpr.lib.athabascau.ca/action/download.php?filename=mais/dagnyduboisProject.pdf.
Duhamel, Karine, and Warren Bernauer. "Ahiarmiut Relocations and the Search for Justice: The Life and Work of David Serkoak." Northern Public Affairs, July 2018.
Dunning, Norma. "Reflections of a Disk-Less Inuk on Canada's Eskimo Identification System." *Etudes/Inuit/Studies* 36, no. 2 (2012): 209–26.
Eber, Dorothy Harley. "Art Centre ... For How Long?" *Globe and Mail*, 18 January 1969.
– "It's Not Magic, It's from My Mind." *The Star*, 5 July 1969.
– "The History of Graphics in Dorset: Long and Viable." *The Canadian Forum*, March 1975.
– "Peter Pitseolak, An Historian for Seekooseelak." In *Peter Pitseolak (1902–1973), Inuit Historian of Seekooseelak*, edited by David Bellman. Montreal: McCord Museum, 1980.
– *When the Whalers Were Up North: Inuit Memories from the Eastern Arctic*. Kingston: McGill-Queen's University Press, 1989.

Edwards, Elizabeth. "Exchanging Photographs: Preliminary Thoughts on the Currency of Photography in Collecting Anthropology." *Journal Des Anthropologues*, no. 80–1 (1 June 2000): 21–46. https://doi.org/10.4000/jda.3138.

– "Material Beings: Objecthood and Ethnographic Photographs." *Visual Studies* 17, no. 1 (January 2002): 67–75. https://doi.org/10.1080/14725860220137336.

– "Objects of Affect: Photography Beyond the Image." *Annual Review of Anthropology* 41, no. 1 (21 October 2012): 221–34. https://doi.org/10.1146/annurev-anthro-092611-145708.

– "Photographs and the Sound of History." *Visual Anthropology Review* 21, no. 1–2 (April 2005): 27–46. https://doi.org/10.1525/var.2005.21.1-2.27.

– "Talking Visual Histories: Introduction." In *Museums and Source Communities: A Routledge Reader*, edited by Laura L. Peers and Alison K. Brown, 83–99. London; New York: Routledge, 2003.

Edwards, Elizabeth, and Janice Hart. *Photographs Objects Histories: On the Materiality of Images*. London; New York: Routledge, 2004.

Ekho, Naqi, and Uqsuralik Ottokie. *Interviewing Elders: Childrearing Practices*. Edited by Jean Briggs. Vol. 3. Iqaluit, Nunavut: Nunavut Arctic College, 2000.

Elkins, James. *What Photography Is*. London: Routledge, 2011.

Erdmann, Friedrich. *Testamentetotak: Josuab Aglanginit, Esterib Aglangit Tikkilugit. Printed for the British and Foreign Bible Society in London, for the Use of the Moravian Mission in Labrador.* Stolpen: Gustav Winterib Nenerlauktangit, 1869.

Eskimo Graphic Art. Cape Dorset: West Baffin Eskimo Co-operative, 1966.

Eskimo Graphic Art. Cape Dorset: West Baffin Eskimo Co-operative, 1968.

Evans, Brad, and Aaron Glass. *Return to the Land of the Head Hunters: Edward S. Curtis, the Kwaka'wakw, and the Making of Modern Cinema*, edited by Brad Evans and Aaron Glass. Native Art of the Pacific Northwest: A Bill Holm Center Series. Seattle: University of Washington Press, 2014.

Fabian, Johannes. *Time and the Other: How Anthropology Makes Its Object*. New York: Columbia University Press, 2014.

Feeney, John. *Eskimo Artist: Kenojuak*. Digital, documentary. National Film Board of Canada, 1963. https://www.nfb.ca/film/eskimo-artist-kenojuak.

"Film in 1965." BAFTA. Accessed 12 June 2019. http://awards.bafta.org/award/1965/film.

Flaherty, Franny, in conversation with Andrea Flaherty. Iqaluit, 7 January 2010. Translated by Rhoda Kayakjuak and Lavinia Flaherty. http://viewsfromthenorth.ca/index.html.

Flaherty, Robert. *Nanook of the North*. Pathé Exchange, 1922.

– *Robert Flaherty, Photographer/Filmmaker: The Inuit 1910–22*. Vancouver: Vancouver Art Gallery, 1979.

Flaherty, Robert, and Frances Hubbard Flaherty. *My Eskimo Friends, "Nanook of the North."* London: William Heiseman, Ltd, 1924.

– *Robert and Frances Flaherty: A Documentary Life, 1883–1922*, edited by Robert J. Christopher. McGill-Queen's Native and Northern Series 45. Montreal: McGill-Queen's University Press, 2005.

Fossett, Renée. "Mapping Inuktut: Inuit Views of the Real World." In *Reading beyond Words: Contexts for Native History*, edited by Jennifer S.H. Brown and Elizabeth Vibert, second edition. Peterborough: Broadview Press, 2003.

Fraser, Crystal, and Zoe Todd. "Decolonial Sensibilities: Indigenous Research and Engaging with Archives in Contemporary Colonial Canada." *L'Internationale Online* (blog), 15 February 2016. http://www.internationaleonline.org/research/decolonising_practices/54_decolonial_sensibilities_indigenous_research_and_engaging_with_archives_in_contemporary_colonial_canada.

Freund, Alexander, and Alistair Thomson, eds. *Oral History and Photography*. New York: Palgrave Macmillan, 2011.

Garneau, David. "Imaginary Spaces of Conciliation and Reconciliation." *West Coast Line #74* 46, no. 2 (Summer 2012): 28–38.

Geismar, Haidy, Anita Herle, Kirk Huffman, and J. Layard. *Moving Images: John Layard, Fieldwork and Photography on Malakula since 1914*. Honolulu; [Cambridge]: University of Hawai'i Press;

University of Cambridge, Museum of Archaeology & Anthropology, 2010.

Geller, Peter. "Pictures of the Arctic Night: Archibald Lang Fleming and the Representation of Canadian Inuit." In *Imaging the Arctic*, edited by J.C.H. King and Henrietta Lidchi, 60–8. Seattle: University of Washington Press, 1998.

– *Northern Exposures: Photographing and Filming the Canadian North, 1920–45*. Vancouver, BC: UBC Press, 2004. http://www.deslibris.ca/ID/404310.

Glenbow Museum. "Qatiktalik (Fullerton Harbour) Photo Narrative Project: Collections in Action." https://www.glenbow.org/art-artifacts/collection-overview/qatiktalik-photo-narrative-project/.

Goldring, Philip. "Historians and Inuit: Learning from the Qikiqtani Truth Commission, 2007–2010." *Canadian Journal of History* 50, no. 3 (2015): 492–523.

Graburn, Nelson H.H. "The Present as History: Photography and the Inuit, 1959–94." In *Imaging the Arctic*, edited by J.C.H. King and Henrietta Lidchi, 160–7. Seattle: University of Washington Press, 1998.

Greenhorn, Beth. "Project Naming: Always on Our Minds." In *Museums and the Web 2005: Proceedings*, edited by J. Trant and D. Bearman. Toronto, 2005. http://www.archimuse.com/mw2005/papers/greenhorn/greenhorn.html.

– "Project Naming / Un Visage, Un Nom." *International Preservation News* 61 (December 2013): 20–4.

– "Project Naming: Reconnecting Indigenous Communities with Their Histories through Archival Photographs." In *Participatory Archives: Theory and Practice*, edited by Edward Benoit III and Alexandra Eveleigh, 45–58. London: Facet Publishing, 2019. https://doi.org/10.29085/9781783303588.

Gustavison, Susan J. *Arctic Expressions: Inuit Art and the Canadian Eskimo Arts Council 1961–1989*. Kleinburg, Ontario: McMichael Canadian Art Collection, 1994.

Hakluyt, Richard. *Voyages in Search of The North-West Passage*. London: Cassell & Company, Ltd, 1886. https://archive.org/details/voyagesinsearchooohakluoft/page/n8.

Hall, Charles Francis. *Arctic Researches and Life among the Esquimaux Being the Narrative of an Expedition in Search of Sir John Franklin, in the Years 1860, 1861 and 1862*.

Hall, Judy, Jill E. Oakes, and Sally Qimmiu'naaq Webster. *Sanatujut: Pride in Women's Work: Copper and Caribou Inuit Clothing Traditions*. Gatineau: Canadian Museum of Civilization, 1994.

Hallendy, Norman. *Inuksuit: Silent Messengers of the Arctic*. Vancouver: Douglas & McIntyre, 2001.

– Telephone interview. Interview by Sandra Dyck, 22 October 2018.

– ed. *Tukiliit: The Stone People Who Live in the Wind. An Introduction to Inuksuit and Other Stone Figures of the North*. Vancouver: Douglas & McIntyre, 2009.

Hallendy, Norman, and William W. Fitzhugh. *An Intimate Wilderness: Arctic Voices in a Land of Vast Horizons*. Vancouver: Greystone Books, 2016.

Hancock, Robert L.A. "Diamond Jenness's Arctic Ethnography and the Potential for a Canadian Anthropology." *Histories of Anthropology Annual* 2 (2006): 155–211.

Hanson, Ann Meekitjuk. Letter to Beth Greenhorn, 14 July 2021.

– "Women Are Natural Leaders." In *Arnait Nipingit: Inuit Women in Leadership and Governance*, edited by Louis McComber and Shannon Partridge, 59–71. Iqaluit: Nunavut Arctic College, 2010.

Harper, Kenn. "The Early Development of Inuktitut Syllabic Orthography." *Études/Inuit/Studies* 9, no. 1 (1985): 141–62.

– "Collecting at a Distance: The Boas-Mutch-Comer Collaboration." In *Early Inuit Studies: Themes and Transitions, 1850s–1980s*, edited by Igor Krupnik, 89–110. Washington, DC: Smithsonian Institution Press, 2016.

– "Taissumani: Inuit Catechists at Blacklead Island – Part 2." *Nunatsiaq News*, 25 January 2019, Digital edition. https://nunatsiaq.com/stories/article/taissumani-jan-25/.

Harrington, Richard. "Padlei Trip: January – April 1950." Typed Diary. Toronto, c 1950. MG31-C5. Library and Archives Canada.

Hicks, Jack. "The Nunavut Land Claim and the Nunavut Government: Political Structures of Self-Government in Canada's Eastern Arctic." In *Dependency, Autonomy, Sustainability in the Arctic*, edited by Hanne Petersen and Birger Poppel. Aldershot, England: Ashgate, 1999.

Hirsch, Marianne, and Leo Spitzer. "Testimonial Objects: Memory, Gender, and Transmission." *Poetics Today* 27, no. 2 (1 June 2006): 353–83.

Houston, James. *Cape Dorset Eskimo Graphic Art 1964–65*. Cape Dorset: West Baffin Eskimo Co-operative, 1965.

Hudson, Anna, Jocelyn Piirainen, and Georgiana Uhlyarik, eds. *Tunirrusiangit: Kenojuak Ashevak and Tim Pitsiulak*. Toronto: Art Gallery of Ontario, 2018.

Hudson's Bay Company Archives, Archives of Manitoba. "Names and Knowledge Initiative: Discovering Indigenous people, places and knowledge in the Hudson's Bay Company Archives." https://www.gov.mb.ca/chc/archives/hbca/names_knowledge/index.html.

Hwang, Priscilla. "Inuk Woman in Ottawa-Area Uses Traditional Know-How to Collect, Recycle Roadkill for Crafts." *CBC News*, 11 February 2017. https://www.cbc.ca/news/canada/north/inuit-ottawa-woman-roadkill-recycle-traditional-craft-1.3976401.

– "Inuvialuit Woman Wants to Change Her Name after Discovering the History behind It." *CBC News*, 14 April 2018. https://www.cbc.ca/news/canada/north/inuit-last-name-journey-1.4615336.

Igloliorte, Heather. "Arctic Culture / Global Indigeneity." In *Negotiations in a Vacant Lot: Studying the Visual in Canada*, edited by Lynda Jessup, Erin Morton, and Kirsty Robertson, 150–7. Kingston: McGill-Queen's University Press, 2014.

– *We Were So Far Away: The Inuit Experience of Residential Schools*. Ottawa: Legacy of Hope Foundation, 2010.

Igloolik Oral History Project. http://cnnro.ca/igloolik-oral-history-centre/.

Inuit Heritage Centre, Qamani'tuaq, "Tuhaalruuqtut, Ancestral Sounds." Community Stories, Digital Museums Canada. https://www.communitystories.ca/v1/pm_v2.php?lg=English&ex=00000370&fl=0&id=exhibit_home.

Inuit Heritage Trust. "Introduction: Place Names in Nunavut." Place Names Program, 2016. http://ihti.ca/eng/place-names/pn-index.html.

Inuit Tapiriit Kanatami. "National Inuit Strategy on Research." Ottawa: Inuit Tapiriit Kanatami, March 22, 2018. https://www.itk.ca/national-strategy-on-research-launched/.

Iqaluit, Nunavut Bureau of Statistics. "2011 National Household Survey." 2011. http://www.stats.gov.nu.ca/en/Census%202011NHS.aspx.

Iqaluit, Qikiqtani Inuit Association. "Cape Dorset." *Qikiqtani Truth Commission: Community Histories 1950–1975*. 2013.

Irniq, Peter (Piita). "Mending the Past: Memory and the Politics of Forgiveness." *Canadian Dimension*, February 2012.

Irniq, Piita. Letter to Beth Greenhorn, 13 July 2021.

Joamie, Akeeshook, in conversation with Sharon Angnakak and Corenna Nuyalia with the assistance of Mike Gardner. Iqaluit, 30 December 2005. Translated by Mike Gardner and Rhoda Kayakjuak. http://viewsfromthenorth.ca/index.html.

Karetak, Joe, Frank Tester, and Shirley Tagalik, eds. *Inuit Qaujimajatuqangit: What Inuit Have Always Known to Be True*. Black Point, NS: Fernwood Publishing, 2017.

Karetak, Kukik, Amy Owin, and Spencer Stuart. "In Conversation." Ottawa, March 2012.

Kayakjuak, Rhoda. Letter to Sandra Dyck, 25 November 2018.

"Kenojuak – Poet of the Arctic." Photo Story 289. National Gallery of Canada Library and Archives, 11 July 1961.

King, J.C.H., and Henrietta Lidchi, eds. *Imaging the Arctic*. Seattle: University of Washington Press, 1998.

Klutschak, Heinrich. *Als Eskimo under Den Eskimos: Eine Schilderung Der Erlebnisse Schwatka'schen Franklin-Aufsuchungs-Expedition in Den Jahren 1878–80.* Vienna: A. Hartlemben, 1881.

Klutschak, Heinrich, and William Barr. *Overland to Starvation Cove: With the Inuit in Search of*

Franklin, 1878–1880. Toronto; Buffalo: University of Toronto Press, 1987.

Kovach, Margaret. *Indigenous Methodologies: Characteristics, Conversations and Contexts*. Toronto: University of Toronto Press, 2009.

Kritzwiser, Kay. "The Camera Captures Canada." *Globe and Mail*, 2 September 1967.

Kublu, Alexina, Frédéric Laugrand, and Jarich Oosten. "Interviewing the Elders: Nunavut Arctic College Oral Traditions Project." In *Introduction: Interviewing Elders*, edited by J.G. Oosten and Frédéric Laugrand, Vol. 1, 1–12. Iqaluit, Nunavut: Nunavut Arctic College, 1999.

– "Listening to Our Past." Nunavut Arctic College. Accessed 10 September 2018. http://www.traditional-knowledge.ca/default.html.

Kulchyski, Peter Keith, and Frank J. Tester. *Kiumajut (Talking Back): Game Management and Inuit Rights, 1900–70*. Vancouver: UBC Press, 2007.

Kunuk, Zacharias. "Keynote Address." Inuit Studies Conference, University of Manitoba, Winnipeg, 2008.

Kuptana, Rosemarie. "Ilira, or Why It Was Unthinkable for Inuit to Challenge Qallunaat Authority." *Inuit Art Quarterly* (Fall 1993): 5–7.

Langford, Martha. "Richard Harrington's Guide: Universality and Locality in a Canadian Photographic Document." In *Photography, History, Difference*, edited by Tanya Sheehan, 33–56. Interfaces: Studies in Visual Culture. Hanover, NH: Dartmouth College Press, 2015.

– "Migrant Mothers: Richard Harrington's Indigenous Madonnas." *History of Photography* 40, no. 1 (March 2016): 28–48.

Laugrand, Frédéric. "Écrire Pour Prendre La Parole: Conscience Historique, Mémoires d'aînés et Régimes d'historicité Au Nunavut. " *Anthropologie et Sociétés* 26, no. Mémoires du Nord 2/3 (2002): 91–116.

Laugrand, Frédéric, and Jarich Oosten. *Inuit Shamanism and Christianity: Transitions and Transformations in the Twentieth Century*. McGill-Queen's Native and Northern Series 59. Montreal: McGill-Queen's University Press, 2010.

Laugrand, Frédéric, Jarich Oosten, and David Serkoak. "'The Saddest Time of My Life': Relocating the Ahiarmiut from Ennadai Lake (1950–1958)." *Polar Record* 46, no. 02 (April 2010): 113–35.

Laugrand, Frédéric, and Pascale Laneuville. "Armand Tagoona and the Arctic Christian Fellowship: The First Inuit Church in Canada." *Polar Record* 55, no. 2 (March 2019): 72–81.

Lett, Stephanie. "The Arthur H. Tweedle Collection, Project Naming, and Hidden Stories of Colonialism." *Past Imperfect* 20, no. 1 (20 October 2017). https://doi.org/10.21971/P71Q17.

Library and Archives Canada. "Co-Lab." Accessed 29 April 2019. http://co-lab.bac-lac.gc.ca/eng.

– ed. *Nations to Nations: Indigenous Voices at Library and Archives Canada*. Ottawa: Library and Archives Canada, 2021. eBook. https://www.bac-lac.gc.ca/eng/discover/aboriginal-heritage/initiatives/Pages/nations-to-nations-indigenous-voices-at-LAC.aspx.

Lonetree, Amy. "A Heritage of Resilience: Ho-Chunk Family Photographs in the Visual Archives." *The Public Historian* 41, no. 1 (February 2019): 34–50.

Lydon, Jane. "'Behold the Tears': Photography as Colonial Witness." *History of Photography* 34, no. 3 (12 July 2010): 234–50. https://doi.org/10.1080/03087291003765836.

– ed. *Calling the Shots: Aboriginal Photographies*. Canberra: Aboriginal Studies Press, 2014.

– "Indigenous Uses of Photographic Digital Heritage in Postcolonizing Australia." *Photography and Culture* 14, no. 3 (September 2021): 269–96.

– "Return: The Photographic Archive and Technologies of Indigenous Memory." *Photographies* 3, no. 2 (23 August 2010): 173–87. https://doi.org/10.1080/17540763.2010.499610.

Manning, Jimmy. "Reflection." *Inuit Art Quarterly* 7, no. 1 (Winter 2014): 44.

Martee, Martha. Letter to Deborah Kigjugalik Webster, August 2018.

Martin, Keavy. "'Are We Also Here for That?': Inuit Qaujimajatuqangit – Traditional Knowledge, or Critical Theory?" *The Canadian Journal of Native Studies* 29, no. 1/2 (2009): 183–202.

– *Stories in a New Skin: Approaches to Inuit Literature*. Winnipeg: University of Manitoba Press, 2012.

McCarthy, Kate. "Case Study: Interview with Sally Qimmiu'naaq Webster, Collaborator on Threads of the Land: Clothing Traditions from Three Indigenous Cultures." *Inuit Art Quarterly*, Focus on: Curatorial Collaboration 15, no. 1 (Spring 2000): 25–9.

McComber, Louis, and Shannon Partridge, eds. *Arnait Nipingit: Inuit Women in Leadership and Governance*. Iqaluit: Language and Culture Program of Nunavut Arctic College, 2010.

McCracken, Melinda. "Film Board Premiere in Gallery." *Globe and Mail*, 25 June 1969.

McGrath, Janet. Letter to Beth Greenhorn. "Email on Behalf of Elder Singuuri," 14 February 2005.

– "Isumaksaqsiurutigijakka: Conversations with Aupilaarjuk towards a Theory of Inuktitut Knowledge Renewal." PhD diss., Carleton University, 2012. https://doi.org/10.22215/etd/2012-13099.

Nakasuk, Saullu, Hervé Paniaq, Elisapee Ootoova, Pauloosie Angmaalik. *Introduction: Interviewing Elders*. Edited by J.G. Oosten and Frédéric Laugrand. Vol. 1. Iqaluit, Nunavut: Nunavut Arctic College, 1999.

"The Names and Knowledge Initiative." Archives of Manitoba, 2019. https://manitoba.ca/chc/archives/hbca/names_knowledge/index.html.

"The Naming Continues: Project Naming Photograph Information Form." Library and Archives Canada. Accessed 29 April 2019. http://www.collectionscanada.gc.ca/inuit/020018-1401-e.html.

"Nanisiniq: Arviat History Project." *Nanisiniq Blog* (blog),Tumblr, n.d. http://nanisiniq-blog-blog.tumblr.com.

Nickels, Scot, Jamal Shirley, and Gita Laidler. "Negotiating Research Relationships with Inuit Communities." Iqaluit: Inuit Tapiriit Kanatami and Nunavut Research Institute, 2006.

Obed, Natan. "How to Overcome the Erasure of Inuit Identity in Archival Photos." *Inuit Art Quarterly* 9 (June 2021). https://www.inuitartfoundation.org/iaq-online/how-to-overcome-the-erasure-of-inuit-identity-in-archival-photos.

Ootoova, Ilisapi, Tipuula Qaapik Atagutsiak, Tirisi Ijjangiaq, Jaikku Pitseolak, Aalasi Joamie, Akisu Joamie, and Malaija Papatsie. *Interviewing Inuit Elders: Perspectives on Traditional Health.* Vol. 5. Edited by Michèle Therrien and Frédéric Laugrand. Iqaluit: Nunavut Arctic College, 2001

Owlijoot, Pelagie and Louise Flaherty, eds. *Inuit Kinship and Naming Customs*. Trans. Pelagie Owlijoot. Iqaluit: Inhabit Media, 2013.

Pauktuutit Inuit Women of Canada. "The Inuit Way: A Guide to Inuit Culture." Ottawa: Pauktuutit Inuit Women's Association, 2010.

Payne, Carol. "Culture, Memory and Community through Photographs: Developing an Inuit-based Methodology." In *Anthropology and Photography*, vol. 5, edited by Christopher Morton et al. London: Royal Anthropological Institute, 2016. http://www.therai.org.uk/images/stories/photography/AnthandPhotoVol5.pdf.

– *The Official Picture: The National Film Board of Canada's Still Photography Division and the Image of Canada, 1941–1971*. Montreal: McGill-Queen's University Press, 2013. http://www.deslibris.ca/ID/444766.

– "Unpublished Text Panel." The Other NFB: The National Film Board of Canada's Still Photography Division, 1941–1971. Ottawa: at Carleton University Art Gallery, 27 May 2017.

Payne, Carol, with contributions by Beth Greenhorn, Piita Irniq, Manitok Thompson, Deborah Kigjugalik Webster, Sally Kate Webster, and Christina Williamson. "Disruption and Testimony: Archival Photographs, Project Naming and Inuit Memory in Nunavut." In *Adjusting the Lens: Indigenous Activism, Colonial Legacies, and Photographic Heritage,* edited by Sigrid Lien and Hilde Nielssen, 125–42. Vancouver: University of British Columbia Press, 2021.

Peck, E.J. *The Book of Psalms*. London: British and Foreign Bible Society, 1917.

– *The Four Gospels. Translated into the Language of the Eskimo of Hudson's Bay*. London: British and Foreign Bible Society, 1897.

– *The New Testament of Our Lord and Saviour Jesus Christ*. London: British and Foreign Bible Society, 1912.

Pedri-Spade, Celeste. "'But They Were Never Only the Master's Tools': The Use of Photography in De-Colonial Praxis." *Alter-Native: An International Journal of Indigenous Peoples* 13, no. 2 (2017): 106–13.

Peers, Laura L., and Alison K. Brown, eds. *Museums and Source Communities: A Routledge Reader*. London; New York: Routledge, 2003.

– *Pictures Bring Us Messages / Sinaaksiiksi aohtsimaahpihkookiyaawa: Photographs and Histories from the Kainai Nation*. Toronto: University of Toronto Press, 2005.

Pelly, David F. "Ukkusiksalik." *Above & Beyond*, April 2011. http://arcticjournal.ca/uncategorized/ukkusiksalik/.

Pinney, Christopher. *Photography and Anthropology*. Repr. Exposures. London: Reaktion Books, 2011.

Pitseolak, Peter. *Peter Pitseolak (1902–1973), Inuit Historian of Seekooseelak*. Edited by David Bellman. Montreal: McCord Museum, 1980.

Pitseolak, Peter, and Dorothy Harley Eber. *People from Our Side: A Life Story with Photographs and Oral Biography*. Translated by Ann Meekitjuk Hanson. Montreal: McGill-Queen's University Press, 1993.

Poignant, Roslyn, and Axel Poignant. *Encounter at Nagalarramba*. Canberra: National Library of Australia, 1996.

Pratt, Mary Louise. *Imperial Eyes: Travel Writing and Transculturation*. New York: Routledge, 2008.

Price, Jackie. "Tukisivallialiqtakka: The Things I Have Now Begun to Understand: Inuit Governance, Nunavut and the Kitchen Consultation Model." University of Victoria, 2007. http://assembly.nu.ca/library/Edocs/2007/001497-e.pdf.

Putulik, Lizzie, in conversation with Faith Kakuktinniq. Kangiqugaapik/Kangiqtiniq, December 2006. Translated by Rhoda Kayakjuak. http://viewsfromthenorth.ca/index.html.

"The Qatiktalik (Fullerton Harbour) Photo Narrative Project." Glenbow Museum, 2019. https://www.glenbow.org/qatiktalik/.

Qikiqtani Inuit Association. "About the Photographs." In *Qikiqtani Truth Commission, Guide to Community Histories and Special Studies of the Qikiqtani Truth Commission*, 6–7. Iqaluit, Nunavut: Qikiqtani Truth Commission and Inhabit Media, 2015. eBook. https://www.qtcommission.ca/sites/default/files/public/thematic_reports/web_guide_english1.pdf.

– "Cape Dorset." In *Qikiqtani Truth Commission Community Histories, 1950–75*. Iqaluit, Nunavut: Qikiqtani Truth Commission and Inhabit Media, 2013. eBook. https://www.qtcommission.ca/en/communities/cape-dorset-kinngait.

– *Qikiqtani Truth Commission, Guide to Community Histories and Special Studies of the Qikiqtani Truth Commission*. Iqaluit, Nunavut: Qikiqtani Truth Commission and Inhabit Media, 2015. eBook. https://www.qtcommission.ca/sites/default/files/public/thematic_reports/web_guide_english1.pdf.

– *Qikiqtani Truth Commission Final Report: Achieving Saimaqatigiingniq*. Iqaluit, Nunavut: Qikiqtani Truth Commission and Inhabit Media, 2010. https://www.qtcommission.ca/sites/default/files/public/thematic_reports/thematic_reports_english_final_report.pdf

Racette, Sherry Farrell. "Returning Fire, Pointing the Canon: Aboriginal Photography as Resistance." In *The Cultural Work of Photography in Canada*, edited by Carol Payne and Andrea Kunard, 70–90. Montreal: McGill-Queen's University Press, 2011.

Racette, Sherry Farrell, Erin Goodpipe, and Tyler Tootoosis. "Arts & Culture: Sakewewak Artists' Collective Annual StoryTellers Festival." RezTV. Accessed 5 November 2018. https://vimeo.com/208195118.

Raheja, Michelle. "Reading Nanook's Smile: Visual Sovereignty, Indigenous Revisions of Ethnography, and Atanarjuat (The Fast Runner)." *American Quarterly* 59, no. 4 (2007): 1159–85. https://doi.org/10.1353/aq.2007.0083.

Rasmussen, Knud. *The Netsilik Eskimos: Social Life and Spiritual Culture*. New York: AMS Press, 1976.

Regan, Paulette. *Unsettling the Settler Within: Indian Residential Schools, Truth Telling, and Reconciliation in Canada*. Vancouver: UBC Press, 2011.

"Returning Photos: Australian Aboriginal Photographys from European Collections." Accessed 18 October 2018. https://ipp.arts.uwa.edu.au/.

Roberts, A. Barry. "Eskimo Identification and Disc Numbers: A Brief History." Ottawa: Social

Development Division, Indian and Northern Affairs Canada, June 1975.

Ross, W. Gillies. "The Use and Misuse of Historical Photographs: A Case Study from Hudson Bay, Canada." *Arctic Anthropology* 27, no. 2 (1990): 93–112.

Ryan, Terry. "Some Notes on the Cape Dorset Prints." In *Eskimo Graphic Art*. Cape Dorset: West Baffin Eskimo Co-operative, 1962.

Saddington, Tony. "Learner Experience: A Rich Resource for Learning." In *Empowerment Through Experiential Learning: Explorations of Good Practice*, edited by John Mulligan and Colin Griffin. London: Kogan Page, 1992.

"Sally Webster." Ottawa Aboriginal Coalition, 2019. http://ottawaaboriginalcoalition.ca/sally-webster/.

Sandals, Leah. "Records Broken at Canada's Fall Auctions." Canadian Art. *News* (blog), 22 November 2018. https://canadianart.ca/news/canada-art-auction-records-fall-2018.

Sangster, Joan. *The Iconic North: Cultural Constructions of Aboriginal Life in Postwar Canada*. Vancouver; Toronto: UBC Press, 2016.

Schultz-Lorentzen, Finn. *Arctic: A Novel.* Toronto: McClelland and Stewart, 1976.

Schwatka, Frederick. *The Search for Franklin: A Narrative of the American Expedition Under Lieutenant Schwatka, 1878 to 1880*. London: T. Nelson and Sons, 1899.

Seesequasis, Paul. *Blanket Toss under Midnight Sun: Portraits of Everyday Life in Eight Indigenous Communities.* Toronto: Alfred A. Knopf Canada, 2019.

Septentrionalium Terrarum Descriptio. Per Gerardium Mercatorem Cum Privilegio. [1605?] [1609?] Map, 40.5 × 48 cm., e004414662. Library and Archives Canada

Siemens, Danielle. "Photographic Encounters in the North: Rosemary Gilliat Eaton's 1960 Trip to the Eastern Canadian Arctic." MA thesis, Carleton University, 2016.

"Social History of the Eastern Arctic Database." University of Manitoba Archives & Special Collections, 14 February 2019. https://libguides.lib.umanitoba.ca/c.php?g=708062.

Sontag, Susan. "In Plato's Cave." In *On Photography*, 3–24. New York: Delta Books, 1973.

Steele, Suzanne. Post on Project Naming. Facebook, 11 March 2019.

Stefánsson, Vilhjálmur. *Report of the Canadian Arctic Expedition, 1913–18*. Ottawa: King's Printer, 1919.

Stern, Pamela. "The History of Canadian Arctic Photography: Issues of Territorial and Cultural Sovereignty." In *Imaging the Arctic*, edited by J.C.H. King and Henrietta Lidchi, 46–52. Seattle: University of Washington Press, 1998.

Tagg, John. *The Disciplinary Frame: Photographic Truths and the Capture of Meaning*. Minneapolis: University of Minnesota Press, 2009.

Tagoona, Armand. "Our Move to Qamanittuaq in 1938." *Inuktitut* 74 (1991): 20–9.

– *Shadows*. Ottawa: Oberon Press, 1975.

Taylor, Miles. "Bull, John." In *The Oxford Dictionary of National Biography*, edited by H.C.G. Matthew and B. Harrison. Oxford: Oxford University Press, 2004.

Tester, Frank, dir. *Beneath the Surface: Inuit Miners at Rankin Inlet, 1957–62*. Spinnaker Productions, 2016.

Tester, Frank, and Peter Irniq. "Inuit Qaujimajatuqangit: Social History, Politics and the Practice of Resistance." *Arctic*, Supplement 1, 61, no. 5 (2008). https://doi.org/10.14430/arctic101.

Tester, Frank, and Peter Kulchyski. *Tammarniit (Mistakes): Inuit Relocation in the Eastern Arctic, 1939–63*. Vancouver: University of British Columbia Press, 1994.

Thomas, Jeff. "At the Kitchen Table with Edward Curtis" (Photo Essay 1). In *Return to the Land of the Headhunters: Edward Curtis, the Kwakwaka'wakw, and the Making of Modern Cinema,* edited by Brad Evans and Aaron Glass, 128–44. Seattle: University of Washington Press, 2014.

– "Emergence from the Shadows: First Peoples' Photographic Perspective." In *The Cultural Work of Photography in Canada*, edited by Carol Payne and Andrea Kunard, 212–28. Montreal: McGill-Queen's University Press, 2011.

– "Jeff Thomas." 2019. https://jeff-thomas.ca/.

Thomson, Aly. "About 80,000 Denied Eligibility for Newfoundland first nation band." *The Globe and Mail*, 7 February 2017. https://www.theglobeandmail.com/news/national/only-18000-eligible-for-newfoundland-

first-nation-band-its-discriminatory/article33925034/.
Thompson, Manitok. "Don't Just Think About It, Do It!" In *Arnait Nipingit: Inuit Women in Leadership and Governance*, edited by Louis McComber and Shannon Partridge, 1:139–56. Inuit Leadership and Governance. Iqaluit: Nunavut Arctic College, 2010.
– Letter to Deborah Kigjugalik Webster, 2019.
Three Thousand. Directed by asinnajaq. NFB Production. 2017. https://www.nfb.ca/film/three-thousand/.
Tippett, Maria. *Between Two Cultures: A Photographer among the Inuit*. Toronto: Penguin, 1994.
Truth and Reconciliation Commission of Canada. *Truth and Reconciliation Commission of Canada: Calls to Action.* 2012. http://trc.ca/assets/pdf/Calls_to_Action_English2.pdf.
– *Honouring the Truth, Reconciling for the Future: Summary of the Final Report of the Truth and Reconciliation Commission of Canada. The Final Report of the Truth and Reconciliation Commission of Canada*. Ottawa: McGill-Queen's University Press, 2015.
– *The Inuit and Northern Experience. The Final Report of the Truth and Reconciliation Commission of Canada*. Montreal: McGill-Queen's University Press, 2015.
Tsinhnahjinnie, Hulleah J. "When Is a Photograph Worth a Thousand Words?" In *Photography's Other Histories*, edited by Christopher Pinney, Nicolas Peterson, and Nicholas Thomas, 40–52. North Carolina: Duke University Press, 2003. https://doi.org/10.1215/9780822384717-004.
Tulurialik, Ruth Annaqtuusi, and David Fraser Pelly. *Qikaaluktut: Images of Inuit Life*. Toronto: Oxford University Press, 1986.
Tunirrusiangit: Kenojuak Ashevak and Tim Pitsiulak. Toronto: Art Gallery of Ontario, 2018.
Ullulaq, Jennifer. Letter to Carol Payne, May–June 2018.
"Umiyaqtutt Festival." Facebook, 2018. https://www.facebook.com/UmiyaqtuttFestival/.
University of Manitoba Archives & Special Collections. "Social History of the Eastern Arctic Database." https://libguides.lib.umanitoba.ca/c.php?g=708062.
Views from the North (cybercartographic atlas). Carleton University: Geomatics and Cartographic Research Centre. http://viewsfromthenorth.ca/index.html. This site was down at the time of publication.
Vizenor, Gerald Robert, ed. *Survivance: Narratives of Native Presence*. Lincoln: University of Nebraska Press, 2008.
Vowel, Chelsea. "Giving My Children Cree Names Is a Powerful Act of Reclamation." *CBC News*, 4 November 2018. https://www.cbc.ca/news/indigenous/opinion-cree-names-reclamation-chelsea-vowel-1.4887604.
Wamsley, Douglas, and William Barr. "Early Photographers of the Canadian Arctic and Greenland." In *Imaging the Arctic*, edited by J.C.H. King and Henrietta Lidchi, 36–45. Seattle: University of Washington Press, 1998.
Webster, Deborah Kigjugalik. *When I Was Young in Nunavut*. Iqaluit: Inhabit Media, 2020.
White, Donny. "In Search of Geraldine Moodie: A Project in Process." In *Imaging the Arctic*, edited by J.C.H. King and Henrietta Lidchi, 88–97. Seattle: University of Washington Press, 1998.
Whitman, Nicholas. "Technology and Vision: Factors Shaping Nineteenth-Century Arctic Photography." In *Imaging the Arctic*, edited by J.C.H. King and Henrietta Lidchi, 29–35. Seattle: University of Washington Press, 1998.
Williams, Carol. *Framing the West: Race, Gender, and the Photographic Frontier in the Pacific Northwest*. London: Oxford University Press, 2003.
Williamson, Christina. "Attatsiaq." In *Uninvited: Canadian Women Artists in the Modern Moment*, edited by Sarah Milroy, 69–74. Toronto: McMichael Canadian Art Collection, 2021.
– "Sewing in Arviat: Inuit Women's Work through Stories and Parkas." PhD diss., Carleton University, 2021.
Wright, Christopher. *The Echo of Things: The Lives of Photographs in the Solomon Islands*. Objects/Histories. Durham: Duke University Press, 2013.
Zawadski, Krista Ulujuk. *Nuvisi: Threading Our Beads at Qatiktalik*. Exhibition, Carleton University Art Gallery, 2021.

CONTRIBUTORS

Murray Angus co-founded the renowned Ottawa-based Inuit post-secondary college Nunavut Sivuniksavut in 1985 and retired in June 2016. The eight-month to three-year program for high school graduates from across Nunavut and the Arctic is acclaimed for its innovative Inuit-centred curriculum. In 2014, he was awarded the Order of Canada by the governor general for playing a vital role in empowering Inuit youth. In 2001, he involved Nunavut Sivuniksavut students in researching the photographs from Library and Archives Canada's collection, an initiative that became Project Naming.

asinnajaq is a visual artist, filmmaker, writer, and curator based in Montreal, QC. asinnajaq's practice is grounded in research and collaboration, which includes working with other artists, friends, and family. In 2016, she worked with the National Film Board of Canada's archive to source historical and contemporary Inuit films and colonial representations of Inuit in film. The footage she pulled is included in her short film "Three Thousand." The film was nominated for Best Short Documentary at the 2018 Canadian Screen Awards by the Academy of Canadian Cinema and Television. asinnajaq was a part of the curatorial team for the Canadian Pavilion at the 2019 Venice Biennale and was long listed for the prestigious Sobey Art Award in April 2020. asinnajaq and three other Inuit are guest curators of the inaugural exhibition, *INUA*, at Qaumajuaq, the new Inuit art centre established at the Winnipeg Art Gallery in 2020.

Sandra Dyck is the director of Carleton University Art Gallery in Ottawa, Ontario. She has curated over fifty exhibitions, published twenty catalogue essays, and won four curatorial writing awards from Galeries Ontario / Ontario Galleries. Her writing has appeared in such journals as *Canadian Art*, *Inuit Art Quarterly*, and the *Canadian Journal of Native Studies*, and in books published by the Montreal Museum of Fine Arts, Art Gallery of Hamilton, and Canadian Museum of History.

Sheena Ellison is an educator and researcher working in Ottawa. She is interested in the role of Traditional Knowledge in Indigenous education, arts, and culture. Sheena has a master of arts in art history from the University of Toronto and is a member of the Ontario College of Teachers. She is a lecturer in the Art History Department at Carleton University and teaches English, history, and Indigenous literature for the Ottawa-Carleton District School Board. She has been involved with the Views from the North project since 2011.

Beth Greenhorn is a senior project manager at Library and Archives Canada (LAC). From 2003 to 2017, she managed Project Naming. In addition to creating web exhibitions and social media content, in 2017, she co-curated the travelling exhibition *Hiding in Plain Sight: Discovering the Métis Nation in the Collections of Library and Archives Canada*. In 2018, she was the co-curator on *Pathways: Following Traces of Indigenous Routes across Ontario*. From 2018 to 2021, she was involved with We Are Here: Sharing Stories. This three-year project was a mass digitization initiative involving archival records and published works containing Indigenous content held at LAC that built upon Project Naming through engagement and collaboration with Indigenous communities. She also coordinated *Nations to Nations: Indigenous Voices at Library and Archives Canada*, an interactive and multi-lingual eBook, which launched in September 2021.

Alexandra Haggert has been a project manager at Library and Archives Canada since early 2017. Before joining LAC, she worked at Veterans Affairs Canada in France and at the Canadian Intellectual Property Office. In 2015, she completed a BA honours in film studies with a minor in French language at Carleton University.

Ann Meekitjuk Hanson is a writer, translator, broadcaster, civil servant, and owner of the business R.L. Hanson Construction Ltd. She was the founding editor of the newspaper *Inukshuk News* in addition to being a councillor, a deputy mayor, a community development worker, and a film actress. Hanson was deputy commissioner of the Northwest Territories from 1987 to 1992 and the commissioner of Nunavut from 2005 to 2010.

Morley Hanson joined the faculty of the Ottawa-based post-secondary Inuit studies program Nunavut Sivuniksavut (NS) in 1988 and served in the main leadership role from 1991 to June 2021 when he retired from NS. NS has been acclaimed for its innovative Inuit-centred curriculum, which has inspired many youth to engage in all walks of life in Nunavut, from the arts and professions to public service and politics. In 2007 and 2013, Morley took year-long sabbaticals from NS to volunteer at the Kigali Genocide Memorial in Rwanda where he worked on the development of Genocide and Peace Education Programming. In 2014, Morley was awarded the Order of Canada by the governor general, who cited his commitment to empowering young people, particularly Indigenous youth. By 2001, the yearly initiative of having NS students research the photographs from Library and Archives Canada's collection had evolved into Project Naming.

Dr Heather Igloliorte (Inuk, Nunatsiavut Territory) holds the Tier 1 University Research Chair in Circumpolar Indigenous Arts at Concordia University, where she is an associate professor in the Department of Art History. She is the director of the Inuit Futures in Arts Leadership: The Pilimmaksarniq/ Pijariuqsarniq Project, which she began because she wanted to see more Inuit in decision-making roles in the arts. Igloliorte and three other Inuit are guest curators of the inaugural exhibition, *INUA*, at Qaumajuaq, the new Inuit art centre established at the Winnipeg Art Gallery in 2020. Among her many publications, Igloliorte's essay "Curating Inuit Qaujimajatuqangit: Inuit Knowledge in the Qallunaat Art Museum" was awarded the 2017 Distinguished Article of the Year prize from *Art Journal*. She is also the president of the board of directors of the Inuit Art Foundation, serves as the co-chair of the Indigenous Advisory Circle for the Winnipeg Art Gallery, and is on the Faculty Council of the Otsego Institute for Native American Art History at the Fenimore Art Museum in Cooperstown, New York.

Piita Irniq is a residential school survivor and political leader. He has extensive experience as a legislator and leader in the North. He served for two terms as a member of the legislative assembly of the Northwest Territories and was a member of the Nunavut Implementation Commission that established the Territory of Nunavut in 1999. From 2000 to 2005, he served as the second commissioner of Nunavut. Since that time, he has remained a tireless advocate of Inuit culture and the Inuktitut language. Now based in Ottawa, he was involved in the development of Project Naming and has participated in the identification of photographic records from his community of Naujaat (Repulse Bay), Nunavut.

Curtis Kuunuaq Konek is an Inuk researcher and youth leader based in Arviat, Nunavut. Between 2011 and 2013, he worked as a researcher, interviewer, translator, and filmmaker with the Nanisiniq: Arviat History Project. He travelled with the Nanisiniq crew making presentations about the history project's findings on climate change and the relocations of Inuit in the Arviat area. As part of the Nanisiniq research program, he also worked with Project Naming to name and connect family members through old photos of relatives in the community of Arviat. From 2013 to 2014, he filmed and instructed youth from Uqsuqtuuq (Gjoa Haven) as part of the first year of the Nanivara History Project.

Jimmy Manning is a Kinngait-based photographer and artist. Manning has been manager of Kinngait Studios and was a member of the board of directors for the Inuit Art Foundation. A grandson of the photographer Peter Pitseolak, Manning photographs the land and people of Kinngait. Among other collections, his photographs can be found at the Musée des Beaux-Arts de Montréal and the Canadian Museum of History.

Kathleen Ivaluarjuk Merritt is an alumna from Nunavut Sivuniksavut, and a Nunavut-based performer, writer, and arts administrator from Kangiqliniq (Rankin Inlet). She was the manager and facilitator of the National Arts

Centre's Music Alive Program in Nunavut, was interim executive director at Alianait Arts Festival, and led the Qaggiq Inuit Performing Arts and Cultural Learning Hub feasibility study. More recently, Ivaluarjuk studied Inuktitut at the Pirurvik Centre in the Aurniarvik Program accredited with the University of Victoria. She currently resides in Iqaluit working as the executive assistant to the president of Nunavut Tunngavik.

Dr Carol Payne is a professor of art history and associate dean (research and international) in the Faculty of Arts and Social Sciences at Carleton University. A historian of photography, she is author of *The Official Picture: The National Film Board of Canada's Still Photography Division and the Image of Canada, 1941–1971* (McGill-Queen's University Press, 2013) and co-editor (with Andrea Kunard) of *The Cultural Work of Photography in Canada* (McGill-Queen's University Press, 2011) among other publications. Between 2005 and 2014, she was the principal investigator in a collaborative photo-based research project, Views from the North, with Nunavut Sivuniksavut, Library and Archives Canada, and Carleton University funded by SSHRC.

Barry Pottle is an Ottawa-based contemporary photo-based Inuk artist originally from Rigolet, Nunatsiavut (in Labrador). His work has been exhibited across Canada. In his photography, he explores Inuit culture, history, and contemporary experience including the experiences of urban Inuit. In his photo conceptual series *Awareness*, he photographed several of the notorious numbered identification discs issued by the Canadian government to Inuit between 1944 and 1969. His work, like his outreach activity as a whole, explores how photography can be used to expose Inuit history – including a history of colonization – and assert Inuit resilience. He is currently interested in using photography to study the uniqueness of urban Inuit communities and the contemporary reality of this world. He is a beneficiary under the Labrador Inuit Land Claims Agreement and has participated as a board member and president of Tungasuvvingat Inuit Community Centre and served on the board of the Inuit Head Start Program.

Paula Ikuutaq Rumbolt is a Qamani'tuaq (Baker Lake), Nunavut–based writer, teacher, and youth leader. She is a graduate of Nunavut Sivuniksavut and holds a BA in creative writing from Concordia University in Montreal. In her writing, she describes Inuit culture from an Inuk perspective. Her book *The Legend of Lightning and Thunder* was shortlisted for the 2014 Canadian Library Association's Book of the Year for Children and her second book, *The Origin of Day and Night*, was published in 2018. She is also the recipient of a Northern Youth Abroad Outstanding Alumni Award as well as a TD Michaëlle Jean Bursary for youth using the arts for social change. She has worked as a child and youth outreach worker with the Government of Nunavut in Qamani'tuaq and is currently an Inuktitut teacher in the elementary school. She is co-founder and owner of Hinani Design, a popular apparel collective based in Arviat, Nunavut.

David Serkoak was born in the northern part of Nueltin Lake, southwest of Arviat, Nunavut. David has worked in many levels in education as a teacher (primary/secondary schools), vice-principal, principal, instructor at Nunavut Arctic College, and curator at the British Museum of Mankind in England. David helped to develop Inuktitut teaching materials at all levels, local, regional, and territorial, in both NWT and Nunavut. In 2012 David retired from teaching, but he still gives workshops on Inuit social history to Canadian Armed Forces and drum making and drumming to Inuit youth in three regions in the Arctic, Nunavut, Nunavik, and Nunatsiavut. After a decades-long effort by Serkoak and the Ahiarmiut Relocation Society, the Canadian Government apologized and came to a settlement agreement for the relocations of the Ahiarmiut between 1949 and 1959.

Dr Frank Tester is a professor emeritus at the University of British Columbia. Tester's work on Inuit focuses on social issues and conditions and has resulted in a number of innovative projects including the Nanisiniq: Arviat History Project, the Nanivara History Project, and several documentaries. His research in southern countries focuses on human rights including land rights, environmental protection, and human security. He is a former chair of the Family Court/Youth Justice Committee, City of Vancouver, and a founder of the long-running One World Community Film Festival. A photographer and filmmaker, he is the recipient of the Gustavus Myers Award for his contributions to the study of human rights in North America.

Manitok Thompson was born in Salliq (Coral Harbour), Nunavut. She graduated from the Teacher Education Program in 1977 and worked in several schools in Nunavut and the Northwest Territories as a teacher and as a consultant. In 1994, she was elected as a municipal councilor for Rankin Inlet, and in 1995, she was elected to the Northwest Territories Legislature, holding different cabinet portfolios. She was elected to the Government of Nunavut in 1999 and served as the territory's first female cabinet minister. After politics, she led the Education Act Consultations for the Nunavut Government. Currently, she is CEO of the Inuit Broadcasting Corporation and cataloguing its vast thirty-five-year collection of videos capturing the life of Inuit. This collection is a documentation of Inuit language, culture, and Inuit Qaujimajatuqangit (Inuit Knowledge). In her spare time, she pastors at Larga Baffin hospice in Ottawa and teaches traditional Inuit skills from her house in Carleton Place.

Deborah Kigjugalik Webster is an anthropologist and curator of Heritage Collections, Government of Nunavut. She is also a writer of many published articles and two books including *Harvaqtuurmiut Heritage: The Heritage of the Inuit of the Lower Kazan River*, a book about the archaeology, oral history, and place names research conducted near her home community of Qamani'tuaq (Baker Lake) in Nunavut, and *Akilak's Adventure*, a children's book. Deborah Webster's most recent book is *When I Was Young in Nunavut* (Iqaluit: Inhabit Media, 2020). Webster has been actively involved with Project Naming for several years. She lives in Ottawa with her two daughters.

Sally Kate Qimmiu'naaq Webster is a revered Elder with a long history of promoting Inuit art and culture. She was born on the land near Qamani'tuaq (Baker Lake), Nunavut, and now lives in Ottawa. She attended federal day school in Baker Lake, later serving as a classroom assistant and as a coordinator at the Baker Lake campus of Nunavut Arctic College. She operated Baker Lake Fine Arts and Crafts for several years, promoting local artists.

Dr Christina Williamson is a public historian and research associate at the Faculty of Native

Studies at the University of Alberta, for the Métis Archival Project. She has a PhD in cultural mediations at Carleton University, where her dissertation examined the history of Inuit women's labour history through the lens of sewing, material culture, and Oral History. She has been involved in a number of public history projects including the *Lost Stories* project and is a former director on the board of the Edmonton Heritage Council.

INDEX

Page numbers in italics refer to figures.